F

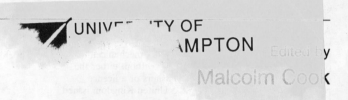

UNIVERSITY OF
HAMPTON

Edited by

Malcolm Cook

LONGMAN
London and New York

Longman Group UK Limited,
Longman House, Burnt Mill,
Harlow, Essex CM20 2JE, England
and Associated Companies throughout the world

*Published in the United States of America
by Longman Publishing, New York*

© Longman Group UK Limited 1993

First published 1993

British Library Cataloguing-in-Publication Data

A catalogue record for this book is
available from the British Library

Library of Congress Cataloging-in-Publication Data

French culture since 1945 / edited by Malcolm Cook.
    p.   cm.
  Includes bibliographical references and index.
  ISBN 0–582–08806–2
  1. France—Civilization—1945– 2. France—Cultural policy.
3. Decentralization in government—France—History—20th century.
4. France—Popular culture—History—20th century. I. Cook, Malcolm.
DC33.7.F727   1993
944.082—dc20   92–28669
                                                  CIP

Set 5E in Times
Printed in Malaysia

CONTENTS

NOTES ON CONTRIBUTORS

Malcolm Cook is Senior Lecturer in French at the University of Exeter and Chairman of the School of Modern Languages. He has written monographs on fiction in France during the French Revolution, on the eighteenth-century writer Lesage and, most recently, on the social reality in French fiction 1775–1800. He is currently the French editor of the *Modern Language Review*. His present research interests are centred on the French author Bernardin de Saint-Pierre, whose correspondence he is editing. His teaching interests range from eighteenth-century literature to courses on contemporary France.

Rachel Edwards is a graduate of Warwick University. She spent a year at Hull University as tutorial assistant and has recently taught English at Nanterre University. She has published articles on Tournier: "Myth and Allegory and Michel Tournier" and "Menstruation and Initiation in Michel Tournier's *Amandine ou les deux jardins*".

A. Greaves is a lecturer in French at the School of Education, Exeter University, where he is also the co-ordinator for International Affairs. He has published on Stendhal, French teacher-training and foreign language teaching. He has current research interests in the French education system.

Alex Hughes is a graduate of London University, and recently completed a PhD on the twentieth-century French author Violette Leduc. She is currently teaching at the University of Birmingham, in the department of French Studies and her research interests lie in the field of contemporary women's writing and feminist theory.

Roger J. P. Kain is Montefiore Professor of Geography at the University of Exeter and is a Fellow of the British Academy. He has written on the history of classical architectural and urban design in France and on urban conservation.

Stephen Mennell is Professor of Sociology at University College, Dublin. Until 1990 he taught at the University of Exeter. His books include, *All Manners of Food: Eating in England and France* (1985), which won the Grand Prix international de littérature gastronomique and the Prix Marco Polo.

Alan Pedley worked in schools and teacher training before joining Exeter University's French Department in 1986. He has published articles on language teaching and on Charles de Gaulle, and produced audio and video teaching materials relating to contemporary France. One of his current teaching interests is the French media.

Gerard Poulet was educated in Lille where he worked as a freelance actor with Le Théâtre Populaire de Flandres. He taught English and French in France and West Africa, before coming to England in 1967 to teach French language, literature and civilisation at Leeds University as a *lecteur*. He has been involved in teacher training at St Luke's College and the School of Education at Exeter University since 1978.

Keith Reader is reader in French Cultural Studies at Kingston University and the author of numerous articles on French cinema, particularly the work of Renoir and Bresson and the films of the Popular Front period. His most recent book, *The May 1968 Events in France*, is to be published by Macmillans in May 1993.

Martin Sorrell is Senior Lecturer in French at Exeter University. He studied at Oxford and Kent Universities. He has written a number of articles on modern French theatre (notably on Jérôme Savary) and was the co-founder of the French-speaking theatre company Bac to Bac. His other main interest is poetry and his bilingual anthology *Modern French Poetry* was published by Forest Books in 1992.

D. A. Trotter is lecturer in medieval French at Exeter University, where he also teaches French linguistics (descriptive and historical). His publications include studies of medieval crusade literature and editions of translations from Latin into French during the Middle Ages. He is currently involved in a complete revision of the Anglo-Norman Dictionary (MHRA).

David Looseley is lecturer in French Studies at Bradford University. His publications include, *A Search for Commitment: The Theatre of Armand Salacrou*, as well as articles on modern French theatre and cultural policy. He is currently writing a book on politics and culture under Mitterrand, funded by the Leverhulme Trust.

CHAPTER 1

Introduction:
French culture since 1945

Malcolm Cook

Our intention in this book is to provide readers with an extensive and authoritative guide to aspects of French culture since the end of the war. Each chapter, written by a specialist in the respective field, provides both a survey and an analysis which will present the reader with a challenging synthesis and a provocative study. Obviously, because of the wide range of areas which are covered in this book, there will be differences of approach and various conclusions. Some, for obvious reasons, will present a more historical analysis: for example, the chapters on architecture, language and food in which the authors attempt to see the evolution of styles as part of an on-going process in which the past is ever present. Indeed, one could say that this was true, perhaps to a lesser extent, of all the sections. French culture did not begin in 1945 and the choice of date has been made for reasons of practicality and history: it may appear, to some, to be slightly arbitrary. Each contributor has been asked to take the survey up to the very moment of writing, the last few months of 1991.

My intention in this introduction is to establish the context in which the various contributors are writing without pre-empting what they will say with far greater authority than myself. My task is to provide a brief background and to examine problems of definition. While preparing the ground for further reading, I do not claim to offer a full survey of all the works on French culture which have been produced since the war. In his book *The French* (London: Collins, 1983), Theodore Zeldin wrote a short chapter entitled: 'How to recognize culture'. He does not provide the reader with an identikit model with which to confront the world ('The essence of French people's culture is that they cannot agree what exactly it is' (p. 362)). Nor, indeed, does he show that there is anything which is specific about French culture. In our book we hope to provide the reader with information which will permit a sensible judgement of French culture, even if we may not be able to achieve a simple definition of it. It would seem, in one sense at least, that culture is related to creativity and reception. It is

huge in dimension and can embrace every aspect of our daily life.
The state can, by its support, provide the environment and the
funds through which cultural activity can flourish. Culture can,
consequently, be political. It was De Gaulle in France who had
the vision and the courage to create the first Ministry of Culture
and who nominated the first Minister, the one-time revolutionary
novelist André Malraux, in 1959. Certainly it is now recognized
that there is a close relationship between culture and politics and
it is one which is at the very heart of a democratic state. Zeldin
gave two functions of culture: first, the defence of the individual
and of small groups against the increasing homogenization of the
media, against passivity before the television screen or the football
match – it is to be the stimulation of individuality – and, second,
as an instrument for creating new forms of sensibility, bringing
individuals from different social groups together in new forms
of common enthusiasm. Zeldin quotes Jack Lang, the present
Minister who wrote when he was organizer of the Nancy theatre
festival: 'Culture is a battle for the right to live freely' (quoted by
Zeldin, p. 363).

   In this introduction, in my examination of context, I shall
concentrate, briefly, on three areas: definitions of culture, French
cultural policy, the evolution of culture since 1945.

Definition

There are as many definitions of culture as there are writers on
the subject. I can only offer a sample here but it is a sample
which will reveal the diversity of opinion. In an excellent survey
which provides an extensive and rich bibliography Sylvie Rab,
in an article entitled: 'Histoire des politiques culturelles' (Paris,
C.N.R.S., 1990) (kindly provided by Mme Schneider of the
French Ministère de la Culture and which is part of an extensive
survey undertaken by the Institut d'histoire du temps présent)
concentrates on 'politique culturelle' and points out the difficulty
of definition:

L'imprécision naît du mot 'culture', dont les interprétations sont elles-
mêmes multiples: de la conception anthropologique du culturel comme
l'ensemble des pratiques et des représentations d'une société (tout étant
culture) à la réduction courante du culturel à l'intellectuel, livresque et
artistique. (p. 88)

We are confronted by a major difficulty and one to which I
can see no easy solution. Is culture to be restricted to that
which is deliberately artistic or is it to be applied to all of man's
creations? François Léotard, himself a Minister of Culture, wrote

in the preface to his *Culture: les chemins du printemps* (Paris: Albin Michel, 1988):

Il y a peu de mots qui se soient autant 'laissés aller' que le mot de culture.

Malraux disait qu'autour de la table du Conseil des ministres il était probablement le seul à pouvoir dire qu'il ne savait pas ce que c'était . . .

Aujourd'hui, de la mode à la chevelure, de l'art du jardin à la bande vidéo, du concert de rock à la peinture sur soie, tout est culture, nous dit-on. (p. 11)

Obviously, no book on French or any culture can include sections on every aspect that some might consider to be culture. What we hope to achieve in this book is to concentrate on aspects which nobody would deny were cultural and in which the French have made a particular contribution.

Louis Dollot in his *Culture individuelle et culture de masse* (Paris: Presses Universitaires de France, 1974) provides two useful frameworks of definition. He quotes the Universal Declaration of the Rights of Man issued by the United Nations in December 1948, article 27 in which it is expressly stated that every individual has the right to take part freely in the cultural life of the community and to enjoy the arts and to participate in the scientific benefits and progress which result from it (p. 39). There can be no doubt that, in this respect, culture in its broadest sense is related to political freedom. Culture is the right of the people so culture becomes a political consideration, as we shall see in detail shortly. On the 29 June, 1972 the Académie Française attempted to provide a definition of the concept of culture for inclusion in its dictionary. Dollot quotes the definition, which I reproduce in part:

Culture: au sens abstrait et général, culture se dit par référence à nature; c'est le génie humain ajouté à la nature pour en modifier, en enrichir, et en accroître les dons. [. . .]

Culture désigne aussi, pour l'homme, l'application méthodique à développer ses facultés natives par l'étude des lettres, des sciences, des arts, ainsi que par l'observation et la réflexion.

Selon le domaine où s'exerce cette application, on peut préciser culture de l'intelligence, du jugement, de la sensibilité; on dit culture physique pour l'entraînement rationnel à des exercices corporels.

Associé à un qualificatif, culture peut désigner des connaissances propres à une discipline particulière: culture philosophique, littéraire, artistique, scientifique etc. Selon les conditions d'acquisitions, ou la forme du savoir, on peut parler de culture livresque, empirique, d'autodidacte, ou de culture classique, moderne, technique, etc. Absolument, une vaste, une solide culture [. . .].

Sur le plan social, culture désigne aujourd'hui l'ensemble des aspects intellectuels, moraux, matériel des systèmes de valeurs, des styles de vie qui caractérisent une civilisation [. . .]. (pp. 7–8)

Such a definition would send many readers to another dictionary in search of precision and clarification. But the Académie's

definition provides a very useful service. It shows the extent
to which the definition has changed since the 1930s, the date
of the previous dictionary, and it emphasizes the plurality of
meanings. Interestingly and in passing it will be apparent to
many readers that culture in France has a status that it does not
share in the English-speaking world. Culture has, for the French
at least, both a specific and a general sense. It can be applied to
different modes of artistic expression and it can be related to the
way of life of the population. In an ideal world, perhaps, the two
are connected, perhaps even indistinguishable. This, I suggest,
is where politics comes in and where de Gaulle's vision becomes
strikingly apparent.

André Maurois, in his *Portrait de la France et des Français*
(Paris: Hachette, 1955) attempted to define the French character
and used the English and Americans as points of reference. He
wrote:

A la vérité, Anglais et Américains se trompent en croyant les Français
logiques [. . .] Ce qui reste exact, c'est que le Français a le goût des
idées et le respect de l'intelligence; en cela contraire à l'Anglais, qui
a la méfiance des idées générales et le respect du caractère. Chez nous
la culture occupe, dans l'échelle des valeurs, une place plus élevée
qu'ailleurs. (pp. 14–15)

Anybody who has an intimate knowledge of France and the
French will find it easy to understand what Maurois was saying
so many years ago. Is it not still the case today? Where, in the
English-speaking world, does culture have the status which the
French give it? In a review of French theatre in the *Guardian* of
31 December, 1991, Michael Billington concluded:

Britain is much richer than France in living dramatists but infinitely
poorer in theatrical organisation. What we urgently need before the
century is out is a French-style Ministry of Culture.

Culture, in other words, had and has a status in French life which
is unique. But it is apparent that, in the modern world, culture has
to be defended and organized. It is part of national life at many
quite different levels, not simply the artistic and the physical.
Moreover, with the evident mechanization of culture since the
advent of mass media, the state has cultural obligations which,
perhaps, it did not have before.

French cultural policy

It may still be too early to offer an authoritative analysis of the
role of the state in the development of French culture since the
war. It is tempting to date the intervention of the state from 1959
when culture was given 'official' status. David Looseley's chapter

will show how wrong such an approach would be. Some critics
well known in the English-speaking world have not been afraid
to make judgements about the role of the state. John Ardagh in
his *France in the 1980s. The Definitive Book* (Harmondsworth:
Penguin, 1982) is outspoken in his conclusion:

> Under Giscard, culture's share of the overall State budget had been
> falling and was down to under 0.5 per cent. Mitterrand in 1981 then
> promised to raise it sharply, speaking of 1 per cent as a 'reasonable
> minimum'. To be Minister of Culture he chose his friend Jack Lang,
> a brilliant, erratic maverick who had founded the Nancy experimental
> drama festival and is always brimming with ideas – some sane, some
> zany – for the popularizing of the arts. What a contrast he makes to the
> smoothies who filled that post under Giscard! (p. 615)

Ardagh goes on to say that under Mitterrand the state budget for
culture doubled. Mitterrand, he concludes, believed that culture
had a crucial part to play in the new Socialist France that he was
seeking to build.

Ardagh's quick and hasty judgements will provide provocative
judgement but lack the authority that only the true specialist
can offer. There can be no doubt that the French allow cultural
debate to be at the very heart of political thinking. Writing *Ici
et Maintenant* (Paris: Fayard, 1980) Mitterrand offers a scathing
analysis of French cultural policy in the 1960s and 1970s. Asked
about the successors to Malraux, he wrote:

> L'œuvre culturelle de la dernière décennie illustre ce jugement que
> Michel Ange portait sur certains paysages des Écoles du Nord 'faites
> sans raison ni art, sans discernement, sans choix ni certitudes, en somme
> sans substance et sans nerfs'. Où sont les promesses d'antan. Une maison
> de la culture par département? Elles sont au nombre de 14. Un orchestre
> symphonique par région. Ils sont au nombre de 6. Seule a progressé à
> pas de géant l'idéologie rentabiliste à courte vue: la télévision prisonnière
> de la loi du racolage, l'histoire et la philosophie reléguées à la remise
> des lampes à huile, les centres dramatiques asphyxiés. Que dire des
> maisons de jeunes ou des universités? Les caprices du prince succèdent
> aux improvisations sans lendemain de serviteurs zélés sans qu'à aucun
> moment un projet culturel ne mobilise les esprits. (p. 159)

Mitterrand agrees that some of the projects undertaken by Giscard
find favour with him (le musée des Sciences et de l'Industrie à la
Villette, le musée d'Orsay and Beaubourg) but he criticizes the
lack of vision of the Giscard régime claiming that, while only
0.50 per cent of the state budget goes towards culture, in Socialist
municipalities the figure is 12 per cent (p. 161).

François Léotard, a former *ministre de la culture*, suggests that
the cultural process is an ongoing one and one which individuals
will find it difficult to influence. He imagines a traveller in
France in the year 2000 asking who was responsible for the
great architectural projects undertaken by France since the war. He

writes in *Culture: Les chemins du printemps* (Paris, Albin Michel, 1988):

La réponse, on le sait, est: personne en particulier. Cet ensemble est le fruit de débats successifs que se sont déroulés dans le désordre naturel des choses de la vie. Le Centre Georges-Pompidou porte l'empreinte de celui dont il honore le nom et de son ministre de la culture Jacques Duhamel; le musée d'Orsay a été décidé par M. Giscard d'Estaing parce qu'il voulait sauver la gare promise à la démolition; l'opéra de la Bastille était recommandé dès 1968 par Boulez, Vitez et Vilar consultés par André Malraux, et décidé sous M. F. Mitterrand; quant au Grand Louvre, il est l'aboutissement d'un débat qui a commencé en 1913 avec l'achèvement du pavillon de Marsan et les premiers projets de déménagement du ministère des finances de l'aile Flore.

L'exemple de Paris vaut aussi pour le reste de la France. (p. 14)

Léotard suggests that important cultural projects are not necessarily in the hands of the Minister of Culture – they are the product of the French people and an essential aspect of a democratic state. The minister's role is to find ways and means by which culture can flourish at every level. Subventions, he argues, are not the only means at the minister's disposal – indeed, he argues that it is by allowing tax concessions that the role of the state can be most influential ('entre donner davantage et prélever moins, il est toujours préférable de choisir la deuxième solution. Elle est non seulement économiquement meilleure, elle est surtout culturellement plus efficace et plus responsable' (p. 16)). What is apparent to anybody who is not French is that culture in France has a high political profile. It is directly related to the democratic process in a way which is inconceivable in many countries.

In *Une Stratégie du Gouvernement* (Paris: Albatros, 1989) presented by Jacques Chirac, Raymond Barre and Valéry Giscard d'Estaing (Club 89 sous la direction de Michel Aurillac) Chapter 9 is entitled: 'Libérer la Culture et la Communication', pp. 145–55; in it the authors appeal for a liberation of culture and communication from state control:

Cette situation est grave pour notre pays. Sans création culturelle vivace, il n'est pas de pérennité de l'œuvre nationale. Sans une communication activement libre, il n'est pas de réelle démocratie. (p. 145)

The authors criticize what they see as the dismal record of the Socialist government in cultural affairs and appeal for a cultural Renaissance in an attempt to give new confidence to creativity: citizens must be allowed a more active choice in cultural projects; and the state must preserve what is called the 'pérennité culturelle française' (p. 148). In particular the state must, it is said, preserve the nation's heritage (*patrimoine* is the word used increasingly to designate the cultural heritage), it must defend French culture on the international stage, and decentralize all that does not require a national approach. All this will sound very familiar when readers finish our book. The preoccupations of the state have changed little since 1945.

However, what has changed is the means of access to culture. The world of the 1990s is vastly different to that of 1945 and one writer, Pascal Ory, has highlighted this transformation in two books: *L'Entre-deux-Mai: Histoire culturelle de la France, Mai 1969–Mai 1981* (Paris: Seuil, 1983) and *L'Aventure culturelle française, 1945–89* (Paris: Flammarion, 1989). Ory concentrates on the political and economic factors which influence cultural activity. He concludes, not surprisingly perhaps, that it is 'la domination économique et la force politique, au choix ou réunies' which determine what he calls the 'hégémonie culturelle' (*L'Entre-deux-Mai*, pp. 247–8). It is increasingly apparent in the writings of the politicians of culture that the state has a role to play at every level: from education (see *Une Stratégie*, pp. 149–59) to the mass media. André-Hubert Mesnard wrote, in his *Droit et politique de la culture* (Paris: Presses Universitaires de France, 1990):

il n'y a pratiquement pas de ministère qui ne soit concerné par la Culture: pour le moins chaque ministère entretient ses monuments historiques, fait fonctionner ses bibliothèques, s'occupe de l'animation culturelle de son personnel [. . .] et subventionne d'innombrables associations aux activités plus ou moins culturelles ou socio-culturelles. (p. 17)

He concludes where we began by appealing for a wider definition of culture. Marc Fumaroli can talk, in 1991, of *L'Etat culturel* (Paris: Editions de Fallois) ('Mais qu'est-ce donc que cette Culture obsessionnelle propagée par des bureaux, et qui a pris les proportions envahissantes d'une religion de la modernité?'). How, he asks, did France manage to survive before 1959 without a ministry of culture – was it a cultural desert before that – and has the ministry transformed it since?

What has changed, without any doubt, is the manner in which culture is purveyed. In a fascinating paper Jean-Marie Domenach analyses what we might call the mechanization of culture:

Ce qui a changé, par contre, c'est l'environnement, ce sont les mœurs. Dans la société de consommation, les valeurs – ce qui ne peut être ni produit ni consommé – perdent de l'importance. Les gens dépensent sans gêne, ils se précipitent dans les supermarchés, ils empruntent, ils ont des dettes. La télévision et l'automobile renforcent le privé par rapport au public. Le livre de poche, l'achat de disques et de chaînes hi-fi permettent d'accéder à un standing culturel plus élevé. ('Le monde des intellectuels', in *Société et culture de la France contemporaine*, ed. by Georges Santoni, Albany: State University of New York Press, 1981, p. 339)

Domenach claims that the physical nature of France has produced a cultural shock which is felt by few other nations. France, he maintains, is in constant dialogue and conflict: between its rural structure and its modernity; there is constant conflict between the permanence of its ancient structures and its technical innovations (p. 323). Domenach takes a pessimistic view of French culture – more, he claims with reference to books, does not mean better:

Il est vrai que, comme l'argent va à l'argent, la culture va à la culture. On s'est aperçu que c'étaient les mêmes en France qui bénéficiaient des festivals, qui achetaient des livres et il faut donc se méfier des statistiques globales. (p. 350)

The same may well be true for all of France's cultural competitors. Domenach thinks that culture is at the bottom of everybody's shopping list and that it is for this reason that the state feels a central responsibility for it. He claims that the problem for the state is one of overcoming French mentality. The French, he claims, think that they are naturally 'cultivés': 'Passer tous les jours devant le Louvre ou sur la place de la Concorde est une chose qui aide, peut-être, mais cela ne suffit pas' (p. 359). For Domenach, therefore, confronted by what he sees as the commercialization of culture and French apathy, the state has simply a 'corrective' role: 'L'Etat a compris que son action culturelle ne pouvait pas vraiment rivaliser avec la puissance des *businessmen* de la culture, ceux qui fabriquent les disques, les livres, les films' (p. 360). The paradox, for Domenach, is that greater commercialization has led to decreased creativity.

Certainly, it is against the background of mechanization, of the industrialization of culture, that the state, in France, understands that it has an educative role (see Mitterrand, *Ici et Maintenant*, pp. 158–9; *Une Stratégie de Gouvernement*, (Paris, Albatros, 1989) pp. 149–50 where the *authors* see the need to 'rendre la culture vivante dans l'enseignement'). What, I think, will be apparent in the course of reading this book is that the words of François Léotard have an evident truth, when he suggested:

Nous sommes entrés dans une période – probablement longue – de bouleversement des comportements culturels, des pratiques de consommation. S'en étonner, le regretter en imputer la responsabilité à un gouvernement ou à un autre, est aussi stupide que de considérer Champollion comme responsable de la civilisation égyptienne. (*Culture*, p. 31)

What will be apparent to readers is that there is an active engagement between creator and state, a constant cultural dialectic between government and public which is, perhaps, unique to France. In a report entitled *La Politique culturelle 1981–91*, (Paris, Ministère de la Culture, de la Communication et des grands travaux, 1991) Jack Lang, the minister of culture at the time of writing, provides a full account of what might be called 'cultural activity' during the ten-year period. The report begins:

Dix ans de priorité gouvernementale:
En 1981, pour la première fois, la culture est devenue une priorité

gouvernementale. Grâce à un spectaculaire doublement du budget de son ministère, elle se trouvait enfin dotée de moyens à la hauteur de ses ambitions. Depuis, cette priorité n'a cessé d'être réaffirmée, hormis pendant la période 1986–1988, et les crédits de progresser, jusqu'à frôler en 1991 le seuil symbolique de 1% du budget de l'Etat. (p. 3)

Lang goes on to express the cultural ambition of the French socialist state: to provide excellence (and he quotes the Grand Louvre project and the courage of the Peï pyramid design), to open up what he calls the frontiers of culture: to use new technology to take culture out of its old fortresses and to make it available to a wider public (here he quotes the 'immense succès de la Fête de la musique'). He concludes that in the last ten years the very perception of culture has changed. Culture no longer has a backward-looking stance. It is very much present and creative. It is a creator of jobs, acts against the exclusion of minorities and opens up dialogues with other countries. And yet, of course, Lang realizes that France cannot turn its back on the past: he is proud of the way in which France has attempted to marry the old with the new: he quotes extensive renovation projects (L'Opéra royal de Versailles, les châteaux de Compiègne et Fontainebleau, la cathédrale de Nantes); archaeologists have, he says, seen their funds multiplied five times; the Archives Nationales in Paris have been provided with a new Centre d'accueil to enable easier access to the archives, using new technology.

Readers of this book will find a portrait of France in which a number of themes can be seen to dominate. In terms of architecture, France has dared to establish new norms and to juxtapose striking new buildings and traditional masterpieces. The desperately poor region which consisted of what the French call 'bidonvilles' or shanty towns which stood shoulder to shoulder with the richer suburban areas of Paris, was transformed into a dramatic office development called 'La Défense'. Designed to take some 100,000 employees out of the congested Paris office areas, it was given the go-ahead as long ago as 1956. The office blocks were intended to dominate this development with towers some thirty floors high and looking, then, arrogantly modern. Many aesthetic sensibilities were offended but this new development gave Paris and France desperately needed new office space within easy reach of Paris. Standing in the Tuileries gardens one could follow the lines of the Champs-Elysées up to the Arc de Triomphe and beyond to the tall Manhattan-style skyscrapers. If La Défense was too close for comfort, what is to be made of the architectural monument which can be seen as its crowning glory, La Grande Arche? Opened to celebrate the bicentenary of the French Revolution, the new edifice was first used officially for the summit of the seven leading industrial powers in July 1989. It has not produced the kind of controversy which surrounded the opening of the Centre Pompidou in 1976. Hated by traditionalists and admired by modernists the Centre Pompidou, set in the historic Marais area of Paris, produced fierce debate about the design of the building and its situation. An article in *Le Point* of 4 September, 1989 asked the question: 'Y a-t-il une esthétique Mitterrand?'. Nobody has had a greater effect on Parisian architecture since Napoléon III, the author claims, and lists the monuments which Mitterrand has encouraged and fostered: L'Arche, L'Opéra-Bastille, la Pyramide du Louvre. It is said, by his opponents, that his only aim is to leave Paris with striking reminders of his periods of office. If these new edifices are symbols of Mitterrand they suggest that the President was innovative, daring and, on occasions, impractical. It looks as if the new library being built to house the national collection will be of greater use to photographers than to readers. Obviously, not all the changes made to Paris since the war can be attributed to Mitterrand. France was changing rapidly in the 1950s and 1960s, shaking off the cobwebs of traditionalism and moving desperately towards a new era.

If the buildings leave us with the obvious physical reminders of regimes, other cultural phenomena should not be overlooked. The role of the state in the protection and encouragement of culture is enormous in France, far greater, I think, than in any other country; the feminist movement, so powerful in France and with an intellectual force which is unrivalled, is a magnificent feature of France since the war. France has attempted to retain those elements of its culture which give it power and status; it has striven to maintain the purity of its language and the international flavour of its culture. As we move towards the year 2000 France can be seen as an example of cultural dynamism, retaining its past values and attempting constantly to innovate and to experiment. This book will show the reader how, in various cultural areas, France has been active and how such activity has been centrally controlled and encouraged. Space does not allow us to cover every aspect of life which could be called cultural: there are gaps that others, no doubt, will want to fill: the visual arts and serious music are just two examples.

It is against this background where the state's role in cultural matters has become very much a political priority that the different contributors to this volume are writing. Our book charts the evolution of culture since the war, showing significant developments and indicating the extent to which France has a cultural commitment to the past, the present and the future.

Acknowledgements

I would like to express my thanks to Mme Schneider of the Ministère de la Culture, 2 rue Jean-Lantier, 75001 Paris for her help in providing useful photocopies and bibliographies and to Hélène Dussauchoy of the Département des Affaires internationales, 14 rue Notre-Dame des Victoires, 75002 Paris who provided important statistical information and a copy of the Lang report.

PART ONE

The arts

CHAPTER 2

Literature

Rachel Edwards

This chapter will deal with the main trends in literature, especially the novel, since 1945. It will include a brief section on literary criticism and poetry. More attention will be given to lesser known authors of the post-war period than to well-documented writers such as Sartre and Camus, who will only be touched on here. The aim is to redress the balance and achieve a more general picture of the period. In addition, writers of the *mode rétro*, whose way was paved by the right-wing novelists of the 1950s, will be discussed. The challenge to Existentialism after 1960 in the domain of criticism will equally be considered, in particular the influence of Structuralism and its successor Deconstruction as well as the role played by the journal *Tel Quel* in the promotion of both criticism and new fiction. A general appreciation of the developments in criticism at this point will facilitate the comprehension of experimental writing such as that of the *nouveau roman*. (It must be noted, however, that advances made by the *nouveaux romanciers* also helped to feed the theory of *Tel Quel*.) Deconstruction will also act as an aid in understanding the work of women writers which proliferated after 1968. Likewise a basic knowledge of Structuralism is particularly useful when tackling writers such as Michel Tournier and Patrick Grainville. The *Beur* writers will also be taken into consideration. Finally, four of the major poets to have emerged since 1945 will be examined, although it must be stressed that this section is intended simply to give a flavour of a domain which, although it does not enjoy the popularity of previous eras, nevertheless has many writers using different techniques within it.

Littérature engagée

In 1945 the single most important influence on all aspects of culture was that of the war itself. Nowhere was its impact more strongly felt than in France. Not only did France have to face the full horrors of the concentration camps and the devastating potential of the atomic bomb, it also had to deal with its own immediate past: occupation by the Nazis since its defeat in 1940. The Occupation brought internal conflicts to the country which did not resolve themselves until many years later (and in some instances solutions are yet to be found). Whilst some people actively collaborated during the war, the majority remained passive in the face of the aggressor and only a small minority actually resisted. The allegiance of writers was also split. Although it is true that most called for resistance and novelists such as Camus, Simon and Duras actively resisted, a small number of quality writers collaborated. Among them were Pierre Drieu la Rochelle and Robert Brasillach. The end of the war brought fierce reprisals. During the *épuration* many people were put to death by the Resistance. Drieu committed suicide to avoid the fate which awaited Brasillach who was executed in 1945. The full extent of the *épuration* was condemned by many left-wing writers including Camus. The end of the war also saw the beginning of the Cold War which was brought about by the division of the world into two blocs and allegiances were once again divided. This also had an impact on literature.

At the end of the war the two most influential writers were Sartre and Camus. Both felt that in order for literature to be authentic, it had to be *engagée*, that is, to manifest commitment to left-wing political values. Existentialism, which was given a new prominence in their writings during the war, now took on a humanist face as Sartre's *L'Existentialisme est un humanisme* (1946) indicates. But, whereas both writers advocated *engagement*, they differed in their approach to the USSR and the Communist Party which had now gained considerable support in France. Differences in this area led to their famous quarrel of 1952 triggered by Camus's *L'Homme Révolté* (1951) which denounced revolution because of its violence and suggested a form of moral revolt in its stead.[1] Camus's dislike of Communism had become more acute in 1951, the same year as *L'Homme Révolté* appeared, after Rousset provided evidence of the Stalinist labour camps. Sartre, however, continued to voice support for the Soviet Union until the latter invaded Hungary in 1956. But, whilst Sartre supported the USSR, he never subscribed to any form of 'controlled' writing, unlike others who wrote novels to order as a means of spreading the message of Socialist Realism. Amongst them were Roger Vailland, André Stil and Pierre Courtade.

By far the most talented of the three writers is Roger Vailland. Originally refused membership of the Parti Communiste Français (PCF) in 1942, he became a member ten years later having proved his commitment to Communism through journalism and two novels, *Bon pied, bon œil* (1950) and *Un Jeune homme seul* (1951). However, it was really with the publication of *Beau Masque* (1954) and, a year later, *325,000 Francs* that this commitment was most convincingly demonstrated. Both novels criticize bourgeois capitalism and individual efforts to improve the workers' conditions are portrayed as worthless: only collective activity will bring about unity and hope for the future. In *Beau Masque*, a tight structure is achieved by the integration of personal and political issues. This is helped by the role Vailland himself plays as journalist, for it allows him to comment on different events and characters without it seeming an overt and unwanted intrusion. The novel sets about examining two political factions. On the one hand, the bourgeois management of a silk factory, which is portrayed as decadent and immoral for exploiting the workers by accepting US financial aid and thus putting their jobs in jeopardy. On the other, the workers, who are depicted as strong and healthy. They are led by the exemplary Pierrette Amable who organizes strike action and an anti-US demonstration. Caught up in the conflict is Beau Masque, an Italian immigrant worker, who, although he has a history of Communist involvement, is nevertheless perceived as an outsider simply because he is an immigrant. The management and Beau Masque are linked on a personal level by Pierrette who becomes Beau Masque's lover (which adds to her credibility as a person but undermines her stature as a political leader in the eyes of the others) but is also admired by Philippe Letourneau, the owner's stepson, who, having fallen in love with her, reveals company secrets. In the end Beau Masque is shot thus becoming, as J.E. Flower notes, 'the symbolic victim of the capitalist system and of CRS aggression' (*Literature and the Left in France: Society, Politics and the Novel since the late Nineteenth Century*, London/New York: Methuen, 1983, p. 164). Despite the fact that her lover is killed, Pierrette is ready to face future conflict. The ending, however, is not without some irony given that victory is achieved as much through the owners' attempt to avoid scandal as it is by strike action. But the final message is that it is only concerted political action which counts in the face of the obvious immorality of the capitalist system.

325,000 Francs has similar aims but goes about achieving them in a different way. In the novel, Busard needs 700,000 francs in order to rise above his station as a factory worker and become the owner of a snack bar on the N7. With his own savings and the dowry which his marriage to Marie–Jeanne will bring him he has just over half the amount and decides to work hard to earn the rest before marrying and moving to the snack bar. During his final term on the machine, which he mans in shifts with another worker, his hand is crushed and, although he now has enough money, he is no longer capable of running a snack bar. Instead he becomes the owner of a local café which is unsuccessful. He then has to consider going back to the factory to work for a lower wage because of his disability. The clear moral of the story is that individual action counts for nothing and that improvements can only come about through collective political action. Busard is punished because he fails to realize this. As Flower points out: 'Busard and Marie–Jeanne are, like so many of their class, largely unaware of their environment or of the forces which control their lives. Escape may be glimpsed but they have been conditioned into imagining it only in clichés or stereotypes – *un vrai métier, un snack-bar, une Cadillac,* for example – most of which, in practical terms, are quite unattainable' (*Literature and the Left in France,* pp. 168–9).

Although not as good nor as successful an author as Vailland, Pierre Courtade is a particularly interesting example of an extreme left-wing writer. Elected to the central committee of the PCF in 1954, he remained publicly faithful to Stalin even after the de-Stalinization of 1957. Whilst Courtade's novel *Jimmy* (1951) betrays a conflict between personal and political demands, his later novel, *La Place rouge* (1961), successfully resolves this conflict. It is a kind of *Bildungsroman* which traces the development of Simon Bordes from youth to political maturity (a time which coincides with, and is equated to, his 'becoming a man') and this via a period of doubt which is eroded by the informative situations in which he finds himself. Throughout the narrative Courtade often uses Bordes to voice his own opinions and as such the novel takes on an autobiographical and even confessional quality which adds to its didactic persuasiveness. The text begins with a meeting at the cinema between Bordes and his friends, who reappear at strategic points throughout the narrative and against whom his progress can be judged. The film they see is Eisenstein's *The Battleship Potemkin* which metaphorically points to the journey which the young people are about to undertake. Later, they gather at the aptly named café, *L'Avenir*, and at this point in the narrative Bordes's political doubts are completely obvious. A change in Bordes's way of thinking is only fully effected when he meets a member of the Resistance, whom he marries after his first wife's death. This encounter coincides with his political coming of age. Where he initially expressed doubt at Prévost's suggestion that the Nazi–Soviet pact was a necessary part of the historical process, he is now ready to accept this explanation when it comes to the Stalin trials. His personal journey is complete and the novel ends with his visit to Moscow where everything points to a golden future.

The Hussards

If Courtade is representative of one extreme of the spectrum in relation to *littérature engagée*, the other extreme is represented by a group of writers who became prominent in the 1950s and who were considered right-wing, more because of their total refusal of *engagement* and their commitment to a completely different literary tradition, than because of any strong political convictions. They consisted of young writers who had reached maturity during the war years and who came together around 1945 and continued to be associated with the reviews *Arts* and *La Parisienne*. The latter was founded in 1953 by Jacques Laurent who became known as 'le Sartre de la droite'. Included in their ranks were Michel Déon, Félicien Marceau, Kléber Haedens and, more importantly, Jacques Laurent, Antoine Blondin and Roger Nimier. They were known as the 'Hussards', a name coined by Bernard Franck which he took from Nimier's novel of 1950, *Le Hussard bleu*.[2] The 'Hussards' looked back to the eighteenth century and Stendhal in particular (*Le Hussard bleu* recalling *Le Chasseur vert*, the title which Stendhal had initially intended for *Lucien Leuwen*). They were also influenced by the writers of the 1920s and 1930s such as Chardonne, Marcel Aymé and Drieu la Rochelle. Their novels were often more a reflection of the gay 1920s in their depiction of parties, alcohol, straight dresses and fast cars than of the 1950s to which they belonged.

This group is also important in that it dared to challenge orthodox presentations of the Occupation. Their protagonists, instead of being heroic members of the Resistance, often collaborated, not so much out of political conviction as out of self-interest or merely boredom. Blondin's *Europe buissonnière* (1949) and *Le Chemin des écoliers* (1952) form a burlesque account of the war years and recount the adventures of several almost picaresque characters. However, the most daring evocation of the war period, given France's need at the time to deny the role it played as collaborator, came from Nimier. His first novel *Les Epées* (1949) tells the story of François Sanders, the son of a professional soldier, who leaves the Resistance to join the German police to whom he hands over his girlfriend, also a member of the Resistance, and whom he calmly watches being shot. He is totally immoral and considers members of the Resistance to be merely victims of what he calls the 'Joan of Arc complex'. However, his allegiance to the *milice* is not based on political conviction and he thinks no more of the collaborators than he does of the *résistants*.

François Sanders reappears in *Le Hussard bleu*. This time he has joined a regiment of the French army which occupies Germany after the war. The novel is largely related through the monologues of characters, who, far from being military heroes, are a mixed bunch of essentially undesirables. It is considered Nimier's best novel and brought him instant literary acclaim as well as much criticism. For many, Sanders's last words in *Le Hussard bleu* sum up his essential character: 'Tout ce qui est humain m'est étranger' (Paris: Folio, 1950, p. 434). This deliberate rejection of moral values seems to be the result of a disillusionment which underlies the work of most of the 'Hussards' and which is voiced by Nimier in *Le Grand d'Espagne* (1950): 'Vingt ans et les fumées d'Hiroshima pour nous apprendre que le monde n'était ni sérieux, ni durable' (Paris: Table Ronde, 1950, p. 136). In their work disillusion is often mixed with melancholy and the bitter/sweet experiences of youth which they know cannot last. In *La Droite buissonnière* Vandromme comments: 'Comme son hussard bleu, Roger Nimier pense que c'est une grâce de mourir jeune; mais elle lui a été refusée, et il se demande comment il va se comporter devant la difficulté d'être' (Paris: Les Sept Couleurs, p. 160). This comment is doubly ironic given that two years later Nimier died in a car accident at the age of only thirty-seven and in so doing solved the problem outlined by Vandromme. That he should die in a car crash also links his fate to his work, as it is largely through Nimier that the Jaguar became a symbol in fiction. It was most notably taken up by the popular novelist Françoise Sagan whose style has often been likened to that of Nimier as Claude Bonnefoy points out: 'S'il fallait, aujourd'hui, chercher un certain style hussard, c'est chez Sagan que nous le trouverions: même goût de la vitesse, de l'alcool, dérivatifs d'une société factice qui éprouve l'ennui à la fleur de peau.'[3]

The 'Mode rétro'

Although the 'Hussards' themselves did not really last beyond the 1950s their work did go some way towards laying the foundations for what was later to become known as the *mode rétro* which began in the late 1960s and flourished during the 1970s. The *mode rétro* came into being precisely to challenge the official view of the Occupation which championed the 'myth' of the Resistance, myth here being used in the sense of a fabricated and therefore false account of history. Although the 'Hussards' had attempted to challenge this myth during the 1950s, it remained intact until the demise of de Gaulle in 1970; de Gaulle being the man who was largely responsible for its origin and perpetration. As Alan Morris points out in his article 'Attacks on the Gaullist "Myth" in French Literature Since 1969' the myth comprised four main tenets: 'First, the number of real collaborators was minute; second, the vast majority of French people were basically patriotic, even if some were misled; third the true cause of France was actively expressed by an elite of heroic *résistants*; and finally, the Resistance was incarnated by Charles de Gaulle.'[4] The effect of this was that a whole part of French history was neglected. The real role played by those who collaborated and the extent of the collaboration was ignored as were the conflicts within the Resistance and the crimes of the *épuration*, which left little to be desired between *résistant* and *gestapiste*. It was not until the end of de Gaulle's political career in 1969, and his death a year later, that the way was opened up for an attack on his ideas. It was now that the writers of the *mode rétro* set about redressing the balance. As Morris points out, many of them had been children during the war and had fathers who collaborated with the Germans. They wrote, therefore, partly to understand and come to terms with their real past which they felt had been denied them. Many sought both to exorcize the mixture of feelings which arose from the knowledge that the man they knew as kind and loving had collaborated and to understand how this might have come about. There are two main ways in which the writers of the *mode rétro* achieved this: by attacking the Resistance and by showing the collaborators in a more favourable light than that in which they had hitherto been shown.

The trend itself is usually said to have begun in 1969 with Marcel Orphüls's four and a half hour film *Le Chagrin et la Pitié*. Initially intended for television, it was banned and not broadcast until 1981, although it did play to packed audiences in the cinemas. Another film which also caused much controversy when it appeared was Louis Malle's *Lacombe Lucien* (1974), the screenplay for which was written by both Malle and Patrick Modiano, one of the *mode rétro's* most exemplary writers. *Lacombe Lucien* takes up most of Modiano's concerns in his fiction: it concentrates on the essential ambiguity of the war years and on the highly ambivalent roles played by what were formerly termed torturer and victim. Criticism of the film initially centred on the fact that the seventeen-year old Lucien, a normal lad of peasant origins, could join the German police purely by chance and without any real convictions. Lucien at first wants to join the Resistance because his friend has done so but he is told that he is too young. Shortly after this, his bicycle has a puncture and he has to push it to a neighbouring town where he arrives after curfew. He is picked up by the Gestapo whilst watching party-goers return to a hotel which houses the police headquarters. He is welcomed by them, given several drinks and inadvertently divulges the name of the Resistance leader in his own village. Offered fine clothes, money and power, he joins their ranks. And all this is simply because he had a puncture. In as much as Lucien is a victim of fate and is someone with no real political convictions, he is reminiscent of the main character of Modiano's *La Ronde de nuit* (1970) who joins the Gestapo by chance and is given the name Swing Troubadour. He is then asked to infiltrate the Resistance, which he does, and assumes the name La Princesse de Lamballe. The Resistance then asks him to infiltrate the Gestapo and so Swing Troubadour/Lamballe becomes a double agent. He hands over the Lieutenant of the Resistance to Le Khédive, the Gestapo's leader, and finally tries to make amends by attempting to shoot Le Khédive, something he fails to do. This doubleness of intention along with his adoption of a surrogate family in the guise of the odd couple Coco Lacour and Esmeralda is also mirrored in the film in Lucien's involvement with the Horns, a Jewish family. Lucien falls in love with Albert Horn's daughter, France.

The normal role of torturer/victim is undermined in *Lacombe Lucien* by the fact that Lucien saves France and her grandmother from the Gestapo by shooting an SS officer and then taking them up into the hills to hide. Even though his motive for saving them is ambiguous, the fact that he does so puts the 'torturer' in the role of 'saviour'. Usual values are further overturned by the fact that Lucien is captured and shot by the Resistance at the time of the Liberation which places the 'saviour' in the place of the 'victim' and the Resistance movement in the place of the 'torturer'.

The Horn family are also the focus of a series of similar conflicts which are very personal to Modiano himself, for he is a Jew whose father lived in hiding in Paris during the Occupation and frequented the infamous black-marketeer Maurice Sachs. In the film, the Horns become Lucien's surrogate family (his real father has been imprisoned). In a sense, Modiano is attempting to reconstruct what might have been his own life at the time, with Horn as his father. (This is completely fictitious as Modiano was not born until after the Liberation, in 1945.) The Horns are not only Jews but they are German Jews. Albert Horn is therefore an ironic example in that the German race which hates Jews also contains Jews. Furthermore, as he is a member of the people who want to persecute him, he is victim and torturer in one. This is strengthened by the fact that he is ensured survival only in as much as he works on the black market and serves those who want to annihilate his race. The same ambiguity is seen in his daughter, France. She is both Jewess and, by virtue of her name, that which is anti-semitic. During the Occupation, France, the country, handed its Jews over to the Nazis.

Lucien, in sleeping with France, not only prostitutes France, Horn's daughter, as Horn says, but also has total power over France, the country. Nazi conquers both Jewess and French soil. In calling his daughter a whore, Horn nominates himself a pimp as he allows Lucien to sleep with her under his roof. This he does not so much for money, although he accepts Lucien's gifts, but in return for his own life. In this way Horn is not dissimilar to Schlemelovitch in *La Place de l'Etoile* (1968), Modiano's first novel, which calls into question the whole issue of what it means to be a Jew. In this novel Schlemelovitch comes to incarnate all possible anti-semitic stereotypes of Jewishness and all aspects of Jewish history. At one point he becomes involved with Lévy-

Vendôme (whose very name betrays an incompatible mixture of Jewishness and Frenchness) and the white slave-trade, sending white women to foreign parts and thereby prostituting France once more.

In *Lacombe Lucien*, Horn eventually becomes his own torturer when, in a combined attempt at martyrdom and suicide, he goes to the hotel to seek Lucien and discuss his daughter's future. He is immediately deported to a concentration camp. This sense of martyrdom is also prevalent throughout much of Modiano's fiction, as seen for example in Lamballe's attempt to shoot Le Khédive which only leads to his own downfall. It is also indicated by the epigraph of *La Place de l'Etoile:*

Au mois de juin 1942, un officier allemand s'avance vers un jeune homme et lui dit:
"Pardon, monsieur, où se trouve la Place de l'Etoile?"
Le jeune homme désigne le côté gauche de sa poitrine. (Paris: Folio, 1968)

Whilst the anecdote plays on the Parisian landmark and Jewish identity, it also shows that, in pointing to the Star of David which the Jews were obliged to wear during the Occupation, the man is giving himself up to the torturer thereby echoing Horn's visit to the hotel. One wonders if, in Horn's case, Modiano is not trying to exorcize some kind of guilt for his own father surviving the holocaust. In giving himself up, Horn makes a moral choice and his ensuing disposal is not only because he is a Jew but also acts as a punishment for his living a lie for so long.

Modiano recreates his father in much of his fiction and this search for his own identity through that of his father's is one of the most important themes in his novels. His texts always focus on the same central points which may explain why he was awarded the Prix Goncourt for his work as a whole after the publication of the *Rue des Boutiques obscures*. This novel again tries to reconstruct the war years through an amnesiac's attempt to discover his past.

The *mode rétro*, therefore, can be interpreted as an essentially ambiguous mode. On the political level, like most post-1968 activities, it challenges the old order and the father figure supplied by de Gaulle through its counter myths; on the other hand, it is also a search for other father figures who were absent in real life and who are needed both on a personal and a political level to give guidance and direction.

Criticism

Just as the writers of the *mode rétro* and the 'Hussards' before them directly challenged the idea of 'littérature engagée' in the domain of fiction, so Structuralism became the dominant trend in criticism after 1960. The major breakthrough had come about earlier in the area of linguistics when Saussure discovered the arbitrary nature of the sign or word (*Cours de linguistique générale*, ed. by Tullio de Mauro, Paris: Payot, 1973). The sign itself is split into two parts: its form, the *signifiant* or 'signifier', and its meaning (the idea which the form conveys) known as the *signifié* or 'signified'. It is the link between *signifiant* and *signifié* which is arbitrary. There is no reason why a fork should be called a 'fork', it could just as well have been called a 'boop' or a 'cat'. The reason we relate the word fork to the object fork is because the word differs from other words such as spoon, knife and cup. What is important therefore is the way in which words differ from each other. In effect, what matters is not the words in themselves but the way in which we combine them, for it is this which enables us to communicate. This same basic linguistic model was then applied to other areas of human science. For example, through his close readings of Freud, the psychoanalyst Lacan discovered that the unconscious is structured in the same way as language (most of his theories are contained in his *Ecrits*, Paris: Seuil, 1966).

In the area of anthropology, Lévi-Strauss set about the structural analysis of myths, in particular those of the North and South American Indians, which are used as tools to resolve cultural contradictions. He found all myths to belong to a basic set and each individual articulation of any specific myth to be a subset or a rearrangement of the elements found in the main set. Again, the breakthrough he made was that, unlike other mythologists such as Jung, who considered basic aspects of myth to be archetypes residing deep in the human psyche, he concluded that as in language what matters is not the elements in themselves but the way in which these elements are combined.[5]

In the domain of French culture, Roland Barthes provided a structural analysis of what he terms modern 'myths' in *Mythologies* (1957) and of fashion in *Système de la Mode* (1967). Following the example of Vladimir Propp, he also worked on the structural analysis of the *récit*.[6] In a later work *S/Z* (1970), a detailed study of Balzac's *Sarrasine*, Barthes shows how meaning in the text is produced by reference to five different codes which are entirely made up of previous literary discourses. Paradoxically, the result is that in analysing the text in terms of the five codes and thereby identifying an underlying structure, the text is opened out and becomes the locus of a number of possible readings. In this way *S/Z* can also be seen as a Deconstructionist reading of *Sarrasine*.

Deconstruction, in fact, grew out of Structuralism and may be viewed as a reaction against it. The basic tenets of Deconstruction are set out by Jacques Derrida in *L'Ecriture et la différence* (1967). Derrida agrees with Saussure's premise that in language there are only differences and no positive terms. However, unlike Saussure, he does not believe that the *signifiant* and the *signifié* are but two sides to the same coin. Instead he concentrates on the concept of what he terms *différance* which carries connotations of both difference and deferral in English. He sees writing as the continual freeplay of the signifier whose meaning is constantly modified by other signifiers and therefore any ultimate meaning is continually deferred. It is this lack of any absolute meaning which opens up considerable space for a variety of interpretations and prevents the text from being reduced to only one meaning.

In this way, Derrida is seen to champion writing over speech, which according to him had wrongly been given precedence over writing in the Western Philosophical Tradition, since it was supposed that in speech precise meaning could be conveyed because of the speaker's intentions. For Derrida, this 'metaphysics of presence' is completely delusory; writing, in as much as it constitutes the freeplay of the signifier, is therefore prior to speech. C. Norris comments:

Writing for Derrida, is the 'free play' or element of undecidability within every system of communication. Its operations are precisely those which escape the self-consciousness of speech and its deluded sense of the mastery of concept over language. Writing is the endless displacement of meaning which both governs language and places it forever beyond the reach of a stable, self-authenticating knowledge. (*Deconstruction: Theory and Practice*, revised edition, London: Routledge, 1991, pp. 28–9)

Deconstruction therefore opened up criticism by allowing the text to be read in different ways rather than reducing it to a single meaning governed by an underlying structure.

It is worth pointing out at this point the role played by the quarterly review *Tel Quel* in the promotion of both Structuralist and post-Structuralist forms of criticism. *Tel Quel* was founded in 1960 and grew up in opposition to Sartre's *Les Temps modernes*. It was at its most influential during the late 1960s and early 1970s when it helped to establish the reputations of Barthes, Derrida, Julia Kristeva and Gérard Genette. It also helped to promote experimental writing by both writers and poets. Among them, Philippe Sollers, who, when *Tel Quel* folded in 1983, became the editor of the *Editions du Seuil, Tel Quel* books as well as editor of *L'Infini*, the journal which replaced *Tel Quel*. Sollers was one of *Tel Quel's* main contributors of both theory and fiction. His novels can be perceived as a development of the techniques inaugurated by the *nouveaux romanciers* of the 1950s and 1960s whose fiction can essentially be identified as an experimental mode which also grew up in opposition to the *littérature engagée* of the time.

The 'Nouveau Roman'

It is worth reminding the reader at this point that writers such as
François Mauriac, notably in *Un adolescent d'autrefois* (1969)[7]
and Aragon in *La Semaine sainte* (1958), also contributed to new
fiction, even if they seem to belong to an earlier period. By 1960,
however, there were six main *nouveaux romanciers:* Alain Robbe-
Grillet, Nathalie Sarraute, Michel Butor, Claude Simon, Bernard
Pinget and Claude Ollier, the first four of whom are the most
important. Although these writers did not form a coherent group
and certainly wrote in different ways, they nevertheless all shared
the same aim: to undermine the traditional novel and to create
new narrative modes. In his preface to Nathalie Sarraute's *Portrait
d'un inconnu* (1947), Sartre describes these types of novel as
anti-romans and explains what they set out to achieve:

Les anti-romans conservent l'apparence et les contours du roman; ce
sont des ouvrages d'imagination qui nous présentent des personnages
fictifs et nous racontent leur histoire. Mais c'est pour mieux décevoir: il
s'agit de contester le roman par lui-même, de le détruire sous nos yeux
dans le temps qu'on semble l'édifier, d'écrire le roman d'un roman qui
ne se fait pas, qui ne peut pas se faire, de créer une fiction qui soit aux
grandes œuvres composées de Dostoievsky et de Meredith ce qu' était
aux tableaux de Rembrandt et de Rubens cette toile de Miró, intitulée
Assassinat de la peinture.[8]

From this it can be seen that the main aim of these novelists is
to undermine the procedures used in the traditional novel thereby
bringing about its destruction and producing a new type of writing.
Sartre's use of 'décevoir', containing the English meanings of
deceive, disappoint and delude, calls into play the role of the
reader, for it is he or she who will often be deceived and deluded
and will also be disappointed in his or her expectations of what
a novel 'should do'. In order to appreciate what the new novel
achieves, the reader must leave behind old expectations and come
to the text ready to confront the new. Instead of being a mere
recipient of information given by the traditional text, the reader
now assumes an active role in the creative process and journeys
through the text with the writing itself. He or she therefore
participates in what Robbe-Grillet has called the 'aventure de
l'écriture' (*Pour un nouveau roman*, Paris: Editions de Minuit,
1963). It is useful at this point to mention Barthes's distinction in
S/Z between the *texte lisible*, which refers us to a stable, outside
reality which is ultimately finite and is therefore easy to read,
and the *texte scriptible* which concentrates on the 'écriture' and
the actual process of writing thereby making reading problematic
as well as part of the creative process (Paris: Seuil, 1970). In
Robbe-Grillet's *Dans le labyrinthe*, for example, the labyrinth in
which one finds oneself is precisely that of the text.

The main way in which the *nouveau roman* challenges the traditional novel is by destabilizing the presentation of character and plot. It does this by pointing to the artificiality of the text and by being self-reflexive, which means that it reflects itself as a piece of writing. Each of the *nouveaux romanciers* have different ways of going about this. As early as 1938 Nathalie Sarraute had written her first series of what might be termed prose poems, *Tropismes*, which contain the seeds of what was to flourish in the rest of her novels. Ahead of its time, it went unnoticed and she only became associated with the *nouveau roman* with the publication of *Martereau* in 1953. *Tropismes*, a scientific term meaning a reflex action in response to external stimuli such as heat or light, is used by Sarraute to designate the semi-conscious workings of the mind which arise in the individual before they become fully articulated thoughts. It is these psychological movements existing in an area of *pré-langage* which Nathalie Sarraute tries to put into writing. She labels this kind of interior monologue *sous-conversation*. Its ruminations provide a strong contrast between what characters say to each other, or the common ground on which they communicate, and what is going on in that proud and egotistical or sometimes anxious and self-effacing area underneath. In this way, the portrayal of a character as a fixed and classified psychological being is undermined. 'Je' is a fluid entity as it refers to whoever is speaking: and one person's 'Je' is another person's 'il' or 'elle'. Robbe-Grillet, incidentally, was against Sarraute's 'psychologie des profondeurs', preferring to remain on the surface of individuals and things.

Since her texts are often largely made up of the psychological movements of the characters, traditional concepts of plot are also done away with. In *Les Fruits d'or* (Paris: Folio, 1963) the plot might vaguely be outlined as the rise and fall of a novel of that very name. Although it is said to be written by Bréhier, there is a sense in which the book about which we are reading *is* the actual book we are reading. This technique, which in this instance points to the self-reflexive nature of the novel, is known as *mise-en-abyme*, and although it is not new (Gide, for example, used it in *Les Faux-monnayeurs)* it is much favoured by the *nouveaux romanciers*.

The title *Les Fruits d'or* also points to another of Sarraute's preoccupations: the at once fluid and yet fixed nature of language which is both living and organic like fruit, in that it is the only way in which we can communicate, and dead, because, once articulated, an expression is fixed. Language therefore exists in that area 'entre la vie et la mort' (the title of Sarraute's next novel (1968) in which we read about the novelist writing about writing). In *Les Fruits d'or*, the reader is also included in the fluid movement of the text and the final sentence rings out ironically:

'Vous en êtes encore . . . aux Fruits d'or?' (p. 158) to which the reader has to reply in the affirmative.

In *La Modification* (Paris: Editions de Minuit, 1957) Butor also employs the second person plural, but here it is the voice in which the whole of the text (apart from very few passages) is narrated. It has various functions and solves certain problems of narration. First, it breaks with tradition in that novels are normally related in the first or third person. Here, the use of the second person plural, or *vous* form, means the reader is being directly addressed and so it is also the reader who finds him or herself on a train about to enter a compartment when the novel begins: 'Vous avez mis le pied gauche sur la rainure de cuivre, et de votre épaule droite vous essayez en vain de pousser un peu plus le panneau coulissant' (p. 7). However, as you read on you discover the *vous* is not only you but is also addressed to Léon Delmont, a man of forty-five who is travelling third class from Paris to Rome with the intention of returning to Paris with his girlfriend Cécile. He has found her a job and intends to live with her once he has left his wife and four children. The *vous* form therefore serves the double function of embroiling the reader in the text but at the same time giving him or her the space to observe the main character. Furthermore, the second person refers us back to a narrator addressing the *vous*. The creative process is therefore firmly kept in view. It is the narrator who animates the character and who is responsible for the words on the page. The illusion of naivety, often achieved by the use of the third person narrator who purports to convey the truth of a given situation in which the reader is intended to believe, is therefore exposed as fictitious.

Butor's use of the second person also helps to solve other problems of narration which he outlines in *Répertoire II* (Paris: Editions de Minuit, 1964). It is this form which most adequately solves the problem of the interior monologue, for in *La Modification* the action may be seen to take place inside Delmont's head. Normally interior monologue is recounted in the first person, but, for Butor, the first person is inadequate because, in order to decide what it is that triggers off the monologue in the outside world, the monologue itself has to be interrupted. This spoils the flow of the text. The *vous* form however allows both thoughts, objects and reflections which prompt these thoughts to be recounted without interrupting the narrative. This is because the entire area which the *vous* form depicts is that of a consciousness which has not yet been formulated into language. In this instance, Butor's preoccupations are not dissimilar to those of Sarraute, for he, too, is putting into writing an area which is really that of *pré-langage*. What we have, therefore, is essentially a monologue in which the narrator reveals to the character those things of which he is not aware, or would sooner not have to face about himself.

In *Répertoire II*, Butor compares this technique to being a judge who reconstructs from the evidence he is given, what he thinks is the 'real' story which the witness or defendant could not, or would not, give him. In the same way as we learn about the character, so Delmont learns about himself. By the time he reaches Rome, he has changed his mind about divorcing his wife and living with his lover. This is the 'modification' of the story.

In Butor's fiction his experiments with language always take place within a fairly reassuring and overtly structured architecture. For example, *La Modification* is structured by the train line between Paris and Rome. In the novels of Robbe-Grillet, however, there is often no such stabilizing factor. His description aims at a complete breakdown of the link between the text and the outside world. This is achieved in the first pages of *Dans le labyrinthe* (Paris: Editions de Minuit, 1963) where the artificial nature of writing is brought to the fore. We are presented with a series of conflicting statements: 'Dehors il pleut', 'Dehors il y a du soleil', 'Dehors il neige' (p. 9 and p. 11) and later, 'Dehors il neige. Dehors il a neigé, il neigeait, dehors il neige' (p. 14).

The text here is working on several different levels. First, the creative process is brought into play. In writing a novel, the author must make a choice from an unlimited number of possibilities. In this case, the narrator eventually opts for snow as opposed to the other weather conditions because it permits him to establish a parallel between the two worlds depicted in the text: the snow on the streets outside and the dust on the objects in the room in which the text is created. The narrative is in continual flux between outside and inside within the text itself. There is no external reality to which the narrative refers, no world beyond the text which the novelist wishes to describe as there is in the Balzacian novel whose language aims at being transparent and purports to describe and copy the outside world. It is because of this that the *nouveau roman* has been likened to music. Music is the least mimetic of modes and need translate no reality outside itself.

The narrator also experiments with tense and finally chooses the present tense since, according to Robbe-Grillet, it is the tense which most accurately reflects human reality, in that everything we do and think (even if it is about the past or the future) can only take place in the present. Because the narrative unfolds in the present and because of its frequent *glissements* from one scene to another, the *nouveau roman* can achieve filmic quality. In fact, Robbe-Grillet has also devoted much of his time to film-making, especially since 1961. His preoccupation with film is further seen in certain novels such as *La Maison de Rendez-vous* in which the characters' names are derived from Hollywood stars. In this text he exploits art and evokes the Surrealist photographer Man Ray through one of the novel's narrators, Manneret, whose name is also reminiscent of the painter Manet. This preoccupation with art is equally prominent in *Dans le labyrinthe*. It has often been suggested that the picture *La Défaite de Reichenfels*, contains the main elements of the narrative.

Another *nouveau romancier* who is interested in trying to achieve on paper with language what the artist is able to attain on canvas with paint, and who actually began his career as a painter, is Claude Simon. As painting can entail depicting what the eye sees, the *nouveaux romanciers* often spend much time describing objects for their own sake without their having any deeper meaning or significance with regard to character or plot. This love of surface detail has often led the writers to be dubbed *chosistes* (Nathalie Sarraute, however, is an exception). When composing *La Route des Flandres* (1960), Simon admits he used different colours for different themes and pasted coloured paper on the walls adding more blue/green/red where necessary in order to achieve the balance he wanted.[9] One of *La Route des Flandres's* central images and one to which the narrative constantly returns is that of the painting of de Reixachs's ancestor who is said to have committed suicide. Art therefore plays a significant role within the work.

In a similar way to Robbe-Grillet, Simon also undermines traditional concepts of character and plot. In *La Route des Flandres*, the narrator is both 'Je' and 'Georges' and as a character he never achieves complete unity. The novel is essentially composed of Georges's reflections on the past and in particular his attempt to discover whether his commanding officer, de Reixachs, committed suicide at the Battle of the Meuse. Because of the constant meanderings between the past and present, time emerges as one of the novel's main preoccupations. As it is depicted according to the dictates of the memory, the story is not subjected to any chronology. The mind may recall the past but it does so in the present. This use of memory has a particular effect on the writing. It is worth noting here Claude Mauriac's similar preoccupation with unchronological time in his ten-volume diary, *Le Temps immobile*, which is written over a period of ten years and which is continued in a rather different form in *Le Temps accompli*. In Simon sentences can be exceptionally long and punctuation is scant. They also often contain digressions within parentheses and sometimes the parentheses are never closed. The effect of this is quite clearly to undermine traditional narrative rules which state that all information in a novel should have some kind of significance, whether overt or symbolic, in relation to the text as a whole. Details can be related for their own sake without further import on the narrative.

As memory works by association one image often recalls another so that the description can change direction. For example, in *La Route des Flandres* a memory of the sun glinting on the 'acier vierge' of de Reixachs's sword immediately brings to mind his wife who was anything but a virgin when they married. The text constantly returns both to de Reixachs and his wife, Corinne, as it does to other memories. Because of this, the novel, as Simon explains, is structured very much like a clover leaf: the narrative turning round in three loops, corresponding to the three parts of the novel. This repetitive nature of the narrative reflects the concept of History as a cyclical process. It is suggested that de Reixachs committed suicide during the battle, thereby following in the footsteps of his ancestor (concerning whose death there was also speculation, when he died in the 1789 Revolution). The exact truth, however, never emerges. George's memories are muddled, reflecting, on a fictional plane, the confusion of the *débâcle* on the Flanders Road in May 1940 when French troops were defeated by the Nazis. In fact, the whole novel can also be read as a means of depicting the events of France's defeat.

Women writers [See also the chapter on Gender Issues, pp. 241–68]

It was another tumultuous moment in French history which helped the next group of writers under consideration to flourish. The writers are women and the time is May 1968. It was really only after 1968 that there was a concerted and conscious attempt by women to produce literature which was not dominated by masculine modes of discourse. However, as early as 1949 Simone de Beauvoir had written *Le Deuxième Sexe* in which she exposes and examines the 'myths', this time meaning fabricated cultural images, which arise in all areas of culture and society and which men have invented in order to categorize and control women. She argues for the equality of all women in the male preserve and is in favour of women adopting masculine values. Although Beauvoir was inspirational for a first wave of women writers, after 1968 she was criticized by some for not suggesting that men should take up traditional feminine values and also for inciting women to be more like men.

In particular this criticism came from a group of women who went under the name of *Psych et Po (Psychanalyse et Politique)* and who claimed the title *MLF (Mouvement de la libération des femmes)* for themselves. Unlike Beauvoir they rejected masculine values completely and urged women to exalt their own specific qualities. One of the most influential and well-known writers of the group is Hélène Cixous. She is perhaps the major exponent of *écriture féminine*, a term which she inadvertently coined to describe a certain type of writing that distinguishes itself from traditional male discourse. The term is not easily defined and it is not necessarily women writers who practise it. Indeed, Cixous considers that prior to 1968 there were only three twentieth-century writers to whom the term could be applied: Colette, Marguerite Duras and Jean Genet. Essentially *écriture féminine* or rather, as she prefers, a *writing said to be feminine*, differs from masculine discourse in that it allows for the inscription of difference and equality in the writing. Here Cixous is influenced by Derrida's theory of *différance*. In the beginning of *La Jeune née*, one of Cixous's most widely read texts, she asks the question *Où est elle?* and supplies the following table:

Activité/Passivité
Soleil/Lune
Culture/Nature
Jour/Nuit

Père/Mère
Tête/Sentiment
Intelligible/Sensible
Logos/Pathos (Paris: UGE, 10/18, 1975, p. 115)

According to Cixous the fundamental duality which underlies the above alternatives is the human couple man/woman. The terms are not only opposites but are also antagonistic and it is always the masculine value which is given positive associations and which is victorious over qualities which are assumed to be feminine. In this way masculine discourse always champions those qualities which have culturally been attributed to the male. Male writing therefore rests upon a death, in that one term only survives at the cost of its opposite. Writing said to be feminine, on the other hand, is inclusive of both terms so that one no longer has to exist at the expense of the other and both sides are invested with value. According to Cixous, feminine writing is therefore essentially bisexual and it is more likely to be women who will be bisexual writers. It is through writing that Cixous claims women will find true emancipation and she calls upon women to take up the pen and write themselves into existence. This means essentially writing their bodies and desires into the text; claiming for themselves those areas which have been kept from them by men and have only been talked about by men for their own convenience.

However, in transcribing the body and feminine desire into the text, Cixous has been accused of highlighting sexual difference and of perpetrating the dualism she has decried. This misunderstanding of what Cixous intends began during the fierce feminist arguments of the 1970s and indeed still largely (mis)informs Anglo-American readings of her work.[10] But to say that in speaking of a feminine and a masculine libidinal economy Cixous is merely recreating a warring duality is to undervalue seriously the intellectual and astute critical rigour which Cixous takes both to her own writing and literary criticism in general. As Sarah Cornell notes in *The Body and the Text*, referring to those who participate in Cixous's *Etudes Féminines:* 'When we speak of "feminine" and "masculine" . . . we are speaking in terms of difference and equality and not in terms of binary opposition nor hierarchy.'[11] For Cixous, the two economies are present in differing amounts in both women and men, although it is true to say that, because of socio-political history, feminine libidinal economy is more fully present in women than it is in men and vice versa.

In her seminars entitled *La Poétique de la différence sexuelle*, which currently (1991–92) take place at the Collège International de Philosophie in Paris, Cixous studies authors whose works are invested with sexual difference. One of her major concerns is the work of the Brazilian writer Clarice Lispector, who, in her refusal to tell a particular story, undercuts the linear plot thereby exploding masculine discourse. As Cixous has noted, Clarice Lispector's work is the locus of hundreds of beginnings and can therefore be taken up at any point in the narrative without the feeling that something essential to the plot has been missed.[12] Writing said to be feminine can also be defined (inasmuch as this is possible, since definitions ensnare and this is precisely what *écriture féminine* tries not to do) in the way that it approaches the 'other'. Whilst masculine writing tries to appropriate the world for the self, the self in feminine writing goes out to meet the other and gives, or is, to the point where this self can become one with the other. In a way, it is perhaps this fluidity between the self and the other, which best describes feminine writing in the way that it is meant and used by Hélène Cixous.

It is because of the insistence on sexual difference that certain feminists, and in particular those whose allegiance lay with a group formed around the journal *Questions féministes*, have condemned Cixous and the *Psych et Po* group. They accuse Cixous of 'essentialism' and of reiterating the qualities already granted them by men. For them it is this that helps to keep women in a position of servitude. One of Cixous's major critics is Monique Wittig, who, for political reasons, left France for the United States in 1976. She considers that the *Psych et Po* group failed to deal with the material reality of women on an everyday basis. For her (and here she hardly differs from Cixous), the concept of 'woman' has no foundation in reality and is merely a socio-political concept designed to keep women in a subservient role. This is made clear in her article, *On ne naît pas femmé*: 'Nôtre première tâche est . . . de toujours dissocier soigneusement "les femmes" (la classe à l'intérieur de laquelle nous combattons) et "la femme" le mythe. Car "la femme" n'existe pas pour nous, elle n'est autre qu'une formation imaginaire, alors que les femmes sont le produit d'une relation sociale' (*Questions féministes*, 8, 1980, 75–84, p. 80). In fact for Wittig, the only real position which escapes the power struggles inherent in male/female relationships is that of the lesbian.

Like Cixous, Wittig also believes in the necessity of rewriting basic cultural stories in order to explode male concepts of women. In Wittig's *Le Corps lesbien* (1973) all the parts of the woman's body are named, both external limbs and internal organs, in an attempt to restore the whole of the body to women, not just those parts which have been championed by men. The novel itself has caused much controversy even amongst feminists because of its violence. However, it has been highly praised by those who consider that the body needs to be torn apart in order to be properly restored.

The unpassive nature of women is also explored in a different way in *Les Guérillères* (Paris: Editions de Minuit, 1969), a novel of prose poems, written in 1968 and appearing the following year. The title of the novel is a combination of *guerrières*, female warriors, and *guérilla*, freedom fighters against the established order. The novel tells of a society made up exclusively of women who wage war against men and emerge victorious. The battle which is fought is also one of language. Wittig introduces new terms and reworks existing stories in an attempt to undermine oppressive male discourse and to write women back into a language from which they have been excluded or reduced to silence. This is more obvious in French than it is in English: in French a mixed group is always designated by the pronoun *ils*, and the mute e, the one which is not heard, is feminine.

Many stories and myths must be rewritten in order for women to take possession of the past, a past in which they have been portrayed as weak and passive and have been exploited. However, the language which belongs to the women does not exist in male language but in the gaps which this discourse does not fill: 'Cela se manifeste juste dans l'intervalle que les maîtres n'ont pas pu combler avec leurs mots de propriétaires et de possesseurs, cela peut se chercher dans la lacune, dans tout ce qui n'est pas la continuité de leurs discours, dans le zéro, le O, le cercle parfait que tu inventes pour les emprisonner et pour les vaincre' (p. 164). In *Les Guérillères* the circle is a recurring symbol and it divides the book into three sections. It is representative of both 'l'anneau vulvaire' and the space of female discourse which is yet to be uttered. Like Wittig, it is precisely this gap in language which Cixous tries to bridge with her bisexual text in order to produce her *écriture féminine*.

In a very different way Marguerite Duras inscribes this space or gap into the very fabric of her texts so that the voice which is not heard becomes the definition of what is most feminine. In *Les Parleuses* (Paris: Editions de Minuit, 1974), a series of discussions with Xavière Gauthier, Duras explains that these *blancs* began appearing in her work after the publication of *Moderato cantabile*. Gauthier equates the previous fullness of meaning with a more masculine type of writing. The *blancs* inscribe themselves into the texts in various ways so that the main themes of her novels, love, death and madness, are invested with new and elusive qualities. Sometimes the spaces occur at the level of syntax. Duras makes it clear that she deals first and foremost with words. It is in the guise of words that things and ideas initially come to her. Only later do they join together and often parts of the sentence are never manifested. Furthermore, explanations as to why characters act as they do and descriptions of their sentiments are also frequently left out. When the heroine closes her eyes (and it is always women in Duras's novels who fascinate) we have no idea what goes on in her mind and we can only observe voyeuristically from the outside. In a way, the reader's role is that of a *voyeur* unable to enter into the drama and only able to look on. It is this very quality which enables Duras's writing to cross the boundaries of the genres of novel, film and theatre. The distance between reader/watcher and what unfolds before her or him is what helps to create a feeling of uneasiness. Duras informs Gauthier that the one phrase which recurs in the letters she receives about her work is 'je suis malade de vous lire'. Her novels however, are not only disturbing to read, they are also painful to write and this is precisely because they touch on an area 'non encore creusée', in other words, that of the feminine. But this absence or gap can manifest itself as a type of illness in her characters. They constantly try to compensate for this *lacuna* and it is the impossibility of doing so which can lead to despair or even suicide. However, it is also because of their incompleteness and elusiveness that her characters are rendered so fascinating.

Le Ravissement de Lol V. Stein (Paris: Gallimard, Folio 1964) is a particular case in point. *Blancs* appear in this novel on several different levels. The narrator is Jacques Hold, Lol's lover: the story he tells of Lol is itself incomplete. He tries to fill the gaps in his knowledge by imagining. The phrase 'j'invente' occurs throughout. As his name suggests Hold tries to hold on to Lol, to pin her down in writing, something he does not succeed in doing. The central omission or *blanc* in the text is the feeling of jealousy on Lol's part, when ten years earlier her fiancé Michael Richardson elopes with Anne-Marie Stretter at a ball held in S. Tahla. The ambiguity of 'ravissement' in the title, meaning at once 'ravish' and 'rapture' adds to the feeling of an absence of any logical explanation. The triangle with Lol as 'voyeur' at the ball is later reproduced with the couple of Hold and Tatiana Karl, Lol's school friend. Lol watches from the rye field as they make love in the hotel. Hold's final analysis is that to know nothing of Lol is to know her already and this emphasizes the significant spaces in the narrative – meaning is undermined because of the refusal of the text to yield all. In a way, it is reminiscent of Duras's statement in the aubiographical *L'Amant* (1985) for which she won the Prix Goncourt: 'L'histoire de ma vie n'existe pas'.[13] At the heart of existence in Duras's texts there is always absence.

In direct contrast to Duras's use of *blancs*, Marie Cardinal insists on employing the totality of vocabulary available. Of the four women writers discussed here, Cardinal is the most traditional in her use of language. Her novels are also the most unproblematic in terms of plot and character. In *Autrement dit* (Paris: Grasset, 1977), a text which consists of discussions with Annie Leclerc and which was produced in response to the many letters she received after writing *Les Mots pour le dire* (1975), she explains what she perceives to be the role of the woman writer:

La difficulté, pour nous qui écrivons, c'est de nous servir de la totalité du matériel qui est à notre disposition, sans tenir compte des interdits d'usage, sans l'adapter, sans créer un autre ghetto, celui d'une écriture féminine. On sait déjà ce que ça vaut une poétesse, une doctoresse, une avocate . . . ça ne vaut pas un clou. Une écrivaine ça ne vaudrait pas plus cher. (p. 89)

The answer is not to try and create a new vocabulary but to use the one already at the writer's disposal and, by naming those things which are taboo, to bring about a change in the perception of women by others and by themselves. She continues:

La meilleure manière de prouver qu'il manque des mots, que le français n'est pas fait pour les femmes, c'est de nous mettre au ras de notre corps, d'exprimer l'inexprimé et d'employer le vocabulaire tel qu'il est, directement, sans l'arranger. Il deviendra alors évident et clair qu'il y a des choses que nous ne pouvons pas traduire en mots. Comment dire notre sexe, la gestation vécue, le temps, la durée des femmes? (p. 89)

How to articulate that which is specifically feminine is a central preoccupation of *Les Mots pour le dire*. The beginning of the text concentrates on the protagonist's constant loss of menstrual blood whilst living in perpetual fear. She descends into a kind of living hell, and the blood, which is psychosomatically induced, is both an excuse for her illness and that which prevents her from finding solutions to the real problems which are ruining her life. In writing about the loss of blood, Cardinal is examining the relationship between a woman and her body in an area which, until recently, was socially taboo and which has remained relatively unexplored outside of the medical dictionary.

Although the words she uses to describe this are familiar, it is by applying them to an area not usually discussed that the feeling of something new is achieved. What is more, by giving a description of an exclusively female phenomenon, reality is claimed by the woman and for once it is the male reader who must attempt to identify with something it is not possible for him to experience.

The narrative which follows describes the birth of a new woman which is brought about by the psychoanalysis that she undergoes, and during which she is able to piece together significant events in her life so that a structure emerges which makes order out of what was before only chaos. Within this context, the narrator is able to explore the major relationships of her life, especially that between herself and her mother. The dynamics of the mother–daughter relationship is particularly important in new feminist psychology. The mother in *Les Mots pour le dire* is seen as a source of many of the daughter's problems. However, by the time of *Les Grands désordres* (1987), a novel which also recounts a mother–daughter relationship in which the daughter is addicted to heroin, the emphasis is different. Here it is the daughter's problem which succeeds in breaking through the superficial layer of apparent order in the mother's life revealing an underlying state of entropy (a term borrowed from physics and in this context meaning chaos) and with which Elsa, the mother, now has to deal. In this novel Cardinal chooses a man as the scribe who will put Elsa's experiences into writing and in doing so overturns stereotypical masculine/feminine roles. Here the man is able to convey sentiment in writing, whereas the woman, whose story he tells, is only at ease with a technical vocabulary. The appointed narrator becomes increasingly enamoured of Elsa and in this sense his fascination is reminiscent of Jacques Hold's obsession with Lol. In both cases it is the woman who leaves the man bemused.

Although the debate in France is still ongoing as to whether an *écriture féminine* actually exists and whether it is in fact detrimental to women anyway to prove that it does, there is certainly a movement away from the preoccupation with texts as a gendered activity. What is certain is that it is hoped by all that enough headway has been made for women to take their rightful place alongside male authors in the literary canon.

A certain amount of ground was gained in this direction when a woman writer who displays none of the above qualities and whose work remains indifferent to the new techniques of many of the authors of the post-1945 period became the first female member elected to the Académie Française in 1981: namely, Marguerite Yourcenar. Whilst there is no doubt as to her quality as a writer, she was perhaps also granted admission to this male-dominated institution precisely because much of her prose fiction, at the same time as being classical, celebrates male characters and their personal quests in what are traditionally masculine roles. This is largely because her novels often draw on historically real people as in the case of the Emperor Hadrian in *Mémoires d'Hadrien* (1951). In *L'Œuvre au noir*, awarded the Prix Femina in 1968, the sixteenth-century alchemist, Zénon, is an amalgamation of personalities. He is an exceptional character and challenges the established order of his time. The title of the novel reflects not only Zénon's work as an alchemist (for we are told that this is the first and most difficult stage of the Great Work) and the fact that much of this work has to be carried out undercover, but it also refers to the constant transformations which Zénon himself undergoes throughout the novel. His quest, therefore, is one of knowledge and above all of self-knowledge. That this takes place at a time situated between the Middle Ages and the dawn of the modern world when religious wars were cruelly waged, makes its appearance in 1968 particularly relevant and in fact highlights many of the analogies between the world of the novel and that of contemporary existence.

A return to myth

Traditional values are also subverted in a different way in the work of other novelists writing just prior to and after 1968. Authors such as Michel Tournier challenge contemporary values through the reworking of well-known stories and ancient myths. This return to story-telling can also be seen as a reaction against more experimental forms of fiction which were prevalent during the 1950s and 1960s. For Tournier, as for almost everyone who uses the term, myth has a specific meaning. It is, amongst other things, 'une histoire fondamentale' (*Le Vent paraclet*, Paris: Gallimard, Folio, 1977, p. 189), and 'une histoire que tout le monde connaît déjà' (p. 189). It is for this reason that Tournier claims his works 'doivent être reconnus–relus–dès la première lecture' (p. 189). For example *Le Roi des aulnes* (1970), for which Tournier won the Prix Goncourt, deals with the well-known figure of the ogre, and *Les Météores* (1975) recounts a version of the ancient story of twins. Both these novels refer us back to primitive beginnings which exist essentially outside of time and of history: in the snow-covered terrain of East Prussia which in *Le Roi des aulnes* is populated by elks and aurochs and is where the ogre Tiffauges hunts his prey, consisting of young boys; and in the timelessness of the 'cellule gémellaire' of the twins Jean and Paul, or Jean-Paul as they are collectively known, in *Les Météores*.

However, as well as belonging to this timeless world, Tournier's narratives also unfold in some area of modern history: the story of the ogre, Abel Tiffauges, takes place between 1938 and 1944. It relates, on an allegorical level, all the horrors of the concentration camps, the exploitation of youth during the war and the devastating revenge of the Red Army as it swept through eastern Europe after the war. Tiffauges is also representative of other ogres who belong to the Third Reich. He first finds affinity with Göring when he becomes the helper of the *Oberforstmeister* of Göring's estate and later graduates to the level of Hitler when he becomes the attendant of several Jungmannen at the *napola* of Kaltenborn. The novel is structured in such a way that history is viewed as a cyclical process and this adds to its disturbing quality. The relationship between fiction and history is an important one in Tournier and it also arises as a concern in *Les Météores*. This novel takes place between 1930 and 1960. Most of the narrative, however, focuses on the initiatory voyage which Paul undertakes when he follows his twin Jean around the world in the manner of Phileas Fogg. The war is only evoked fleetingly by the scandalous uncle, Alexandre, who has inherited his brother's waste disposal business. He likens the infernos of the new depots for incinerating rubbish to the methods used in Nazi concentration camps for disposing of prisoners. The war is also an issue when Maria-Barbara, the twins' mother, who becomes involved in the Resistance, disappears. Even in heroism she manages to outdo her poor husband Edouard who, since he was prey to the whims of heterosexual fancy, was shown by the prevailing attitudes of the novel to be fit for nothing else. The question therefore naturally arises as to what constitutes 'history' and whether, in fact, what we know as history is but another version of a subjective story related in much the same way as were the ancient stories which purported to tell the truth, but which we have now named 'myths'. It must be remembered that the whole of the theory of the Third Reich was itself based on a myth. Myth, therefore, in many guises, emerges as one of the central preoccupations of Tournier's novels.

In fact, he views myth as a multi-tiered structure which, at its most basic, is 'une histoire pour enfant' and which then becomes, on another level, 'toute une théorie de la connaissance, à un étage plus élevé encore cela devient morale, puis métaphysique, puis ontologie, etc., sans cesser d'être la même histoire' (p. 188). Although this formula can be applied to all his fiction, it is perhaps truest of his first and most influential novel to date, for which he won Le Grand Prix du Roman de l'Académie Française: *Vendredi ou les limbes du Pacifique* (1967 and revised in 1972). This novel is an explicit parody of Daniel Defoe's *Life and Adventures of Robinson Crusoe*. Instead of Robinson making a civilized being out of Friday, it is Vendredi who initiates Crusoé into his way of life. The simplest level of this story is further exploited in *Vendredi ou la vie sauvage* (1971), a version which is more accessible to children in that it leaves out the explicit sexual scenes as well as the metaphysical passages. In *Vendredi ou les limbes du Pacifique* philosophical ruminations abound especially in Crusoé's logbook which has a particularly twentieth-century quality to it. This, in turn, adds to the novel's multi-dimensional time-scale. It is set in the eighteenth century in the Enlightenment, exactly one hundred years after Defoe's narrative. The fact that Vendredi and Crusoé enter into 'les limbes du Pacifique' projects them into a golden age which has the quality of beginnings, and which exists outside of time. That Vendredi overthrows the established order brings us up to date once again in that it is reminiscent of the then recent political upheavals of 1968.

In some ways, *Vendredi* is also a fictional interpretation of Gaston Bachelard's philosophy which had a great impact on literary criticism during the 1960s. This is particularly evident in the depiction of Robinson's development in terms of the elements of earth, wind and fire, manifested in the sun. Tournier is also indebted to the anthropologist Claude Lévi-Strauss, whose immense structural study of the myths of other cultures has given us a greater understanding of the concrete science of peoples hitherto dubbed 'primitive'. Tournier claims that in *Vendredi* he wanted to include *l'essentiel* of what he had learned 'au musée de l'Homme sous la direction notamment de Claude Lévi-Strauss' (*Le Vent paraclet*, p. 194). Crusoé gives up his existence for a more immediate way of life, which, although it cannot be said to represent any particular culture, does however, provide a significant alternative.

In Tournier's later novel *La Goutte d'or* (1986), Vendredi recurs in the guise of Idriss who comes to France from the Sahara and never manages to fit in with French culture, although he certainly adds colour to French life by his very 'otherness'. This story is particularly relevant to modern times in that it deals with a member of an ethnic minority and Tournier might have dedicated it to the very people to whom he wanted to dedicate *Vendredi*: to the 'trois millions d'Algériens, de Marocains, de Tunisiens, de Sénégalais, de Portugais sur lesquels repose notre société et qu'on ne voit jamais, qu'on n'entend jamais qui n'ont ni bulletin de vote, ni syndicat, ni porte-parole' (*Le Vent paraclet,* p. 236).

A similar kind of story is told by J. M. G. Le Clézio in *Désert* (1980). The main character this time is a girl, Lalla, who like Idriss in *La Goutte d'or*, comes from the Sahara where she communes with the wind, the sand and the sea. She is also in contact with the sacred *homme bleu* of the desert – *Es Ser* or *le Secret*. After having run away with Hartani, the mute goat-herd by whom she becomes pregnant, Lalla is sent to Marseille where she lives a life of complete drudgery. The drabness of life there is set in direct contrast to the brightly illuminated, pure world of the desert, untainted by occidental values, to which she is eventually able to return. However, like Idriss, she too brings colour to Marseille in that her luminosity is captured in the photographs taken of her by a fashion photographer. Again essential non-western values are prized above those which are promoted in occidental cultures.

A Vendredi type figure also appears in Patrick Grainville's novel *L'Orgie, la neige* (1990). He comes into contact with the novel's narrator, who relives the experiences of his youth when, like a kind of Robinson Crusoe, he goes hunting alone in the vast winter snows of Normandy. The Robinson-narrator and his Vendredi meet when a ship from a banana republic is stranded in the estuary. Vendredi, in the shape of Nirou, this time accompanied by three girls, comes ashore. His characteristics are reminiscent of Tournier's Vendredi, especially in the church episode when his iconoclastic laughter, and that of the three girls, booms in the face of occidental religion.

Grainville provides an inversion of this story in *Les Flamboyants* which won him the Prix Goncourt in 1974. This time it is an insipid Robinson figure, William Néant Blanc, who ventures into the realm of the African King, Tokor Yali Yulmata, and is befriended by him. Tokor is the incarnation of passion and this passion is what makes him both a cruel monster and an endearing individual who sometimes displays the innocence of a child. He takes Néant Blanc on a quest to capture the sacred tribe, the Diorles, and this ends in a bloodbath and Tokor's downfall. But again, the novel champions those values which are immediate and natural and even Tokor's death is eventually a triumph for he is dissected and incorporated into the forest he so much loved. The colourfulness of Tokor's character is equally matched by Grainville's writing which is often considered to be 'baroque' in its extravagance, unlike the more classical styles of Tournier and Le Clézio.

The type of alternative lifestyle depicted in these novels is very much a feature of post-1968 fiction and the new Crusoé/Vendredi story, inaugurated by Tournier, might be said to constitute the 'contemporary myth' par excellence. For it is now Western civilized values which are exposed as undesirable in the light of the more lyrical, natural and more sacred ways of life of peoples from cultures which are very different from our own.

'Beur' fiction

Whilst writers such as Michel Tournier and Claire Etcherelli in *Elise ou la vraie vie* (1967) discuss the problems faced by Vendredi-like immigrants plunged into a culture very unlike their own, a group of writers have emerged in the last decade, most of whose parents emigrated to France either shortly before, during or after the Algerian War of Independence of 1954–62. These second generation immigrants (or *immigrés*, the word usually retained for the unskilled workers in France) have become known as the *Beurs*. The term was originally used by North Africans on the radio in 1981 when the Socialist government came into power in France abolishing a law which stated that immigrants could not form groups of any kind without the consent of the Minister of the Interior. The word *Beur* was then taken up by the press especially during the coverage of what has become known as the 'Marche des Beurs' which took place in 1983 across the length of France mainly in response to the ground gained in the Spring elections of that year by Jean–Marie Le Pen's party, the *Front National*. The march is covered in Bouzid's novel *La Marche* which appeared in 1984. The word *Beur* comes from *verlan*, a type of slang originally adopted by the French underworld and quickly taken up by other marginal groups. It consists in inverting the syllables of words, *verlan* itself meaning (*à*) *l'envers*. According to Alec G. Hargreaves who quotes Nacer Kettane, the President of Radio Beur, the word *Beur* has its roots in 'arabe' which gives 'rebe', which when inverted gives 'ber' or 'beur', as it is written (*Voices from the North African Immigrant Community in France: Immigration and Identity in Beur Fiction*, New York and Oxford: Berg, 1991, p. 21).

As Hargreaves points out, lying at the core of *Beur* fiction is the personal identity crisis undergone by writers who have found themselves at the crossroads of two very different cultures: that of their parents who see Algeria as their home and try to impose upon their children their own Islamic values, and that of the French society in which they live and have to survive and which cannot be excluded from the home because of media such as the television. Equally, however, those values learnt at home have ways of undercutting accepted Occidental values. *Beur* writing is more concerned with exploring a sense of personal crisis and the search for a stable identity rather than with the question of how one social group can fit into another. It is interesting that most works concentrate on two main areas: home and school, the workplace being a significant omission. On the one hand, this reflects, as Hargreaves notes, the relatively young age of the writers concerned, on the other, these years of their lives are the most significant in terms of establishing an identity and of trying to bridge the two conflicting areas of home/Algeria and school/France. Even more than being *Bildungsromans*, these novels are ones of initiation, common not only to *Beur* fiction, but to much fiction of the post-1945 period – whether it is initiation into a more immediate way of life, as in the case of Tournier's Crusoé, or, as with the *Beurs*, into Occidental life. The dilemmas with which they are faced helps us to see our own culture as 'different' rather than 'natural', as Barthes, Lévi-Strauss and others have also tried to point out.

The conflict between school and home is most acutely seen in Farida Belghoul's *Georgette!* (1986) which is narrated through the interior monologue of a seven-year old girl whose real name we never learn but who imagines herself being called Georgette, a name unheard of in Arabic and which, for her, embodies all the coquettish Frenchness she feels her father will accuse her of as she adopts the codes of French society. This taking on of otherness is largely explored in the novel through the little girl's learning to write. Her father's knowledge is undermined when he tells her to do her homework at the back of her exercise book (Arabic writing going from right to left rather than from left to right). At school she learns that writing from left to right is the normal French way.

Language and writing actually become a key focus in the novels of the *Beurs*, for most of the first generation immigrants were illiterate and therefore spoken Arabic, or more often Berber, is equated with material poverty, whereas spoken and written French is seen as the language of progression. Much of the conflict within families and between generations also hinges on language. For example, when in Mehdi Charef's *Le Thé au harem d'Archi Ahmed* (1983), the main character Madjid is asked by his mother to go and look for his father, he refuses saying her French accent is too bad for him to understand and when she speaks Arabic he pretends to have even more difficulty. He protests by playing the Sex Pistols at full volume. This is not, as one might suppose, his way of adopting French culture instead of Islamic culture, for he has chosen to play an anarchic British rock group which completely rejects all aspects of bourgeois culture. The music therefore suggests his position not only outside of his parents' society but also outside of the French bourgeois society to which his school encourages him to belong. This love of anarchic music is something he shares with other teenagers whatever their origins – all those, in fact, who feel uprooted and apart (see, for example, Marie Cardinal's *La Clé sur la Porte* (1972)).

A sense of separateness is also explored in Azouz Begag's *Le Gone du Chaâba* (1986). As the title suggests, the gap which the novel tries to bridge is that between French and Arabic (*gone* is a slang Lyonnais term for *enfant* and *Chaâba* is the Arabic name given to the *bidonville*, or slum, in which the main character Azouz lives). When Azouz changes school, he decides he will be more easily accepted if he pretends to be Jewish like two of his classmates. When his mother turns up to fetch him from school, her obviously Algerian appearance makes him deny that he knows her and this is a matter of great shame for them both. The whole episode is, however, highly ironic. In choosing to be Jewish rather than Arabic, Azouz is aligning himself with the most persecuted peoples of all time and those who not half a century ago were freely handed over by the French to the Nazi authorities.

In the sequel to this novel, *Béni ou le paradis privé* (Paris: Seuil, 1989), the main character tries to integrate himself by adopting the name Béni rather than keeping the name Ben Abdallah which he dislikes: 'Béni, c'est moi, "mon fils" dans la langue du Prophète, béni dans celle du Christ, anagramme du bien dans celle du Petit Robert' (p. 35). In this way he tries to combine Islam, Christianity and French secular society. But the struggles which he undergoes throughout the narrative indicate that he never succeeds.

Full integration into French society is most often seen as impossible and other solutions are therefore sought. In Sakinna Boukhedenna's *Journal: nationalité immigré(e)* (Paris: Harmattan, 1987), the narrator, unable to put up with the racism to which she is subjected in France, goes back to Algeria. However, once there, she finds it impossible to live with the sexism inherent in the Islamic way of life and she returns to France preferring to fight against racism, rather than not being allowed even a voice with which to fight in Algeria. At the beginning of her journal she says that in France she learnt to be an Arab and in Algeria she learnt to be an immigrant, and this seems to sum up the precarious identity of immigrants on the whole (p. 5).

However, the *Beurs'* situation is not always without its humour. The prejudice to which they are subjected can be used to their advantage as Madjid and Pat demonstrate in *Le Thé au harem d'Archi Ahmed*. They become pickpockets on the metro and Madjid having stolen something passes it over to his French friend, Pat. When he is accused of stealing, Madjid takes great pleasure in being indignant and in accusing the person of racism – which is true as the person never assumes that the thief could be the French boy and that the two could possibly be in league. It is uncertain what direction fiction of this nature will take in the future, but at present, with the increasing popularity of the extreme-right in France, it seems all the more important that such fiction should be read so that the problems faced by immigrants in a foreign society can be more fully appreciated.

Poetry

In the domain of poetry, although some preoccupations are shared with the novel, such as the search for the sacred in the natural and a concentration on language, the post-1945 period has essentially been one of crisis which is situated at the centre of language itself. On the one hand, poetry must use language to name the outside world and to communicate to the reader, on the other, there is an acute awareness that, by virtue of the free play of the signifier, language cannot name anything beyond itself and that writing and poetry are essentially self-reflexive activities. This dual dilemma of having to name and of the impossibility of doing so is at the core of the work of many poets of the period.[14]

In addition to this tension, and despite the fact that the poets who will be discussed here are politically *dégagés*, there is a strong feeling amongst them that it is the duty of poetry to give back to the world the hope which was lost during the devastation of the Second World War. In a lecture first given in 1958 entitled *L'Acte et le lieu de la poésie*[15] Yves Bonnefoy equates poetry and hope. In a similar way, André du Bouchet seeks to re-establish a harmony which was lost as a result of the Occupation. In an interview in *Le Monde* (10 June, 1983) he comments on how he felt when France fell in 1940 and people took to the roads: 'C'était une expérience très violente, le monde était détruit. C'est à ce moment que j'ai écrit pour la première fois avec la volonté de rétablir quelque chose, de rendre compte d'une relation qui, à peine entrevue – j'avais juste 15 ans – était balayée.' It is therefore with the aims of restoring a kind of spiritual or emotional peace that much post-1945 poetry is written.

Perhaps the most important poet to have emerged since the war is Yves Bonnefoy. Bonnefoy came to poetry via Surrealism, which was dominant between the wars. His relationship to Surrealism and his rejection of it are symptomatic of the new demands which were now being made on the poetic imagination. Having founded a Surrealist review entitled *La Révolution la nuit* in 1946, his definitive break with the movement came the following year when he refused to sign the Manifesto which he considered too 'occultist'. Bonnefoy's main concern was to find the sacred in what could be perceived by the senses, not in what could not. According to John E. Jackson in *Yves Bonnefoy* (Paris: Seghers, 1976) two further factors contributed to his rejection of Surrealism: his reading of the French Symbolists, Mallarmé in particular, and his trips to Italy where he was influenced by the work of many artists who had managed to resolve the conflict between the depiction of the world in terms of Platonic ideas, according to which words signify essences, and the world as perceived by the senses. This is particularly true of the work of de Chirico, who in defining the moment is also able to capture the eternal, thereby revealing what Bonnefoy terms an underlying *présence* or *vrai lieu*. It is this *présence* which Bonnefoy seeks to capture in his own poetry, and which, although he never fully defines it, points to a feeling of universal unity.

The revelation of an underlying presence seems, as Joseph Frank points out, to go directly against what he calls 'the fierce campaign waged by Jacques Derrida . . . to uncover and expunge all the lingering traces of the "metaphysics of presence".'[16] Also Bonnefoy's preference for certain words over others seems equally to betray a return to the realm of essences or Platonic ideas. In his work entitled 'La Poésie française et le principe d'identité'[17] Bonnefoy states that words such as stone, silex, laugh and cry are preferable to brick, silicate, grimace and sneer because they reflect the roots of the human situation in the world, whereas the latter terms only describe appearances.

However, although these terms might attempt to capture an underlying essence they can also, as G. D. Martin notes, lead to a bewildering ambiguity (*Anthology of Contemporary French Poetry*, Edinburgh, Edinburgh University Press, 1972). But it is precisely this sense of ambiguity which words must convey if they are to remain fluid signifiers. For as Bonnefoy states in his inaugural lecture given at the Collège de France in 1981, words are not things and what they signify changes according to circumstance.[18] This is directly in opposition to Platonic ideas and in favour of Derridean Deconstruction. What remains is a twofold situation, or a type of layering: the word is distilled down to its roots or its essence, whilst at the same time it proliferates above the surface in a multitude of meanings. In the one instance stability is achieved, in the other, the word retains its fluidity: the one aspires to death, the other to life.

In fact, the life/death dichotomy is seen to be at the heart of Bonnefoy's poetry. For him, death is an integral part of life and it is only by admitting death into life that what he terms *la vraie vie* can be experienced. This contradiction is always heralded by the epigraphs with which his collections of poetry begin. For example the quotation taken from Hegel at the beginning of *Du Mouvement et de l'immobilité de Douve* (1953) reads: 'Mais la vie de l'esprit ne s'effraie point devant la mort et n'est pas celle qui s'en garde pure. Elle est la vie qui la supporte et se maintient en elle.' Although this is not said without irony, it is indicative of the preoccupation of the entire work. Two later collections *Pierre Ecrite* (1965) and *Dans le leurre du seuil* (1975) take their epigraphs from Shakespeare's *The Winter's Tale*. The first epigraph informs us: 'Thou mettest with things dying; I with things new born', and the second: 'They look'd as they had heard of a world ransom'd or one destroyed'.[19] Each, then, focuses on the integration, indeed the necessity of death at the heart of life. *The Winter's Tale*, it must be remembered, is a tragi-comedy putting the emphasis here on the final expression of hope. The last quotation which talks of 'a world ransom'd or one destroyed' points to the precarious nature of language in the poem. Once it names it dies, but it is also reborn or reprieved in that meaning can never be stable for the fluidity of the signifier ensures that at the heart of death new life is rekindled.

Language is also one of the central preoccupations in the work of André Du Bouchet. He has stripped his vocabulary down to an even greater degree than Bonnefoy and his poetic universe consists of the barest of elements: for the most part heat, wind and dazzling light. Two kinds of reality are depicted, the immediate world and a higher reality which is just beyond reach. The quest is to re-establish what Du Bouchet has termed a lost relationship between the two. This 'relation perdue' is also to do with the loss of wholeness within the self and the feeling of being at one with the world.

The self is always on the move walking along 'la route' which is constantly evasive and which 'se perd'. Moreover it is fraught with obstacles typified by the mountain and the glacier. The glacier, as an image, displays Du Bouchet's fondness for the changing texture of matter. Once liquid, the water is now frozen. In other poems the earth can be drunk and the air forms clods. The day is likened to 'un papillon glacé', at once lively and yet frozen. The entire subject matter of his poems finds its reflection in the very fabric of the text itself. After *Dans la chaleur vacante* (1968) appeared it was thought that Du Bouchet lived in the mountains whereas he really lived in the flat plains of Vexin in Normandy. Talking of this work he says:

Je crois que le mot 'montagne' qui y revenait assez souvent n'était autre que la langue que je commençais à habiter et à laquelle je me heurtais . . . Lorsque, bien des années plus tard, je me suis arrêté dans les Préalpes, pour y vivre, la montagne réelle est venue comme la confirmation d'un mot que j'avais éprouvé profondément, mais qui n'était pas du tout le reflet d'un paysage. (*Le Monde*, 10 June, 1983)

André du Bouchet had spent ten years in America where English was the language in which he learned to formulate his intellectual concepts. He was now trying to put an essential experience into French which often resisted his efforts. The quest which is undertaken in his poems is therefore also that of the language or *écriture*. And the 'glacier' or 'montagne' which it must cross is that of the white page.

Typography in Du Bouchet's poetry is very important and the page, white, like the light and objects in the poems, is an integral part of the meaning. The use of white has been familiar since Mallarmé and Reverdy (Du Bouchet's favourite poet), but Du Bouchet goes to greater lengths in his use of it. Single words and phrases are separated by expanses of white. The reader has to get from one word to the next like stepping over a crevasse or climbing a mountain, the feeling is similar to walking which is mirrored in much of the content itself. But the whiteness, like most things in Du Bouchet's poetry, has contradictory roles. It is both silence and voice. As silence, it is but the empty page, a nothingness, a mirror of the absolute which is also void or 'vacant'. On the other hand, it is the silence which gives rise to the voice. It is only in this silence that words can be heard. The word, in fact, even disturbs the silence but its effort fails in that it tries to capture that which cannot be named. The silence is the most perfect expression of itself. On the one hand it is dead space, on the other it is exemplary of what is most vital once it is traversed and filled by breath when the poetry is read.

The visual appearance of thin black traces on the white page is reminiscent of the almost skeletal figures sculpted by Giacometti, whom Du Bouchet admires greatly and who similarly tried to solve the dichotomy of being and nothingness. In fact, Du Bouchet's comments in *Qui n'est pas tourné vers nous* (1972), which consists of six essays on Giacometti, can be applied to his own work. His view of the sculptor whose work becomes rarer as it is built is similar to his own poems in which white space becomes increasingly pervasive.

Unlike André du Bouchet whose mountains existed in his poetry long before they existed in his surroundings, Philippe Jaccottet uses the mountainous countryside where both he and Du Bouchet now live in the Drôme to the north of Provence, as inspiration for his writing. And so it is in more than a literal way that Jaccottet can say of himself and his neighbour that 'une montagne nous sépare . . .' (*Une transaction secrète*, Paris, Gallimard, 1987, p. 267). As Mark Treharne points out in the introduction to his translation of *Beauregard*, Jaccottet's 'landscapes in prose' belong to a mode of writing which he has made very much his own (*Comparative Criticism*, 1, 1989, 171–77, p. 171). Not that Jaccottet's observations of the countryside are limited to his prose, they also form the main substance of his poetry. Indeed, a strict line cannot actually be drawn between prose and poem, since his prose is merely a less condensed form of the feeling that gives rise to the poem. As Treharne says: 'One of the functions of his prose in his writing is to provide a broader context for the dense nexus of feeling that a poem represents (p. 173).' Both prose and poetry also often treat the same subject. For example, the almond trees in *A travers un verger* are already seen in the poems *Airs*. Intertextuality is therefore something which Jaccottet and Du Bouchet have in common, but again, in different ways.

For Jaccottet the entire poetic experience is bound up with the contemplation of the natural world. There is a deep sense in which seeing is actually being. In *La Promenade sous les arbres* (Paris: La Bibliothèque des Arts, 1980) Jaccottet sums up this experience as a moment of intense contemplation when the self becomes at one with the object. It is in these fleeting moments that a rare presence is felt, the *ailleurs* in the *ici*, or the *illimité* in the *limité*. In this sense what his poetry aims at is similar to Bonnefoy's *presence* or *vrai lieu*. It is exactly this sense of the sacred moment which exists outside of time that Jaccottet tries to capture.

Because his subjects are simple, he also searches for a vocabulary which is unembellished and dreams of what he has called the absolute transparency of the poem. Jaccottet is very aware of the traps of language. He wants to describe reality as it is and this means avoiding the pitfalls of using various phrases and images which our culture has built up and with which we have tried to organize our world. He wants to respond directly to the world, but not through the mask of easy and deadening clichés taken from our literature. In *A travers un verger* (Montpellier: Fata Morgana, 1975, p. 17) the message is 'Méfie-toi des images'. Similarly in 'L'Approche des montagnes', a section in *La Promenade sous les arbres*, he resists the temptation of describing the mountains using language usually associated with them and tries to depict them as they really appear to him. However, as he says: 'Les mots traînent après eux des représentations machinales qu'il me faut d'abord écarter' (p. 57). All images, in fact, are to be regarded with suspicion and avoided as far as possible. But the necessity of communicating a feeling to the reader (which is one of the reasons he writes poetry) and of grasping reality in its totality often necessitates the use of images. As far as possible, however, he keeps his language very simple and tries not to give his writing the stamp of his own personality and this in itself has become a distinguishing feature of his poetry.

The attempt to describe things as they simply are and without intervention of personal bias is one of the characteristics of the Japanese *HaiKu* with which Jaccottet became acquainted in the early 1960s through an anthology compiled by Blyth. Although they have certainly influenced his poetry as the poems in *Airs* bear witness, there is one decisive way in which Jaccottet's writing will never be like the *HaiKu* and that is because of his acute awareness of the presence of death in that which is natural. In *A travers un verger* the almond blossom whose beauty he tries to describe soon gives rise to thoughts about death. Normally death is associated with autumn but here it is the end of winter and the beginning of spring and new life which prompts these thoughts. Death is therefore present at the very heart of life.

In fact one of the central preoccupations in some of his works pivots around notions of life and death: 'J'ai toujours eu dans l'esprit, sans bien m'en rendre compte, une sorte de balance. Sur un plateau il y avait la douleur, la mort, sur l'autre la beauté de la vie' (p. 19). In some of his work the scales tip to the side of death. *A travers un verger* is one of them as is *L'Obscurité* (which represents a kind of crisis in his writing). The life and death duo are heralded by light and shade which, far from being clichéd terms, are rejuvenated in Jaccottet's work because of their relationship to what is seen with the eye and it is through vision that the world is questioned. When the eyes are open the beauty and sacredness of the world can be appreciated and it is light which makes this possible. When the eyes are closed there is only darkness and when they do not open again this is death: 'Tous ces regards fermés qu'il y a dans la terre, sous nos pieds, depuis le commencement de la terre! Que des fleurs s'ouvrent et se ferment, sortent de terre et y retournent, on n'en éprouve guère de tristesse, et on s'en étonne à peine. Mais les regards!' (p. 25). For Jaccottet 'seeing' is therefore both being and poetry.

In contrast to the three poets already discussed, who use a reduced vocabulary in order to capture the 'essence' of things, Michel Deguy's vocabulary is all-inclusive. For him, nothing lies beyond poetic discourse. He therefore employs a mixed vocabulary taken from the realms of philosophy, linguistics, history, geography, criticism, ethnology, sport and nature. In this way, his poetry achieves the most surprising and unexpected contrasts. In his poems the theory of poetry and poetry itself are woven together so that the two become part of the same whole. There has, however, been a progression in his work. His first three collections *Fragments du cadastre* (1960), *Poèmes de la presque-île* (1962) and *Biefs* (1964) have more references to the outside world, in particular to the landscapes of the Brittany he loves, than his later poetry does. Since the publication of *Actes* (1966), his semi-theoretical essays, followed by *Figurations* three years later, his poems have become more self-reflexive, the main reality being that of the poem itself.

Deguy splits open words making us aware of the play of possibilities within them of which we are normally unaware. So it is with the term 'abdication' in *Le Tombeau de Du Bellay* (1972). In an interview with Mary Ann Caws he explains: 'c'est un acte . . . d'ab-dication. (Je cherche le lien entre "acte", "dire", et "abdiquer"; y a-t-il quelque grand livre qui ne soit un acte dans la mesure où il abdique la tradition qui ne cesse de le porter?)' (*Esprit Créateur*, 15(3) 1975, 387–93 p. 391). In fact, all Deguy's poetry may be said to constitute a voiced act which runs counter to tradition. What he tries to capture in his work is not so much a superior reality, as is the case with the other poets discussed, but the very space of definition in which words and things meet: the area between the words as they exist in the dictionary, and as they are imagined by us, and the things to which we apply them in the outside world. The subject or speaker inhabits this very space given that it is he or she who chooses which words to apply to which things.

Between these two poles there are poets, many of whom are women, expressing themselves both by drawing on the vast corpus of the poetic tradition and by branching out into new areas. In a way, their endeavour is similar to that of the novelists of the period whose work sometimes uses the past as a millstone to be cast off and at other times as a stepping stone towards the promotion of the new. In many instances both old and new are combined.

Conclusion

What is certain, is that the latter half of this century has seen a period of crisis in all domains largely brought about, in the first instance, by the moral devastation of the Second World War and, in the second, by the political upheavals of 1968. The attempt to reconstruct a world which had been blown apart and then the systematic deconstruction of this new-found reality is perhaps in keeping with the impending feeling of apocalypse which tends to accompany every *fin de siècle*. There is also an increasing anxiety surrounding what many consider to be the demise of the intellectual. As John Flower has pointed out in his article 'Wherefore the Intellectuals?', many believe that the intellectuals and the debates with which they were concerned have passed away with the two figures who dominated French intellectual life since the war – Sartre and Raymond Aron (*French Cultural Studies*, 2, 1991 275–90). The deaths of other thinkers such as Barthes and Foucault adding to this unease. However, during the 1970s, and coinciding with the rise in the New Right, a number of thinkers known as the *Nouveaux Philosophes* emerged: a term applied to all those who saw it as their duty to remain outside the political arena and to stand alone when discussing all issues. They grew up especially in opposition to Sartrean *engagement*. Flower indicates two figures of particular importance: Bernard-Henri Lévy and Alain Finkielkraut. In his *Eloge des intellectuels (Paris: Grasset, 1987)*, an obvious allusion and challenge to Sartre's *Plaidoyer pour des intellectuels* (1972), Lévy suggests a definition of the intellectual: 'Intellectuel, nom masculin, catégorie sociale et culturelle née à Paris au moment de l'affaire Dreyfus, morte à Paris à la fin du XXe siècle' (p. 48). The probable reason for this demise is that class structures have been levelled. This view is shared by many and emerges as the common denominator in the *Magazine Littéraire's* survey on the role of the intellectual in an issue entitled *Le Rôle des intellectuels de l'affaire Dreyfus à nos jours* (December, 1987). It is echoed in Finkielkraut's *La Défaite de la Pensée* (1987) in which he suggests that the equality of societies has resulted in the deadening of the critical faculties. The demand is now for instant culture and this is given added impetus by the all-pervasive power of the media. As Flower suggests: 'In a society when a comedian like Coluche or a singer like the ever-present and seemingly ageless Johnny Hallyday both have claimed to be intellectuals and are even treated as such something has changed' (pp. 288–9).

But the fact that this is being taken up and debated within France and without suggests that this very change has provided much food for thought. However, the latest challenge to the French intellectual is the American Frances Fukuyama's suggestion that history itself has come to an end: democracy now being perceived by one and all as the best state of affairs. If this is in fact the case, then it is suggested that there may soon be nothing left for the intellectual to debate.

This sense of an ending, to use Kermode's term, is all the more acute given that the death of the intellectual and indeed that of the novelist need not only rest on a metaphorical plane. Aids has become very much of a reality already claiming the life of structuralist and philosopher, Michel Foucault, in 1984. This is alluded to in Hervé Guibert's novel *A L'Ami qui ne m'a pas sauvé la vie* (1988) in which Foucault is seen in the character of Muzil. It also treats Guibert's own homosexuality and the illness which claimed his life in December 1991. Two of his works have appeared posthumously. *Cytomégalovirus* (1992), a journal of his hospitalization, and *L'Homme au chapeau rouge* (1992).

The question which finally remains to be answered is whether literature will continue to exist given the competition it now faces with cinema, the *bande dessinée* and computer technology. It is perhaps significant that Bernard Pivot's programme *Apostrophes* which helped to promote writers and intellectuals alike has gone off the air. Pivot now has a new programme called *Brouillon de culture* which is exactly that, in that it involves all the arts and not just literature. Only time will tell if literature is to be replaced by other modes of narration. But what remains constant, as the centuries have proved, is humanity's need to narrate itself. What can change, however, is the mode in which we choose to do so.

Notes

1. For Jeanson's reply to Camus see *Les Temps modernes* (May, 1952). For more information on the debate in general see John Cruickshank's chapter 'Revolt and Revolution: Camus and Sartre', in *French Literature and its Background*, vol. 6 (Oxford, Oxford University Press, 1970)
2. The name was coined in Bernard Franck's article 'Grognards et Hussards', *Les Temps modernes*, vol. 8 (juillet–déc, 1952) 1005–1018
3. Claude Bonnefoy, *Panorama de la critique littéraire*, textes recueillis

et présentés par Tony Cartano, Maurice Lever, Georges Londeix et Daniel Oster (Paris, Belfond, 1980), p. 102

4. Alan Morris 'Attacks on Gaullist "Myth", in French Literature since 1969', in Ian Higgins, ed., *The Second World War in Literature* (Edinburgh, Scottish Academic Press, 1986), p. 75. For another appraisal of literature generated by the Second World War see Colin Nettlebeck's 'Getting the Story Right: Narratives of World War II in Post-1968 France', in *Journal of European Studies*, 15 (1985), 77–116

5. In particular see Claude Lévi-Strauss, *Anthropologie structurale* (Paris, Plon, 1958), *La Pensée sauvage* (Paris, 1966) and *Mythologiques*, four volumes written between 1964 and 1971

6. Barthes's essay and those by other structuralists are collected in *L'Analyse structurale du récit, Communications*, 8 (Paris, Seuil, 1981)

7. See John Flower, 'Temporalité et jeu de l'écriture dans *Un Adolescent d'autrefois*', in *Le Temps dans l'œuvre de François Mauriac, Cahiers François Mauriac*, 16 (Paris, Bernard Grasset, 1989), 144–52.

8. Jean Paul Sartre, preface to Nathalie Sarraute *Portrait d'un inconnu* (1947 for preface, this edition Paris: Folio, 1956) p. 9

9. Claude Simon, *Claude Simon: Colloque de Cerisy*, dirigé par Jean Ricardou (Paris, Union Générale d'Editions, 1975), p. 428

10. See, for example, Toril Moi's *Sexual/Textual Politics* (London/New York, Methuen, 1985) in which Moi gives a good account of the way Cixous deconstructs in her writing but then goes on to accuse her of falling back onto biologism therefore contradicting her own argument more successfully than she manages to contradict Cixous's.

11. Sarah Cornell, 'Hélène Cixous and *Les Etudes Féminines*', in *The Body and the Text: Hélène Cixous, Reading and Teaching*, ed. Helen Wilcox, Keith McWatters, Ann Thompson and Linda R. Williams (Hemel Hempstead, Harvester Wheatsheaf, 1990)

12. See, for example, Lispector's very rich novel *La Ville assiégée,* (Des Femmes 1991) which in terms of plot can only be said to be about a woman without further elaboration.

13. Marguerite Duras, *L'Amant* (Paris, Editions de Minuit, 1984), p. 14. At present in France (February, 1992) controversy is raging round Jean-Jacques Annaud's adaptation of *L'Amant* for the cinema, a production which Duras herself dislikes.

14. The poets dealt with in this section belong to the older generation of French poets. For an anthology which includes a more contemporary collection of poetry see, for example, Martin Sorrell's *Modern French Poetry: A Bilingual Anthology covering 70 years* (London/Boston: Forest Books, 1992)

15. Yves Bonnefoy, 'L'Acte et le lieu de la poésie', translated as, 'The Act and the Place of Poetry', by Jean Stewart and John T. Naughton, in John T. Naughton ed., *The Act and the Place of Poetry* (Chicago/London, University of Chicago Press 1989)

16. Joseph Frank, foreword to John Naughton ed., *Yves Bonnefoy: The Act and the Place of Poetry* (Chicago/London, University of Chicago Press 1989), p. xi

17. Yves Bonnefoy, 'La Poésie française et le principe d'identité', translated as 'French Poetry and the Principle of Identity', in

John Naughton ed., *Yves Bonnefoy: The Act and the Place of Poetry* (Chicago/London, University of Chicago Press 1989)
18. Yves Bonnefoy translated in John E. Naughton ed., *Yves Bonnefoy: The Act and the Place of Poetry* (Chicago/London, University of Chicago Press 1989), as '"Image and Presence": Inaugural Address at the Collège de France,' by John E. Naughton
19. Epigraphs from Shakespeare's *The Winter's Tale* at the beginning of Yves Bonnefoy's *Pierre Ecrite* (Paris, 1965) and *Dans le leurre du Seuil* (Paris, Gallimard 1975) respectively

Further reading

The Novel

Bersani, J, Autrand, M., Lecarme, J. and Vercier, B., *La Littérature en France depuis 1945* (Paris, Bordas 1970)
Flower, J. C., *Literature and the Left in France: Society, Politics and the Novel Since the Late Nineteenth Century* (London, Methuen 1983)
Heath, Stephen, *The Nouveau Roman: A study in the Practice of Writing* (London, Elek Books Ltd 1972)
Jefferson, Ann, *The Nouveau Roman and the Poetics of Fiction* (Cambridge, Cambridge University Press 1980)
Marks, Elaine and de Courtivron, Isabelle, eds., *New French Feminisms: An Anthology* (New York/London, Harvester Wheatsheaf 1981)
O'Flaherty, K. *The Novel in France 1945–1965* (Cork, Cork University Press 1973)
Ricardou, J., *Problèmes du nouveau roman* (Paris, Seuil 1967)
Tilby, Michael, ed., *Beyond the Nouveau Roman: Essays on the Contemporary French Novel* (New York/Oxford, Berg 1990)
Vercier, B. and Lecarme, J., *La Littérature en France depuis 1968* (Paris, Bordas 1982)

Criticism

Culler, Jonathan, *Structuralist Poetics: Structuralism, Linguistics and the Study of Literature* (London, Routledge and Kegan Paul 1975)
On Deconstruction: Theory and Criticism after Structuralism (London, Routledge and Kegan Paul 1983)
Tadié, Jean-Yves, *La Critique littéraire au XXe siècle* (Paris, Belford 1987)

Poetry

Bishop, Michael, ed., *The Language of Poetry: Crisis and Solution: Studies in Modern Poetry of French Expression, 1945 to the Present* (Amsterdam, Rodolphi 1980)
Delaveau, Philippe, *La Poésie française au tournant des années 80* (Paris, Corti 1988)
Hackett, C. A., *New French Poetry: An Anthology* (Oxford, Basil Blackwell 1973)

Jaccottet, Philippe, *L'Entretien des Muses* (Paris, Gallimard 1966)
Richard, J. P., *Onze études sur la poésie moderne* (Paris, Sevil 1964)
Sabatier, Robert, *Histoire de la poésie française: la poésie du vingtième siècle, vol 3, Metamorphoses et modernité* (Paris, Albin Michel 1988)

CHAPTER 3

The theatre

Martin Sorrell

Introduction

Judged by certain criteria, French theatre in the 1990s is in good shape. The central positions of the playhouses of Paris and its suburbs remain assured, and all around in the provinces there is a wealth of highly regarded Centres Dramatiques and Maisons de la Culture – the fruit of the rather hesitant *décentralisation* of the last few decades. After the apparent decline in significance of the playwright in the late 1960s and 1970s, and the corresponding ascendancy of the director, as well as a vogue for collective creation, the mid and late 1980s began to see a slow reinstatement of the writer for the stage. *Metteur en scène* and writer now have just about equal status within the profession, if not always in the eyes of the public, who may still prefer to know who is directing a play rather than who has written it. It is also worth considering that, by most standards, French theatre is quite substantially subsidized. (True, Germany gave and still gives larger subventions, but this is an exceptional case.) How the subsidies are divided and used, though, is a prickly and contentious issue, and the rôle of the Socialist Minister of Culture, Jack Lang, in the distribution of resources over the last two decades has been the object of heated controversy.

The thirty-nine annual theatre festivals (the best-known of which is the Festival d'Avignon, founded in 1947 by one of France's greatest-ever directors, Jean Vilar) are flourishing, and attest to the health not only of the major companies but also of small, independent and fringe groups, some of which spring into life but all too often vanish just as quickly. Finally, an interesting token of the prestige of French theatre, its great traditions as well as its most recent explorations, is that it continues to experience the considerable worldwide exposure it has always enjoyed. Whether in the original or in translation, French plays are staged around the world with dependable regularity. The theatre of France, then, is alive and apparently well, and it is held in high regard.

After a short historical survey, this chapter will focus on theatre in France during the last three decades in particular. Where important names have received little or even no attention, it is because they have already been expertly dealt with in numerous publications which are readily available. Details of significant productions are set out in the chronology given at the end of the book.

From the late nineteenth to the mid-twentieth Century

The truly modern theatre in France can be said to originate from the end of the last century, when the director André Antoine brought a somewhat out-dated overstylized stagecraft up to date with his blunt, powerfully naturalistic *mises en scène*. The central position of the stage director in France dates from then, as does what may be called 'Absurd' theatre, for 1896 saw the first production of the celebrated *Ubu roi*, written by the schoolboy Alfred Jarry. This dark, violent comedy anticipates some of the most important writing for theatre of the 1950s and 1960s. Its apparent anti-theatricality was reinforced by Jarry's own characteristically provocative pronouncement that theatre must rid itself of its awful, incomprehensible accretions – notably sets and actors.

Jarry's experimental style was continued to an extent by Guillaume Apollinaire in his play of 1917, *Les Mamelles de Tirésias*, and by some of the Surrealists of the 1920s, such as Roger Vitrac. But a seemingly more orthodox type of writing held sway in the first part of the present century, especially the interwar years, when the best-known names included Jean Cocteau, Paul Claudel, Jean Giraudoux, Jean Anouilh and Henry de Montherlant. At the same time, the importance of the director's newly acquired status was affirmed by the legendary Jacques Copeau, around the time of the First World War, and by the celebrated Cartel des Quatre, four directors who followed him, Charles Dullin, Louis Jouvet, Georges Pitoëff and Gaston Baty, who together dominated Parisian theatre between the two world wars. One lonely, strident and altogether extraordinary voice crying out during that period was that of Antonin Artaud, playwright, *metteur en scène*, performer, theoretician and visionary, the elaborator of the so-called 'Theatre of Cruelty', not greatly influential during his own lifetime, but much more so in the 1950s and beyond. Artaud lays great emphasis on performance, for him both a fragile thing and the supreme element of drama. Among important playwrights, Jean Genet and Armand Gatti are arguably the two who most call to mind Artaud's view of theatre.

The German Occupation of France, perhaps surprisingly, did not mean the suppression of theatrical life, despite heavy censorship. On the contrary, in Paris particularly, good plays continued to be staged. If the 1940s was a decade of high intellectual and political questioning, its two leading thinkers, Jean-Paul Sartre and Albert Camus, brought ideology and philosophical discourse on to the stage. Of the two, Sartre has been the more performed, and much of his substantial output is regularly revived. Most recently, his *Kean* has had successful runs, but there appears to be renewed interest in Camus, especially his skilful *Caligula*.

The Theatre of the Absurd, and the example of René de Obaldia

The 1940s also marked the emergence of the 'Theatre of the Absurd'. The best-known play of that so-called school, Samuel Beckett's *En attendant Godot*, was written in 1947, although it was not given its first performance until 1953, in Paris, under the direction of Roger Blin. Beckett simply could not find a producer to take it on, nor an editor to publish it, for a number of years, so controversial and unprecedented did it seem. But the 1950s saw Beckett's reputation grow, alongside that of Eugène Ionesco, the two of them too readily grouped together despite their very considerable differences. Other practitioners of 'Absurd' theatre in France at the same time were Fernando Arrabal, Arthur Adamov, Robert Pinget and a playwright who has been performed around the world more than any other of his French contemporaries, but whose popularity has declined in recent years, René de Obaldia.

Obaldia manages to avoid the portentousness and weighty gloom which is the risk the Absurdists run, yet his world is as disconcertingly incoherent as any. He is worth pausing over, the more so as English critics have devoted relatively little space to him. Like Ionesco (from Roumania), Arrabal (from Spain) and Adamov (from Russia), Obaldia comes from outside France. He was born in Hong Kong in 1918, the son of a French mother and a Panamanian father. He came to France as a young child, and went to school in Paris. He started writing plays as a way of entertaining friends. His ambition was therefore modest and not too serious, which goes some way to explaining the freshness and off-beat humour of his comedies. From his considerable output (it runs to ten published volumes), his greatest success has been *Du vent dans les branches de sassafras*. But *Le Cosmonaute agricole*, of 1965, can serve as an admirable example of Obaldia's style. It is the story of a couple of farmers in central France, both of them by turns simple and ferociously intellectual, and whose son, bored and needing to spread his wings, has taken off to outer space at the age of four. In the middle of the play, he returns to engage in scholarly – and scholastic – discourse with his parents on a variety of metaphysical matters. The characteristics of Obaldia's style of Absurdist writing are apparent; the incessant thwarting of all the firm judgements we would like to make both about events and people; nothing is at all what it seems; the mix of surface whimsicality and underlying seriousness; a kind of happy mental dislocation in individual minds; and a brilliant use of stylized language, full of plays on words, literary and philosophical allusions, anachronisms and aphorisms. Taken all together, these elements make for a play in which the spectator is as much thrown off any possible scent as in a piece by Ionesco, Beckett or whoever. Perhaps the best word to describe the effect is *féerique* (magical). For some people's taste, however, Obaldia comes too close to boulevard theatre. It is true that he is reminiscent of this kind of commercial theatre, but another crucial aspect of his writing clearly shows that he has distanced himself from it: namely, parody. He imitates and distorts the work of other playwrights and other traditions, in order to send them up. His last play, *Les Bons Bourgeois*, is a virtuoso reworking in modern alexandrine verse of Molière's *Les Femmes savantes*, a comedy about educated women's search for autonomy in a male-dominated world. A satire for our times, as Obaldia has described it, it may have struck audiences as reactionary. Certainly, unlike some of the playwrights of the 1980s, Obaldia is not political in a doctrinaire way, but he is socially and politically aware in a broader sense. Three of his plays were revived at the 7th Festival de la butte Montmartre, Paris, in the summer of 1991.

A key feature of Obaldia's plays, as of all Absurdist theatre, is what may be termed its non-mimetic quality. This type of theatre does not seek to imitate life, to replicate it in any cinematic way, in contrast to the productions mounted by Antoine at the end of the last century. What appears to have asserted (perhaps re-asserted) its presence in French theatre from Beckett, through Ionesco and others, to Genet above all, is what might be termed theatricality. That is, the truths and insights which theatre provides are not to be separated from an audience's understanding that it is witnessing something artificial, a contrived event, a rite or ritual. The meaning and value of this type of theatre is inherent in its performance; it is not literature acted out.

Jean Genet: Antonin Artaud

Nowhere in post-war French theatre is this sense of what might be termed undisguised illusion more powerful than in the five plays of Genet, spanning the years 1947 to 1961. This small output (a novelist and essayist as well, Genet stopped writing anything of substance during the last twenty years or so of his life) is distinctive, often demanding for audience, actor and director alike, and characterized by an unblinking, ferocious search for identity and authenticity. But, if this sounds intellectual, Genet's plays when seen on stage, most of all *Le Balcon*, are rich, heady, colourful, making use of sumptuous, elaborate rites which suggest religious ritual. Genet's world is a cruel one. Characters are harsh; they are unforgiving towards one another and to the spectator. We are made to feel that the on-stage characters are holding up blinding mirrors of truth not only to themselves but also to us in the auditorium. This is a variant of Artaud's idea of cruelty in the theatre. The correct performance unlocks in subconscious ways the submerged sensibilities of the spectator, often by brutal ('cruel') methods – for example, powerful lighting, violent noise and movement and a highly stylized, exaggerated acting technique. Then, the actor, while still aware that he/she is acting, doing something artificial and ritualistic, goes to the edges of pain, to which we as audience respond equally painfully, the understanding being that a theatrical representation, shared as a communal rite, can push us through a pain barrier and into a fuller and more naked awareness of our humanity. As good an example as any of how Artaud's ideas work out in practice is the film version of Peter Weiss's *Marat/Sade*, with Glenda Jackson, which Peter Brook had originally staged. In 1964, Brook and Charles Marowitz ran a Theatre of Cruelty season at LAMDA, London. An English version of one of Artaud's plays, *The Spurt of Blood*, was put on during this event.

It is perhaps no coincidence that Artaud's delirious vision led him into madness, and that he ended his days in an asylum. Genet does not go all the way down that line. The search for authenticity in his plays, which are sometimes over-long and too intricate, seems to stop short of finding it, and his characters are all too wryly aware of the distance between reality and illusion. Through his often used device of *trompe l'œil*, a form of play-within-the-play, Genet never lets us or his characters or the actors playing those characters forget that we are all attending a ritual of make-believe which is called theatre. Part of his message appears to be that this is preferable to what is called real life, because, paradoxically, it is *more* real.

Artaud's legacy probably has been most apparent outside France: in Jerzy Grotowski's remarkable Laboratory Theatre, from Poland, and in the equally extraordinary work of The Living Theater and The Bread and Puppet Theatre, both from the USA. The first two of these three paid several visits to France during the 1960s.

Bertolt Brecht

If Artaud was one major guru of French theatre after the war, then an equally powerful, though very different one, was Bertolt

Brecht. This great German all-round man of the theatre was known in France up to the late 1950s only for *The Threepenny Opera*, which had been produced twice in Paris in the 1930s. *Mother Courage* was put on in 1951 by Jean Vilar at the Théâtre National Populaire (TNP), in its Chaillot premises near the Eiffel Tower, but the play was not a resounding success. However, the first two visits to France of Brecht's Berliner Ensemble in 1954 and 1955 changed all that. Their production, on the first of these visits, of *Mother Courage* took the theatre world by storm, and opened French eyes to what Brecht was about. For the Ensemble's second visit, the choice of play was *The Caucasian Chalk Circle*, produced with the greatest success. Brecht's work now received serious attention, it was much discussed in newspapers, journals, etc. An important review, *Théâtre Populaire*, which started at that time, published Brecht's work, and espoused his Marxist ideology of theatre.

One by-product of the 1954 and 1955 visits was a number of significant productions of Brecht's work in France. One of his major champions, the director Roger Planchon, did two productions very soon after, as did Jean Dasté, Cyril Robichez and André Steiger. The Berliner Ensemble paid a third visit to France in 1960, the year of the biggest flowering of Brechtian activities. The Ensemble itself staged four different productions, while Vilar and an equally renowned director, Jean-Louis Barrault, did *Arturo Ui* and *The Caucasian Chalk Circle* respectively.

Where Beckettian Absurdist drama is largely non-political and aims for a kind of universality, Brecht's concept is thoroughly political, left-wing, localized in time and space. He wants a drama which is no longer classically Aristotelian but rather what he calls 'epic'. That is to say, he rejects the passive, agreeable and compliant role into which audiences traditionally are cast as they watch a continuous spectacle unfold. Instead of this semi-hypnotic submission to the pleasures of agreeable acting, rich costumes and lighting, in short the pleasures of illusion, Brecht wants his audiences to be made to take a thoughtful, critical stance in front of the episodic, interrupted action, to eschew too-easy identification with heroes. Brechtian action is presented in the form of a story, an account, composed of discontinuous episodes, thus placing it at one remove from the immediacy of the classical play, and also 'historicizing' it. The actors should make clear to the spectators that they, the actors, are essentially outside the action, that they know the whole play, the story, the dénouement. They must *show* their character, not *be* it. This is Brecht's epic theatre. The spectator must work to understand fully the dramatic events, he/she must not lose critical self-awareness, or the understanding that to go to the theatre must *not* mean that one loses oneself. These imperatives are a large part of what is meant by Brecht's celebrated *verfremdungseffekt*, or 'distancing effect', often referred to as 'alienation'. It does not mean, as it is frequently interpreted, that the audience should feel unabsorbed by what is happening on stage, or that there should be no pleasure other than a fiercely intellectual one in going to the theatre. On the contrary, Brecht's plays are full of variety, interest, changing focuses, songs and music, clips of film, etc.

Brecht's influence on French theatre over the last thirty or so years has been huge, particularly in the 1960s, and has created a strong current of socially aware and committed theatre, leaning leftwards at various angles, and employing many of Brecht's techniques of stagecraft. Brecht has had a liberating and a rejuvenating effect. Ever since the mid 1950s, French theatre has looked with admiration on its German counterpart. Undoubtedly, Planchon has been the most important Brechtian in France (though he is a freer spirit than this might imply, and was initially an admirer of Artaud). Over a good many years, he strove to bring his Brecht-inspired productions to new and working-class audiences in Villeurbanne, an industrial suburb of Lyon. It was there that in 1957 he set up his Théâtre de la Cité, which in 1972 took over the title of the TNP, relinquished by the troubled Chaillot theatre in Paris.

Decentralization

Certain tendencies in French theatrical life of the 1960s which perhaps were not fully apparent, or which simply did not attract enormous attention, surfaced with *brio* in the watershed year of 1968, the year of the famous *événements* when France came close to revolution. If part of the malaise which almost tore France apart that year had to do with that perennial issue in French life, centralization and the pre-eminence of Paris in most domains, then it certainly permeated the world of theatre. Ever since the last war, there had been a government-sponsored programme of *décentralisation*. The moving spirit of this programme in the 1940s was Jeanne Laurent who, on the basis of her own observations and of a report written by the director Charles Dullin at the request of the Front Populaire socialist government of the mid 1930s, decided to create a number of entirely new Centres Dramatiques Nationaux (CDN), to be funded both by central and local government. She also established a competition for new theatre companies, offering substantial prizes; and a subsidy for new writing, 'l'aide à la première pièce'. Five CDNs were created by Mme Laurent. In order, these were: the Centre Dramatique de l'Est, Colmar, 1946; St Etienne, 1947; l'Ouest, Rennes, 1949; Le Grenier de Toulouse,

1949; and the Comédie de Provence, Aix-en-Provence, 1951. Today, there are twenty-five CDNs, plus five others specifically for youth audiences. They are dotted all over the country, including the industrial suburbs of Paris.

The pattern of decentralization during and after the 1950s was a little erratic. The creation by André Malraux, de Gaulle's Minister of Culture, of the Maisons de la Culture targeted towns and areas hitherto deprived of the best in artistic and cultural activity, including theatre. But there were often sharp differences of opinion between administrators and artistic directors, leading to dismissals, resignations, and so on. By the mid 1960s there were six Maisons open and a further six near completion. Only the ones at Caen and Bourges housed permanent theatre companies. However, the burgeoning CDNs and the new Troupes Permanentes (established companies) constituted expansion and real decentralization. The hallmark of the work of these places and companies was their adherence to the principles of Brecht. Political theatre performed with a good deal of experimentation marked French theatre of the 1960s.

The noted contemporary playwright Michel Vinaver gave a paper on decentralization at a conference on regional theatre, held at Birmingham University in April 1990. On the plus side, Vinaver concluded, decentralization has shown the commitment of France to non-profit-making theatre, and an unflagging attempt by local and central governments to finance it, irrespective of their political colour. It has also brought about a modest increase in attendance figures, at a time when theatres are having to fight harder than ever for audiences. Therefore, decentralization has slowed down considerably the undeniable erosion in public support for theatre, especially in the provinces. And there has been a trickle of new spectators from social classes which traditionally do not go to the theatre. On the whole, the administration at central and local government levels have been enlightened and constructive. And finally, one of the results of decentralization is that the art of *mise en scène* has been much enlivened.

On the minus side, said Vinaver, the Utopian hope of a large, enthusiastic blue-collar class clientèle regularly flocking to the theatre (the dream of Vilar and Planchon, among others) has not been realized. Part of the blame for this lies at the door of television, probably theatre's most dangerous challenger. Interestingly, there is some evidence that television makes people want to *do* theatre rather than *go* to it. The risk, therefore, is that there will be more and more companies bidding for smaller and smaller audiences. Another perceived negative is what can be called retrenchment, theatre people closing in and working mainly for themselves. Too many theatre practitioners are doing theatre for theatre's sake; there is a lot of navel-gazing.

This narcissism has helped create an escalation in costs, with ever more extravagant demands being made on the funding bodies. Then, there is the increasingly wide gap between the three 'leagues' in French subsidized theatre, the big, middle and small, which do not enjoy the cross-fertilization that they should. However, Vinaver's strongest criticism, perhaps not surprising coming from a playwright working in the current climate, was for the disproportionate power of directors, so many of whom have achieved star status, with the result that new writing, the life-blood of any theatre which wants to move forward, has withered away. There is scarcely any new and independent writing being done for the theatre.

Despite all this, however, decentralization has progressed over the decades, and borne some rich fruit. And, to pick up an observation at the start of this chapter, compared to some countries, French theatre is quite handsomely subsidized and sympathetically administered.

Total theatre: Jean-Louis Barrault

From the 1940s, although its origins were pre-war, there has been a flowering of what has come to be known as 'total theatre'. The person most closely associated with this concept is Jean-Louis Barrault. Before the war, he attracted the attention and praise of Artaud with his experimental production of a Faulkner adaptation, *Autour d'une mère*, which relied on a very marked physical expressivity while it downgraded more orthodox features, such as scenery and costume. Echoing a popular tradition of theatre, Barrault favoured open-air, energetic and athletic performances, full of physical humour, acrobatics, song and dance. Later, particularly in the 1950s and even more the 1960s, Barrault did some most distinctive productions whose common thread was a thorough exploration of the means of theatrical expression beyond the written word. He has played a major part, arguably right up to the present day, in that trend of recent decades to move away from the imperatives of the text and to act on the understanding that a performance is a complex system of signs – non-linguistic as much as linguistic. In a country such as France, where the literary, written tradition is very strong, the new 'total theatre' has always been controversial, at least in some quarters.

When the events of May 1968 erupted, the *esprit de contestation* in French theatre was already well honed. Provincial companies, highly politicized and revolutionary in spirit and resentful of the capital's unchanging supremacy, were ready to join their Parisian comrades in their occupation of theatres. 'Revolutionary' tribunals of inquiry met to scrutinize the records of the luminaries of the stage, and to subject them to thorough cross-questioning. Barrault was one such, and he had to defend himself against what he thought were most unfair criticisms by the students; he saw himself as the well-proven purveyor of a theatre in touch with contemporary youth. The result, however, was that Barrault left the Odéon in 1968, and continued his career at the Elysée-Montmartre and the Théâtre d'Orsay. In theatres all around France, similar soul-searching took place. Theatre workers were accused of being aloof, elitist. Largely, they conceded the point, and promised shake-ups and reforms. In some cases, current programmes during that early summer of 1968 were cancelled on the spot, and more 'relevant' performances, such as agitprop pieces, were hastily substituted. A working-class potential audience which knew nothing of the theatre was identified and labelled 'the non-public'. But a different kind of play, of performance, was necessary if this non-public was going to be won over. And radical departures in the whole organization of the theatrical enterprise were needed. In the spirit of democracy and egalitarianism, theatre companies henceforth should abolish hierarchies, too much power and control should never be allowed to fall into any one individual's hands, every theatre worker should have equal rights and an equal say. All of this taken together amounted to a vastly different style of theatre ideology, which came to be known as *la création collective* (collective creation), and which had far-reaching effects in the 1970s above all.

Collective creation

La création collective took non-text-based theatre as far as it has ever been. As the appellation implies, plays, productions, performances were elaborated jointly, corporately, in the often chaotic fervour of 1968 and post-1968 France. The dictatorial exigencies of the author and the written script were rejected with some passion, though it can be argued that the growing dominance of the director in French theatre was rapidly accelerated by this 'demise' of the writer. Nevertheless, a breath of fresh air stirred up the French theatre world from the late 1960s onwards and introduced experiments and experiences which the general public had not encountered before. There was a new wildness, a kind of controlled anarchy (not unconnected with the 'anything goes' approach to life of the free-wheeling 1960s) which led to some extraordinarily inspired and exhilarating theatre, a blend of carnival, street theatre, circus and outrageous provocation. And there was a more studied, intense, political theatre exploring a new and astonishing stagecraft. The first of these trends is best exemplified by a company which came to prominence in the early 1970s, Jérôme Savary's Grand Magic Circus, the second by what was the outstanding company of the 1970s, if not of the 1980s, Ariane Mnouchkine's Théâtre du Soleil. Their stories are exemplary, and are worth looking at in some detail.

Jérôme Savary and Le Grand Magic Circus

Savary is now a firmly established mainstream director. In 1988, this Frenchman of international background – distantly related to a former Governor of New York, a childhood partly spent in Argentina, much of his work seen in the USA, Canada and Europe – took up his appointment as director of one of France's five National Theatres, the Chaillot, formerly the TNP. But in the 1960s, at the start of his career, he was very much in the vanguard of experimental and subversive theatre. From 1965, when his Compagnie J. Savary was founded, the majority of his productions were devised collectively by the group. In this way he laid down a principle which was to sustain his work for a good many years after. 1965 saw the production of *Les Boîtes*, which he scripted jointly with Fernando Arrabal. This was a loosely constructed piece, and it made use of film, and two other elements which are very much Savary hallmarks, namely, on-stage music and animals. The collaboration with Arrabal arose out of Savary's association with this playwright and with Roland Topor and Alexandro Jodorowsky, who together formed the so-called Théâtre panique, named after the deity Pan and intended (by Arrabal at least) to show that they had distanced themselves from Absurdist theatre. What exactly Panic theatre amounted to remains confusing, but it led Savary to change the name of his company in 1966 to Grand Panic Circus. The *panique* 'anti-movement' was shortlived, however, and influenced only one of Savary's productions, *Le Labyrinthe*.

With its emphasis on filth, physical misery and extreme violence, Savary's 1967 production of *Le Radeau de la Méduse* was an embodiment of a certain notion of cruel theatre. 1967 also saw the staging of Savary's production of Arrabal's *Le Labyrinthe*. The fact that he was working from a text did not embarrass him. He cheerfully doubled the original cast of five by adding a goat and some chickens. Generally, it was a chaotic spectacle. Actors were constantly changed. The final, multi-national cast randomly delivered their lines in French, Spanish or English. The often improvised action took place on several different platforms, sequentially or simultaneously, and Savary himself was Master of Ceremonies, high on a raised platform, banging a drum, playing his trumpet or addressing the actors through a microphone. With *Le Labyrinthe*, Savary moved towards that festive, carnivalesque circus which in his next productions was to make him internationally well known. *Le Labyrinthe* amounted to Savary's rejection of orthodox theatre. To be tied to a text was to be tied to literature and thus to the Establishment. And, as France careered towards the momentous and revolutionary days of May 1968, Savary identified orthodox theatre with the repressive forces of bourgeois high culture. He placed himself firmly in the camp of revolt.

In 1968, Savary's troupe adopted its final and most celebrated name, Le Grand Magic Circus et ses animaux tristes. The sad animals were human beings, sad because we are animals who have lost animal joy and spontaneity. There followed a series of amazing productions over the next few years which for many theatre devotees and critics alike represent the peak of Savary's achievement. The classic Magic Circus productions were *Zartan, frère mal-aimé de Tarzan, Les Derniers Jours de solitude de Robinson Crusoë, De Moïse à Mao, 5000 ans d'Aventures et d'Amour*, and *Good Bye Mister Freud*, all dating from the early 1970s.

These productions were highly distinctive. The choice of venue, to begin with, was as non-theatrical as possible. Sometimes huge tents were used, or sports halls, or the friendly, rough-and-ready space of the Cité Universitaire, which is where the Magic Circus gained major fame with *Zartan*. Then, in the pre-performance period of a show, the arriving audience would be entertained by a circus-like warm-up, involving brassy music, strongly coloured lights, and the chatter and activity of the troupe itself (a style developed in a more refined way by the Théâtre du Soleil). The printed publicity outside the venue as well as the hand-outs for the audience were flamboyant and full of cartoons. The plays themselves took the form of loosely linked tableaux performed in several areas of the space. In *Zartan*, for example, there were eight such areas. Besides this, the company constantly moved among the spectators, creating yet another performance area, and coming as close as possible to abolishing the distinction between players and audience. For those not used to it, this was certainly a theatre of assault and embarrassment, at least in the early stages of the evening – by the end, audiences tended to be won over and to lose any inhibitions. Joy and exuberance eclipsed the darker potential inherent in its subject, such as the history of colonialism in *Zartan*. Political messages in the Magic Circus's work tended to get lost in light and lightness.

The rambling plot of Magic Circus shows never quite lost coherence, thanks to the familiarity of the original stories to most of the audience, to the largely self-contained nature of the episodic tableaux, and to the controlling, ringmaster presence of Savary himself, guiding and shifting the action with a flourish of his trumpet and some rudimentary commentary on the action for the spectators' benefit (an eccentric adoption of some of Brecht's principles; Savary has said that he is a Brechtian). The dominant aesthetic was exactly that suggested by the company's apt name, the wide-eyed and intoxicating magic of the circus. The action was fast and acrobatic, the players' make-up garish, the costumes extravagant and glittering, the lighting powerful, and the whole spectacle was propelled by loud music, often with a Latin beat. If all of this sounds innocent enough, the spice and the controversy lay in the deliberate offence to good taste which ran through the whole of these shows. The most obvious form of this 'offensiveness' was the sexual near-explicitness, the very frequent nudity of the performers, who were never shy of keeping themselves indelicately close to the audience; and the creation of well-known characters from real life who were then made to behave in outrageous fashion. For example, in *Zartan* there was a moment when an actress looking startlingly like Queen Elizabeth II arrived on stage piggyback on a man's shoulders, a cigarette in mouth, tiara on head, royal blue sash awry and one regal breast exposed. The real danger to a largely defensive post-1968 society was that the Magic Circus's message of anarchic spontaneity might be heeded. These shows were subversive. They questioned how we live, asked why society accepts repression and collective depression. There was obviously nothing original in the Magic Circus's simple political message; but it was powerful. Audiences were enchanted, they came to life. Feelings of freedom were in the air, and the shows would close with exhilarating dancing by audience and cast alike. Savary has said that he wanted his productions to be 'taken over' by the spectators turned protagonists. In the collision of social philosophies which marked 1968 and its aftermath, Le Grand Magic Circus was in the forefront of the movement for total renewal.

From the mid-1970s, however, the character of Savary's company began to change. For one thing, the 'swinging 60s' (which swung into the early 1970s too) had died a natural death, and the Magic Circus, whatever else, was a product of the flower-power years. The company carried on working, it put on a considerable number of shows which were toured a good deal, frequently in Germany, a country with whose theatre Savary has always had a special rapport. There was a handful of productions before the interesting 1980 staging of Savary's version of Molière's *Le Bourgeois Gentilhomme*, seen at Aulnay-sous-Bois, and then at the Théâtre de l'Est Parisien, one of France's National Theatres. Savary's view of Monsieur Jourdain as a naïve but sympathetic man whose genuine search for knowledge and self-improvement is triumphantly vindicated in the play's final scene stood the conventional interpretation of the play on its head. What Jourdain had *really* been searching for was a vibrant, popular culture, not the upper-middle-class, so-called 'high' variety.

Today, the Grand Magic Circus exists no more, though its influence can still be seen in Savary's productions at Chaillot. Some of the Magic Circus's actors have continued to work with him. But the subversive quality has largely gone out of Savary's work now that he is in charge of a Théâtre National. And it is difficult to see who has picked up where he left off. Society and artistic fashions have changed in the last two decades. The exciting novelties Savary brought to the theatre – a total theatre, with music, dance, acrobatics, nudity, near-pornography, audience participation – have either been assimilated into the mainstream or have fallen out of favour.

Ariane Mnouchkine and le Théâtre du Soleil

Ariane Mnouchkine's Théâtre du Soleil, which has been in existence for over a quarter of a century now, is one side of a coin whose other is the Grand Magic Circus. Soleil's work, politically to the left, has always been, if not exactly subversive, then certainly provocative. Mnouchkine and her company have radically re-thought the nature of theatre, of what it is to be present at a performance both as theatre worker and as spectator, and they have employed a battery of startling new techniques which have made their theatre unique. Their ambitions have been greater than those of the Magic Circus, their results infused with a weightiness, a seriousness which Savary never would claim for himself. Soleil is more adult than the Magic ever wanted to be; it is also less joyous.

Ariane Mnouchkine discovered theatre as a student in Oxford and then at the Sorbonne in the late 1950s. She worked in student theatre, putting on productions in the early 1960s, until, in 1964, her Théâtre du Soleil was officially born. An essential principle from the start was that the organization of the company should not be hierarchical. It was to be rigorously a cooperative. All areas of work as well as salaries were to be equal, profits to be shared, everyone to have a vote. Actors were to be technicians and vice versa, as well as cleaners, sweepers, ushers and bar staff, box office attendants, telephone receptionists, etc. And everybody was to take part in the process of creating a production (not 'writing' it). Soleil set out to be a genuine theatre collective, and it has maintained that principle to this day. In its first few years, it led a nomadic life, staging productions of Gorki's *Les Petits Bourgeois*, of Wesker's *The Kitchen*, of *A Midsummer Night's Dream*, and its own collectively devised spectacle, *Les Clowns*, in whatever venues it could negotiate. In

1970, Mnouchkine was offered a disused munitions factory, the Cartoucherie, in the Bois de Vincennes on the edge of Paris. This vast building, like an aircraft hangar, suited the generous kind of *mise en scène* which the company was evolving. Soleil is still there, twenty years on, still creating a truly gigantic style of theatre. In the last decade, its major productions have been of Shakespeare's history plays, of *Norodom Sihanouk* (about the recent history of Cambodia), and *L'Indiade ou l'Inde de leurs rêves*. The prominent feminist writer Hélène Cixous has been closely associated with Soleil for a number of years.

However, Soleil sprang to national and international prominence with a production entitled *1789*, arguably its most impressive work to date. It opened in Milan in 1970 before transferring in the following year to the newly acquired Cartoucherie, and it was also seen in 1971 at the Roundhouse, London. This collectively devised, patiently rehearsed play about the first year of the French Revolution was truly . . . revolutionary. In the first place, it was a promenade performance. That is, there was little seating for the audience, who instead stood to watch, moving around the large space following the story as it unfolded in different areas, on five separate raised wooden stages (copying the *tréteaux* of old French open-air theatres) linked one to the other by a series of walkways and steps. On to these stages stepped heavily made-up actors, dressed in the most sumptuous costumes, richly lit, and acting in a stylized way, full of simplified but exaggerated, expressionistic gesture. The production took the form of ten scenes, depicting the rise and fall of the ordinary people's hopes during the first months of the Revolution. As set out in the programme for the Roundhouse run, these scenes were: Prologue; An Allegorical and Realistic Description of the Conditions in the Kingdom before 1789; The Summoning of the States General and the Request for Lists of Grievances; The Puppet Show and the 'Bed of Justice'; The King's Betrayal; The Storming of the Bastille; The Great Fear; the 4th of August 1789 and Its Consequences; Martial Law; Unspeakable Comedy (The Massacre of the Champs de Mars). The use of capital letters, incidentally, highlighted the epic, Brechtian feel of the production, as did the plentiful facts and figures about late eighteenth-century French history also printed in the programme. Indeed, the way in which the episodes were introduced and commented on revealed the company's intention to create a distancing effect which would encourage the audience to think critically about the historical events being represented. Occasionally, different 'readings' of events were offered, as at the very beginning, when the play seemed to be launching itself with a predictable account of the flight to Varennes of the King and Queen, only to stop, pass comment, and start again on a different tack. Mnouchkine, the director of *1789* as of all the big Soleil productions, successfully created theatre magic while making it clear that what was going on was not to be a comfortable source of easy identification for the spectators. At every opportunity, she had her actors make plain that this was exactly what they were, actors. Thus, they changed items of costume (virtually every actor took more than one role) and applied make-up in full view of the public, a feature of Soleil's ideology which persists today. Then, some huge and magnificent puppets were used in the fourth tableau, again making the spectator stand back from the action. The actors played their characters non-naturalistically. A sickly, fairytale king hobbled on to one of the stages on his crutches, accompanied by two players in bird-masks who represented the Nobility and the Clergy, and who themselves were riding on the back of the Donkey, that is, the People. They whinnied, and they threw King, Nobility and Clergy to the ground, then removed their masks, bowed and exited. The controlling image of the fairground was never far away. In the manner of total theatre, *1789* used a broad range of theatrical expression including music, much of it pre-recorded and very potent (in subsequent productions, music played by an on-stage band led by Jean-Jacques Lemêtre became an integral and equal part of the performance), and wrestling and fighting. One of the most memorable episodes was the sixth, in which an impassioned account of the Storming of the Bastille was given. Instead of attempting to portray the storming, Mnouchkine had her actors tell it, but in a most original way. At a given moment, various members of the cast came down off the platform stages and dispersed among the audience. Each one invited his or her section of spectators to gather round and listen to the story of how the Bastille had been taken. Apparently separate and autonomous, these accounts in fact were skilfully orchestrated, the actors' voices coming to a synchronized crescendo on the words 'the Bastille has fallen!' Apart from an intrinsically exciting, climactic moment in the play, this account subtly involved the audience directly, gradually turning it, as a body, from uninvolved onlooker into active participant. Mnouchkine made her audiences unwittingly and unavoidably become The People. It was a *tour de force*. On the 14 July, 1971, Soleil gave a free performance of *1789* in the Cartoucherie and, when the sixth episode was reached, the performance was stopped and the evening turned into a Bastille Day *fête*, with the 5,000-strong audience singing and dancing, eventually spilling out into the summer night.

The sequel to *1789* was the less impressive *1793*, given in 1972. This production used some of the innovative techniques of *1789*, but somehow they did not combine so effectively. Soleil has not sought to imitate *1789* so closely in its subsequent productions, although a distinctive Soleil house-style clearly exists.

But for many years, perhaps even still today, a production at the Cartoucherie was the most exciting event in the whole of Paris theatre. If any French company has developed a bold, innovative, revolutionary ideology, shaking up virtually every preconception of what theatre is, and then continued to re-assess its direction, energetically refusing to rest on its laurels, then that company surely is the Théâtre du Soleil.

The dominance of the director

One much-discussed and often deplored feature of French theatre life which the careers of Mnouchkine and Savary exemplify is the all-powerful place of the director. It has become almost a cliché to talk about the demise of the playwright from the mid 1960s virtually to the present. Certainly, there has been a plethora of respected directors in recent years (though it could be said that this phenomenon dates back to Antoine via Copeau, the Cartel, and others). On the plus side, however, the high-profile directors of roughly the last forty years have generated enormous interest, excitement and respect, ensuring the continuing good health of theatre in France. There has been a constant stream of absorbing *mises en scène* from indigenous and non-indigenous directors alike, such as Roger Blin, Roger Planchon, Jean-Marie Serreau, Peter Brook, Jacques Kraemer, Marcel Maréchal, Victor Garcia, Jorge Lavelli, Guy Rétoré, Patrice Chéreau, Jean-Pierre Vincent, Antoine Vitez, Giorgio Strehler, Daniel Mesguich, Gildas Bourdet, Georges Lavaudant, to name several, but there are others too. Some of these have been the driving forces behind an intriguing aspect of theatre life in Paris, the handful of prestigious, somewhat avant-garde playhouses which have grown up in its communist 'red belt' suburbs. Awkward to get to by public transport (an unfortunate irony, considering their desire to attract large audiences of low-paid workers), nonetheless their consistently exciting work has guaranteed them a loyal if predominantly middle-class following. The best-known are the Théâtre des Amandiers at Nanterre, the Théâtre de la Commune at Aubervilliers, the Théâtre des Quartiers d'Ivry, the Théâtre Gérard Philippe at St Denis, and the Théâtre de Gennevilliers (publishers of the impressive review *Théâtre/Public*). All of these houses, all the directors listed, have distinctive styles, and their work has been very well detailed by a number of recent critics.

Peter Brook

One of the most absorbing contemporary men of theatre, not just a director but also an important film-maker, an essayist, a visionary of the theatre, is the Englishman Peter Brook, who has made France his home, and who in 1970 established his Centre International de Recherches Théâtrales (CIRT) in Paris. From his stunning *A Midsummer Night's Dream* at Stratford-on-Avon in 1970, just before he moved to Paris, to his *Mahabarata* of 1985, seen in Paris, Avignon, Glasgow and around the world, Brook has done work unlike anyone else's. For one thing, he devises and executes productions on a colossal scale. So too does Mnouchkine, incidentally, but nothing quite as long as the twelve-hour *Mahabarata* given for the first time in a quarry by the Rhône at Avignon as part of the Festival. Brook devises, meditates, plans, rehearses over very long stretches of time, working with a varied, international cast, and taking his productions to venues all around the world, such as Iran, and the Sahara and north-west Africa. It is always fascinating to go and see what is being performed at the somewhat inappropriate former music-hall which has been his base since 1974, the Bouffes du Nord, near the Gare du Nord in Paris.

The re-emergence of the playwright

It is not only directors' voices which are being heard in the French theatre. The playwright is making a comeback. There appears to be a slow but sure redressing of the balance between the two, and it is safe to say, that, while the 1970s were particularly difficult years for new writers, the last decade has indicated that the tide may be slowly turning. A small but significant number of contemporary playwrights command attention and respect. Michel Vinaver, who has already been encountered in this chapter, is perhaps the best known. His career dates back to the 1950s, and he has been writing more or less steadily ever since. And though sometimes it has been a struggle, he has got his plays staged. Indeed, he has been sympathetically produced outside of France on quite a few occasions. Some other playwrights to note are (in no particular order) Bernard-Marie Koltès (who works closely with the director Patrice Chéreau), Hélène Cixous (linked with the Théâtre du Soleil), Jean-Claude Grumberg, Michel Deutsch, René Kalisky, Jean-Paul Wenzel, Daniel Besnehard, Arlette Namiand, Jean-Gabriel Nordmann, Brigitte Jaques, Jérôme Deschamps, Jean-Marie Besset, Yasmina Réza, Valère Novarina. An older generation of established writers, including Nathalie Sarraute and Marguerite Duras, has also continued to write for the stage. Among the newcomers, Brigitte Jaques caused a wave of interest with her 1986 production of *Elvire Jouvet 40*, an unusual play about a Jewish actress called

Claudia trying to get to grips, during the last war, with the part of Elvire for a production of Molière's *Dom Juan* under the direction of Louis Jouvet. The heart of the play is Jouvet's rehearsal-room where day after day he persuades, inspires, even bullies Claudia until finally she gives him the Elvire he wants.

Though theatre subsidy has doubled in France over the last few years, the bulk of it has gone to directors and not to writers. However, the cause of aspiring playwrights has been kept alive by one or two organizations, including the Théâtre Ouvert. Founded in 1970 by the broadcaster and publisher Lucien Attoun, its original activity was to hold play-readings at the Avignon Festival, to do broadcasts on the France-Culture channel of French Radio and to engage in some small-scale publishing. Now, it employs an eight-person team to read and assess unpublished plays. Théâtre Ouvert receives some forty plays per month, all of which are carefully read, and it commissions around eighty plays per year. The aim is to encourage new writers, and the hope is to discover new talent. Some of the plays submitted are published by Théâtre Ouvert, and others are tried out by what it calls 'mise en espace'. That is, the plays are rehearsed by actors over a twelve-day period, with the help of a director, and then given four performances on stage, over four days, but without costumes or sets. The audiences contain a substantial number of theatre professionals, but the general public is there too. If a play is well received, then a full-scale production, either in Théâtre Ouvert's own premises or elsewhere, is arranged. The undertaking is subsidized by grants from the Ministry of Culture and from the city of Paris. Financial assistance is given for the publication side of Théâtre Ouvert's work by the *Société des auteurs dramatiques*. This society has created its own forum for new work. In the mid 1980s it came up with the idea of one-voice readings, and these take place once a month in a small theatre in Paris. The society's committee selects the work of a totally unknown author, and an actor gives it a public reading. At the end of the year, the best of the plays are given a public performance at the Théâtre de l'Odéon as part of an 'Author's Week'. Mention must also be made of the series of plays published by the Actes Sud press, and entitled *Papiers*. Actes Sud has played a prominent part in bringing the work of unknown new playwrights to general attention.

Conclusion

France has a long tradition of writing for the stage. The central importance of the playwright was never questioned and certainly never seriously threatened until the post-war period. Now, in

the early 1990s, despite some signs that the recent golden age
of the director may be coming to an end, and that the writer
may be poised to retake old ground, a glance at the programme
of productions in Paris during the 1991–2 season does not seem to
bear this out. True, there is, at the time of writing, keen interest
in one or two emerging writers for the stage. Valère Novarina's
Je suis, a long play written in a delirious and sometimes exciting
language, opened in September at the Théâtre de la Bastille
to very enthusiastic reviews. Earlier in 1991, the same theatre
was host to Eric da Silva's *No Man's Man*, also greeted with
acclaim. And other younger writers are making their presence
felt. Eugène Durif, Jean-Marie Besset, Yasmina Réza all have
had recent critical successes.

But the talk in France, and Paris especially, is still mostly of
directors. Now that Vitez is dead, the running of the Comédie-
Française is in the hands of Jacques Lassalle, formerly of the
Théâtre National de Strasbourg. One of the more interesting
productions scheduled at the *Français* is of Camus's *Caligula*,
directed by Youssef Chahine. But overall, the programme is
safe – Molière, Racine, Hugo, Beaumarchais. At other national
theatres, the accent is also on somewhat unadventurous plays put
on by celebrated directors. The new productions of Chéreau,
Lavelli and Savary are eagerly awaited, as much for the fact
that it is they who are doing the *mises en scène* as for the
choice of texts. Other established directors, such as Brook,
Bourdet, Vincent, Mnouchkine, Planchon, Villégier, Françon,
will all have productions around Paris. And then there are
some new directing talents. Brigitte Jaques (a director as well
as writer), Chantal Morel, Eric da Silva (founder of the Théâtre de
l'Emballage, which has made something of an impact), François
Tanguy (working with the equally interesting Théâtre du Radeau),
represent the rising generation of directors.

The fresh talent, writers and directors alike, is a welcome
indication of the evolving life of French theatre. And yet, the
fact that there are no fewer than nine productions of Racine
due in Paris in the winter of 1991–2 can only fuel the regular
complaint that the old authors are crowding out the new, and
that the celebrities of *mise en scène* are still hogging the stage.
A cursory glance at the programmes for all of Paris in the
1991–2 season reveals a disproportionate number of classics and
of revivals, a substantial fraction of which is to be directed by big
names. Despite good levels of subsidy, these are straitened times
for the theatre in France as much as for elsewhere in the world.
Managers have to do their utmost to ensure that they sell seats
in their theatres. To have celebrated directors staging safe texts
is perhaps the surest way of sustaining public interest in what, in
reality, is a minority cultural activity. In the theatre as in so much

else in French life, the events of May 1968 made for revolutionary change. Some of this change has become institutionalized, not to say ossified. But the early 1990s do not seem ripe for another theatrical revolution. If theatre in France is changing, it is doing so quietly and in a spirit of cautious evolution. A little nervously, tradition and innovation have joined hands to tread the boards together in the hope that a healthy audience will continue to occupy the seats beyond the footlights.

Acknowledgements

Probably the best books in English on recent and contemporary theatre in France are those by David Bradby and by David Whitton, and they have been an invaluable source of information in the preparation of this chapter. Details are given in the further reading at the end. Grateful acknowledgement is also made to Professor Christophe Campos and Ellen Gendron of the British Institute in Paris, who kindly made available their unrivalled collection of reviews and cuttings about productions in Paris during the 1980s and 90s.

Further reading

Artaud, Antonin, *Le Théâtre et son double* (Paris: Gallimard, 1964).
Bradby, David, *Modern French Drama, 1940–1990*, 2nd edition (Cambridge: Cambridge University Press, 1991).
  'A Theatre of the Everyday: The Plays of Michel Vinaver', in *New Theatre Quarterly*, 7 (1991), 261–74.
Bradby, David and McCormick, John, *People's theatre* (London: Croom Helm, 1978).
Bradby, David and Williams, David, *Director's theatre* (London: Macmillan, 1988).
Dort, Bernard, *Lectures de Brecht* (Paris: Seuil, 1960).
  Théâtre public (Paris: Seuil, 1967).
  Théâtre réel (Paris: Seuil, 1971).
  Le Théâtre en jeu (Paris: Seuil, 1979).
  La Représentation émancipée (Arles: Actes Sud, 1988).
Esslin, Martin, *Artaud* (London: Fontana, 1976).
  The Theatre of the Absurd (Harmondsworth: Penguin, 1980), (revised edition).
Godard, Colette, *Le Théâtre depuis 1968* (Paris: Lattès, 1980).
Jomaron, Jacqueline, *Le Théâtre en France*, 2 vols. (Paris: Colin, 1989).
Knapp, Bettina, *Off-stage voices* (New York: Whitston, 1975).
Knowles, Dorothy, *French Drama of the inter-war years, 1918–1939* (London: Harrap, 1967).
  Armand Gatti in the theatre (London: Athlone, 1989).
Laurent, Jeanne, *La République et les beaux-arts* (Paris: Julliard, 1955).

O'Connor, Garry, *French Theatre Today* (London: Pitman, 1975).

Puaux, Paul, *Avignon en festivals* (Paris: Hachette, 1983).

Roubine, Jean-Jacques, *Introduction aux grandes théories du théâtre* (Paris: Bordas, 1990).

Vinaver, Michel, 'Decentralisation as Chiaroscuro', in *New Theatre Quarterly*, 7 (1991), 64–76.

Whitton, David, *Stage directors in modern France* (Manchester: Manchester University Press, 1987).

CHAPTER 4

French cinema since 1945

Keith Reader

The beginnings

The first commercial screening of a moving picture took place on 28 December, 1895, when ten short documentaries (as they would now be called) made by the Lumière brothers of Lyon were shown at the Grand Café in Paris. In pre-Hollywood days, France rivalled Germany as the world leader of the cinematic industry, and it is this historical pre-eminence, along with the early interest in the medium's artistic potential shown by such figures as Cocteau and the Surrealists, that accounts for the cinema's particular importance in French cultural life. Courses in French cinema figure on an increasing number of educational syllabuses, from school to postgraduate level.

Yet cinema attendances in post-war France have not been so high as the medium's culturally privileged position might suggest. In 1950, the average French inhabitant went ten times per year to the cinema, compared to twenty-nine visits for her/his British counterpart (René Bonnell, *Le Cinéma exploité*, Paris: Seuil, 1978, p. 27); in 1986 less than half the French population over the age of fifteen went to the cinema once a year or more (*Quid*, Paris: Laffont, 1989, p. 496). Pierre Sorlin points out that in the 1950s 'France, which statistically was the country least interested in movies, had the most publications and gave Europe, in 1953, what would soon become the most influential of her film-monthlies, *Cahiers du Cinéma*' (*European Cinemas, European Societies, 1939–1990*, London: Routledge, 1991, p. 87). Sorlin attributes this to France's large rural population; the polarization between Paris – unchallenged capital of the cinema as art-form – and the provinces, so characteristic of French society, has certainly had a great effect on the development of cinematic culture before the war and since.

French cinema found itself in a sorry plight after the Liberation. Many of its leading directors – René Clair, Jean Renoir, Julien Duvivier – had left for the USA to avoid the Occupation; many other leading figures, such as Sacha Guitry and the actress Arletty, were excluded or marginalized for collaboration with the Germans. The American cinema (which had not been able to show its post-1940 productions in occupied France) represented formidable competition, accentuated by the 'Blum-Byrnes agreements' of 1946, which imposed quotas on the screening of French films within France as part of the price of American economic aid. The Centre national de la cinématographie was set up to foster national production in 1946, but its resources, human and material, were inevitably inadequate.

The productions of the ten or so years after the Liberation have long fallen into disfavour, dismissed by the *Cahiers* critics of the late 1950s as 'cinéma de qualité' – a term connoting studio-bound filming, an emphasis on traditional production values, and often literary adaptations using scripts by the team of Jean Aurenche and Paul Bost. These latter, vilified as the epitome of constipated and unimaginative cinema, have recently returned to prominence with their scripts for Bertrand Tavernier (*Coup de torchon* of 1981, *La Vie et rien d'autre* of 1989), and we shall see that a technicolor, location-shot variant of this kind of cinema has been one of the two dominant tendencies of the late 1980s and early 1990s. Its leading post-war practitioners were Jean Delannoy (*La Symphonie pastorale* of 1946), Christian-Jacque (*La Chartreuse de Parme* of 1948), René Clément and Claude Autant-Lara. Clément praised the working-class resistance in the moving *La Bataille du rail* (1946) – evocative in many ways of the Italian neo-realist cinema – and achieved his greatest success with *Jeux interdits* (1952), about two children, one orphaned by the war, who exorcize their distress by creating a pet cemetery. His Zola adaptation *Gervaise* (1955), scripted by Aurenche and Bost, is more typical of the 'cinéma de qualité' than either of these works.

Autant-Lara was briefly a member of the Communist Party after the war, but his later membership of the Front National (which at the time of writing he still represents in the European Parliament) might be thought closer to the truculent populism displayed by many of his films. *Le Diable au corps* (1946), an adaptation of Raymond Radiguet's novel about the passionate affair between a school student and a young woman whose husband is a soldier at the front in the First World War, caused a scandal when it was first screened because it seemed to condone adultery and implicitly attack the military. It remains remarkable now because of the impassioned performances by Micheline Presle and Gérard Philippe, the latter of whom was to die of cancer only thirteen years later – one of the last great French acting careers to have been divided between the cinema and the live theatre.

Autant-Lara's other major post-war work, *La Traversée de Paris* (1956), starring Jean Gabin, a black comedy about black-marketeering in occupied Paris, is in sharp contrast to the rose-coloured heroism that dominates so many occupation and resistance films. This is based on a text by Marcel Aymé, a right-wing anarchist writer whom, in many ways, Autant-Lara resembles and whose novel *Uranus* was to be filmed thirty-four years later by Claude Berri – a further example of the revival of highly scripted, big-star cinema.

A major pre-war genre that remained popular for some years afterwards was the *film noir*, 'characterised by the theme of doomed lovers, the setting of urban backstreet squalor and an all-pervading air of fatalism' (Roy Armes, *French Cinema*, London: Secker and Warburg, 1985, p. 129). Marcel Carné, whose *Quai des Brumes* and *Le Jour se lève* had been the greatest examples of the genre, returned to it in 1946 with *Les Portes de la nuit*, marked like his earlier work by a morbid poetry of destiny that seemed more self-indulgent than in pre-war years, and might have appeared hopelessly dated if it were not for the film's music (*Les Feuilles mortes* – *Autumn Leaves*), and the first appearance in a starring role of a young variety singer – Yves Montand. Yves Allégret, whose directing career had begun under the Occupation, distinguished himself in this genre with *Dédée d'Anvers* (1948) and *Une si jolie petite plage* (1949). The former starred Simone Signoret – at the time married to Allégret, later to form half of French cinema's most famous couple with Montand – in a drama of love and revenge set in a portside bar-cum-brothel; the latter featured Gérard Philippe as the desperate young man whom Madeleine Robinson (like him, like the central couple in *Le Jour se lève* brought up in an orphanage) vainly attempts to save from blackmail and suicide.

If films such as these (and the three I have mentioned are all in my view powerful and moving) rapidly went out of fashion and were soon spoken of condescendingly, this is doubtless because they represented the survival of a cinematic style and mood associated with the years leading up to defeat. The work of Henri-Georges Clouzot is closely akin to *film noir*, but was associated less with defeat than with collaboration, for his *Le Corbeau* (1943), a vicious tale of poison-pen letters, had caused him to be suspended from film-making for two and a half years after the Liberation, ostensibly because the film had been used in Germany to 'montrer la dégénérescence du peuple français à travers les habitants d'une petite ville provinciale' quoted by Jean Tulard, (*Guide des films*, vol. 1, Paris: Laffont/Bouquins, 1990, p. 503). He resumed his career in 1947 with *Quai des orfèvres*, a bleak murder story starring Louis Jouvet, and was to reach his peak with *Le Salaire de la peur* (1953) and *Les Diaboliques* (1955). *Le Salaire de la peur* stars Yves Montand as one of four French lorry-drivers driving nitroglycerine over perilous South American roads to put out an oilwell fire; the tension is masterfully sustained over two and a half hours and the atmosphere of desperation, cynicism and loss among the ne'er-do-well expatriates evokes an atmosphere close to *film noir* in spite of the baking heat. Hitchcock was later to prove a major influence on New Wave directors such as Chabrol and Rohmer, but the closest approach to his work in French cinema remains *Les Diaboliques*, set in a squalid boarding-school on the outskirts of Paris. Simone Signoret and Véra Clouzot (the director's wife, who in real life suffered from a similar heart condition to that which kills her in the film) star in a murder triangle which for much of the time appears to be a ghost story, and the bizarre final sequence suggests that it may all along have been just that. The horrifying bathtub sequence near the end is re-used in Adrian Lyne's Hollywood success *Fatal Attraction* (1987). The sour relentlessness of Clouzot's pessimism is rendered tolerable in these films through his mastery of suspense, which is why they have hardly dated.

Jacques Becker's *Casque d'or* (1952), again starring Simone Signoret, can scarcely be described as a *film noir*. There are too many passages of sunlit happiness and of popular celebration for that, and its setting in the Paris of 1902 would alone be enough to disqualify it. But its inexorable movement through gangster rivalries towards a tragic ending has something in common with the genre; Signoret watches her lover's guillotining from a window with the same Mona Lisa-like impassivity as Humphrey Bogart watches Mary Astor taken away by police through the lift-grille at the end of John Huston's *The Maltese Falcon*. Becker (an assistant to Renoir before the war) has suffered unduly from the general neglect of the cinema of this period. He extracted perhaps Jean Gabin's greatest post-war performance in *Touchez pas au grisbi* (1954) – an authentic *film noir* in colour – and in his last work *Le Trou* (1960), an extraordinary minimalist drama about a prison escape, gave us what has been called 'la charnière entre le cinéma dit "de qualité" des années d'après-guerre et la formidable explosion des années 60' (Tulard, II, p. 945).

The old and the new

Directors celebrated before the war continued to be active after it, though almost never with the same success. Jean Renoir lived for most of the time in California, and it may be his consequent lack of close contact with French society that deprives even his best post-war work – such as *French Cancan* (1955), with Gabin and Edith Piaf, or the acerbic *Doctor Jekyll and Mr Hyde* adaptation *Le Testament du docteur Cordelier* (1961) – of the subtle ironies of *La Règle du jeu*. Jean Grémillon, whose *Lumière d'été* (1943) remains the great undervalued masterpiece of the Occupation years, could get funding for very few post-war projects, and was obliged to work in the documentary field. René Clair (*Les Grandes Manœuvres* of 1955) and the German Max Ophüls (*Lola Montès* of 1955) shot what appeared to be (and were received as) 'just' period melodramas, but were – *Lola Montès* above all – also lyrical and tragic dissections of the mechanisms of desire. The interaction between cinema, theatre and literature characteristic of French culture bore fruit in the later works of Sacha Guitry (*Si Versailles m'était conté* of 1954) and, far more richly, in Jean Cocteau's *Orphée* (1950). *Orphée*'s ironic staging of the relationship between poetry and death reworks a romantic literary tradition, while its use of mirrors and special effects looks back to the Surrealists and forward to *L'Année dernière à Marienbad*. It would be wrong to see this at once glacial and impassioned work as totally unconnected with a social context, for the coded messages of the motorcyclists of death evoke those used by the Resistance a matter of years before.

Three film-makers whose feature careers had begun hardly or not at all before the Liberation hinted very soon afterwards at what was to come. Jean-Pierre Melville's adaptation of Vercors's *Le Silence de la mer* (1947) is with hindsight significant less for its resistance subject-matter than for the cinematic presentation of it. It is the anonymity and muteness of the resistance shown by a French family in opposition to the cultivated and well-meaning German officer billeted on them that provides the film's drama, rather than any epic feats of arms; and this is articulated through a cinema of silences, gaps, hesitations that shows how the cinema could become, to quote Alexandre Astruc, 'a means of writing as subtle and supple as the written word' (quoted in Penelope Houston, *The Contemporary Cinema*, Harmondsworth: Penguin, 1963, p. 97). Such cinematic writing is even more strikingly characteristic of Robert Bresson's third feature, the Bernanos adaptation *Journal d'un curé de campagne* (1950), where it has a specifically spiritual resonance and density. The young, incurably sick priest's writing of his diary is set before us in its materiality, with silences and gaps as we see the pen in its often faltering progression across the page and hear the priest's voice reading the text he is writing. The effect is of a journey towards salvation, a linguistic Way of the Cross – the Cross that fills the screen after the priest's death at the end, as a voice relates his dying words: 'Tout est grâce.' Bresson's use of non-professional actors (he prefers the term 'models') and ascetic editing that eschews any hint of psychological 'explanation' have remained the defining factors of his style ever since.

Jacques Tati began as a music-hall comedian before turning to the cinema, and his first feature, *Jour de fête* (1949), shows the dulcet debunking of modernity and the perfectionist timing of gags that characterize all his work. He is best known and loved for *Les Vacances de M. Hulot* (1953), set in a Breton beach resort and proving that the French have a 'seaside', almost in the British sense, as well as a coast, but Tati aficionados tend to rate *Playtime* (1967) as his greatest work. The gags here are so elaborately and immaculately choreographed as often to be invisible until a second or third viewing. The corollary of this, alas, was a heavily overspent budget and a contraction of his audience which meant that in the fifteen years before his death Tati was to make only one more feature (*Traffic* of 1971).

Melville's subsequent career was on the whole divided between two types of film: literary adaptations in the wake of *Le Silence de la Mer* (the Cocteau-based *Les Enfants Terribles* of 1950), and ever more elaborate reworkings of the gangster movie, for which his name came to stand much as Tati's did for the slapstick genre. *Bob le flambeur* (1956) and *Deux hommes dans Manhattan* (1959) are among the works that caused him to be regarded as the founding father of the New Wave (he has a cameo role in Godard's *A bout de souffle*). Bresson's relationship to the New Wave is a more problematic one; revered by its directors, he nevertheless maintained a ferocious independence throughout his career, making only thirteen features in all. His spiritual intensity is most apparent in *Pickpocket* (1959), a Dostoevskyan parable pared to the bone, and *Au hasard Balthazar* (1966), in which a donkey comes to represent the force of goodness in an extended *mise-en-scène* of the Beatitude 'Blessed are the meek'. The bleakness and austerity of his work is often enough commented upon, less so its paradoxical optimism; the pickpocket Michel is redeemed by love, the country priest's death is a transcendence of suffering, the central character's suicide in *Mouchette* (1966) is a rejection of the cold brutality around her made affirmative by the sounds of Monteverdi's *Magnificat*. Redemption is dramatized through the selection and foregrounding of the significant detail, not only in the images but on the soundtrack (the raking of the leaves as the priest and the Countess converse in *Journal d'un curé de campagne*, the sound of the racecourse turnstiles like a mechanism of destiny in *Pickpocket*). Bresson's remains one of the most distinctive of all cinematic styles.

'Le réalisateur essaie de se dégager des carcans traditionnels du scénario, des dialogues, de l'interprétation' (*Dictionnaire du cinéma français*, ed. by Jean-Loup Passek, Paris: Larousse, 1987, p. XX) – this remark suggests what Bresson's work and that of the New Wave directors have in common. The term *nouvelle vague* was coined by Françoise Giroud to refer to the work of a number of directors – they never formed anything so cohesive as a 'group' – who had worked for the journal *Cahiers du cinéma*.

Their critical work was characterized by a stress on the cinema as a mode of writing in its own right (whence their scorn for the *cinéma de qualité* type of literary adaptation), an enthusiastic championing of American cinema and directors such as Fuller, Hitchcock and Hawks (seen as the authors of their films much as European art-cinema directors such as Renoir or Bergman had always been), and the consequent advocacy of a laconic, elliptical, unsentimental cinema that would nevertheless draw widely on other types of culture – theatrical, philosophical and artistic. This was in different ways what they themselves went on to make, aided by the availability of new lightweight equipment and coerced by financial constraints.

The New Wave

The year 1959 was the year in which the government-underwritten *avance sur recettes* scheme was introduced, making it less difficult than hitherto for aspirant directors to start their careers. It is no coincidence that it also, famously, saw the 'start of the New Wave' – the first features of Claude Chabrol (*Le Beau Serge*), François Truffaut (*Les Quatre Cents Coups*), Eric Rohmer (*Le Signe du lion*) and Jean-Luc Godard (*A bout de souffle*).[1] Jacques Rivette began at about the same time shooting *Paris nous appartient*, though this was not to be released until 1961. It is essentially these five directors, with their shared *Cahiers* background, that constitute the New Wave. I shall first of all look at the début features mentioned before following through the widely divergent career of each of them in more detail.

Le Beau Serge (which Chabrol shot with inherited money) tells the story of a Parisian who returns to his native village in central France and saves a childhood friend from alcoholic despair; its *Doppelgänger* theme is echoed in *Les Cousins* (also 1958/9), in which a young provincial student's relationship with his brilliant but amoral cousin (a para-Nietzschean dandy) ends in a tragic accidental shooting. These films introduced actors and actresses prominent in the early days of the New Wave (Jean-Claude Brialy, Bernadette Lafont, Stéphane Audran), and *Les Cousins* in particular, with its cynical construction of a world in which style counts for more than the canons of conventional morality, was a foretaste of much to come. *Les Quatre Cents Coups* introduced another key New Wave actor, Jean-Pierre Léaud, in the role of Antoine Doinel, and with him Truffaut's lifelong preoccupation with the feelings and problems of childhood. The plot here counts for far less than its *mise-en-scène*, and the crane-shot of a group of schoolboys out for a supervised walk – a direct homage to Jean Vigo's *Zéro de conduite* – like the film's final freeze-frame of the young Doinel seeing the sea for the first time, remain memorable examples of how a young director (Truffaut was twenty-seven) could celebrate and revel in the possibilities of the medium as earlier, more script- and set-bound directors had not been able to do. (Truffaut was by some way the most pugnacious of the *Cahiers* critics, energetically reviling and being reviled by Autant-Lara in particular and getting himself banned from the Cannes Film Festival in 1958.)

Le Signe du lion, about a bohemian painter in Paris whose overtrustfulness all but ruins him, reveals in embryo two of the preoccupations Rohmer was later to develop in what many found an increasingly mannered way – a fascination with ethical ambiguities deriving from French *moraliste* writers such as Montaigne and Musset and a related pleasure in filming social interaction among groups (here in the numerous party and bistro scenes). What remains most striking about the film, however, is its location shooting of Paris deserted by its inhabitants in the heat of August. The cinematic Paris of the 1930s, 1940s and 1950s had been largely a studio construction (and overwhelmingly the work of one man, the Hungarian Alexandre Trauner); the New Wave changed that for very nearly twenty-five years.

This is strikingly illustrated in *A bout de souffle*, not the first film of the New Wave but probably its best loved. Jean-Paul Belmondo plays a small-time gangster who almost inadvertently kills a policeman, in a performance whose mingled arrogance and vulnerability recalls Gabin, but which has a defiant modernity in its self-mockery and frequent remarks made straight to the camera. The film's editing was noteworthy for the constant use of jump-cuts (moving swiftly from one action to another), contrasted with long scenes of faltering conversation between Belmondo and his American lover (Jean Seberg), who eventually denounces him to the police. Jump-cuts and faltering conversation alike create a world of uncertainty and improvisation – strategic, emotional and ethical – that was something new in French cinema at the same time as being a rewriting of the *film noir*.

Paris nous appartient lasts 135 minutes – half as long again as other New Wave films, yet brief by Rivette's subsequent standards. The setting is theatrical (an abortive production of Shakespeare's *Pericles*), with a whiff of political conspiracy and mysterious death in the air. The plot matters less through its resolution – like most of Rivette's it runs itself into the ground – than through its bringing together of characters in the creation of an atmosphere of paranoid dreams. Rivette more than any of the other New Wave directors was to find it difficult to make the films he chose, if only because of his obsession with length. *Out Un* (1974) initially lasted twelve hours forty minutes, and was reduced to just over four hours – the same length as his intense scrutiny of painterly creation, *La Belle Noiseuse* of 1991 (starring Michel Piccoli). *Céline et Julie vont en bateau* (1974) has been his most successful work in English-speaking countries, probably because it is a homage to the Hollywood screwball comedy as well as to the dreamlike world of Cocteau. His most conventionally narrative film was also his most controversial; *La Religieuse* (1966) was banned by the government for its portrayal of sexual and spiritual humiliations in a convent, and could be released only after the title had been changed to *Suzanne Simonin, la religieuse de Diderot*. This, predictably, made it his major French commercial success.

Chabrol's career has been almost exclusively devoted to what might be called the 'social thriller' – films using a suspense format often akin to that of Hitchcock to comment on the deviousness and duplicity of French society. *Les Bonnes Femmes* (1960) details the often tawdry lives and dreams of a group of young women working in an electrical shop (indicative of the newly prosperous France of the time), the most imaginative and sympathetic of whom is strangled by a sex-killer. With *Que la bête meure* (1969) and *Le Boucher* (1970), the murder-thriller plot acquires spiritual overtones; Jean Yanne's wish to avenge himself on the hit-and-run driver who killed his son and Stéphane Audran's rejection of the love of the butcher (also played by Yanne) who then turns to killing, set acute ethical dilemmas against the skilfully evoked settings of Brittany and the Dordogne respectively. His work of the 1970s and 1980s is far less distinctive and well focused, and he began the 1990s with a lavish adaptation of Flaubert's *Madame Bovary* (1991), starring Isabelle Huppert, which, ironically, distils the very production values against which the New Wave had begun by reacting. This film has not been distributed in Britain, largely because it did very poorly in the USA – a good example of how important the American market is.

Truffaut was to take Léaud-Doinel through a trilogy of films evoking now wittily, now sentimentally the passage from adolescence through marriage to divorce (*Baisers volés* of 1968, *Domicile conjugal* of 1970, *L'Amour en fuite* of 1979). *Baisers volés* is assured a place in cinema history as the film that reopened the Paris Cinémathèque in April 1968 after the dismissal and triumphant reinstatement of its director, Henri Langlois – an event that galvanized the French cinematic world and gave a hint of the complex relationships between culture and politics that were to explode in May 1968. Truffaut's most innovative films, however, remain his earliest. *Tirez sur le pianiste* (1960), starring Charles Aznavour as an emotionally wounded concert pianist who seeks refuge by playing in a bar, combines Godardian jump-cuts with the revival of 'old-fashioned' devices such as the use of irises-in and -out to link scenes. The palpable delight in the medium is shared by *Jules et Jim* (1961), a Belle Époque tale of love and friendship told in an unmistakably New Wave manner. Jeanne Moreau as the capricious Catherine, who wavers for twenty years between her French and her German lovers, gives one of the great female performances of the post-war period, and in this film she became a more 'intellectual' rival to Brigitte Bardot. Both actresses made a considerable impact as avatars of the so-called 'new woman', exercizing a freedom of sexual and personal choice that was exhilarating but also – to the men in their lives at least – threatening.

Truffaut's other major works include *La Nuit américaine* (1973), his only Oscar-winner, commercializing the perennial New Wave concern with cinema's self-reflexivity in a film about the making of a film, *La Chambre verte* (1978), a morbid Henry James adaptation that seems with hindsight a premonition of Truffaut's early death in 1984, and *Le Dernier Métro* (1980), bringing together the quintessential French cinematic female and male of the time, Catherine Deneuve and Gérard Depardieu, in an Occupation melodrama whose strengths and weaknesses alike reside in its transposition of politics into the theatre in which the action is set. The iconoclastic vigour and irony of his earliest works was not long in turning to sentimentality, but all else apart it should not be forgotten that – as the work for him of Léaud, Moreau, Deneuve, Depardieu, and Isabelle Adjani (in *L'Histoire d'Adèle H* of 1975) proves – he is one of post-war French cinema's greatest directors of actresses and actors.

Rohmer has the distinction of being, at the time of writing, the only one of the five key New Wave directors still making films that are regularly distributed in Britain. This is largely because his work, full of conversations where subtlety, misunderstanding and embarrassment chase one another, is perceived as a distillation of the emotional *finesse* believed to be characteristic of 'the French', from Laclos through to Maurice Chevalier; and also because it is actually relatively undemanding to watch (though not to listen to). Its 'effacement de la représentation' (Passek, p. 362) and straightforward – often banal – story-lines enable the eye to dwell with innocent pleasure on the sensitivity of Nestor Almendros's camerawork, and somewhat less innocently perhaps on the young women in gauzy summertime surroundings who people his later films, in a manner characteristic of 1980s French cinema in particular.

Rohmer's *œuvre* is made up of two major cycles, *Six contes moraux* and *Comédies et proverbes* – a classification and a choice of title suggestive of his literary antecedents. *Ma nuit chez Maud* (1969) evokes Pascal in its Clermont-Ferrand setting and its view of humans' relationships not only with God, but with one another, as a (transcendental?) wager. Transcendence and the divine disappear altogether in the later cycle, whose social comedy at once disguises and articulates a sense of ethical uncertainty (as, though far more uproariously, in Woody Allen). *Le Beau Mariage* (1982) hints at the 'new puritanism' in its heroine's determination to get married; *Pauline à la plage* (1983) rests on an explicitly sexual imbroglio; in *Conte de printemps* (1990) the prurient male gaze is explicitly present in the character of the father of one young woman who is also the lover of another – a surrogate for Rohmer himself? Even those unhappy with or bored by Rohmer's latter-day *marivaudage* are likely to recognize his subtle choice and use of location settings (Le Mans, the Normandy coast, and Paris and the Ile-de-France respectively).

Godard and others

Of all French post-war directors (and despite being Swiss), Godard is assuredly the most celebrated. His work represents a two-fold exploration of contradictory evolutions – that of modern French society and of cinematic language – like no other, along with a journey from apparent political nihilism (the Algerian War film *Le Petit Soldat* of 1960 was branded fascistic by left-wing critics and banned for three years by the French government), through intense commitment to the far left, to an apparent flagging of interest in politics. The 'apparents' are there because (as Colin MacCabe admirably shows in *Godard: Images, Sounds, Politics*, London: BFI/Macmillan, 1980) Godard's career-long interrogation of the relationships between image, sound and represented reality is nothing if not political in its ceaseless problematizing of questions of language and power, in which respect it complements the work of such contemporary film theoreticians as Christian Metz or Jean-Louis Comolli. His analysis of the filming of a factory occupation in post-1968 France, *Tout va bien* (1972 – co-directed by Jean-Pierre Gorin, with Jane Fonda and Yves Montand), opens with a hand signing the cheque that is to finance the making of the film; *Numéro deux* (1975) shows not only the bleak existence of a working-class couple in a modern development in Grenoble, but Godard's own periodic despair (slumped in front of his editing-table) at how best to articulate this; *Sauve qui peut (la vie)* (1979), marking his return to the 'commercial' cinema after a seven-year absence devoted to video, gives the theme of prostitution, so frequent in his films, its most savage working yet in its portrayal of a sex-chain, organized by and for, a managing director, that suggests the persistence of industrial relationships of domination and exploitation into post-industrial society.

Godard's filming of women is likewise charged with ambiguity. His marriage to Anna Karina produced seven films in which she magnetizes the camera's gaze; greatest of these is *Pierrot le fou* (1965), assembling elements of the gangster film, the musical, the political thriller (via a murky sub-plot about gun-running) and – in its heart-rending climax – even a modernist Technicolor rewriting of the *film noir*. Belmondo's performance in the title-role ranks with that of Gabin in *Le Jour se lève* as a *tour de force* of fatalism. In *Le Mépris* (1963), he had given Bardot what was to remain (along with Clouzot's *La Vérité* of 1960) her major dramatic role; the film opens on a shot of her all-but-unclothed body that is ambivalently celebratory, exploitative, or a parody of her exploitation elsewhere (and probably all of these). More recently, *Je vous salue Marie* (1985), which rewrites the Virgin Birth into contemporary Switzerland, was attacked by the Catholic Church (Godard, ironically, is of Protestant origin), but also by certain feminist critics for its presentation of the female body.

Among his most remarkable films are two, both dated 1967, that pre-figure the events of May 1968. *La Chinoise*, in which a Brechtian influence is particularly strong, lampoons (not unsympathetically) the activities of a dedicated cell of Maoist Marxist–Leninists, and features a conversation between a Communist philosopher and a far-left student on a train bound for Nanterre which uncannily pre-echoes the debates that erupted the following year. *Weekend* is the most savage of his social satires, eviscerating that lazily right-wing society of acquisitiveness against which May 1968 was to react. His most recent work (such as *Nouvelle vague* of 1990, with Alain Delon) lacks the polemical bite of its predecessors, but Godard's articulation of word and image remains unlike any other.

Other directors associated with the New Wave were Roger Vadim and Louis Malle. Vadim 'discovered' Brigitte Bardot with *Et Dieu créa la femme* (1956), at the time the frankest treatment of sexuality in the post-war French cinema; his penchant for exposing to the camera the body of his current wife or partner (as with Annette Stroyberg in *Les Liaisons dangereuses*, 1960) soon became tedious, and overtook any wider innovativeness. Malle's work is often seen as lacking that last flourish of individuality that makes the true *auteur*, an impression reinforced by his departure to work in the USA between 1977 and 1987. He gave Jeanne Moreau her first major roles in *L'Ascenseur pour l'échafaud* (1958) and *Les Amants* (also 1958, and at the time considered scandalously erotic), and adapted a Raymond Queneau novel in a manner reminiscent of Tati-plus-dialogue in *Zazie dans le métro* (1960). Best known among his French films, however, are the wartime dramas *Lacombe Lucien* (1974) and *Au Revoir les enfants* (1987). The former intensified the debate around wartime collaboration launched by Marcel Ophüls's *Le Chagrin et la pitié* – a documentary montage made for French television in 1969, banned by them, and released in the cinema in 1971. *Le Chagrin et la pitié* called into question not simply the universality of resistance to the occupier, but the Gaullist and post-Gaullist social and political order that had been built upon the Resistance myth. That order can be said to have fallen in 1974, with the death of Pompidou and the election of Giscard d'Estaing, so that the release of Malle's film in that year was ironically well-timed. Its tale of a youth in south-western France who collaborates with the Nazis after being turned down by the Resistance, and falls in love with a young Jewish woman, provoked intense debate in journals such as *Cahiers du cinéma* and *Les Temps modernes*. *Au Revoir les enfants*, based on an episode from Malle's autobiography (the denunciation and deportation of Jewish pupils and the priest who sheltered them in his school), is a far less challenging companion piece; to quote Jean-Pierre Bertin-Maghit, 'le coup de griffe donné par *Lacombe Lucien* à l'imagerie d'Épinal des Français sous l'Occupation avait suscité bien des polémiques. En 1987, *Au Revoir les enfants* fait l'unanimité' (Tulard, I, 145).

Films such as these acquired a quasi-documentary veneer through their careful period reconstructions and presentation of hitherto hidden pages of French history. The documentary itself is associated primarily with two directors: the ethnographer Jean Rouch, who made a great many important anthropological films in Africa (*La Pyramide humaine* of 1959, *Cocorico, monsieur le poulet* of 1974), and collaborated with the sociologist and cultural critic Edgar Morin on *Chronique d'un été* (1960), a montage of interviews with Parisians of all classes and backgrounds that remains among the most telling self-interrogations of Gaullist society. Chris Marker has probably travelled more widely with a camera than any other film-maker, which is emphatically not to insult him by reducing him to the rank of tourist; his strong left-wing political commitment and constant questioning of his own relationship to the places and societies he films preclude such a judgement. *Cuba Si!* (1961) features an interview with Fidel Castro, while *Sans soleil* (1982) counterposes the former French African colony of Guinea-Bissau and Japan – the latter as much a source of fascination for French political exoticism in the 1980s as Cuba or China had been in the 1960s. Like Rouch, he 'takes the temperature' of contemporary Paris via documentary interviews in *Le Joli Mai* (1963), and his most ambitious work, *Le Fond de l'air est rouge* (1977), juxtaposes footage from all round the world to present a four-hour survey of the 'revolutionary decade' that began in 1967.

The best-known French documentary of our period, however, is by a director who subsequently devoted himself to features – *Nuit et brouillard* (1955), by Alain Resnais. Its intercutting between harrowing footage of the concentration camps (in black-and-white) and their buildings nowadays (in colour) figures Resnais's constant concern with time, place, memory and their interconnections. The film acquired shocking renewed relevance when shown on all French television channels in the wake of the desecration of Jewish graves in Carpentras in 1990.

Resnais's feature début, with a script by Marguerite Duras, was *Hiroshima mon amour* – from the *annus mirabilis* of 1959. The film can be understood as a meditation on the duality of the word *histoire*, for the central character's love affair with a Japanese architect while filming in Hiroshima woundingly evokes for her an earlier *histoire d'amour* with a German soldier shot during the Occupation, and major historical traumas flow into and out of what the heroine herself describes as a 'petite histoire de quatre sous'. Different layers of memory coexist here as in Proust, and this novelistic strand in Resnais's filmic writing is even more marked in *L'Année dernière à Marienbad* (1961), scripted by the prominent *nouveau romancier* Alain Robbe-Grillet. (Duras and Robbe-Grillet went on to direct feature films of their own, something it is difficult to imagine a British novelist being able to do). *Marienbad*, as it cultishly became known, can be read as a tale of seduction – of an enigmatic woman (Delphine Seyrig in her first major, and for me her greatest, screen role), by a mysterious stranger in a vast, frozen baroque hotel. Past, present and future, real and imagined, indicative and conditional become impossible to distinguish clearly, which led to frustrated diatribes against the work's 'pretentiousness' but, more perceptively, also to a recognition that it exploits more thoroughly and suggestively than virtually any other film the chronological ambiguities inherent in the moving image – an image always in the present, yet (as the 'moving' indicates) always entering it from, or leaving it behind for, somewhere else.

Resnais's subsequent work includes *Muriel* (1963), again with Delphine Seyrig, a startling mosaic construction set in the rebuilt town of Boulogne-sur-Mer and evoking the trauma of the Algerian War that had just ended, *Providence* (1976), scripted by David Mercer and starring John Gielgud and Dirk Bogarde, and *L'Amour à mort* (1984), which links love and death in a manner reminiscent of *La Chambre verte*, whose director Truffaut died in that year (his companion Fanny Ardant plays a leading role in the Resnais film). Resnais remains all but unique among French directors in commissioning his scripts and filming them unaltered, which paradoxically brings out his distinctive 'authorial' qualities.

Jacques Demy, like Resnais, began his career in the documentary film before his first feature, *Lola* (1961), with Anouk Aimée, in which two of his main stylistic features are already apparent – the importance of music and the seaport setting. Both of these refer back to a pre-war cinema; the last (and the first) major French director to make musicals, as Demy was to do, had been René Clair (*Sous les toits de Paris, A nous la liberté*), and the 'poetic realism' of Demy's settings – Nantes here, Nice, Cherbourg and Rochefort subsequently – in many ways evokes that of a more bitter-sweet Carné-Prévert (whose *Quai des brumes* had been set in Le Havre). One of Catherine Deneuve's best-known roles is in *Les Parapluies de Cherbourg* (1964), where the young lovers' idyll is destroyed by the Algerian War, here present as sentimental background rather than as in *Le Petit Soldat* or *Muriel* insupportable context of history and memory. Deneuve co-starred with her sister Françoise Dorléac (killed in a car crash) in *Les Demoiselles de Rochefort* (1967), the closest French cinema has come to the 'all-singing all-dancing' musical of MGM's Hollywood heyday.

Women directors

Demy's work, while unique of its kind, has to take second place for cinematic inventiveness to that of Agnès Varda, his wife and virtually the only woman film-maker to have enjoyed a major feature-making career in the period of our study. Marguerite Duras directed a number of films often based on her literary texts (*India Song* of 1975, *Le Camion* of 1977, with Depardieu), and Yannick Bellon has made a number of features since 1972 (*L'Amour violé* of 1978, *Les Enfants du désordre* of 1988), though twenty-four years separated her first feature from her documentary début. Coline Serreau has recently enjoyed immense commercial success in both France and in English-speaking countries with *Trois hommes et un couffin* (1985), about three hitherto carefree bachelors who take on the responsibility for a six-month-old baby (and needless to say love every minute), and *Romauld et Juliette* (1989), about the 'odd-couple' love-affair between a white managing director and his black cleaning-woman. Serreau, however – like Diane Kurys whose *Coup de foudre* (1982) movingly explores the friendship between two women (Isabelle Huppert and Miou-Miou) which outlives, and from the husbands' point of view destroys, their marriages – tends to downplay the importance of her gender, and Varda's *œuvre* remains the most significant feminist body of work in the French cinema. (To those who may object that I have dispatched woman film-makers in two over-hasty tokenist paragraphs I would reply first that this alas accurately mirrors the space given to them by the industry, and secondly that so inevitably rapid a survey as this could scarcely do otherwise).

Varda's *Cléo de 5 à 7* (1962) is one of the few features set in something like 'real' time (its eighty-five minutes correspond to two hours' narrated time), and takes its central character, a singer, through the nerve-racking wait for the results of her examination for cancer. The tentative optimism of its conclusion, from which Cléo emerges empowered if not medically in the clear, is ironically inverted in *Le Bonheur* (1965), whose pastel colours and Mozartean lyricism throw into relief its bitterly cyclic view of human relationships. Its central character, happily married, begins an affair that for him complements his love for his wife; when the wife, not seeing things altogether in the same way, drowns herself, he marries his lover. If the women in this film are victims, that cannot be said of Mona (a magnificent performance from Sandrine Bonnaire) in *Sans toit ni loi* (1985), who wanders round the south of France in a bitterly cold winter until she perishes from exposure, rejecting any relationship that might entail dependence and any discourse that might 'explain' her behaviour (a good many of these are proferred in documentary-style interviews with people who meet her, but none of them as it were 'takes'). To quote Susan Hayward, 'we cannot fix the text any more than we can fix Mona and it is in this de-fetishization of the text as well as the body-female that Varda asserts her own brand of feminist film-making practices' (*French Film: Texts and Contexts*, ed. by Susan Hayward and Ginette Vincendean, London and New York: Routledge, 1990, p. 294).

The return of 'quality'

Whilst the film-makers associated with or close to the New Wave continued, as we have seen, to work with varying degrees of success through the 1970s, that decade also signalled the beginnings of the return to the *cinéma de qualité* that was to become so important in the 1980s. One obvious reason why was that television, as more or less everywhere else in the developed world, became the dominant form of popular audio-visual entertainment, and growing numbers of people went to the cinema only a few times a year, often to large-scale big-screen spectaculars that constituted an 'event' in themselves rather than part of the typical week. Another was the increase in production costs, which combined with the graduation to 'superstar' status of many actors and actresses who had come to prominence since the War (Belmondo, Delon, Deneuve, Montand, Moreau) to bring about higher-budget, more conservative forms of film-making. Claude Sautet is a good representative of this, analysing the problems of the French bourgeoisie less acerbically than Clouzot or Chabrol and relying on established stars (Michel Piccoli and Romy Schneider in *Les Choses de la vie* of 1970, Schneider, Montand and Isabelle Huppert in *César et Rosalie* of 1971).

It obviously becomes more difficult as we approach the present day to choose which film-makers to include in what is already perforce a perfunctory survey. Of those who made their débuts in the 1970s, however, it is (relatively) safe to assert that Bertrand Tavernier is among the most influential. Tavernier's work is characterized by more humanistic, less dialectical left-wing politics than that of a Godard or a Marker, so that more than anybody else he may be seen as representing the 'film-making wing of the Parti Socialiste'. Lyon, his native city, is frequently evoked in his films; *L'Horloger de Saint-Paul* (1974) stars Philippe Noiret as the Lyonnais artisan initially bewildered by, then sympathetic to his son's involvement in left-wing 'terrorist' activity. *Une semaine de vacances* (1980) gave Nathalie Baye one of her earliest starring roles as a schoolteacher going through a professional crisis that becomes a personal one – an archetypal narrative of the 1980s. Family rather than broader social problems characterize his later work, as in the Renoir-influenced period piece *Un dimanche à la campagne* (1984) and the touching three-hander *Daddy Nostalgie* (released in Britain as *These Foolish Things*) of 1990, in which Jane Birkin and Dirk Bogarde give among their best screen performances.

If one film of the 1970s represents an antithesis to the *cinéma de qualité*, it is Jean Eustache's *La Maman et la putain* (1973). Eustache's earlier work, such as *La Rosière de Pessac* (1969), resembles *cinéma-vérité*, as, at nearly four hours in length, does *La Maman et la putain*. A seemingly interminable love-triangle in black-and-white, involving Bernadette Lafont, Françoise Lebrun and Jean-Pierre Léaud, endless talking and even more endless drinking, the film's narrative eventually runs itself into the ground in an at once despairing and exhilarating apotheosis of the 'generation of 1968'. Eustache's growing problems in funding the films he wanted to make were at least partially responsible for his suicide in 1981.

The rawness of the emotional confrontations that is one of *La Maman et la putain*'s most striking qualities was to become a virtual trademark of the work of Maurice Pialat. The increasing focus on family problems that marks French cinema through the 1970s and 1980s is nowhere more pronounced than in Pialat's work, right from *Nous ne vieillirons pas ensemble* (1972), in which the odiously phallocratic Jean Yanne, Macha Méril and Marlène Jobert form one among the most acrimonious of screen triangles. His early reliance on non-professional actors (as in *L'Enfance nue* of 1969) may seem reminiscent of Bresson, but Pialat's films make wide use of non-scripted, 'spontaneous' elements in a manner that would be anathema to Bresson. In *A nos amours* (1983), an actress violently slaps Pialat himself (her screen husband), in an unscripted gesture by all accounts fairly typical of the atmosphere during the shooting of this harrowing account of a teenager's early sexual life in an increasingly fractious family atmosphere. Sandrine Bonnaire became a star with her first screen appearance as the young Suzanne, and it was for Pialat in the title role of *Loulou* (1980) that Gérard Depardieu, whose extraordinary emotional energy makes him by far French cinema's greatest male star at the time of writing, gave one of his outstanding performances.

The other director with whom Depardieu was particularly associated at this time is Bertrand Blier, who exploited his intense sexual ambiguity in *Les Valseuses* (1974) and *Tenue de soirée* (1986). The former film is noteworthy because it introduced a trio of actors – Miou-Miou, Patrick Dewaere and Depardieu – who had hitherto been principally associated with the Montparnasse alternative theatre Café de la Gare. The film's vigour and its periodic misogyny rapidly became Blier's trademarks, making him along with Pialat one of the two undisputed *enfants terribles* of this period. They were among the first French directors to make films about the *marginal* world of petty criminals and drop-outs increasingly characteristic of the 1970s and 1980s; *Tenue de soirée* takes one such couple and details the disruptive implosion into their lives of Depardieu, a burglar who takes them under his wing because of his intense desire for the man (played by Michel Blanc). The film's final sequence, with Depardieu in drag, has already become (paradoxically for the iconoclastic Blier) iconic.

It has, however, been those French films associated with the *cinéma de qualité* that have been most lucrative at the British box-office and also most successful in the USA in recent years. Claude Berri's Pagnol adaptations *Jean de Florette* and *Manon des sources* (1985–6), and Jean-Paul Rappeneau's *Cyrano de Bergerac* (1990), based on the Edmond Rostand play, have been immensely successful both in the cinema and on video. Berri had been making features for well-nigh twenty years before (such as *Tchao Pantin* of 1983, starring France's leading alternative comedian of the time, Coluche). The Pagnol adaptations are quintessentially a montage of generations: the author's wry 1950s Provençal dialogue set against the landscape evoked in technicolor and Dolby sound, Yves Montand dying of grief when he discovers that the man he has hounded to his death was his illegitimate son – played by Depardieu. Nostalgia, the yearning for countryside roots, the pleasure of a tragedy set just far enough away (and endowed with just enough inevitability) to move without truly disturbing are all assuredly among the reasons for these films' success.

Cyrano de Bergerac adapts a nineteenth-century play set in the seventeenth century – an unlikely source, it might be thought, for the most successful French film ever in Britain. Depardieu plays the title role to the hilt in what must be regarded as one of the greatest of romantic acting performances, and the play's

Alexandrine metre (rendered in rhyming subtitles by Anthony Burgess) is paralleled, along with its emotional fluctuations, by the mobility and fluidity of the camera movements. *Cyrano* is a very long way from what Astruc meant when he spoke of 'a means of writing as supple and subtle as the written word', yet that observation is no less appropriate to it than to (say) *A bout de souffle*, as though to emphasize how widespread the concept of cinematic writing had become since its original polemical use in the New Wave heyday.

'Forum des Halles' cinema

The lavish revival of the *cinéma de qualité* is one of the two dominant tendencies in French cinema since about the mid-1980s. The other is what has been dubbed the 'Forum des Halles' genre (after the modern, or post-modern, space in central Paris that is the focal point for endless youthful parades of style). The work of directors such as Luc Besson, Jean-Jacques Beineix and Léos Carax is characterized by often determinedly non-realistic settings, flimsy and/or implausible plots that serve largely as showcases for a new generation of younger actresses and actors (Juliette Binoche, Mireille Perrier, Jean-Hugues Anglade), and a relentless foregrounding of style, that inescapable founding value of the 1980s in France as in Britain. Their films – in this if in no other respect like those of Berri and Rappeneau – proudly reclaim cinema's escapist role and tradition, and there is more than a touch of old-style Hollywood mythologization of the director in the way that Beineix's *La Lune dans le caniveau* (1983) or Carax's *Les Amants du Pont Neuf* (1991) massively exceeded their production budgets.

Their visual style, however, is determinedly contemporary, influenced above all by the video clip and the language of advertising. Besson's *Subway* (1985), with sets designed by Alexandre Trauner who, more than forty years before had designed those for the great Carné/Prévert films, imagines a bizarre sub-culture (including itinerant musicians and a roller-skating pickpocket) dwelling in the tunnels of the Métro – perhaps an analogy for the Forum des Halles, much of which is underground. *Le Grand Bleu* (1987) is a tale of divers and dolphins shot in real-life locations ranging from the Greek islands to Peru; its ecological kitsch made it an extraordinary cult success in France, though it failed no less spectacularly in Britain and the USA. *Nikita* (1990), starring Besson's wife Anne Parillaud, plays with drug addiction, espionage and romance under a false name – 'MacGuffins', as Hitchcock would have said, on which to hang a string of spectacular visual set pieces.

Beineix's *Diva* (1981) now clearly appears as the inaugural film, and still among the best, of this genre. Its fascination with classical music (the hero is infatuated with an opera singer), with the technologies of cultural reproduction (he clandestinely tapes her recitals because she has always refused to have her voice recorded), with marginal social groups presented more whimsically and less savagely than in Blier, in many respects set the mould for a decade. *37°2 le matin* (English title *Betty Blue* – 1986) sets its neurotic and finally self-mutilatory heroine against the easy-going unrecognized literary genius of her lover Zorg, in a classic contrast of gender stereotypes scarcely redeemed by the film's inventive use of colour.

Carax's work is inextricably associated with that of his alter ego Denis Lavant, star of his three features to date – *Boy meets girl* (1984), *Mauvais sang* (1986) and *Les Amants du Pont Neuf*. Lavant's blend of rebarbativeness and seduction is reminiscent of the early Belmondo, and allusions to Godard as well as to Cocteau, Bresson, Jean Vigo abound in Carax's work, making him more of a cinephile's director than Besson or Beineix. *Les Amants du Pont Neuf* is a *tour de force* of visual inventiveness that also comments incisively on the France of the late 1980s – that of the 'new poor' (Lavant and Juliette Binoche, the lovers of the title, sleep out on the Pont Neuf while it is closed for repair) and of the sumptuous bicentennial celebrations of the French Revolution, evoked in hyperrealist bursts of fireworks.

Between them, the *revived cinéma de qualité*, the 'Forum des Halles' genre and the continuing work of the 'old New Wave' largely account for, but by no means exhaust, the most important work in current French cinema. The comedies of Claude Zidi (*Les Bidasses en folie* of 1971, *Les Ripoux* of 1984) outgrossed virtually all their contemporaries at the French box-office, while a generation of film-makers of North African extraction have brought the *cinéma beur* to prominence (Mehdi Charef's *Le Thé au harem d'Archimède* of 1985, Rachid Bouchareb's *Bâton rouge* of the same year). Éric Rochant's work examines the problems of contemporary French youth at once more realistically and more traditionally than that of Besson or Carax (*Un monde sans pitié* of 1989, *Aux yeux du monde* of 1991). And, while the 'Forum des Halles' directors drew extensively on the language of advertising, the leading advertising director to branch out into features, Étienne Chatiliez, has produced grotesque, caricatural work far less glossily self-indulgent than theirs. Chatiliez's *La Vie est un long fleuve tranquille* (1988) uses the archetypal narrative of babies exchanged at birth to satirize two families – one *haut bourgeois*, the other lumpenproletarian – with even-handed venom, while the winsome stereotype of the 'dear little old lady' is somewhat more clumsily taken apart in *Tatie Danielle*

(1990). The bite of Chatiliez's work is a rare enough quality in contemporary French film-making, perhaps a reflection of what has seemed until recently a tranquil social consensus eschewing ideological extremes. The approaching end of the Mitterrand years, the growing disillusionment with their style of high-gloss, high-budget (and some are increasingly saying megalomaniacal) cultural funding, and the upsurge of racism will undoubtedly have their impact upon the 'cinema(s) of tomorrow', though at this stage it is impossible to predict what that impact will be.

Notes

1. Some reference works give either 1958 or 1960 as the dates for some of these films. All, however, are listed in at least one major work as dating from 1959.

Further reading

Armes, Roy, *French Cinema* (Oxford: Oxford University Press, 1985).
Forbes, Jill, *The Cinema in France: After the New Wave* (London: BFI/Macmillan, 1992).
Hayward, Susan and Vincendeau, Ginette, eds, *French Film: Texts and Contexts* (London: Routledge, 1990).
Jeancolas, Jean-Pierre, *Le Cinéma des Français* (Paris: Stock, 1979).
Quinze ans d'années trente (Paris: Stock, 1985).
Monaco, James, *The New Wave* (Oxford: Oxford University Press, 1976).
Passek, Jean-Loup, ed., *Dictionnaire du cinéma français* (Paris: Larousse, 1987).
Reader, Keith, and Vincendeau, Ginette, eds, *La Vie est à nous: French Cinema of the Popular Front* (London: National Film Theatre, 1986).
Williams, Ian, *The Republic of Images*, (Cambridge, MA: Harvard, 1992).

CHAPTER 5

Conserving the cultural heritage of historic buildings and towns in France since 1945

Roger J. P. Kain

In France since the Renaissance, major building works have been closely linked with the power of the state and have both reflected and enhanced that power. François I in the sixteenth century initiated the construction of the great *château* of Chambord and the rebuilding of the Louvre palace. In the seventeenth and eighteenth centuries the construction of *places royales* (squares of town houses dedicated to a particular monarch) and the successive extensions of the palace and town of Versailles were quintessential expressions of state and aristocratic power.[1] For architects and town planners, the Revolution meant little more than a change of client. Napoléon I ushered in a century of monumental architectural works ranging in scale from the construction of individual monuments such as the *Arc de Triomphe* at Etoile in Paris, to the complete restructuring of the whole of central Paris, a programme that was largely achieved during the twenty years of the Second Empire.[2] During the Third Republic the Eiffel Tower was constructed, and today it is probably still the most widely recognized feature of the Parisian skyline. Contemporary reactions to this startlingly new structure, fabricated from metal girders, were no less polarized than people's reactions to the post-Second World War *grands projets* in France. These include buildings such as 'Europe's' airport of Roissy-Charles de Gaulle, the Centre National d'Art et Culture Georges Pompidou, the Grande Arche de la Défense, the Grand Louvre and its Pyramide, the Opéra at the Place de la Bastille in eastern Paris and the new Ministry of Finance at Bercy in outer Paris.[3] It would seem that men of power in France since the Second World War have subscribed to Napoléon I's dictum that 'men are only rendered great by the monuments they leave'. De Gaulle, Pompidou, Giscard d'Estaing and Mitterand have, in their different ways, continued linking both state power and themselves personally to architectural and town planning works and in so doing have added a particularly French ingredient to the broader, pan-European trends in architectural design which have affected French towns and cities since 1945.[4]

A somewhat quieter and more conservative counterpoint to this headline catching and loudly sung new building work has been the extension of protection over, and the conservation of, the historic building heritage of France. Though in many senses less spectacular than the *grands projets*, it is nevertheless an area of cultural affairs in which France can claim to have established a 'model and exemplar' for other European countries to follow.[5] The subject matter of this essay is a review of the ways in which the French government has cherished and nurtured its cultural building heritage since the Second World War.

By comparison with the United Kingdom, France is favoured with a particularly rich architectural and urban heritage. This richness is derived in part from the great flowering of classical architecture and town planning which dominated French building and town extensions from the adoption of Renaissance design in the sixteenth century through to the nineteenth century. Of equal importance, but a phenomenon of quite a different character, is that industry-led urbanization in the nineteenth century, and urban renewal in the twentieth century, by-passed much of southern, central and western France. As a result, many ancient ruins from as long ago as the Middle Ages and even Roman times have survived in these areas in particular (figure 5.1). War damage

Figure 5.1 Nîmes: the Maison Carrée, an original Roman temple used today to house a small museum (author's photograph). Its survival reflects both the high degree of romanisation in this part of France, some very early attempts by the French government to protect Roman remains, and also that this part of France was not much affected by industry-led redevelopment in the nineteenth century or by urban renewal in the present century.

in both world wars was also a northern and eastern phenomenon so that little of the historic heritage outside these areas was lost through these causes. Even in such an avowedly 'historic' English town as Exeter, true medieval secular buildings are hard to find; an English visitor to almost any western or southern French town cannot fail to be impressed by the sheer number of old buildings which have survived to the present (see figure 5.2).

At the end of the Second World War, France had already enjoyed almost exactly a century of European supremacy in the field of architectural protection and preservation.[6] The effective beginning of this was in 1837 when the infant Department of Historic Monuments set out to draw up a massive inventory of all the historic buildings of France.[7] Its first Inspector General, Prosper Mérimée, estimated that this could take more than 200 years

Figure 5.2 Bourges: late medieval houses on the rue Cambounac (author's photograph). Many thousands of such timber-framed houses survive in French towns; by comparison in England the genuine articles, as distinct from nineteenth-century 'replicas', are few and far between.

to complete so he reduced its scope and in 1840 published one of the first 'lists' of buildings in Europe. Today the listing of historical buildings in a register, and then according statutory protection to all of them by virtue of their having been listed, is a normal procedure in all western countries.

In keeping with the contemporary Gothic revival idea that only medieval relics were worth valuing, all the monuments on the first French lists were of medieval and earlier date. At this time 'restoration' of historic buildings meant just that – the process of removing all later additions and alterations and returning structures to their actual (or more usually imagined) medieval form. The 'restoration' of the southern town of Carcassonne by Viollet-le-Duc is a quintessential example of this kind of activity (figure 5.3).

*Figure 5.3 **The medieval cité of Carcassonne in south-west France 'restored' by Viollet-le-Duc (author's collection). In the nineteenth-century, restoration ideas of the Gothic revival movement were very important and represent a significant cultural 'export' from England to France. The object was to remove all later additions and alterations so as to 'restore' a structure to its medieval splendour. This meant that much renaissance and later building work, now of course greatly valued in its own right, was destroyed in the restoration process. Furthermore, architects had often only the sketchiest of notions of what a building, or in this case a small town, was actually like in the Middle Ages so many of these Gothic-revival-inspired restorations were very much the products of their architects' imagined ideals.***

The twentieth century began with France scoring another 'first' for Europe when, by an act passed in 1913, two categories of historic buildings were established and the top division of 'classified buildings' benefitted from the fact that all structures and land within a circular zone of 500 metres were also protected from demolition or development. These 'protected perimeters' pioneered the now generally accepted view that it is important to protect the immediate environs of major monuments. It was then but a short step to recognizing that it is important to conserve the whole townscape not just the most important individual historic buildings within it. It was a step first taken in France.

A difficulty with the 1913 Act, and one that has not been entirely removed by later amending legislation, is that, if demolitions or alterations to buildings on the list were disallowed, then owners could claim compensation for the loss of development value. With rising urban land prices in the twentieth century, particularly in town centres where most classified buildings are to be found, these sums could be very large. This fact in part explains why, despite the evidently much richer and numerically much greater heritage of buildings in France by comparison with England, the English lists contain more than ten times the number (about 500,000) of listed buildings than the French.

What France and the United Kingdom have in common in this context is that, for both countries, it is their nineteenth century and especially inter-war buildings which are under greatest threat. This fact was recognized in 1974 by the French Minister of Cultural Affairs when he announced that a further 200 unprotected post-1800 buildings were to be listed, including, for example, buildings such as the Eiffel Tower in Paris, most of the Second Empire Parisian theatres, the Casino at Vichy and some important early twentieth-century modernist architecture at Lyon by Tony Garnier.

The listing procedures described above, even with the widening of scope which occurred in the 1970s, were still directed at 'important' buildings; the more ordinary, mostly residential buildings that made up the protected perimeters around the major monuments in the 'classified' category of the lists were included only because of their contextual value rather than in their own right.

France in the immediate post-Second World War period, in common with most other European countries, suffered chronic housing shortages brought about in the short term by the loss of some 450,000 dwellings due to war damage. Probably about a quarter of the total housing stock was either destroyed or damaged.[8] Squalid urban housing conditions were further exacerbated by processes of rural-urban migration associated with the drive to re-industrialize the economy. After lagging well behind West Germany in the 1950s, the quantity of new housing completions in France rose to some 300,000 per annum in the late 1950s, 400,000 by the mid-1960s and to over 500,000 in the 1970s.[9] Much of this was accomplished by 'comprehensive redevelopment' involving slum removal and rehousing in the now notorious *grands ensembles* of high-rise appartments on the peripheries of cities. High-rise living brought with it its own set of social and psychological problems for rehoused residents. A further problem with such an approach, and comprehensive redevelopment was far from unique to France, was that properties demolished could be at once slum housing in social amenity terms but also of significant historical and/or architectural value notwithstanding their run-down physical condition.

It was against this background of the mass destruction of the historic quarters of French cities in the name of housing improvement that, in 1962, at precisely the time this activity was at its climax, the French government once again enacted reforms which were radical, not only for France, but for the whole of Europe.[10] An act, known since as the 'Malraux Act' after André Malraux the then Minister of Cultural Affairs who was its chief sponsor, provided for the designation of *secteurs sauvegardés* (conservation areas) within historic towns and gave powers for state intervention to enhance their historic qualities.

Publicly funded work was carried out by defining an 'operational area' of perhaps one or two street blocks within the *secteur sauvegardé* and on which expenditure was to be concentrated. The idea was to effect quick results by focusing resources and thus create some spectacular results which it was hoped would encourage private property owners to invest in restoring their own properties themselves. The actual work was done by setting up a *société d'économie mixte* (a company funded with part public, part private finance and a mechanism used to effect much urban development and infrastructural work in France). These companies received delegated powers from the state to effect the conservation work which included the now notorious draconian powers to expropriate properties from their owners.

The Malraux Act involved much more than the mere repair and preservation of old buildings, though the rescue of historic areas from the advancing demolition teams was an essential aim, but it also proposed the demolition of eyesores within the historic areas designated as *secteurs sauvegardés*, the conversion of old buildings to modern uses, the upgrading of housing by providing baths, sanitation and proper sewage disposal, the management of traffic and parking and, most radically, provision for the integration of new buildings with the old where restoration was not practicable. Of fundamental significance were to be attempts to introduce new economic activities to help retain populations and provide some positive functional role for *secteurs sauvegardés* within the wider urban context. It was certainly not the intention that they become open-air museums of historic architecture but rather that their historic qualities be retained in a restructured functional context.

The French Malraux Act, legislation without precedence anywhere else in the world, was a landmark by virtue of its philosophy of positive enhancement rather than just restoration and protection. It was held up as a model of excellence in the 1960s by other European countries and was, for example, closely studied by Britain's Civic Trust when the United Kingdom's Civic Amenities Act (1967) was being drafted; the emphasis on an area-based approach to historic buildings heritage is shared by both.

From the perspective of today we can see that the *secteur sauvegardé* approach to urban and architectural conservation, while undoubtedly producing some spectacular individual beauties, has not brought about the general renaissance of the French urban past that André Malraux had planned. Designation has been slow (only some seventy-five *secteurs sauvegardés* out of about 400 initially proposed – see figure 5.4), and the work of enhancement has progressed equally slowly and has been dogged by political problems, not least the fact that local communities had little say in what the central, Paris-based authorities intended to happen in each town. There has also been equally powerful popular political protest at the social changes that conservation in *secteurs sauvegardés* encouraged.

Responsibility for protecting and enhancing the building fabric of the past in France has always been, and in many ways still is, very much within the province of the Ministry of Cultural Affairs rather than the ministries more directly concerned with physical planning such as *Equipement*. The Ministry of Cultural Affairs' *Direction du Patrimoine* and *Sous-direction des Monuments Historiques* work in close conjunction with the *Caisse Nationale des Monuments Historiques et des Sites* (a semi-public agency with particular responsibility for publicity about, and presentation of, the past) to formulate policy.[11] Though in the 1960s the French were very much in the vanguard of philosophical and methodological innovation in urban conservation, in matters of defining what it was that was worth conserving, France was very much in line with the international community. The Ministry of Cultural Affairs accepted the usual definition of 'an historical monument' as defined in the international Charter of Venice as 'an architectural creation, isolated or part of a group, which is evidence of a particular civilisation, or an evolutionary process, or an historical event'. This broad definition incorporating both architectural and historical values could be applied to both individual monuments and also to architecturally or historically important quarters of whole towns.[12] The critical element is its implied

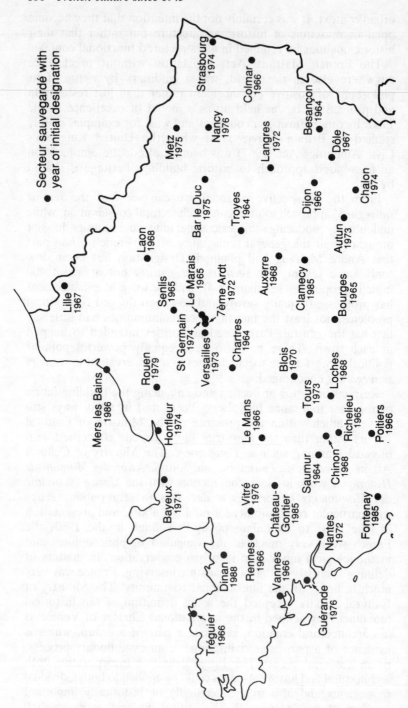

Strasbourg
1974

Colmar
1966

Nancy
1976

Metz
1975

Besançon
1964

Langres
1972

Dôle
1967

Bar le Duc
1975

Troyes
1964

Chalon
1974

Laon
1968

Dijon
1966

Autun
1973

Senlis
1965

Le Marais
1965

7ème Ardt
1972

Auxerre
1968

Clamecy
1985

Bourges
1965

Lille
1967

St Germain
1974

Versailles
1973

Chartres
1964

Blois
1970

Rouen
1979

Loches
1968

Mers les Bains
1986

Le Mans
1966

Tours
1973

Richelieu
1965

Poitiers
1966

Honfleur
1974

Chinon
1968

Bayeux
1971

Vitré
1976

Saumur
1964

Château-
Gontier
1985

Fontenay
1985

Dinan
1988

Rennes
1966

Vannes
1966

Nantes
1972

Guérande
1976

Tréguier
1966

● Secteur sauvegardé with
  year of initial designation

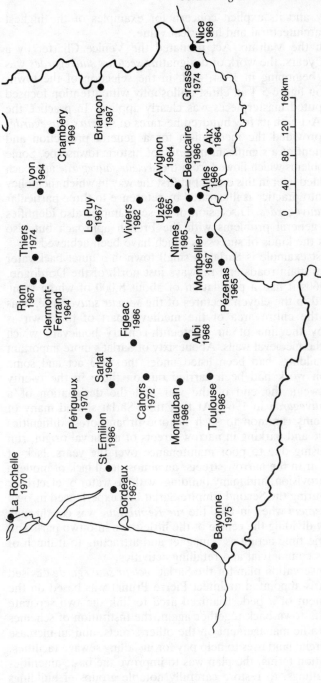

Figure 5.4 **Secteurs sauvegardés designated in France to 1990.**
Source: Ministère de l'Equipement, du Logement, des Transports et de la Mer – DAU.

selectivity and its explicit concern for examples of the highest order of architectural and historical value.

Though the Malraux Act predated the Venice Charter by a couple of years, the work of designating *secteurs sauvegardés* was only just beginning in 1964, and, in the selection of the towns mapped on figure 5.4 an elitist philosophy with attention focused on undisputed masterpieces was clearly applied. In practice the Malraux Act with its few hundred hectares of *secteurs sauvegardés* has not provided the mechanism for a general protection and enhancement of a significant *quantity* of historic townscape. Some of the problems which flowed from the *secteur sauvegardé* approach are examined later in this essay, but first the way in which the policy was put into practice is illustrated by reference to three particular *secteurs sauvegardés*. Discussion of these examples also identifies incipient general problems with the French approach but also highlights the kinds of successes which have been achieved.

The first example is Sarlat, a small town in a quiet backwater away from main roads and railways just north of the Dordogne. In the 1960s it had a population of about 8,000 of whom some 1,300 lived in the eleven hectares of the *secteur sauvegardé*. This included the entire area of the medieval part of the town as defined by the line of an eighteenth-century boulevard which replaced the medieval walls. About sixty of Sarlat's more important historic buildings had been listed under the 1913 act and some restoration work had been carried out on these in the twenty years between the end of the war and the designation of a *secteur sauvegardé* in 1964. At that time Sarlat shared many of the problems common to such historic urban cores: difficulties with traffic and parking in narrow streets of medieval origin, run down housing due to poor maintenance over the years, lack of light and air in the narrow streets, an almost total lack of modern sanitary provision, and many buildings with no water or electricity supply. During the Second Empire Sarlat had experienced its own *bouleversement* when in 1860 the *rue République* was cut through effectively dividing the centre of the little town into two parts and at the same time acting as a magnet and attracting to it much of the town's commercial and retailing activities.

The conservation plan for the Sarlat *secteur sauvegardé* devised by the Paris-appointed architect Pierre Prunet was based on the establishment of a pedestrianized area to link the two separate parts of the town back together again, the institution of schemes of strict traffic management on the other streets, and an increase in commercial land uses to help pay for installing sewage facilities. In restoration terms, the plan was to improve the basic amenities of all dwellings, to restore carefully notable groups of buildings while actually demolishing some others in order to increase the proportion of open space in the densely built-up *cité* (figure 5.5).

Figure 5.5 Sarlat: restored stone buildings and repaved streets in the secteur sauvegardé (author's photograph). Work in secteurs sauvegardés is characterised by close attention to architectural veracity; it is expensive, particularly as here in Sarlat where there is a lot of stone construction.

The essential need in Sarlat in the 1960s was to bring population and economic activity back into the town centre – a need still shared by many historic inner city areas in western Europe in the 1990s. The Malraux programme has largely succeeded in this aim in Sarlat.

At Avignon, the *secteur sauvegardé* is quite different. At six hectares it is one of the smallest, it extends over only a fraction of the historic town rather than the whole as at Sarlat, and it contains not a single classified building. Its importance lies not in the quality of its architecture which is patently of a very low order, but in its relationship to the magnificent medieval papal palace complex, constructed when the papacy resided in Avignon after exile from the city of Rome. This part of Avignon, known as the *quartier de la Balance*, was occupied by the lowest socio-economic groups, many residents were squatters and a large proportion of the population was made up of north African immigrants.

The enhancement plan drawn up in the years after 1964 was based on housing improvement and the provision of restaurants and luxury shops oriented towards the tourist trade as tourism was to be the economic rationale of the enhancement plan. All this led to inevitable changes in the socio-economic composition of the resident population; conservation work in Avignon heralded one of the great difficulties with all such work, that of disadvantaging the indigenous population and thus offending concepts of social justice as gentrification (displacement of low socio-economic groups by higher-income residents) took place. Also in Avignon there has been much more emphasis on demolition and rebuilding than on the restoration of existing dilapidated buildings which reflected their very poor state and general low architectural value. In rebuilding, the grouping, massing and scale of the original structures have been retained so as to protect views across the *secteur sauvegardé* to the papal palace (figure 5.6).

Figure 5.6 Avignon: rue de la Balance showing new buildings under construction in the secteur sauvegardé *to replace existing buildings which were very dilapidated and of little architectural worth (author's collection). The new buildings respect the general style of the old, notably the arcaded ground floors, and also the mass and scale of those which have been demolished.*

The third example to illustrate the Malraux approach to urban conservation is the *secteur sauvegardé* of the Marais in Paris. This is usually considered the showpiece of post-Second World War urban conservation in France but at the same time it is where the political weight of popular protest about social change has been greatest. At 126 hectares it is one of the largest *secteurs sauvegardés* in the country yet it covers but a tiny fraction of

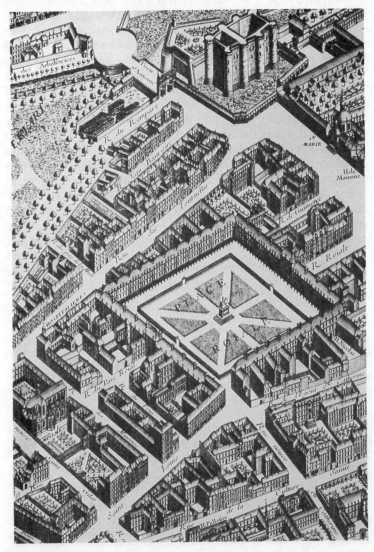

Figure 5.7 Paris: Place Royale constructed circa 1610 and dedicated to Louis XIV (now Place des Vosges) as represented on Turgot's plan of Paris, 1739.

historic Paris. By contrast with say the *quartier de la Balance* at Avignon, it is a veritable anthology of high quality French classical architecture. From the time of the Revolution onwards, the Marais experienced decline in social prestige as areas of Left Bank Paris such as Saint Germain were ascending, and in the nineteenth century its great buildings were sub-divided, their courtyards and gardens were built over as a response to the chronic housing shortage that industrializing and redeveloping Paris experienced. The Marais changed fast from an aristocratic residential district to one based on small-scale, craft industries with a population living at high densities in slum conditions. The nadir of the Marais's fortunes was reached around the First World War and it was designated an official slum area in the 1930s. Attitudes changed gradually after the Second World War; the planned comprehensive redevelopment did not occur before a campaign to save the Marais achieved momentum in the 1950s and the opportunity to declare the area a *secteur sauvegardé* for enhancement under the Malraux Act was taken early in 1965.

The basic philosophy of the Marais plan is to cut away all the accretionary structures built for workshops and slum housing in the nineteenth century and to return the Marais to the general pattern of open space and buildings which it displayed at the time of Turgot's great cartographic survey of Paris's streets and buildings in 1739 (figures 5.7 and 5.8). A small area of three hectares centred on the *hôtel* Carnavalet was selected as the first experimental or 'operational' area. State finance was concentrated on the enhancement of these few streets to show what could be done with a run down inner city area. The Carnavalet operational

Figure 5.8 **Paris: restoration in progress in the Place des Vosges in 1978 (author's photograph).**

area shared many of the problems common to other parts of the Marais, notably the very fragmented pattern of property ownership which made expropriation and consolidation of properties difficult, the presence of accretionary structures in the courtyards, buildings in a poor state of repair and congestion caused by on-street parking. Its conservation plan also included a typical mix of activities, from complete rebuilding behind restored street facades to the careful architectural scholarship applied to restoring some of the old town mansions, such as the *hôtel* Salé (figure 5.9) and a group of *hôtels* in the *rue du Parc Royal* (figures 5.10 and 5.11).

With the opening of the Centre Georges Pompidou which houses an extensive modern art collection, the monopoly of Left Bank Paris as *the* location for art galleries was broken. Today many private galleries are locating in the area of the *Centre*, not least in properties in the Marais: the Galerie Maeght in the *hôtel* de Rebours was one of the first. Museum has also followed on museum in the Marais: the latest being the transfer by the Ville de Paris of the *Musée* Cognac-Jay into the *hôtel* Donon (Ernest Cognac was the founder of the first of Paris's great department stores, La Samaritaine). In many respects a world away from what Malraux had intended, this *secteur sauvegardé* is now neatly described by phrases such as 'Le Marais *entre galeries et musées*'. The Marais has fast become a part of Paris which depends economically on cultural tourism and luxury retailing as

Figure 5.9 **Paris: Hôtel Salé restored as a museum, a project like so many in the Marais characterized by a high degree of architectural scholarship but achieved at an equally high monetary cost (author's photograph).**

Figure 5.10 Paris: one of a group of town mansions on the rue du Parc Royal in the Marais **secteur sauvegardé** *photographed in 1979 just before restoration began (author's photograph).*

a '*quartier de luxe*' rather than continuing to be characterized by the activities of artisans which the conservation plan has singularly failed to retain in significant numbers.

Economic change has caused social change and the most difficult of the problems faced by conservation planners have been in the social arena. With hindsight we can see that it was perhaps unrealistic to expect a large proportion of the original residents to be able to live and work in the Marais after the conservation programme as was originally intended at designation in 1965. It is inconceivable that restoration work of the thoroughgoing type envisaged in the Marais plan could be carried out without rehousing existing occupants while the work was undertaken. The intention was that such displacement would be temporary with residents able to move back in when their properties had been restored. Many, however, had inhabited what were euphemistically called 'accretionary structures' now demolished and thus simply not there for reoccupation. The position is not much better with most

Figure 5.11 Paris: the same hôtel as pictured in Figure 5.10 with restoration almost complete in 1982 (author's photograph).

restored flats which are either let at much higher rates or sold. In either case they are beyond the reach of the indigenous population so that temporary displacement is proving to be permanent as the process of gentrification takes its seemingly inevitable hold. Certainly there has not been a shortage of takers for chic city centre flats among the middle classes with their much more 'urban' residential preferences than, say the English. A walk around the area with its luxury shops confirms the overwhelming social change that has taken place.

Though the Malraux law did not succeed in effecting the renaissance of the past that was hoped for and has indeed brought about some catastrophic social consequences, it is important because it adopted a strategic view of conservation by establishing broad zones (the *secteurs sauvegardés*) over which control of the heritage could be exercised, and at the same time provided a mechanism for small-scale 'tactical' projects (the operational areas) within the strategic framework which contributed to the long-term, overall goals. In criticizing it from a standpoint of today, it must also be remembered that the political and economic worlds of the present and thirty years ago are so very different, particularly in the sense that the threats to historic quarters of towns come no longer from the comprehensive redevelopers but from the inexorable processes of physical decay fuelled by economic stagnation and decline in inner city areas. Nevertheless, the very limited public participation and an equally low order of local input to the decision-making process are now politically unacceptable.[13]

The Malraux Act then has protected some historic areas in towns from the threat of comprehensive redevelopment associated with the accelerating attack on the housing problem in France. In itself, it did little to contribute to the improvement of housing in inner cities as a whole because the tiny proportion of the total old housing stock included in *secteurs sauvegardés* was but a drop in the ocean of the problem. Moreover, with the close attention to exact architectural scholarship which is characteristic of restoration activity in *secteurs sauvegardés*, progress of work on this minority was also very slow.

In 1975 in what proved to be an analysis of the first importance, Pierre Nora and Bertrand Eveno reported to the French government that, despite all the attempts in the thirty years since the end of the Second World War, 39 per cent of the national housing stock represented by more than 6.5 million dwellings was still substandard. Very nearly two-thirds of the housing constructed pre-1948 (more than six million dwellings) provided living conditions which the Nora-Eveno report considered intolerable in the context of the 1970s.[14] Their report underlined the perhaps not unexpected fact that it was the lowest income sector of the population, particularly the elderly, which suffered the worst conditions and who were effectively trapped. Nora-Eveno highlighted the scale of the reservoir of old, and in many cases 'historic' housing stock for rehabilitation and recommended that this could only be remedied by government action. They justified rehabilitation rather than renewal on social and economic grounds as well as for reasons of cultural heritage conservation.

The indictment of the failings of post-war housing improvement in France by the Nora-Eveno report and recognition of the political opposition and the social problems consequent on the *secteur sauvegardé* approach, brought about in 1976 and 1977 a radical change of government policy. First in 1976 a new, single body the *Fonds d'Aménagement Urbain* (FAU) was instituted to be responsible for the administration of all government funding of urban works; part of its brief was to establish a socially just approach to restoration. *Opérations programmées d'amélioration de l'habitat* (OPAH) introduced in 1977 were the specific instruments designed both to avoid the local opposition which was slowing down work so much in the *secteurs sauvegardés* and to do something more in quantitative terms to improve the poor housing stock of French towns. The aims of OPAH are much more modest, the areas they cover are much smaller, perhaps about 300 dwellings on average. The almost infinite timescales of some *secteur sauvegardé* programmes are replaced in OPAH by contracts between the local authority, the state and property owners of just three years duration. Larger projects have to be organized in separate three-year plans. Gone also is the sweeping *curetage* of 'alien' structures built in recent times to return a *secteur sauvegardé* to a 'pure' state in which it was known to have (or more likely imagined to have) existed at a particular time in its past. Instead the object with OPAH is to upgrade existing buildings to statutory norms of amenity and effect necessary structural repairs to buildings, *providing* that the continued survival of the indigenous population can be assured. Enshrined in the policy is the principle that low-income households should have the same right to comfortable accommodation as better-off households.[15]

By contrast with the Parisian domination of decision-making under the Malraux Act, OPAH are based on voluntary agreements by the local and national state and property owners; the whole process of designation is determined locally rather than nationally. Particularly significant is the role accorded to social criteria in deciding whether or not an OPAH ought to be approved; social justice is accorded at least equal weight as matters of architectural quality of buildings and their historic interest and importance. Local communities were not slow to designate OPAH; almost 400 were underway within three years with the more regionally conscious provinces, particularly Brittany, proceeding most quickly.[16]

In practice, however, reality does not match up to these ideals. The principle of voluntarism which underpins them means that municipalities can declare an OPAH but are not obliged to do so. Furthermore, even where an OPAH has been declared, owners are not required to do work on their properties. Barbara Reid's recent analysis of the working of an OPAH in the Toussaints-Parcheminerie quarter of Rennes in Brittany reveals many cases of poor targeting of funds with the result that those dwellings which would most benefit have not always been included, partly as a consequence that available funds are often concentrated in small areas within a district, and partly because the voluntary principle of the measures requires individuals to respond to grant incentives to carry out work on their properties. Superficial appearances of improvement belie the fact that a high proportion of funds is spent on external stone cleaning works rather than on the much-needed internal improvement of dwellings. More controversially still, her findings suggest that in the allocation of building and other contracts within an OPAH a small number of contractors and consultants have been favoured.[17]

In the three OPAH of Bordeaux – Trois Places, Saint-Michel and Saint-Pierre – Michel Genty finds that all the restoration activity of the 1980s has resulted in only a modest number of rehabilitations of low-rented dwellings. By contrast some 500 dwellings a year for uncontrolled letting have been produced and this process is bringing about substantial changes in the socio-economic structure of these historic areas. In place of low-income families there is a temporary and transient population of students and single people and childless couples who value a city centre living environment, appreciate the historic aura engendered by the old buildings, and are prepared and able to pay for it.[18] *Plus ça change?*

Despite some misgivings, these OPAH procedures must be judged on success. More than 1,500 OPAH programmes have been completed to date which compares with just seventy-three *secteurs sauvegardés* designated and with work on none of these

Dans un ilot de calme et de charme au cœur historique et vivant de Paris

Figure 5.12
Figures 5.12, 5.13 and 5.14 Paris: Quartier d'Horloge – conservation or comprehensive redevelopment? Building façades along the rue Saint-Martin have been retained but are the only fragments of authentic historic fabric. Behind these walls everything else has been demolished and rebuilt new (author's photographs).

Figure 5.13

Figure 5.14

completed in its entirety. A figure of about 500,000 properties enhanced, however imperfectly, under OPAH procedures can be set against the annual achievement of some 1,800 to 2,000 dwellings improved throughout the whole *secteurs sauvegardés* system in the heyday of this work in the late 1960s to the mid 1970s.

The final three illustrations in this essay are of the *quartier d'Horloge* in Paris described in its publicity material as '*un îlot de calme et de charme au cœur historique et vivant de Paris*' (figure 5.12). As the photographs illustrate, the only authentic historic fabric which remains is the external street façade along the *rue* Saint-Martin (figure 5.13). Everything else has been demolished and rebuilt anew (figure 5.14). Is this then, an example of urban conservation, or does it belong to a different category? It respects the height of the old buildings but in every other respect is a pure pastiche trying to associate itself with the past in order to attach to it the aura of past times and so increase its marketability.

For much of the time period with which this book is concerned and for a long time previously, France has been at the forefront of cultural heritage preservation and conservation in the western world. No one approach has proved universally successful but nor should this be expected of policies concerned with dynamic cultural phenomena like urban systems which necessarily reflect and change with the social, political and economic milieux of their times. Who, in 1945, imbued with the futuristic architectural visions of the likes of Le Corbusier then constructing the first of his high-rise appartment blocks, the *Unité d'Habitation* at Marseille, could have foreseen that forty years later the French middle classes would be clamouring for a restored flat in the very same slum property that Le Corbusier was trying to empty?

Notes

1. R. J. P. Kain, 'Classical urban design in eighteenth-century France: the rebuilding of Rennes', *Connoisseur*, 190 (1975), 248–57; 'Classical urban design in France: the transformation of Nancy in the eighteenth century', *Connoisseur*, 202 (1979), 190–7.

2. R. J. P. Kain, 'Napoléon I and urban planning in Paris', *Connoisseur*, 197 (1978), pp. 44–51; 'Urban planning and design in Second Empire France', *Connoisseur*, 199 (1978).

3. An up-to-date review in English of *Les Grands Projets* in post-war Paris is provided in the text and printed discussion of the three Royal Society of Arts Bossom Lectures for 1991 *viz.* M. Mead, '*Gloires*, past and present'; E. J. Biasini, '*Les Grands Projets*: an overview'; P. Andreu and R. Lion, '*L'Arche de la Défense*: a case study'. All are published in *Royal Society of Arts Journal*, 139 (1991), 555–80. Also in English see H. D. Clout, 'The chronicle of La

Défense', *Erkunde,* 42 (1988), pp. 273–82. F. Chaslin, *Les Paris de François Mitterrand* (Paris: Gallimard, 1985) examines several of the *grands projets* being pushed forward in the 1980s, while the most recent developments in French architectural theory and practice are reviewed in J. Lucan, *France architecture 1965–1988* (Paris: Editions Electa Moniteur, 1990).

4. A recent, well-illustrated book on twentieth-century architectural design is D. Sharp, *Twentieth century architecture: a visual history* (London: Lund Humphries, 2nd edition, 1991).

5. R. J. P. Kain, 'Europe's model and exemplar still? – The French approach to urban conservation, 1962–1981', *The Town Planning Review*, 55 (1982), 403–22.

6. R. J. P. Kain, 'Urban conservation in France', *Town and Country Planning*, 43 (1975), pp. 428–32; 'Développement des politiques de restauration du patrimoine historique des villes d'Europe occidentale', in *Géographie Historique des Villes d'Europe Occidentale*, ed. by P. Claval (Paris: Université de Paris-Sorbonne, 1986), pp. 173–88.

7. In this nineteenth-century context when the western world was infused with gothic revival ideas, 'historic buildings' were limited to those of medieval age or earlier. This was the time of the 'restoration' of places such as the *cité* of Carcassonne by Viollet-le-Duc; concern for monuments of the classical renaissance did not come until much later. Cf. R. J. P. Kain, 'Gothic revival, restoration and preservation of historic buildings in the nineteenth century', in *Il Neogotico nel XIX e XX Secolo*, ed. by R. Bossaglia and V. Terraroli (Milan: Edizione Mazzotta, 1990), pp. 43–65.

8. I. Scargill, *Urban France* (London: Croom Helm, 1983), p. 83; for an illustrated discussion of the architectural forms employed in post-war reconstructions see the exhibition catalogue prepared by J.-D. Pariset, *Reconstructions et modernisations: La France après les ruines 1918 . . . 1945 . . .* (Paris: Archives Nationales, 1991).

9. J. Pearsall, 'France' in *Housing in Europe*, ed. by M. Wynn (London: Croom Helm, 1984), pp. 9–54.

10. R. J. P. Kain, 'Conservation planning in France: policy and practice in the Marais', *Planning for Conservation: an international perspective*, ed. by R. J. P. Kain (London: Mansell, 1981), pp. 199–233.

11. J.-B. Bleynon, *L'Urbanisme et la protection des sites: la sauvegarde du patrimoine architectural urbain* (Paris: Librairie Générale de Droit et de Jurisprudence, 1979).

12. See C. B. A. Reid, 'The improvement and repair of housing in inner urban areas of France and the policy of *Opérations Programmées d'Amélioration de l'Habitat*: a realist analysis', University of Exeter Ph.D. thesis, 1990, pp. 65–6.

13. See J. Tuppen, *France under recession, 1981–1986* (London: Macmillan, 1988) for a discussion of the revitalization of cities.

14. P. Nora and B. Eveno, *L'Amélioration de l'habitat ancien* (Paris: La Documentation Française, 1976).

15. Kain, 'Europe's model and exemplar still? . . .' (1982).

16. C. Fontanel, 'La répartition géographique des OPAH', *Les Cahiers de l'ANAH*, 18 (1981), 10–11.

17. Reid, 'Improvement and repair of housing in inner urban areas', pp. 467–72.

18. M. Genty, 'Stratégies immobilières et mutations résidentielles dans les quartiers historiques de Bordeaux', *Revue Géographique des Pyrénées et du Sud-Ouest*, 60 (1989), 27–47.

Further reading

In addition to the specific references noted in the text, the following items of further reading are suggested:

Burtenshaw, D., Bateman, M. and Ashworth, G. J., *The city in western Europe* (Chichester: John Wiley, 1981) employs a valuable comparative approach and contains a chapter on conservation in western European cities.

Coing, H., *Rénovation urbaine et changement social: îlot no. 4, Paris 13ème* (Paris: Les Editions Ouvrières, 1966) is a classic study of the social effects of the kinds of urban redevelopment undertaken in the 1960s and against which the Malraux Act and its system of *secteurs sauvegardés* was to provide some protection.

Duclaud-Williams, R. H., *Politics of housing in Britain and France* (London: Heinemann, 1978) contrasts the very different approaches to solving the post-war housing crises in the two countries.

Lévy, J. P., *Centres villes en mutation* (Paris: CNRS, 1987) takes a comparative France/North America approach to decline, rehabilitation and restoration from the 1950s and presents some detailed findings on towns in south-west France.

Lowenthal, D. *The past is a foreign country* (Cambridge: Cambridge University Press, 1985) is a fundamental study of the history and philosophy of heritage conservation, though written mainly from an Anglo-American perspective.

Pitte, J. R., *Histoire du paysage français* (Paris: Tallandier, 1983, 2 vols.) reviews the historical evolution of French landscape and townscape.

Topalov, C., *Le logement en France: histoire d'une marchandise impossible* (Paris: Presses de la Fondation Nationale des Sciences Politiques, 1987) sets post-war housing into its temporal and political contexts.

The best source for up-to-date comments, news and reviews of the French historic building heritage and its conservation is the bi-monthly journal *Monuments Historiques* (formerly *Les Monuments Historiques de la France*) which is published by the Caisse Nationale des Monuments Historiques et des Sites from the *hôtel de* Bethune-Sully, 62 *rue* Saint-Antoine, Paris 75004. The current annual subscription from the United Kingdom is 375 francs. Issue no. 161 (1989) was devoted to '*Vingt ans de patrimoine*', and reviews a wide range of examples of recent conservation projects in France and looks ahead to the effects of the single European market on the country's cultural building heritage.

PART TWO

Popular culture

CHAPTER 6

Sport in France

A. Greaves

Preamble: sports, games and pastimes

The principal problem with a subject such as this is one of definition. Georges Magnane, in *Sociologie du sport* (Paris: Gallimard, 1964) offers his own provisional specification of sport:

Une activité du loisir dont la dominante est l'effort physique, participant à la fois du jeu et du travail, pratiquée de façon compétitive, comportant des règlements et des institutions spécifiques, et susceptible de se transformer en activité professionnelle. (p. 81)

This looks fine except for the phrase which introduces the 'pratiquée de façon compétitive' element. For this clearly excludes what the French call simply 'activités physiques', which embrace, but are not in themselves necessarily games where a score is recorded, or a performance measured. Hang-gliding, mountaineering or cross-country skiing, for example, fall readily, and most often, into a non-competitive category where the activity is undertaken for its own sake rather than as a means of assessing achievement against time, distance or other people; and yet most would qualify these activities as sports.

Again, hundreds of thousands of Frenchmen regularly practise fishing (not to mention shooting birds the flesh of which is so exiguous as to necessitate a minimum of twenty corpses for the most modest *pot-au-feu*), and both Formula 1 racing and the Paris-Dakar Rally sustain a following beyond even that which the British generate for such motorized activities. Nothing will persuade me that fishing and Formula 1 racing are physical activities, still less sports, but armies of people (and not just the French) will have their well-considered and sincere reasons for disagreeing. Perhaps it is useful that the distinction between *sports* and *activités physiques* exists as an understood working tool in the French language, as indeed it does in the English. The two terms neatly differentiate the competitive and recreational elements of physical activity, and between them offer some pretty sound criteria for excluding fishing and motor-racing (and billiards, pin-ball and clay-pigeon shooting, for that matter – all of them very popular activities in France). I shall, therefore, examine sport in France as personal physical exertions, some of which are games. Magnane's definition above is close to how the French would perceive sport today, but it would not include their perception of all physical activity. For sport can be distinguished from pastimes by the physical effort involved, and physical activities can be just as clearly differentiated from sport by the presence or absence of winners and losers. A Sunday morning cycle ride is a simple *activité sportive* until or unless one of the group tries to reach home before the others – in which case it becomes a sport. This distinction is important in that it informs much of the developments in France in the last twenty years or so.

Administration

France was for decades held up in England as one of the illustrative instances of a centralized country. The administration of everything emanated from Paris. We recounted the exemplary anecdote of every French pupil in *quatrième* studying Act Three, Scene One of *Andromaque* on the second Friday of November, between 10 a.m. and 10.55 a.m. We all knew it was not really like that, but took pleasure in the story because it captured something of the rigidity of French administrative systems, to the implied benefit of our more flexible British procedures. Much has changed since the decentralization laws of 1982. The basic structures are still largely in place, but responsibilities and decision-making have been significantly loosened up. Sport and recreational activities have been affected by this as much as other areas of French life.

The French equivalent of the British Department of Education and Science is the *Ministère de l'Education, de la Jeunesse et des Sports*; since 1984, it has had a Secretary of State with specific responsibilities for Youth and Sport, and, in most respects, 'Education' and 'Sport and Leisure' have become separate administrative entities. The Secretary of State for *Jeunesse et Sports* and his Heads of Department (Equipment, Finance, Sports Medicine, Sport for All, for example) liaise closely with regional bodies (both government and individual sports), often through the *Comité National Olympique et Sportif Français*, itself a natural and sensible merger in 1972 of the old *Comité Olympique Français* and the *Comité National des Sports*. One of the effects of the decentralization laws of 1982 and, more specifically, of the 1984 Act has been to establish regional and departmental (in the French sense of 'county') bodies to coordinate the administrative and financial contributions of both central government and local councils (not to mention private enterprise). So the centralized lines of communication have been streamlined, but many executive powers radically devolved, particularly in the areas of finance and the appointment of personnel.[1]

There is government funding for sport and recreational physical activity. This is very largely administered through the *Fonds National pour le Développement du Sport* (FNDS). Originally created in 1976 for the funding of top-level sportsmen and women, its revenue came from the tax levied on all sports events where the public paid to attend. It is an interesting notion that all monies generated solely by sporting occasions should by right be fed back into the system, in that it displays a kind of common sense and justice which one might think are self-evident. The FNDS has been expanded both in the acquisition and the distribution of its revenues. Funds now come from the taxes levied on alcoholic drinks (about £3.5 million allocated for 1990), on the betting on horse-racing through the *Pari Mutuel Urbain* (about £2.3 million), the National Lottery (£30 million) and the new, nationalized football pools known as the *Loto Sportif*. It was hoped that the pools would raise over £50 million, but the figure is in fact much lower than that – nearer £35 million is estimated for the current year. Nevertheless, this represents an important budget to be shared between national and local sporting bodies. Of course, regional and more local clubs receive funds from private enterprise as well, and professional clubs are heavily sponsored, as they are in Britain, but the level and the nature of state involvement in underwriting sport and physical activities reveal a commitment in principle to the wider propagation of the healthier life-style which participation brings. Tangible results of this commitment are not readily available if one's criteria are Olympic medals or European football trophies; but they are if we consider that the 12 million or so paid-up members of sports clubs in 1989 represent a near ten-fold increase since the early 1950s.

Participation; the 'goût du spectacle'; media influences

So which sports do the French play, which physical activities do they practise? When Georges Magnane was writing his eminently readable work in the 1960s, the most popular French sports were football, cycling, boxing and wrestling (p. 51). This was not surprising, given that (a) football has throughout the century been universally the most popular of all sports, and (b) austerity was still a strong memory, and all these sports offered the possibility at least of an escape from poverty. We cannot tell where Magnane obtained his evidence for naming these sports, although other sources (*L'Equipe* and *Miroir des Sports* of the period, for example) bear him out. There is, though, an inherent problem with the word 'popular' in that it does not differentiate between spectating and participating; I suspect that Magnane's observation refers to those sports which most attracted French interest or support. It is highly unlikely, for example, that boxing and wrestling would have had more participants than basketball, handball or rugby. By contrast, we do have figures for 1988 which reveal the numbers of paid-up members of the various sports federations (in France, when you join a rugby club, for instance, you automatically join the national association and become a 'licensed' player). The figures for active involvement in sport or physical activities, therefore, are especially interesting, and more indicative of a nation's commitment to them than those for spectators.

In 1988, there were 1,769,179 footballers, 1,364,902 tennis players, 921,191 skiers, 420,885 judo-men/women, 346,263 basketball players and 223,726 rugby-players – all paid-up members of their respective federations. Horse-riding, sailing and golf all have well over 100,000 'licensed' participants, whilst serious keep-fit gymnastics has just over 300,000 (*REPS*, p. 44). This clearly reflects a number of modern social trends. In the 1950s and 1960s, tennis was an élite activity reserved for the comfortably off. Municipal tennis courts existed, but were poorly maintained and irregularly used. Decent facilities were available only in private clubs, which were prohibitively expensive. The astonishing rise of tennis revealed by these figures certainly underlines the increase in the nationwide standard of living, and the improvement in leisure possibilities which better transport has helped to bring. The same can be said for the near-million skiers. Again, tennis (not to mention football, basketball, rugby, etc.) is one of those sports which has had enormous media coverage since the middle-seventies. Wimbledon, the US Open, the Australian Open, the Davis Cup and, of course, the French Open at Roland Garros all receive massive attention of the sort which we might easily (but wrongly) associate exclusively with the *Tour de France*. The main French news programmes on television frequently carry the lead item from Roland Garros, the latest stage of the *Tour de France*, football's World Cup, or the French rugby Cup Finals (especially Union). Clearly, the combination of such exposure and increased wealth has had an important effect on the aspirations of young people; the rise in the popularity of tennis, therefore, is not so astonishing, after all.

And yet there is more to it than this. Roland Barthes's notion that 'La culture . . . est un contrat passé entre les créateurs et les consommateurs' (*La Chambre Claire*, Paris: Seuil, 1980, p. 51) points to the element of supply and demand in the context of culture, and sport certainly belongs within a nation's culture in the sense that it is part of the 'ensemble des formes acquises de comportement dans les sociétés humaines' (dictionary definition in *Le Petit Robert*). Television programme-planners might well be manipulators of national perceptions or modes of expression ('les techniciens de l'illusion dirigée', as Georges Magnane calls them (p. 33)), and so of certain aspects of a nation's culture, but they are astute readers of situations, too. They know that the French want and expect to be exposed to spectacle and pageant. This brings us to a fascinating aspect of French life which can be qualified as *le goût du spectacle.* Notwithstanding the notion of 'an event' which is attached to, say, the English FA Cup Final, a Test Match at Lord's, or Wimbledon, few nations give themselves over to spectacle in the way that the French do. It is inconceivable, for example, that the BBC news should lead with the latest developments from Lord's or Wembley (though some of us might consider this a matter for regret), and we have nothing which grips the nation's imagination even remotely like the *Tour de France*.

The *Tour de France* represents to most French people much more than a cycle race; it is the pitting of wits and strength against opponents on a machine which properly belonged to a pre-1919 (even pre-1914) age and which was long ago superseded by various forms of motorized transport. There is a national pride involved, and I do not mean that this is expressed only in terms of the winner: in the twenty-one years since 1970, the *Tour de France* has been won by a Frenchman only nine times, and 1985 was the last of those occasions (Bernard Hinault). The Tour, first run in 1903, has a wider significance: in French minds and as represented by the French media, it is an event which celebrates the rich diversity of their country. Of course, interest in the contest itself is keen and genuine, but for the millions who line the routes of each stage and/or follow them on the daily television broadcasts, the *Tour de France* is a unifying, jubilant and ritual spectacle. From the fertile fields of Normandy to the rock-strewn landscape of Provence, from the vineyards of Bordeaux or Burgundy to the factories of the north and east, from the awesome presence of the Pyrénées or the Alps to the sophistication of the capital itself, the French are reminded of the abundance and variety which are their enviable patrimony. All this happens through the medium of a sporting event which is above all a spectacle, a festival of France. As long ago as the mid 1950s, Roland Barthes saw the Tour as even more than this. Well before the attendant possibilities of our television age, the Tour already represented for Barthes a gigantic, modern-day epic being lived out before our very eyes:

Le Tour est un conflit incertain d'essences certaines; la nature, les mœurs, la littérature et les règlements mettent successivement ces essences en rapport les unes avec les autres: comme des atomes, elles se frôlent, s'accrochent, se repoussent, et c'est de ce jeu que naît l'épopée . . .

Je crois que le Tour est le meilleur exemple que nous ayons jamais rencontré d'un mythe total, donc ambigu; le Tour est à la fois un mythe d'expression et un mythe de projection, réaliste et utopique tout en même temps. Le Tour exprime et libère les Français à travers une fable unique où les impostures traditionnelles (psychologie des essences, morale du combat, magisme des éléments et des forces, hiérarchie des surhommes et des domestiques) se mêlent à des formes d'intérêt positif, à l'image utopique, d'un monde qui cherche, obstinément à se réconcilier par le spectacle d'une clarté totale des rapports entre l'homme, les hommes et la Nature. (*Mythologies*, Paris: Seuil, 1957, pp. 118–19)

If, indeed, the *Tour* does this it is because the French can readily find in a sporting spectacle a natural channel for that expression of the national character, for liberation from the chains of daily existence through a heightened and stylized version of mankind's struggle. If Barthes was right (and his piece reads as old-fashioned today only because he invokes the names of Louison Bobet and Charly Gaul, for example, rather than Indurain, Fignon or Lemond), then sport can quite properly be seen as an essential part of a nation's culture, of that implicit contract between consumer and producer which results in the different forms of cultural expression – albeit manipulated forms, in the commercialized world of professional sport, at least.

Sport is, by extension, a celebration of French 'style', the desire and ability to present an event in a manner which is attractive by the incorporation of what can only be called flair. We see it, too, in the means of expression used by French national football, basketball, handball, and (perhaps especially) rugby teams. The English were rightly proud of their Grand Slam rugby union side of 1990–1, but two of the French tries (by Saint-André and Mesnel) in the deciding match will be cherished even by many English spectators much longer than the fact that France was defeated. The French have for years (and especially since the massive influence during his playing days of that immensely gifted full-back Pierre Villepreux) been characterized as fifteen individuals of huge talents who only rarely perform together as a team; in contrast to the English, for example, who perform well as a team with much less talented individuals. But this widely held view seems to beg as many questions as it purports to answer. There have been occasions recently when English rugby players (and more consistently, in the 1970s, the Welsh) have performed with a freedom and flair which we maintain is a characteristic of the French. There have also – sadly, in my view – been times recently when the French have played with the self-imposed limitations commonly associated with the pragmatic English. I think it is superficial and misleading to assume that the French are more gifted, with a greater degree of personal skill, than the other teams in the Five Nations; the perceived difference is less in ability than in the players' conception of what it is they are involved in (even if, as a kind of self-fulfilling prophecy, this necessarily produces the differentiation we were disposed to see initially). At Twickenham in March 1991, for example, both teams were there to win. That was their principal objective, and clearly so, since the winners would take the Grand Slam as well as victory in the match. Yet that objective was pursued in two quite different fashions: the one through a subsumption of individual contributions into a collective effort, the other through an awareness of participation in a great *spectacle*. On that occasion, the collective ethic defeated the celebratory glorification of man's virtuosity, although the latter provided the two most memorable moments of the feast. At the time of writing, the English XV has just defeated the French and the Scots to reach the final of rugby's World Cup. This represents an immense achievement, but even the violence which marred the France–England match in Paris cannot invalidate the comment by one of the French coaches that the game signified the end of romanticism in rugby. We could argue with the terminology, but we know what he means. Professional sport is about winning, not about expressing yourself or demonstrating to spectators that imagination and creativity on the field can illuminate otherwise drab lives. So the purpose of the spectacle is changed from that of a diversion to that of a collective wish-fulfilment, and there is something in the French mentality which instinctively rejects this. When a French rugby team takes the field, the point they want to make is not so much that they are better disciplined or less inclined to make errors than the opposition as that their *spectacle* is more attractive, more creative, more fantastical than the others'.

I use rugby as an example here, but followers of other sports can point to football, table-tennis, skiing or basketball for similar illustrations. A French friend of mine thinks that it has something to do with the Catholic and Protestant traditions of our two countries, although neither of us has researched this. 'Chez nous la présentation est très important en tout, que ce soit à la boucherie, au stade ou à l'église; chez vous, tout est beaucoup plus pragmatique, plus *pratiqué*.' This is not to suggest that what is offered in the butcher's shop, in the stadium or in the church is insubstantial or superficial; it is to suggest that ritual, ceremony and display are important elements in French life, that presentation and content go hand in hand much more naturally than for the English; that, in sports, winning in itself is not enough without style to ornament it. Whether it is in a shop display or a French three-quarter movement, the trappings in a church or Michel Platini 'arranging' the patterns of mid-field play, there is something aesthetically pleasing to the senses which is a necessary accompaniment to the content or purpose.

This is an element which has consistently aroused the suspicions of the reserved and pragmatic English, offering some of our more celebrated writers occasional opportunity for delicious (or misplaced) irony.[2] Perhaps it should not surprise us that the dissimilarities in the way we play should manifest themselves in other aspects of our lives as well.

'Le goût du spectacle' is a phenomenon of French sport which has been nourished and strengthened by the influence of media developments, and by television in particular. As for the press, the French have very few 'national' newspapers compared with Britain; most French readers buy the local regional paper rather than *Le Monde, Le Figaro* or *Libération*, for example. Sports coverage is generally comprehensive in the regional papers, but minimal in the nationals (with the exception of *Libération*, although even here attention is restricted to one feature article and a part column of 'snippets'). Local sports and the less seriously competitive stuff are well reported in the regional newspapers; for the *grands spectacles*, the French read *L'Equipe*, a daily newspaper devoted uniquely to sport. Now in its 46th year of publication, the coverage is very full, from professional football (including results and brief reports from abroad: the edition of 9 September, 1991 carries substantial reports on the rugby matches between England and the Soviet Union – including a photograph – and Scotland and the Barbarians) to water-skiing, polo or cyclo-cross, not to mention pages of reports on the dreaded Formula 1 races. Over a million people buy the Monday copy (results' day); it is a revered national institution, playing a complex role in the 'contrat passé entre les créateurs et les consommateurs'. I suppose *L'Equipe* serves both kinds of clientèle: the participant-enthusiasts and those who are drawn by the *goût du spectacle*. Certainly it actively promotes spectacle, both implicitly by its coverage and explicitly by its underwriting and organization of the *Tour de France* (although, today, other enterprises are involved, both financially and administratively). But it sells, which tells us something about the level of interest in sport, about the willingness and the desire to be involved in or informed about this side of the nation's activities – rather like the fact that, every year, there is a nationwide competition to decide 'la ville la plus sportive de France'. When Brive-la-Gaillarde won the title in 1989, municipal pride was tastefully and professionally reflected in the publication of the town's *Journal Municipal d'Informations* for March 1990. Brive's success was seen in terms of local policies and initiatives effected during the last nine or ten years, precisely matching the period of decentralization by the national government.

Recent trends

There is an interesting trend of the last fifteen years or so which, for participants, seems to be heading in the opposite direction from that of the *goût du spectacle*. According to the figures for *licenciés* given earlier, the 'basic' team games like football, rugby and basketball are all holding their own. There has always been and always will be a steady number of men and women attracted to team ball-games. What is more noticeable is the very significant rise in the participant figures for 'individual' sports or physical activities which are, more often than not, non-competitive. I have already commented on the case of tennis as an example of the democratization of a sport. It is also an example not so much of a move away from team games, but rather of the fact that the greatly increased participation in sport activities as a result of increased wealth and leisure time (in 1982, the government increased the statutory paid holiday period by an extra week) has been in the areas of individual and recreational activities. Tennis is certainly a competitive sport, but only for the few. The vast majority of those 1,364,902 paid-up members of tennis clubs are recreational players. This trend is further illustrated by the figures for skiing (nearly a million), judo and associated disciplines (nearly half a million – an extra 167,000 if we include karate and other martial arts), sailing (over 150,000), golf (135,000), and over 596,000 in non-competitive gymnastics. If we add to these numbers the thousands of people who walk, climb, swim or practise the 'Californian' sports (surfing, hang-gliding, wind-surfing, etc.), then it is clear that the new participants in sport are being attracted to these individual, non-competitive activities of self-expression rather than to traditional team-games. Pursuits which incorporate escape, individualism, contact with nature, danger, and a break with traditions – especially for the young – are the ones which are attracting the new, previously 'non-sporting' adherents to physical activity. In a way, they are at the same time highlighting the individual, spontaneous, imaginative characteristic of French team sport performances which the English have often been quick to qualify as indiscipline.

Joffre Dumazedier sees this movement as due to something more than the active financial support given by government, especially during the 1980s:

Malgré une politique positive menée en faveur des sports depuis 1981, les changements les plus importants des pratiques corporelles viennent non de la politique mais de l'évolution de la société elle-même.[3]

Throughout western Europe, the last 150 years have seen a reduction of nearly 60 per cent in the time spent at work. The principle of paid holidays, first introduced in France just before the last war by the socialist government of the *Front Populaire*, has been extended since then to the point where, now, the French are entitled to a minimum of five weeks paid holiday per year. In addition, the French have generally benefited from increased spending power since, say, the 1950s and 1960s, just like the other countries of the west. One of the results of these developments, according to Dumazedier, is that awareness both of one's own personality and of one's relations with others has been perceptibly sharpened in recent years:

1) D'abord une valorisation de la personne: une partie de ce qui était égoïsme hier se nomme aujourd'hui dignité. Des désirs, des aspirations, des volontés autrefois réprimés tendent à s'exprimer dans les pratiques corporelles plus individualisées, plus psychologisées ou plus libérées, pour la performance ou la sensation comme dans toutes les autres pratiques du loisir. Les ascèses inutiles sont moins acceptées.
2) Une valorisation des relations plus spontanées avec autrui: les systèmes de relation trop hiérarchiques ou trop strictes sont davantage contestés. Les genres de relations quasi militaires sont limités à la stricte nécessité. Ce sont des relations plus spontanées, plus authentiques qui sont valorisées dans tous les clubs et malgré les résistances expertocratiques, bureaucratiques ou gérontocratiques. Les groupes inorganisés d'activités physiques ou autres se multiplient. (p. 33)

When Dumazedier highlights the in-built conservative resistance to this trend, he finds an echo in a reaction to the recent power struggle within the French rugby world. The policies and the personality of Albert Ferrasse, the President of the Rugby Federation, have for some time now provoked much controversy, an unrest or unease which has affected the composition of the French national team on the field. *L'Express* recently noted the 'atmosphère de fin de règne qui empoisonne son entourage. La gérontocratie gangrène notre société. Et le rugby n'y échappe pas' (23 November, 1990, p. 23). This is not to present the view as definitive. It is, nevertheless, illustrative of a mood which resents and rejects the ageing hands at the controls of society. *La vie sportive* is one area where individuals can exert at least some influence, if only by embracing fresh activities and outlooks.

Certainly, increased leisure-time and greater economic freedom have strikingly widened people's horizons, as they have done in Britain, too. I think that the French have another advantage in this context. The sheer size of the country (about twice as big as the United Kingdom, with a population more or less the same) necessarily offers the French space in which they can express themselves; they have available choices not offered to the British, or at least, only on a much reduced scale. Skiing (including the cross-country version) and canoeing are obvious examples of activities which flourish more widely in France than in Britain.

Physical Education in schools and the 'Associations sportives'

This expansion of recreational, largely open-air activities has to be fuelled by something more than economic evolution. Some of the answers lie in the world of education, and especially in Physical Education. After the Second World War, France was in a state of collective shock which is near-impossible for us to comprehend. Not that she had suffered the structural damage which Warsaw had, for example, or London, or the cities of Germany. For France, strictly speaking, the war had been over since the signing of the armistice at Compiègne on 22 June, 1940. Whilst hostilities continued to ravage much of eastern Europe, and the rest of the world, France herself was officially at peace. The convulsion which the French suffered during the war was not so much the bombing of her cities (though I do not wish to trivialize that) as the fact of the Occupation, with its sharply opposed reactions of collaboration or resistance. The stories (and there is no single definitive account) of the Occupation are well documented elsewhere, but for us it is important to grasp that France in 1945 was both delirious with liberation and seriously traumatized by national guilt and recrimination.[4] Rebuilding the infrastructure of the country was the same task facing all European governments in 1945; for the French, rebuilding national morale was something different because the population was so divided against itself.

One of the perceived ways through which morale might be restored was Physical Education in the schools. For example, after the war, the authorities revived the *Associations Sportives* which had fallen by the wayside during the dark days. These associations are a phenomenon which bear some examination, since they have no equivalent in Britain. Owing their origins to the establishment, in 1928, of the *Union Française des Œuvres d'Education Physique*, and to the popular development, during the 1930s, of the *Associations d'Etudiants Universitaires* (which had filtered down to the secondary schools, too), the *Associations Sportives* were revived as an obligatory element of secondary schools and then, though less widely and not obligatorily, of primary schools. They were designed to offer children the opportunity to practise a sport of their choice (there would be a different association for each sport, although nowadays some associations are multi-sport) on Thursdays, when French schools were closed (at the present time the free day is Wednesday, notwithstanding moves in a very few parts of the country towards an 'English' weekend, with school running Monday to Friday). The most interesting principle in their conception was that PE staff would run these 'clubs', with the hours spent on Thursdays counted towards their weekly teaching responsibility. Indeed, in 1950, it was established by government decree that all PE teachers should spend three of their statutory weekly hours working within that school's association. At first, it was only the traditional activities which formed an association: team games, athletics, swimming and traditional gymnastics. In the primary schools, it was largely swimming and gymnastics, or what many of us will now remember as 'PT'. All these activities lent themselves naturally to the spirit of self-discipline and to the cult of *mens sana in corpore sano* as an expression of a separation of these human characteristics rather than an integration of them. Since much of the teaching in schools was in those days of the very regimented variety, and since those same teachers were running the associations, it is hardly surprising that Thursdays represented more of the same. Few girls were involved in the very early days, but the associations soon began to demonstrate that they would be a force in the development of female participation in sport: they were, in fact, the first federations to introduce the notion of paid-up, registered female members of sports clubs.

However, today presents a very different picture, and this difference stems from the changes in society which we have already noted, changes which are both reflected in and result from the new trends in the teaching of Physical Education. For today's associations are wide-ranging, with a particular growth in the individual activities like athletics, gymnastics, tennis, swimming, table-tennis and badminton, not to mention the outdoor pursuits which are naturally especially favoured in the warmer southern regions of the country. In the secondary sector alone, the latest figures (for 1990) show 975,000 pupils *licenciés*, practising forty-one different sports or activities, twenty-seven of which are organized as national championships. This represents 15 per cent of all secondary pupils who are voluntarily spending their Wednesday afternoons (at least) on some sporting or physical activity. Alain Hébrard tells us that, in addition, '28% des élèves font une activité sportive (parfois plusieurs) en dehors de l'école (clubs sportifs)'.[5] In primary schools, 802,855 children are *licenciés*, and 13,528 schools have an *Association Sportive* (*REPS*, pp. 26–7). One of the features of this trend, both in and outside school, has been the increasing number of women and girls who are becoming involved in physical activity, whether members of associations or not. Indeed, the rise in popularity of these non-competitive, individual sports or activities is due almost entirely to the increased participation of women:

plus la pratique se codifie et s'institutionnnalise, moins les femmes y sont présentes. Il y a beaucoup d'hommes parmi les licenciés, y compris chez les plus jeunes. Par example, pour la pratique compétitive, les données sont assez nettes: sur 100 compétiteurs, 75 sont des hommes. Autrement dit il y a 2 à 3 fois moins de femmes pour faire de la compétition, y compris chez les 12–17 ans . . .

Autrement dit, l'exercice physique de loisir ou d'entretien reste plutôt 'une affaire de femmes', alors que la pratique instituée, codifiée, plutôt 'une affaire d'hommes' . . .

Le travail d'entretien physique, c'est-à-dire les activités où l'on prête attention à l'esthétisation du corps, la pratique individuelle, caractérisent plus souvent les pratiques des femmes, alors que le travail physique, sportif, instrumenté, technique, performant et compétitif, voire collectif, caractérise plus fréquemment les pratiques des hommes.[6]

So whereas there has certainly been, as in Britain, a much reduced prejudice against women's football or rugby, for example, these trends pale into insignificance when viewed alongside the move away from competition and team-games which the increased number of participating females illustrates. What started, after the war, as a movement to build the *Associations Sportives* as a means to restoring national morale (and so perceived by the public as largely a male matter) inexorably became something else which has contributed to the functioning of the individual rather than to the collective morale.

The traditional element within the association network still functions smoothly, of course. The British pattern of school fixtures built up over a long period between autonomous institutions operating their own 'circuit' has suffered greatly during the last twenty years, at least in the state sector. By contrast, school fixtures in France flourish, and it is tempting to surmise that this is because the whole structure has been, since 1950, built into the PE teachers' responsibilities, and not left to their voluntary good will, and so an obvious target in times of industrial dispute. Matches between schools, in all team sports and for both sexes, are organized as part of a national competition through the *Associations Sportives*; winners emerge from town groupings, then *Académie*, then regional, and finally national. A pool system in the early stages ensures that weaker school teams are not left with no matches soon after their season has started. Teams which are eliminated then arrange other fixtures through their association on a town or *Académie* basis. This nationwide structure, plus the contractual involvement of PE staff, means that, in state secondary schools, all the children who want to can participate in properly organized fixtures; it is not just the privileged from fee-paying schools who are offered this facility, although French private schools (largely Catholic schools) have their own, similarly run system.

Whether they offer a traditional team game experience or the increasingly popular individual and open-air activities, the *Associations Sportives* are clearly perceived by the authorities nowadays as important in a wider context than just that of physical activity itself. In the text of the law of 16 July, 1984 (*Organisation et Promotion des Activités Physiques et Sportives*), article 2 states:

L'éducation physique et sportive et le sport scolaire et universitaire contribuent à la rénovation du système éducatif, à la lutte contre l'échec scolaire et à la réduction des inégalités sociales et culturelles.

This move is part of a larger concern to reduce the percentage of pupils leaving school before the baccalauréat stage. It is interesting that the government has identified a problem within the education system and is looking to Physical Education as one of the means of rectifying it, just as they did after the war with the problem of national morale. The difference now is that the influence of Physical Education is perceived as something significantly dissimilar to the old regimented activities of the 1950s. The modern, more broadly based *Associations Sportives* are actively encouraged by this law as a principal element in the fight against urban degeneration, unemployment and disaffected youngsters leaving school with few or no qualifications. All secondary schools have an *Association Sportive*, and money is available for the establishment of new ones in primary schools and universities (although many of these institutions already have them). Government funding is not sufficient to allow these associations to function without further sources of income, nevertheless. Pupils pay an average 30 francs subscription (it might be more or less, depending on the nature of the activity), and local private firms do sponsor them on an *ad hoc* basis. Again, financial aid is offered to industry to set up associations at the workplace, a facility which is becoming more and more widespread.

Yet another aspect of physical activity in French schools can be seen in the phenomenon of *classes de neige*. The first of these were set up in 1953, still in the post-war period of recession and rebuilding. They provided the opportunity for children to decamp from their habitual school surroundings for a week in the mountains. 'Academic' lessons in the mornings would be followed by an afternoon's skiing, thus combining in a more intensive way the cerebral and the physical elements which were perceived as separate constituent parts of our existence. Since those early days, those constituent parts have come to be perceived as more closely related to one another, and the facility has developed in a number of different directions, which reflects the more enlightened thinking about the curriculum in recent times: 'Ne dites plus classe de . . . neige: aujourd'hui les enfants partent en classe "de découverte" ' (*Le Monde de l'Education*, Décembre, 1987, p. 55). The principle behind the original *classes de neige* and *classes de mer* has been adopted by teachers of other disciplines to the point where children can now spend a week at a centre working on geographical or scientific projects, for instance. It is an example of the rest of the school embracing the benefits of a scheme pioneered by PE teachers (enhanced social skills, team-work/cooperation, building on lived experiences rather than theory, improved classroom atmosphere on return). *Classes de découverte* or *classes vertes* are a feature of life in both primary and secondary French schools, but do depend on the voluntary commitment of the staff. For the primary sector, there are small subsidies available from the *municipalité* but, for the most part, the parents pay. Notwithstanding this, they are an extremely popular and common characteristic of school life in France.

Physical Education teachers: training, equipment, status

Both implicitly and explicitly, much of this chapter has been concerned with Physical Education, the teachers and the system within which they operate; so it is worth examining in greater detail the training of Physical Education teachers and the place of their subject in the schools. The law of July 1989 ushered in what were intended to be radical changes in the initial training of teachers (although the extent to which these changes will be truly radical remains to be seen). As a result of this law, all recruits to teacher-training will, from September 1991, enter a two-year postgraduate course at the newly established *Instituts Universitaires de Formation des Maitres* (IUFM), which are themselves an amalgamation of the old *Ecoles Normales* (which trained primary teachers) and the regional *Centres de Formation Pédagogique Régionaux* (secondary).[7] For primary teachers, the training in Physical Education will be very similar to that received by English students; that is to say as a module or element of their overall course at the IUFM. Intending secondary teachers will first read a degree course in Physical Education (four years) at one of the *Unités de Formation de Recherche en Sciences et Techniques des Activités Physiques et Sportives* (UFR STAPS), which are faculties of the university, and which subsume since 1984 the old *Unités d'Enseignement et de Recherche en Education Physique et Sportive* (UEREPS). There are at present nineteen of these university departments, with approximately 12,000 students. The UFR STAPS can all carry students up to the level of what is called *2e cycle* (roughly the equivalent of our Master's degree), and a few have been granted the necessary status to be involved in the *3e cycle* and its *agrégation* and *doctorat* work (doctorate level). To be accorded this recognition, the institution has to demonstrate its competence in research and teaching at the highest level, and it is clearly prestigious if the students are able to prepare their *agrégation* there. It is also much to the advantage of the PE teaching body that they can now become *professeurs agrégés* in their subject area, with all the attendant benefits that brings (the better qualified you are in French schools, the better you are paid and for fewer contact hours). The first degree course is rather like a Sports Science degree in this country, with the kind of options we would expect to find available. Throughout their four years Physical Education degree, students also receive introductory modules to the teaching of the subject. These modules are compulsory, but for most students they point the way to what is their first-choice career. On graduating, students who apply for teacher-training are recruited to the IUFM on interview and past record.

The first year of their training here is largely theoretical, the second largely practical, with two teaching practices as crucial hurdles to overcome. The new IUFM aim is to give a thorough professional training to potential secondary as well as to primary teachers (in the past, secondary trainees have received training almost uniquely in the methodology of teaching their own subject). What is peculiarly French about this arrangement is that, at the end of the first year of professional training, all students have to take an examination (a *concours*) before passing into year two. An examination *per se* is not something which we might find strange for people hoping to enter the teaching profession; but this examination is not simply aimed at weeding out those who are unsuitable teacher material. It is a competitive examination where the numbers who will pass are known beforehand, based as they are on the official statistics available from government sources for the number of posts which will be vacant in any given subject. To balance this apparently harsh procedure, it has to be noted that students who are accepted into the second year of training are paid a salary (the lowest point on the teachers' scale) for that final year, during which they are known as *stagiaires*. To give an idea of the fiercely competitive climate of the *concours*, an average of 2,000 Physical Education students per year take the examination for places which have varied in recent years between 125 and 600. These figures are not expected to change dramatically in the near future under the new IUFM system, although it is hoped that the number of available posts will rise to a steady state of nearer 800, in the light of the government's recently announced plans to bring 80 per cent of the school-leaving population to the level of the Baccalauréat. Those Physical Education students who fail the *concours* do not, on the whole, remain long in unemployment. Opportunities exist as *animateurs* or *moniteurs* in sports clubs or in the *Maisons des Jeunes et de la Culture*; some become *maîtres auxiliaires* in schools, in the hope of becoming fully qualified through internal qualification 'in post'.

There is no doubt that the Physical Education teacher in

a secondary school now enjoys a much enhanced reputation compared with that of the 1950s or 1960s. This is partly due to the improved, more widely based teacher-training courses and partly also to the social trends we have noted towards physical activities as a healthy and enjoyable part of life. Perhaps the biggest single factor, nevertheless, in this move to 'respectability' has been the government decision in 1981 to remove Physical Education from the jurisdiction of the *Ministère de la Jeunesse et des Sports* and place it under the *Ministère de l'Education Nationale*. The *Ministère de la Jeunesse et des Sports* is evidently charged with the responsibility for recreational activities as well as organized sports, and has thus always suggested an image of leisure and relaxation rather than one of a serious component of the education process. Indeed, when it was first created by the government of the *Front Populaire* in 1937, the new ministry immediately attracted the nickname *Ministère de la Paresse*, a detraction which always hung, albatross-like, around the necks of PE teachers.

Now, with this latest move, Physical Education is perceived, and can perceive itself, as a mainstream 'subject' along with all the other components of the secondary curriculum. It has always had an important role to play in French schools, but now, symbolically as well as administratively, PE teachers can feel properly integrated with the rest of the staff. In any case, it does seem a logical move in the sense that all pupils taking the Baccalauréat examination have, since the 1950s, been obliged to undergo a Physical Education test as a compulsory part of the package, whichever version of the Bac. they take. Furthermore, and again to the advantage of Physical Education and its teachers, the PE element of the Bac. has, since 1984, been included in the range of principal subjects which determine the first round of marks of candidates. In other words, it is no longer a subject which is only taken into account in the case of candidates who score well in it. Each subject has a coefficient, or weighting, which is used to arrive at the final total mark. PE has a weighting of only 1, compared with 3 to 5 for French (depending on the type of Bac. in question), but this does mean, for all candidates, a figure of 8 per cent of the overall total.[8]

This has given a much higher profile to Physical Education in the *lycées*, encouraging fresh thought on methods and content of PE courses. For the Baccalauréat, the teaching staff have to plan a programme based on the following seven areas: Athletics, Swimming, Gymnastics, Outdoor Pursuits, One-against-one Sports/ Games (tennis, for example), Expressive Dance and Team Games. The examination assesses candidates in one of the first three here (Athletics, Swimming or Gymnastics) as a compulsory element, plus one other (free choice). The final mark is reached through an evaluation structure based on practice (what the candidates can do) and the continuous assessment of pupils' progress during the year by the staff, including their knowledge of basic physiology of movement.

One of the major difficulties which teachers have not yet been able to overcome is that of facilities. It is a curious feature of many French secondary schools that their PE facilities are often worse than those to be found in the average English comprehensive. This is partly due to the 'bulge' period of the 1960s and early 1970s, when many new secondary school buildings were erected. Cost restrictions meant that far too many of these new schools were built without fields or gymnasia. *Le Monde de l'Education* noted in 1980 that:

Depuis 1964, on peut construire un établissement scolaire sans gymnase ni terrain de sport. Les équipements sont municipalisés. Officiellement, c'est pour mieux les utiliser et assurer une liaison avec les associations sportives locales. (Février 1980, p. 11)

In fact, as *Le Monde de l'Education* implicitly suggests, there was more to it than that. The tradition of cooperation with the local *municipalité* was used as a means of cost-cutting which today still has a serious effect on the efficiency of PE teaching. For those schools without their own gymnasium or playing-fields, municipal facilities are usually available; no charge is made to schools for day-time use. In a way, it can be argued that this is sensible use of community facilities. The problem is that it is the wrong way round. Instead of basing the facilities on the school sites, and opening them in the evenings and weekends to the public, school classes are obliged to waste valuable time travelling – time lost which inevitably cuts into that which is available for the lesson. The nominal five hours per week (established in 1945, and re-affirmed by government decree in 1967) given over to Physical Education in the *collèges* (11–15 secondary schools) and the *lycées* (15–18) are rarely met anyway. The reality of the current situation is that, largely, the *collèges* get three hours per week, and the *lycées* two. It has been traditionally argued that, for those who want to, the missing hours can easily be made up in clubs outside school. This specious argument neatly avoids the point that Physical Education has a wider remit than simply that of training people for competitive sport.[9] A shortage of teachers is part of the problem; time spent crossing from one side of the town to another exacerbates it. It seems that the problem has at last been officially acknowledged, since article 40 of the Loi No 84–610, 16 July, 1984, states that:

il est tenu compte de la nécessité d'accompagner toute construction d'un établissement scolaire des équipements nécessaires à la pratique de l'éducation physique et sportive.

It remains to be seen, of course, how soon this will be translated into reality. Authorities do not build new schools simply because the existing ones have no gymnasium or sports field; there is a certain distance between taking account of a need and meeting it. Again, on the question of contact-time in Physical Education, the *Comité National des Programmes* (a curriculum advisory body) has in 1991 officially asked the Ministry to implement three hours per week of PE in the *lycées*: at the time of writing, no reply has yet been received.

PE in the primary schools is a more difficult case again, as it often is in England. Immediate post-war efforts were concentrated on the secondary sector and the primary pupils who received more than half-an-hour per week of Physical Education were rare. In 1969 the government introduced a measure which aimed to allocate a third of primary school time to Physical Education (the famous *tiers temps*). Since the school day amounts to five hours, this clearly means that about eight hours per week should have been devoted to PE. It is well known that this has simply not been the case in practice. More recently, five hours per week has been fixed by the Ministry as the obligatory figure in primary schools: even this has not been realized, and for a number of identifiable reasons. First, primary teachers are *polyvalents* (all-rounders, jacks-of-all-trades), as they are in England. As we have already noted, it is only since 1981 that PE has been brought under the umbrella of the *Ministère de l'Education Nationale*, so the great majority of teachers in post were trained in a system where it would have been a lower priority (unless the teacher/student in question was keen on sport). Again, most primary teachers are women, for whom, traditionally, Physical Education has had little appeal. Finally, appropriate facilities in primary schools are even more scarce than in the secondary sector. What happens in fact is that nearly all children in primary education are taught to swim, and this usually by specifically qualified *moniteurs* employed not by the school but by the *municipalité*. Anything in addition to this is a bonus which depends on the competence and enthusiasm of individual teachers. Primary teachers do, after all, have to respond to a huge range of demands, and PE is often the one which comes bottom of the list. The employment of *moniteurs* is not the unequivocal advantage it might seem: on the one hand, the children do receive expert help in a particular skill (although the *moniteurs* themselves are not trained teachers, and so not guaranteed good communicators), and, on the other hand, the profession itself is undermined by the necessity to employ them in the first place for delivering what is an obligatory part of the school curriculum.

Notwithstanding these reservations, and even if it still has some way to go to meet the aspirations of its teachers, the future for Physical Education in schools looks brighter than it has ever done. The importance of physical activity is now acknowledged; involvement in it is respectable. When Catherine Soullard can write in *Le Monde de l'Education* that:

il en résulte, entre autres bénéfices, pour eux une meilleure maîtrise du langage parlé, puisque ces acquis sont conditionnés par le bon développement de la fonction motrice et de ce qui la commande: le système nerveux . . .
. . . l'activité physique est un excellent moyen de se sentir mieux dans sa peau. Bref, le sport est indispensable à l'épanouissement de l'enfant.
. . . La pratique à l'école a beaucoup évolué ces dernières années. Le 'sport-éducation' a remplacé la 'gymnastique-dressage'. (Octobre 1990, pp. 86–7)

we can feel that, with its professional readership, the message is getting through.

Conclusion

There are so many different facets of a subject like 'sports' that it is difficult accurately to identify readers' expectations; indeed, it is impossible to decide whether or not one should even try. I have not paid much attention in this chapter to professional sport, and this might disappoint some. The recent scandals within professional football in France, for instance, offer fascinating possibilities for study of the less desirable sociological influences of sport – what *L'Express* calls:

l'arrogance de l'argent, la banalisation de la violence et la multiplication des magouilles. (10 January, 1991, p. 20)

Indeed, three first division football clubs were relegated to division two last year on the grounds of financial irregularities, and Bernard Tapie's 'ownership' and direction of Olympique Marseille provide serious sports writers with plenty of copy. I have not examined the way in which the French football league is organized, or her rugby championship (for the record, football has a first division of twenty clubs, a second division divided into two regional groups of eighteen clubs each, a third division with six regional groups of sixteen clubs each, and a fourth division with eight regional groups of fourteen clubs each. Rugby Union operates in pools from the start of the season: the first 'division' made up of four pools, the second 'division' of another four pools, each with ten clubs, provide, in the final weeks, the winning teams to compete in the knock-out stages of the championship). I have passed over the contribution to French social and political life of her black sportsmen and women, as rôle-models for disaffected youngsters in a country where Jean-Marie Le Pen has a sinister level of support. As in Britain, the picture of black athletes doing well offers a vision of potential success to ethnic groups who otherwise have little to encourage them. The French sprint relay quartet which earlier broke the world record and then won the silver medal behind the Americans in Seoul is perhaps the best known example.

As with any aspect of national life, it is impossible to be definitive, to give specific truths. France is a developed, western European country: by definition, this means that many of the influences and trends to be observed in Britain, or Germany, or Italy, for instance, are familiar here, too. The increased involvement of women in sport and physical activity is not a French phenomenon, any more than is the movement towards more individual, non-competitive activities. The same can be said for the developments in the teaching of Physical Education, and if I have here granted a significant place to physical activities in schools, that is because the schools are the base of the pyramid, the ground where attitudes and practices are nurtured. I have tried in fact to give some indication of the ways in which these trends are peculiarly French, how they fit into the established fabric of French administrative and cultural life. Whereas the movement towards individual physical activities might in one country be principally a result of an increased awareness of the medical benefits, in France it forms part at least of the policies of decentralization in recent years. For it is not just the decentralization of procedures which is in question: it is the decentralization of minds, of spirits, too.

I have not tried to identify sports which are specifically French, because that leads to all kinds of blind alleys which might serve to confuse rather than explain or enlighten. That would be to raise the question of whether sports emerge from the dominant culture or contribute to it. The whole direction of Magnane's book argues persuasively for the latter:

le sport tend, non pas à s'intégrer à une culture dont les portes lui demeurent sévèrement interdites, mais à en créer une nouvelle. (p. 23)

For instance, it is easy to observe that the French 'play' cycling, or *pétanque*, or *pelote*, and not cricket. What is not so easy is to explain why. In fact, I suspect that it is impossible to explain why the French do not play cricket, or why the English do not play *pétanque*, other than on the grounds of pure chance; and I certainly think that it would be much more interesting to examine what characteristics the different nations bring to the playing of games. The argument that cricket would not suit the French national temperament (whatever that might be) seems to me to be very shaky indeed when one considers the way the 'excitable', 'extrovert' and 'impatient' (French characteristics, as we perceive them?) West Indians have come to master the game. The French simply happened to be excited by cycling, for example, because a rich sponsor decided to initiate the *Tour de France* in 1903 and, in so doing, provided them with a spectacle which had seemingly endless potential for development. Cricket, equally simply, did not happen; the fact that it was a thing of the British Empire and not of the francophone countries was also pure chance, although one could argue interestingly, I think, that the French would never accept an activity which eliminated players for lengthy periods of the game. Recent efforts by Belmont and Milne to establish a cricket centre in the Ardèche certainly failed because of unpropitious circumstances: the product and the moment in history did not happily coincide. But it also failed because, by now, cricket is firmly fixed in the French mind as a characteristic of the illogical, devious and ultimately impenetrable English. *Pétanque* occupies a similar position as a convenient signifier in our philosophy, rather like eating snails or garlic. But we should not forget, as Magnane tells us, that 'étymologiquement, illusion (*inlusio*) signifie: entrée dans le jeu' (p. 165). If we were to keep this in mind, rather than the *illusions dirigées* that are fed to us daily, then sport and physical activity would remain one of the most strongly fashioned links between peoples. Fortunately for the French and the British, *pétanque* and cricket are atypical; there are many other games experiences which we share, and so which ought to unite us. Whether or not we will ever reconcile the differing spirits through which these experiences are lived and shared remains the subject of endless debate.

Notes

1. Specific details of administrative structure seem inappropriate here. The interested reader can find a wealth of information in *Revue Education Physique et Sport* (henceforth, *REPS*) (available from 11 ave. du Tremblay, Bois de Vincennes, 75012 Paris), No. 223, pp. 34–5 and 62–3. For this, for many other official documents and for checking the facts in this chapter, I should like to thank Madame Emilienne Cosson, Directrice of the UEFR STAPS, Université de Rennes II. Her interest and support have been invaluable.
2. See, for example, George Eliot, *Middlemarch*:
   the vastness of St. Peter's, the huge bronze canopy, the excited intention in the attitudes and garments of the prophets and evangelists in the mosaic above, and the red drapery which was being hung for Christmas spreading itself everywhere like a disease of the retina. (Boston: Houghton Mifflin, 1956, p. 144).

3. *Pour un sport ouvert sur la vie, actes du IVe colloque international de la Fédération sportive et gymnique du travail*, Sport et Plein Air, 1983, pp. 30–1.
4. See, for example, R. Paxton, *Vichy France* (London: Barrie and Jenkins, 1972); H. Kedward, *Occupied France* (Oxford: Blackwell, 1985); Ted Morgan, *An uncertain hour* (London: Bodley Head, 1990); Pierre Laborie, *L'opinion française sous Vichy* (Paris: Seuil, 1990).
5. *L'éducation physique et sportive – réflexions et perspectives*, Coéditions Revue STAPS et Revue EPS, 1986, p. 54.
6. Catherine Louveau, 'Toutes les femmes, toutes les pratiques?' in Irlinger, Louveau et Metoudi, *Les pratiques sportives des Français* (Paris: INSEP, 1987).
7. For further details on these training institutions, see A. E. Greaves and K. E. Shaw, 'A new look in French teacher education?', in *Cambridge Journal of Education*, Vol. 22, No. 2, June 1992, pp. 201–214.
8. For a clear explanatory diagram of the Baccalauréat examinations, see E. J. Neather, 'A level and Baccalauréat', in *Language Learning Journal*, No. 4, September 1991, p. 10.
9. In any case, for highly talented youngsters in a particular sport, it is possible to be educated in one of the *Sections Sports-Etudes*. There are nearly 150 of these, offering over twenty different sports specialities. Pupils are taught all the normal school curriculum subjects during the morning and then train and/or practise their sport during the afternoon rather like the English School of Soccer Excellence at Lilleshall.

Further reading

Andreff, W., Nys, J.-F. and Bourg, J.-F., *Le sport et la télévision* (Paris: Dalloz, 1987)

Bourg, Jean-François, *Le sport en otage* (Paris: Table Ronde, 1988)

Bressan, Serge, *Le sport et les femmes* (Paris: Table Ronde, 1981)

Collomb, Pierre, editor *Sport et décentralisation* (Paris: Economica, 1988)

Dumazedier, Joffre, *Vers une civilisation du loisir* (Paris: Seuil, 1962)

Gritti, Jules, *Sport à la une* (Paris: Armand Colin, 1975)

Holt, Richard, *Sport and society in Modern France* (London: Macmillan, 1981)

Lassalle, Jean-Yves, *Sport et délinquance* (Aix-en Provence: Presses universitaires d'Aix-Marseille, 1988)

Lavigne, Pierre, *Le sport dans la fonction publique* (Paris: Documentation Française, 1984)

Mazeaud, Pierre, *Sport et liberté* (Paris: Denoël, 1980)

Nicholson, Geoffrey, *The Great Bike Race* (London: Magnum Books, 1978)

Praicheux, Jean and Mathieu, Daniel, *Sports en France* (Paris: Fayard: Reclus, 1987)

Seidler, Edouard, *Sport à la une: 35 ans de journalisme*, (Paris: Callmann-Lévy, 1986)

Sport et changement social, Actes du colloque de la Société Française de Sociologie du Sport, Bordeaux 3-7 avril, 1987, Maison Sciences de l'Homme Aquitaine, 1987

Weber, Eugen, 'Pierre de Coubertin and the introduction of organised sport', in *My France: Politics, Culture, Myth*, Harvard University Press, 1991, pp. 207–25

CHAPTER 7

The media

Alan Pedley

The decline of the Parisian daily press

Born in the late eighteenth century, the daily paper, *le quotidien*, did not become a cheap, popular consumer item in France until the 1870s when total sales topped the million mark for the first time. By 1914 there were 322 titles with a total circulation of 9.5 million. With 244 per thousand inhabitants buying a daily paper, the French had become, jointly with the Americans, the world's leading consumers. By 1985 the situation was very different: a mere eighty two titles with only 178 sales per thousand inhabitants. The French had sunk to 27th position in the world and 18th in Europe.

The situation of the press in France in 1945 appeared relatively healthy, following the inevitable slump in sales during the war period. Many titles had voluntarily ceased publication or had been banned during the German Occupation and those papers which remained consisted mainly of boring propaganda. After the liberation of Paris in August 1944 two government edicts forbad the publication of all papers which had continued to appear under the German Occupation: after June 1940 in the occupied zone and after November 1942 in the Vichy zone. Although the number of daily titles had changed little if we compare the 1939 figure with the 1946 figure, the Second World War represents a remarkable watershed in the history of the French press. Only twenty-eight of the 206 dailies appearing in 1939 reappeared in 1946, notably *Le Figaro* and *L'Humanité*. In terms of diversity and multiplicity of titles, as well as circulation figures, the French daily press had reached an apogee which has never been seen since. A total circulation figure of 15,124,000 (France's population was 41 million), with a purchasing rate of 370 per thousand inhabitants. By 1988 values the average price of a daily paper was 1.32 francs, which would reach a post-war low of 1.10 francs in 1947.

These circulation figures can be explained partly by the very small size of the dailies (two to four pages) due to paper shortages, and partly to post-war euphoria. Inspired by the high-minded ideals of the Resistance, daily papers mushroomed all over France. 'The press' proclaimed La Fédération de la Presse in 1945 'is not an instrument of profit. It is free when it depends not on the power of government or of money, but only on the conscience of the journalists and the readers.'[1]

Since then, the French daily press has experienced a continuous decline in both the number of titles and in the total circulation figures. In 1988, when France's population had risen to almost 56 million, there were only eight dailies published in Paris (plus three specializing in sport or economic affairs) and sixty-five in the provinces, giving a total circulation of ten million. It must, however, be remembered that today's papers contain considerably more pages than those of 1946.

Undeniably the French have been buying and reading fewer and fewer daily papers over the past four decades. With the exception of the period 1962–73, when total circulation showed a number of annual increases, reaching a new post-war peak of 13 million in 1968, the decline has been constant.

A significant feature of this evolution, however, has been the marked difference in the rate of decline in Paris-based dailies and that of the provincial dailies. Already in 1939 the provincial papers had equalled for the first time the circulation of the Parisian papers (5.5 million each). The twenty-eight Paris-based dailies of 1946 had dwindled to eleven in 1988; their circulation had dropped from 5.9 million to 2.9 million. The 175 provincial dailies had admittedly dropped to sixty-five but their circulation had only fallen from 9.1 million to 7.1 million. In terms of circulation then, the daily provincial press in France is far more important than the Paris-based daily press: 70.86 per cent compared with 29.14 per cent. Indeed France's most popular daily is the Rennes-based *Ouest-France* which averaged 765,195 daily sales in 1988.

How can we explain this imbalance, so different from the situation in Britain where the dominance of London-based papers is almost unchallenged in most regions? There are no clear-cut reasons but two contributory factors may be mentioned. During the war years the provinces, particularly in the Vichy zone, were cut off from Paris papers which were in any case, like the capital's radio station, instruments of Nazi propaganda ('*Radio Paris ment, Radio Paris est allemand*' ran the Free French radio jingle), and would have been regarded by any potential readers with suspicion. Secondly, the traditional freedom of expression introduced in France by the Declaration of the Rights of Man in 1789 (article XI) and enshrined, as far as the press was concerned, by the Law of 29 July, 1881, has perhaps acted as a spur to the provinces to defy in one domain at least, the centralized, Paris-based, administrative and political systems.

To what extent can television be blamed?

While the decline of the French daily is not unique – the Italian daily press for example has undergone a comparable decline – reductions in circulation in many other countries enjoying a similar standard of living have been less marked (e.g., Britain, United States and Australia) and in some countries (notably Holland, Denmark, Norway, Sweden and Japan) sales have been rising over the past thirty years. In Japan 562 out of every thousand inhabitants were buying a daily paper in 1984 as opposed to only 396 in 1960. The decline in France cannot therefore be wholly attributed to the spread of television.

Competition from television, both as a source of information and entertainment, and as an increasingly important rival vendor of valuable advertising space, must nevertheless be recognized as an important factor. Over the past three decades, year by year, the press in France has been receiving a smaller percentage of the total national expenditure on advertising. The main beneficiary of course has been television. The situation for daily papers is being further exacerbated by the fact that advertisers are spending more and more on weekly magazines with their colour and glossy paper and less and less on newspapers. Minitel, the home and office terminal network of the French telecommunications system with its electronic keyboard and instant visual display of up-to-date information, is beginning to eat into the small ads market dominated until recently by the press. From 10,000 terminals in 1982, the Minitel network has grown to 5.8 million (1991). Free local papers and magazines are also depriving the press of some of its small ads income.

In spite of competition from television, Minitel and free papers, the French press relies increasingly on its advertising revenue: 36.8 per cent of its income came from advertising in 1975 and 43.2 per cent in 1988. However, compared with the press in Germany, Belgium, Switzerland and Britain, the French press claims a substantially smaller proportion of national expenditure on advertising.

Economic difficulties caused by falling income from sales and underachievement in advertising revenue are major factors in the dailies' decline. Much needed expensive investment in modernization has created further financial pressure. Increases in the price of daily papers have probably been counter-productive. The average price (4.50 francs in 1988, 5 francs in 1991) of a daily paper not only compares unfavourably with British prices, but also represents a four-fold increase, in real terms, compared with the price in 1947.

The increased pace and pressures of daily life, particularly in cities, have obviously diminished reading time. A daily newspaper offers hours of potential reading material and demands the effort involved in seeking and selecting items of interest, whilst radio and television offer ready made news digests requiring no page-turning, no searching and no selecting. Even people who are not averse to a little reading can switch over, without even leaving their armchairs, to instant teletext news, travel or weather updates supplied by Antiope,[2] providing they are equipped with an appropriate *télécommande* (remote control handset). Fast news for consumers of fast food. It must be remembered that urbanization has been more rapid and more marked in France than any other European country during the second half of the twentieth century. Moreover it is interesting to note that if readership is analysed on a regional basis, the more urbanized the region, the lower the percentage of readers of daily newspapers. The Paris region with a total readership figure of 31.41 per cent (i.e., percentage of homes receiving a daily newspaper) came bottom of the list out of twenty-one regions in 1986, while predominantly rural regions like Brittany (62.84 per cent) and Limousin (57.95 per cent) were at the top of the list (Pierre Albert, *La Presse française* (Paris: La Documentation Française, 1990), p. 96).

Would more Parisians buy papers, if there were more popular titles? With the advent of radio, and especially television, the French public have become increasingly accustomed to receiving their news in a more familiar style of language. Oral presentation obviously tends to be less formal than the printed word and the gap between these two registers is even wider in French than in English. French journalists however, even those writing for less serious papers, like to flaunt their literary prowess, which perhaps explains to some extent the relative lack of really popular, easy-to-read, downmarket papers which thrive in Britain.

Finance, production and distribution

Despite the suspicion with which France's most illustrious political leader since the war, President de Gaulle, regarded the press (*'tout ce qui grouille, grenouille et gribouille'*), the state has traditionally been a generous financial benefactor in its dealings with this ailing sector of the economy which has nevertheless sometimes been called the Fourth Estate (after the executive, legislative, and judiciary powers). In 1989 state aid accounted for 12 per cent of the turnover of the French press. Among western nations France is the most generous contributor, after Italy, to the revenue of its national press.

Financial aid is both direct and indirect. The preferential telephone, fax and rail charges enjoyed by the press are financed by state subsidies to the PTT (Postes, Télégraphes et Téléphones) and the SNCF (Société nationale des chemins de fer français). There are government grants to encourage sales abroad and to help daily papers with lower revenues from advertising. Indirectly the press benefits from the state's compensatory payment to the PTT to cover losses due to reduced postal rates for newspapers and magazines, from reduced VAT rates, from *taxe professionnelle* (a local tax on non-salaried professional people, introduced in 1975) exemption and from tax concessions granted to encourage investment. Leading papers such as *Le Monde* and *Le Figaro* do not receive any direct state aid; a paper with a smaller circulation, *L'Humanité*, received 1.9 per cent of its income from the state in 1988.

As far as expenditure is concerned, staff salaries are invariably the major item: in 1988 *Le Monde* paid out 29.53 per cent of its annual expenditure to its employees; other significant items were distribution costs 23.95 per cent, social security contributions 11.94 per cent, paper 11.5 per cent and overheads 10.33 per cent (Albert, p. 75).

With regard to the production of newspapers, paper is obviously the major expense once the equipment and machinery required for composition and printing have been bought and installed. Over the past forty-five years there have been in France, as in other countries, considerable advances in production methods. Photogravure and offset have gradually replaced letterpress techniques at the printing stage; photocomposition, computerized programming and electronic page-making have replaced linotype at the composition stage. Fax, first used in France in 1975, has allowed instant long-distance duplication of fully composed newspaper pages. These innovations, which have brought increased automation, efficiency and quality, have also brought redundancies and industrial strife, to which reference will be made later in this chapter when the fortunes of individual newspapers will be chronicled.

In addition to printworkers, employees of the newspaper distributors have also lately taken industrial action in protest against modernization. In the Paris region, unlike in the provinces where dailies are usually responsible for distributing their own copies, most newspapers resort to middlemen known as *messageries de presse*. Five of the eight cooperatives involved are controlled by the NMPP (Nouvelles messageries de la presse parisienne) and three by the Transport presse.

Apart from in Alsace, where home deliveries are common, most daily papers are sold direct to the customers in newsagents and kiosks on the streets. The virtual non-existence of the French paperboy (or girl) no doubt adversely affects paper sales, if we compare France with Britain. Of the total daily production in

1986, 59.6 per cent of the copies were sold to the public in shops and kiosks; 16.7 per cent were sold to readers who paid by subscription and received their copies either by post or by special delivery; 3.3 per cent were free or complimentary; 20.5 per cent were unsold (Albert, p. 66).

This high proportion of unsold copies takes us back to economic and financial matters. The industry of the press in France had a total turnover of 47.87 thousand million francs in 1988 and employed 51,343 people, nearly half of whom were journalists (Guillauma, p. 108). While often enjoying a privileged status, in that it fulfils social, political, religious and cultural needs, the French press, like other industries, has been ultimately subject to the laws of the market economy, depending on the consumers who buy its products, on advertisers who pay for the publicity it offers and on financiers who invest their money in it.

In 1988 there were fourteen press (or in many cases multimedia) conglomerates whose annual turnovers exceeded a thousand million francs. By far the most important were the Hachette and Hersant groups. Among the publications controlled by Hachette (originally publishers only, founded in 1829) are the provincial dailies *Le Provençal* and *Les Dernières Nouvelles d'Alsace*, a 36.4 per cent stake in the Paris daily *Le Parisien*, the Sunday papers *Le Journal du Dimanche* and *France-Dimanche* and the weeklies *Télé 7 Jours, Elle, Ici Paris* and *Le Journal de Mickey*. Robert Hersant's publishing activities date back only to 1950, but the expansion in his activities in the field of newspaper publishing since those modest beginnings (as founder of *Auto-Journal*) has been spectacular. His group controls *Le Figaro* and its supplements, *France-Soir* and 22 per cent of the total circulation of provincial dailies.

Hersant has been at the centre of considerable controversy over the issue of concentration of newspaper ownership. Not only has the number of French daily newspaper titles diminished since the war (203 in 1946, 76 in 1988), but there has also been a significant reduction in the number of groups controlling these remaining titles. The Law of 26 August, 1944 had protected pluralism but the dramatic takeovers by the Hersant group in the seventies giving it control of almost 25 per cent of the French dailies provoked fears, particularly on the left, of a possible monopoly of newspaper ownership by a small band of increasingly powerful press groups. Following the Laws of 1 August and 27 November, 1986, no single press group can control more than 30 per cent of the total circulation of daily newspapers in France.

Before we examine individually the principal daily and weekly publications of the French press, mention should be made of an important aspect of news-gathering concerning all these titles, namely the press agencies. There are about 100 such agencies operating in France, some of which are highly specialized (e.g., suppliers of photographs, comic strips, serials, information on science, medicine, the economy, the stock market, etc). All the international agencies such as Reuters, Associated Press and Tass are of course represented in France, but the indispensable and most reliable source of information as far as French papers are concerned is the Agence France-Presse. Created in 1945, but successor to the oldest agency in the world, the Agence Havas, which was founded in 1832, this agency is represented in 129 countries and has twenty-six offices in France in addition to its headquarters in Paris. It employs 950 journalists and 150 photographers, half of whom are based abroad. Its independence and impartiality are guaranteed by a law passed in 1957. Its national and international importance as a gatherer and disseminator of information gives it a key role in the domain of the French media.

The Paris dailies

Le Figaro is one of the few French dailies which can boast of a pre-Second World War history. Founded in 1854, daily from 1866, it voluntarily ceased publication in November 1942 when the Germans occupied the Vichy zone. (Following the fall of Paris in June 1940 it had continued to publish first in Tours, then in Clermont-Ferrand and finally in Lyon.) Allowed to resume publication after the liberation of Paris, this serious, conservative paper went from strength to strength under the guidance of its highly respected editor Pierre Brisson, benefitting from the disappearance of all its right-wing rivals in 1944. Its daily sales reached a peak of 439,000 in 1969. Today it continues to flourish, having survived a number of crises, such as Brisson's death in 1964, and a further tragedy in 1975 when its proprietor Jean Prouvost sold it to Robert Hersant, provoking the resignation of fifty journalists. Under its current editor Franz-Olivier Giesbert, opposition to the Socialist regime has been toned down and circulation figures have steadied (428,736 in 1989). Sub-titling itself *'le premier quotidien national français'* (more or less true in terms of circulation), *Le Figaro*, printed in the larger format, is usually the weightiest of the French dailies, the number of its pages depending on whether it includes one or more of its supplements, e.g., *'économie'* or *'littéraire'*. Much of the financial stability of the paper is due to its successful, separately sold supplements: *Le Figaro Magazine* (created in 1978, 665,000 copies in 1988), *Madame Figaro* (originally monthly when it was created in 1983, now weekly, 650,000 copies in 1988) and *TV-Magazine* (weekly, 4 million in 1988).

In terms of sales strictly in France the more popular (but also right-wing) tabloid *Le Parisien* has in fact recently overtaken *Le Figaro*. Founded in 1944 as *Le Parisien libéré*, this paper reached a peak of 785,000 sales per day in 1975 before being hit by an industrial dispute which lasted for two and a half years and which eventually halved its sales. The decision of the proprietor, Emilien Amaury, to modernize production methods and alter the working conditions of his printworkers provoked an all-out strike. When the paper eventually reappeared, in offset, it was boycotted by the distributors, the NMPP. This dispute in turn severely disrupted sales of the other Paris dailies. Over the past ten years, however, *Le Parisien* ('*libéré*' was dropped in 1986) sales have been progressing continuously (405,000 in 1989). Although undoubtedly popular in its style, this paper, with its coloured outer pages, strikes a good balance between information and entertainment. Since 1960 it has produced separate editions for the different areas of the Paris region.

France's most prestigious daily paper is *Le Monde* which averaged 381,558 sales in 1989. The fact that 17.09 per cent of its sales were abroad in 1988 (compared with 3.68 per cent for *Le Figaro* and 0.22 per cent for *Le Parisien*) speaks for itself. *Le Monde* is a publication with an international reputation for reliable and comprehensive news coverage and intelligent analytical comment. Founded by Hubert Beuve-Méry (who remained editor until 1969) in December 1944, it aimed to fill the role occupied during the Third Republic by *Le Temps* (1861–1942). *Le Monde*, which appears later in the day than the morning papers, is an austere (it contains few photographs), centre-left quality tabloid. It specializes in in-depth articles and is particularly strong in its coverage of foreign news. Its progress has been slow but sure: 110,000 copies sold daily in 1946, 200,000 in 1957, 350,000 in 1968 and 445,00 in 1980 its peak year. Since 1968 the staff (especially the editorial staff) have owned a considerable number of the newspaper's shares (49 per cent in 1968). Following the retirement of Jacques Fauvet (Beuve-Méry's successor) in 1982, there were financial problems which began to be solved by André Fontaine's rescue package which involved salary reductions, the sale of the paper's premises in the Rue des Italiens and the raising of more capital by increasing the number of outside shareholders. With its new modern printing works at Ivry, its computerized newsroom and new offices in the Rue Falguière, *Le Monde* is recovering well in spite of a recent leadership crisis (editors are elected by the journalists and the battle to find a successor to André Fontaine proved to be painfully divisive). Like *Le Figaro*, *Le Monde* publishes a number of successful magazines (*Dossiers et documents*, and the monthlies *Le Monde Diplomatique*, *Le Monde de l'Education* and *Le Monde des Philatélistes*). There are also *Sélections hebdomadaires* sold abroad both in French and English.

Last of Paris's big four in terms of circulation comes *France-Soir* (301,716 copies in 1988) which in spite of its name is now a morning paper. For many years France's leading daily, it was selling 1.4 million copies a day during 1956–8. Founded in 1944, this popular paper flourished under the editorship of Pierre Lazareff but had already started to decline even before his death in 1972. In spite of its colourful outer pages, this paper (not a tabloid), less sensational and scoop-orientated than in its heyday, fairly apolitical although slightly more right-wing than left-wing, runs at a loss and would appear to have a rather insecure future.

As *France-Soir* goes down, *Libération* goes up. Founded as recently as 1973 as a left-wing protest daily, this paper (a tabloid) only really started to flourish with the appointment as editor of Serge July in 1981. It became less left-wing and ended its boycott of advertising. It has become a quality paper respected for its serious investigative approach. Although its circulation figures are modest (180,045 in 1989), they continue to improve.

Only two other Paris papers have circulations of over 100,000: *L'Humanité* and *La Croix*. *L'Humanité* (109,313 in 1988), the organ of the Communist party, was founded in 1904 by Jean Jaurès. Despite efforts to modernize its format – it became a tabloid in 1985 – its sales have been in constant decline ever since reaching its peak of 400,000 in 1946. *La Croix* (104,291 in 1989) is a Catholic evening paper founded in 1883, 88 per cent of whose readers pay by subscription. Sales have been in slow decline since 1971.

Le Quotidien de Paris, founded in 1974, is another loss-making daily (30,000 copies in 1988). As an anti-Socialist paper in the early eighties, it reached its peak in 1982 with 70,000 copies. Today it is a rather slim, quality tabloid. The other Paris dailies specialize in either sport or economic affairs. *L'Equipe*, which organizes the Tour de France cycle race, was founded in 1944 and averaged 267,876 sales in 1989. *Paris Turf* sold 126,029 copies daily in 1989. *Les Echos*, founded in 1908, with 103,931 daily sales in 1989 and *La Tribune de l'Expansion* (57,112), while trailing far behind their British counterpart *The Financial Times* (287,265 in 1990), have been recently progressing steadily.

Before we leave the Parisian daily scene, mention must be made of the three most important casualties since 1945. Significantly, all three of these victims of financial crises and competition from television were popular papers: *Paris-Presse* (1970), *Paris-Jour* (1972) and *L'Aurore*, which, having been taken over by *Le Figaro* in the late seventies, ceased to appear as a separate paper in 1980.

The provincial press and national weeklies

The limited nature of this survey does not allow a detailed description of the provincial dailies in France. Suffice it to say that in 1989 there were nineteen regional dailies with sales averaging over 100,000 including *Ouest-France* (produced in Rennes) which outsells all the Paris dailies with an average total of 786,525 in 1989. Like most other provincial dailies *Ouest-France* issues a large number of local editions (forty). Founded in 1944, it is a colourful, middlebrow paper, produced by ultra-modern techniques, costing significantly less than its Parisian rivals. Ten other provincial dailies have circulation figures of over 200,000, namely (in order of importance) *La Voix du Nord* (Lille), *Sud-Ouest* (Bordeaux), *Le Progrès* (Lyon), *Le Dauphiné libéré* (Grenoble), *La Nouvelle République du Centre-Ouest* (Tours), *Nice Matin*, *La Montagne* (Clermont-Ferrand), *L'Est républicain* (Nancy), *La Dépêche du Midi* (Toulouse) and *Dernières Nouvelles d'Alsace* (Strasbourg).

The somewhat depressing overall situation of the national daily press in France is not echoed by the performance of periodicals. Many weeklies (*hebdomadaires*) are thriving, especially those covering television and women's interests, hence the success of weeklies such as *Télé 7 Jours* (over three million copies), *Femme Actuelle* (two million), *Télé Star* (1.7 million), *Télé Poche* (1.7 million), *Télé Z* (1.1 million) and *Télé Loisirs* (1.1 million). Four monthly (*mensuels*) publications also top the million mark: *Prima*, *Bonheur*, *Modes et Travaux* and *Notre Temps*.

As far as weeklies covering current affairs are concerned, there are first of all the so-called news magazines: on the right of the political spectrum, *L'Express*, founded in 1953, which sold 579,858 per week in 1989 and *Le Point* (1972; 316,268); on the left, *Le Nouvel Observateur* (1950; 403,328) and *L'Evénement du Jeudi* (1984; 179,726). These four magazines are all modelled on the American publication *Time* and in contrast to most national dailies in France their sales have been progressing steadily over the past few years. *L'Evénement du Jeudi*'s rapid success is due in large measure to its dynamic editor Jean-François Kahn. Of the other weeklies covering current events, the best known is *Paris-Match* (founded in 1949), which specializes in photographic reportage, often of a sensational nature. From its peak of 1.5 million sales a week in 1961, it has slipped to 875,392 in 1989: an obvious victim of competition from television. *VSD (Vendredi-Samedi-Dimanche)*, founded in 1977, is also in decline after a promising start (266,019 copies per week in 1988).

Finally mention must be made of the famous satirical weekly, *Le Canard enchaîné*: founded in 1916, this paper, thanks to its fearless investigative approach in the field of politics, has been a thorn in the flesh of many public figures and governments. It sold 423,100 copies in 1988, and it is the only French newspaper to refuse advertisements.

The fairly healthy weekly press in France compensates to some extent for the virtual non-existence of Sunday newspapers. *Le Journal du Dimanche* with 350,734 copies in 1988, is the only Paris Sunday apart from the Sunday edition of *L'Humanité* and the sensation paper *France-Dimanche* (928,603 in 1988).

Radio

By 1945 radio in France had attained a very impressive level of popularity, complementing the equally popular daily newspaper of the day. Its media role had been greatly enhanced by the events of the previous six years throughout which virtually every French family had at times been huddled around its wireless set to receive instant news of declarations of war, capitulations, appeals to continue the war, allied landings and victories. Never had the voice, whether it be that of General de Gaulle or Maurice Chevalier, enjoyed such prestige. The French, like all other Europeans of the time, were a nation of listeners. Television, regarded as a gimmick, was still in its infancy; the experimental broadcasts which had started in 1937 had been suspended during the war and would not resume until 1946. Even future audio rivals such as tape recordings and LP discs had yet to break on to the scene.

Both radio and television broadcasting were at the time state monopolies and the government decree of 8 November, 1945 had created RDF, Radiodiffusion française, which became RTF, Radiodiffusion–Télévision Française, in 1952. Given industrial and commercial status in 1959, it acquired a new legal status, along with a new name in 1964, ORTF, Office de Radiodiffusion-Télévision Française.

The sixties brought an enormous boost, if not a revolution, in listening habits: the transistor radio. General de Gaulle, now President of the new Fifth Republic, had launched his career as a world leader thanks to radio, on 18 June, 1940. On three occasions during his presidency his prompt and direct appeal through radio to the French people, many of whom would have been listening to their transistors in the street or in the barracks, helped to save his regime: on 29 January, 1960 during the Week of the Barricades in Algiers, on 23 April, 1961 during the Generals' Putsch in Algeria and on 30 May, 1968 during the Events of May. For de Gaulle, who was deeply suspicious of the press, radio and television were legitimate instruments of power and state authority.

These instruments of power, along with the power itself, tottered of course during the extraordinary events of May 1968. TV and radio journalists who had rocked the boat during this storm were rooted out in the ensuing witch-hunts and by the time Pompidou had succeeded de Gaulle calm had been restored. As President Pompidou said unashamedly in a press conference, 'Like it or not . . . the television journalist is no ordinary journalist; he has extra responsibilities. French television is thought of as the voice of France, at home and abroad.'

The monolithic nature of the French state radio and television system began to look vulnerable during the liberal presidency of Giscard d'Estaing. One of his first reforms in 1974 broke up ORTF into seven independent organizations, one of which was Radio France. The final blow to the state monopoly was struck, paradoxically, by the Socialist government in 1982. The Law of 29 July, 1982 boldly proclaims that 'audio-visual communication is free.' A few months before, on 9 November, 1981, a law had already been passed authorizing the setting up of private local radio stations, under the supervision of the Haute Autorité, the newly created overseeing audio-visual authority. At first these local stations could not broadcast advertisements but the government finally removed this prohibition on 1 August, 1984. Radio France currently runs five national stations, two Paris stations and forty-seven local stations in the provinces. According to a recent survey these fifty-four stations command an average audience of 22.8 per cent of the total national radio audience.

France Inter, created in 1947, which broadcasts on long wave and FM, is France's second most popular radio station with an estimated audience share of 13.6 per cent and Radio France's flagship. It offers a very wide range of programmes twenty-four hours a day but is, on the whole, fairly middlebrow. France Info, created in 1987, broadcasts (FM only) non-stop news and information, except between 1 a.m. and 7 a.m. when music fills the gaps between news flashes at half-hour intervals. France Culture (FM), which lives up to its name, also broadcasts twenty-four hours a day, although during the night programmes are repeats. France Musique (FM) also broadcasts twenty-four hours a day and tends to include rather more speech – admittedly relating to music (serious) – than the name of the station would lead us to expect. Radio Bleue, created in 1980 (medium wave), is aimed at the over fifties and only broadcasts from 7 a.m. to 7 p.m. The two Paris stations are FIP (France Inter Paris) which broadcasts (FM) non-stop music (popular) and travel news and Sorbonne Radio France which broadcasts lectures on medium wave, thirty hours a week during term time. Since 1 July, 1989 listeners in Europe (including Britain) and North Africa have been able to receive a daily package of live programmes, VICTOR, twenty-four hours a day in FM stereo, made up of a selection of items from all the Radio France national stations, through the D2 Mac transmission system of the TDF 1 satellite. RFI, Radio France internationale, France's world service, broadcasts in thirteen languages on short wave and also has a channel on the TDF 1 satellite.

Even before the end of the state broadcasting monopoly, two of France's most popular radio stations were outside the state system: RTL and Europe 1. These two stations, along with RMC and Sud-Radio make up what the French call the *radios périphériques*, which have always transmitted their programmes from just outside the national frontiers. These stations have been financed largely by advertising, a source of income not available to the Radio France public service stations. The French government not only tolerated these outside stations but, until quite recently, actually owned a significant proportion of their shares.

RTL, formerly known as Radio Luxembourg, based in the Duchy and founded in 1929, is the oldest and most popular of these *radios périphériques*, claiming in 1989 a 20 per cent share of France's listeners.[3] Its powerful long wave transmitters cover the whole of Belgium, Germany and most of Britain as well as France. RTL did lose some of its audience after the creation of Europe 1 but star presenters such as Patrick Sabatier and Philippe Bouvard have ensured its continued success. Audience participation through phone-in programmes has been one of its strong points. Although transmitting from Luxembourg, RTL's studios are now in Paris.

Europe 1, which transmits from the Sarre in Germany but also has its studios in Paris, was created in 1955. Its programmes (long wave) can be heard in most areas of north-west Europe and its popularity in France (13.4 per cent share in 1989) rivals that of France Inter. In the sixties, under the dynamic direction of Maurice Siégel, Europe 1 introduced French listeners to authentic political debates and gave teenagers the highly successful programme *Salut les Copains*.

RMC, Radio-Monte-Carlo (long wave), was created in 1942 and commanded a 6 per cent share of the national audience in 1989. It is best received in south-east France and its popularity understandably increases appreciably during the summer months. Sud-Radio, set up in 1958 in Andorra, and originally financed totally by the French government, covers the Pyrenees and the south-west. It was privatized in 1987.

The local private radio stations, some of which existed as

pirate stations before they were legalized in 1982, command an impressive 36.7 per cent share of the total listening public. The most popular – and popular is the right word – in order of importance, are NRJ, Nostalgie, Europe 2, Fun, Skyrock and Kiss FM.

Radio has of course been profoundly affected by competition from television from the sixties and especially in the seventies. However, transistors, personal stereos and car radios, along with the proliferation of available programmes and the improvement in sound quality brought about by VHF and stereo broadcasts, have helped to keep listening figures higher than viewing figures at certain times of the day. According to a recent survey, for example, between 7 and 9 a.m. 43.2 per cent of the French listen to some radio compared with only 8.3 per cent viewing some television (CESP, quoted by Cayrol, p. 271). The evening figures are of course very different: from 8 to 10.30 p.m. radio claims only 11 per cent as compared with 76.1 per cent claimed by television.

While television has obviously overtaken radio in France in terms of popularity, it has by no means killed it. Estimates of average consumption of the media are of course difficult to make, but according to some recent surveys, while the average French person only spends twenty minutes a day reading a newspaper (Albert, p. 23), he or she spends 127.6 minutes a day listening to the radio and 190.1 minutes watching television (CESP, quoted in *Proscop Media Data 1989*, (Paris, 1989), p. 290).

Television: from state monopoly to privatization

So television, in spite of its spectacular rise over the past twenty-five years, is not quite the all-consuming monster it is often made out to be. One of the factors accounting for its success must be the increase in leisure time available to the French, if we compare the nineties with the forties and fifties. Today people are living longer, retiring earlier, working fewer hours each week and enjoying longer holidays. In 1981 the Socialist government introduced the thirty-nine hour week, the fifth week of paid holidays and retirement at sixty.

It was not until October 1946 that television transmissions (to the Paris region only), begun in 1937, were resumed after their suspension during the war. The 441 lines per frame pictures were transmitted from the Eiffel Tower. On 26 July, 1948 came the first outside broadcast: the finish of the Tour de France cycle race in Paris. Regular programme schedules did not begin until 25 April, 1950, on 819 lines. From 1950 reception gradually spread to other parts of France. Popular events such as the coronation of Queen

Elizabeth II in 1953 (relayed live to France) encouraged sales, but it was not until the sixties that television sets started to be fairly common household objects in France.

In April 1964 a second channel was opened (on 625 lines) and it was this channel that offered the first colour pictures to the French on 1 October, 1967. The colour system adopted, SECAM, was in fact the invention of a Frenchman, Henri de France. A third channel, FR3 (France Régions Trois) was inaugurated on 31 December, 1972, again on 625 lines and also in colour. As previously mentioned, the national radio and television service, known as ORTF, was split up into seven organizations in 1974 (7 August), while remaining a state monopoly. Apart from Radio France, there were the three existing television channels, TF1, A2 (Antenne 2) and FR3, TDF (Télédiffusion de France) which is responsible for the transmission (by whatever means) of television programmes, the SFP (Société française de production) which makes radio and television programmes and finally INA (Institut National de la Communication Audiovisuelle) which is the archive department of Radio France and the national television channels.

The ending of the state monopoly of radio and television broadcasting brought about by the Law of 29 July, 1982 was accompanied by the creation of an independent overseeing authority known as the Haute Autorité de la Communication Audiovisuelle. This body consisted of nine members, three of whom were chosen by the President of the Republic, three by the President of the National Assembly and three by the President of the Senate. Its main functions were to exercise overall control over the various stations and channels run as a public service, including the responsibility for the appointment of the directors of Radio France and each of the three national television channels (previously in the hands of the Minister of Information), the licensing of the *radios libres privées* and the private television channels yet to be created and, finally, to establish and guarantee a pluralistic policy particularly in the domain of political representation and electioneering. Although the setting up of this authority was a significant step towards an independent broadcasting system in France, criticisms of political bias could still be levelled against the Socialist government of the time as its majority in two of the nominating areas gave it, in theory at least, six out of the nine places.

Another blow against the state monopoly was struck with the launching of the ambitious *plan-câble* on 3 November, 1982. Under the DGT (Direction générale des Télécommunications), the whole of France was to be covered to receive not only telephonic communications, but also television transmissions by cable, thanks to the remarkable potential of fibre optic cable. We will return to the outcome of this plan a little later.

On 4 November, 1984 the first private television channel was launched: Canal Plus. It was also the first television channel (transmitted terrestrially) in the world to send out a scrambled (*crypté*) signal. Viewers have to buy a decoder and pay a monthly subscription. Private television broadcasting was given further encouragement following President Mitterrand's declaration on 4 January in favour of '*l'ouverture de l'espace audiovisuel*'. Controversy surrounded the creation of France's fifth national channel, La Cinq, in February 1986. The leading figure in the consortium which had controlling shares in the company (to whom the broadcasting concession had been granted in November 1985) was Silvio Berlusconi who, on account of his involvement in a distinctly downmarket brand of television in Italy, had become a symbol in the eyes of many French Socialists of the worst kind of commercialism. The last concession granted (January 1986) by the Haute Autorité was the private channel TV6 (later to be known as M6) which was to focus on music. Still under the Socialist regime came the founding of a production company and future channel, la SEPT (Société d'édition de programmes de télévision), which partly in conjunction with FR3, had a dual cultural and European mission.

With the defeat of the Socialists in the legislative elections of March 1986 and the advent of the cohabitation period coupling of left-wing President of the Republic and a right-wing government led by the RPR leader Jacques Chirac, came more upheavals in the audio-visual field. The *Loi Léotard* (named after the Minister of Culture) or the *Loi relative à la liberté de communication*, of 30 September, 1986, introduced a number of reforms. The Haute Autorité was replaced by the CNCL (Commission nationale de la Communication et des Libertés), which consisted of thirteen members appointed for nine years. Two were chosen by the President of the Republic, two by the President of the National Assembly and two by the President of the Senate; one was a member of the Conseil d'Etat and elected by that body, one was a member of the Cour de Cassation (Court of Appeal) and elected by that body, one was a member of the Cour des Comptes (Revenue Court) and one was a member of the Académie française and elected by that body; finally three were qualified personalities coopted by the other ten members. Although the CNCL had more power than its predecessor, it proved to be equally complaisant toward its political creators, i.e., the government.

Secondly, consistent with the new government's general economic and social policies, the oldest and most popular of France's television channels, TF1, was to be privatized. A consortium led by the Bouygues group was granted the controlling interest for a period of ten years by the CNCL in April 1987. Thirdly, the state monopoly of television transmission was abandoned. TDF (Télédiffusion de France) was turned into a company which was to compete with private companies. Finally the *Loi Léotard* introduced a measure designed to protect pluralism: no person can hold more than 25 per cent of the capital of a national television company.

Following the return of a Socialist government in May 1988, the main audio-visual reform has been the replacement of the independent controlling body, the CNCL, by a new body, the CSA (Conseil supérieur de l'Audiovisuel) on 17 January, 1989. The nine members of this body are chosen exactly like their antecedents of the Haute Autorité (1982–6). One third of its members are replaced every two years. The powers and functions of the CSA closely resemble those of the CNCL. It should be noted incidentally that governmental involvement in media affairs is maintained by the Minister of State (Ministre délégué) with special responsibility for communication, and the Minister of Culture.

The rise of the French televiewer

The French today are, of course, like most of their European neighbours, more or less totally equipped to receive all their national television channels both technically speaking and in terms of television set ownership. According to INSEE, 94.3 per cent of French homes possessed at least one television set in January 1989; this compared with 97 per cent of British homes (statistics quoted by Cayrol, pp. 268–70 and p. 353). The development of television from a luxury to a standard domestic consumer item has occurred much later and more rapidly than in Britain. In 1960 there were only 1.9 million television sets in France (7 million in Britain in 1957); in 1965, 6.5 million (12 million in Britain in 1963). The dramatic rise in ownership in France came in the seventies: 9.25 million in 1968, 15.97 million in 1980. The current estimates range from about 19 million (licensed) to 29 million (including unlicensed sets). The French have become major television consumers and viewers: in 1989 25 per cent of French homes had videotape recorders (still lagging behind Britain where the figure was 53 per cent), 29 per cent had more than one television set and 55.4 per cent had remote control facilities. In 1988 the average French person was watching television three hours ten minutes each day (*Proscop*, p. 290). Bearing in mind that this figure was only two and a quarter hours in 1976, one wonders if the French may not catch up with the Americans (four and a half hours in 1988) by the end of the century!

What are the French watching every day during these three hours ten minutes? Audience research in France is carried out by three methods: Audimat (gradually being replaced by the more precise Médiamat), an electronic device plugged into a thousand representative television sets in France; *sondages* (interviewing) carried out either in the street or by telephone; and *panels postaux* which consist of representative viewers' watching diaries. Viewing shares vary significantly according to the time of day, the day of the week, the month of the year and of course the programmes on offer. According to the *Financial Times* (3 February, 1992), during the first half of 1991 the average distribution was as follows: TF1 43.8 per cent, A2 21.4 per cent, FR3 11.4 per cent, Canal Plus 4.5 per cent, La Cinq 10.9 per cent and M6 8 per cent. Following the disappearance of La Cinq in April 1992 TF1's share rose to 50 per cent and M6 to 11 per cent. There are variations of course depending on the time of the day: for example from 7 to 9 a.m. (on weekdays), A2, which has a popular breakfast programme, regularly attracts almost twice as many viewers as TF1. During evening prime time, however, TF1 usually attracts at least three times as many viewers as A2.

The above figures show an alarming imbalance between public and private channel viewing. The British figures (1990) are much more balanced: BBC 1 and 2, 47 per cent; ITV and Channel 4, 53 per cent (Cayrol, p. 359). The two key factors behind this imbalance, particularly between the two traditional rivals TF1 and A2, are financial and role-related. It would seem that in spite of enjoying (since 1 October, 1968) the financial bonus of revenue from advertising (18.9 per cent of its total income in 1990) on top of television licence (*la redevance*: 540 francs for a colour receiver and 300 francs for black and white in 1991) revenue (58.8 per cent of its income) and revenue from sales of programmes and other products and services (22.4 per cent) (Cayrol, p. 282), the public channels (A2, FR3 and more recently La Sept) are underfunded compared with some of their private competitors. The most blatant contrast is provided by the TF1-A2 rivalry: in 1986 these two channels operated on more or less identical annual budgets; in 1991, whilst A2 worked on a three thousand million francs budget, TF1 enjoyed a six thousand million francs budget (Hervé Bourges speaking on France Inter, 14 June, 1991). Economies including staffing cuts, and government subsidies will certainly help to reduce current financial problems, but the long-term prospects of the public channels are certainly threatened by the ever-increasing popularity of TF1.

The question of what role the public service channels should play is also a key issue in the so-called *guerre des chaînes*. To what extent do they have a duty to inform, educate and innovate as well as entertain, and thereby attract larger audiences and increased revenue from advertising that such increased audiences create? Should A2 and FR3 compete with each other or complement each other? If they cooperate to make economies how can they keep their separate identities? Since December 1990 A2 and FR3 are jointly controlled by a single director general, Hervé Bourges. His plans, announced in June 1991, to increase cooperation between the two channels could herald a merger.

Advertising and quotas

Advertising is obviously a key element in French television, whether in the private or the public sector. Public channels such as A2 are limited to twenty minutes of advertisements per day. Private channels can show more but cannot show more than twelve minutes of advertisements in any hour during which the channel is operating. Films on the public channels cannot be interrupted by advertising and on private channels they can only be interrupted once. The cost of advertising time varies according to the projected audience. In 1990 a thirty-second *spot publicitaire* could cost as little as 5,000 francs at 11 a.m. on A2 on a Monday morning, to as much as 470,000 francs at 9.15 on a Sunday evening on TF1. On 29 May, 1991 a thirty-second commercial is reported to have cost 800,000 francs if shown on TF1 during the half-time interval of the European Cup Final between Marseille and Red Star Belgrade for which the estimated audience in France was 19.3 million.

Since advertising was allowed on public channels (1968) and since the privatization of TF1 (1987), advertisers have been investing increasingly in television and less in other areas of the media. The following figures which give the proportion of advertising expenditure through the various media in 1987 and the projections for 1991 speak for themselves: cinema 1.8 per cent→1.6 per cent, radio 9.6 per cent→8 per cent, hoardings and posters, 14 per cent→11.9 per cent, press 47.7 per cent→43.5 per cent, television 26.9 per cent→35 per cent (J. Mousseau and C. Brochand, *Le PAF*, Paris: Retz, 1987, p. 109). The press still claims a larger share than television but the gap is narrowing.

Restrictions regarding television programming, to which reference was made above, do not only involve advertising of course (and mention could also have been made of the ban on the advertising of tobacco and alcohol). The other major restriction concerns the screening of films and especially non-French films. In the course of a year at least 50 per cent of the films shown must have an original French dialogue, and 60 per cent must be of

EC origin. This does not mean that 50 per cent will have a foreign language (notably English) dialogue because virtually all imported films and dramas are dubbed into French. Apart from attempting to protect the French viewing public from an excess of American culture and to encourage French productions, the CSA restrictions are aiming to protect the cinema industry as a whole. Each television channel has to comply with regulations relating to the number of films shown each year, to the times at which they are shown and to the minimum delay required following their release (normally three years, apart from Canal Plus, which specializes in recent films, five or six a day, only viewable to subscribers of course).

From TFI to culture

What can French viewers watch on a non-specialist channel such as TFI? An analysis of programmes shown during 1988 divides them into seven categories. *Fiction, films* and *séries* led the way with a 29.5 per cent share of the total programmes; *magazines* and *documentaires* came second with 17.6 per cent; *variétés*, which presumably included game shows (such as *La Roue de la Fortune*) which are as popular in France as in Britain, 15 per cent; *information*, 14.2 per cent; *jeunesse* (children's programmes), 10 per cent; *sports*, 5.7 per cent; *divers et publicité*, 8 per cent (Cayrol, p. 288).

Fiction of course fills a vital role. After the fatigue and tensions of the working day, including the increasingly stressful experience of travelling by car or public transport, the French understandably turn in the evening to the escapist world of *films, téléfilms, dramatiques* (which could be part of a *série*), *feuilletons* (serials), *dessins animés* (cartoons), and *sit-coms* (recently become a French word as well as a French product, e.g., *Maguy* and *Tel père, tel fils*). Many of these programmes are of anglo-saxon origin, e.g., *Les Voisins, Dallas* and *Chapeau melon et bottes de cuir* (*The Avengers*). Magazine and documentary programmes have the virtue of being much cheaper to make than *fiction* or *variétés*; the trail-blazer in this field was the prestigious *Cinq colonnes à la une* (1959–68) produced by two of the famous names in the history of French television, Pierre Desgraupes and Pierre Lazareff.

Variétés have always been immensely popular with French viewers. Although occupying half the annual air time devoted to *fiction, variétés* account for approximately the same annual expenditure; stars are expensive. Probably the best-known figure over the years in this field has been Guy Lux whose successes in the seventies and eighties have included *Intervilles, Jeux sans frontières, Le Palmarès de la Chanson* and *Le Schmilblic*.

Talk shows (used in French in spite of opposition from the *Commissariat à la langue française* who prefer *conversades*), belong to both the *magazines* and the *variétés* categories. Some of the best-known presenters (and producers) in this field are Jacques Chancel (also well known for his France Inter radio interviews such as *Radioscopie* which ran from 1968 to 1990, *Quotidien Pluriel* and *Guetteurs du Siècle*), who has been presenting *Le Grand Echiquier* (A2) since 1972, Eve Ruggieri (equally well known for her radio work on France Inter) who presents such programmes as *Musique au cœur* (A2) and Patrick Poivre d'Arvor who presents the book programme *Ex-Libris* on TF1.

Information is a highly competitive area in French television; the main evening news bulletin is shown by both TF1 (*Le Journal à la une*) and A2 (*Le Journal*) at 8 p.m. and tends to be more dominated by the personality of the presenters than is the case in Britain. News presenters such as Christine Ockrent, Patrick Poivre d'Arvor and Bernard Rapp, play a more important editorial and journalistic role than their British counterparts and consequently enjoy more of a media star status.

Programmes for children in France do not generally match the quality of those shown in Britain; there seems to be a greater reliance on cartoons (usually American) and studio talk. Glowing exceptions, which were successfully exported, include the puppet series *Le Manège enchanté* (*The Magic Roundabout*). Wednesday mornings and afternoons, when most children are free of school commitments, are dominated by programmes for the young on TF1 (e.g., *Club Dorothée*) and A2 (e.g., *Eric et toi et moi*). Finally, sport is as well covered in France as in Britain.

In spite of its relative decline in popularity, A2 has enjoyed some remarkable successes in addition to the programmes mentioned above. For many years the game show *Des chiffres et des lettres* has been a national institution and has even been exported to Britain (*Countdown*, Channel 4). The book programme *Apostrophes* (1975–90), produced and presented by Bernard Pivot, was watched by millions, most of whom were not in the least bookish. FR3, the other public channel, has an identity problem. In the seventies it enjoyed the privilege of being allowed to show more films than its rivals. Following the Socialist government's regionalization policy in the early eighties, its regional role was reinforced. It has a complex structure, having to coordinate productions and programmes provided by twelve regional stations and twenty-five information centres spread over the country. Recent management problems, strikes and budget deficits have turned FR3 into a problem channel. It still produces some successful programmes, however, such as *Thalassa*, a travelogue with a maritime flavour.

To conclude this brief survey of the national channels, mention must be made of the two remaining ones, Canal Plus and M6, and two which disappeared in 1992 La Cinq and La Sept. Canal Plus, which enjoys the second highest budget in the world among the subscription channels (*les chaînes à péage*), is a highly successful company whose main shareholders were Havas (24.72 per cent) and Compagnie générale des Eaux (21.35 per cent) in 1990. Ninety-three per cent of its income is derived from subscriptions (2.8 million in 1990) and 5 per cent from advertising. The channel concentrates on showing recent films and sport. M6, originally TV6, is a private *chaîne généraliste* with a strong *fiction* interest. Its biggest shareholders are CLT (Compagnie luxembourgeoise de Télévision) who also own the radio station RTL, and Lyonnaise des Eaux (25 per cent each). La Cinq did not have complete national coverage. It offered much live sport along with a fairly wide range of mainly popular programmes including news bulletins and current affairs programmes intended to rival those of TF1 and A2. Its capital was reallocated in 1987, giving 25 per cent each to the Hersant and Berlusconi groups, and again in 1990, when Hachette became the principal shareholder. Its annual deficits became gradually bigger and it was forced to close in April 1992. Up to April 1992 some of the programmes of La Sept, the public cultural channel, were screened in the evenings on FR3 which in fact contributed 45 per cent of its budget. From 1990 it had a channel on the TDF 1 satellite and was also available through cable television. Following the demise of La Cinq, the government decided to replace it (in the evenings) by La Sept, renamed Arte. This is a Franco-German cultural channel, financed by the two governments.

Cable and satellite

What of the much heralded cable and satellite television? Cable television with its promise of an aerial-free landscape, interference-free reception and a multiplicity of channels, has had its teething problems. The French government's *Plan-Câble* launched in 1982 was going to create a national cable network. Scared by mounting costs and a tepid response from subscribers, investment in this ambitious project, originally in the hands of the DGT (Direction générale des Télécommunications), later to become France-Télécom which no longer has the cabling monopoly, has lagged behind projected needs. Of the two million homes lucky enough to be in a *ville câblée* which could now receive cable television, only 250,000 have bothered – or been rich enough – to become subscribers. The planned figure of ten million cabled homes for 1992 now seems highly unrealistic and France will continue to lag behind most of her European neighbours in this field. Among the most successful cable channels available are Canal J (for young people), TV Sport, Canal Infos (news), Planète (current affairs and magazines), Canal Santé (medical), Ciné Cinéma (films), TV Mondes, Paris première, Canal bis and some foreign channels like Sky. There are also a number of channels of a strictly local interest.

Satellite television in France is very much in its infancy. With her satellite launching facilities at Kourou in French Guiana, France has, nevertheless, played a key role in satellite television development in collaboration with her European partners. The first French communications satellite, Télécom 1A, was launched in 1984. Homes in the greater part of western Europe equipped with an appropriate 'dish' (*une antenne parabolique*) can receive TF1, A2, Canal Plus, La Cinq, M6, Canal J and a number of radio stations via the satellite Telecom 1C. The satellite TDF1 and its back-up TDF2, launched in 1988 and 1990, carry six channels: Canal Plus, Canal Plus Allemagne, Canal Enfant, Euromusique, Sport 2/3 and La Sept. The TDF satellite offers enhanced picture quality with its D2 Mac standard, Europe's high definition (TVHD: *Télévision Haute Définition*) answer to the Japanese NHK system, but only to viewers with very recently acquired receivers. Better-off French viewers also have the option of acquiring facilities for the reception of programmes beamed by another dozen or so European satellites, some of which show programmes in French: Eutelsat 1-F4 carries TV5 (founded in 1984), which consists of a selection of worldwide francophone television and Olympus (launched in 1989) carried educational programmes in French.

Television: monster or panacea?

Of the three main branches of the media we have been considering, television, in France as in other developed countries, provokes the most discussion and the most controversy. The major question concerns the overall influence of television on French society: has it been beneficial or harmful? *Bilan globalement positif ou négatif*? This question, which this introductory study cannot hope to answer, sub-divides into many others. With its obsessive interest in the high life (particularly in serials) and its encouragement of consumerism – even the viewer of public service channels cannot avoid commercials – has television made the French more materialistic and greedy? Does television portray too much violence and sex? Are viewers, particularly younger ones, corrupted by such portrayals? In 1961 the French introduced a little white square (which became a rectangle in 1964) on television screens when films deemed unsuitable for younger viewers were being shown. This practice was abandoned in 1974, although there have been occasional experimental warning symbols since, for example TF1 introduced a warning blue triangle in 1989. Controlling authorities, such as they are, have undeniably become increasingly liberal and permissive with regard to the portrayal of sex and violence on television, particularly since May 1968, when so many French people decided that *'il est interdit d'interdire'* ('it is forbidden to forbid'). Censorship is virtually dead today in France; it has been replaced by self-censorship. Occasional protests are made by outraged individuals such as the Socialist deputy Ségolène Royal who unsuccessfully introduced in the National Assembly an amendment to the law establishing the CSA in 1988 which would have forbidden the screening of unseemly sex and violence before 11 p.m,

The question of the influence of television on children is perhaps the most interesting of all; they will be running tomorrow's television channels and creating tomorrow's television programmes. The average French child spends 900 hours a year at school and 1,200 hours in front of a television set. Are these 1,200 hours spent in this *école parallèle* contributing to or hampering his or her educational development?

Another contentious issue concerns the proportion of imported American programmes (films, serials and cartoons). Although each channel has to respect certain quotas relating to the balance between foreign and French programmes, an English or American visitor to France will be immediately struck by the high number of British and especially American programmes being screened each week on the national channels. Almost without exception these programmes are dubbed into French, so excessive exposure to the English language is not the problem. What does worry many people is the danger of an excessive Americanization of the French way of life and the consequent threat to French culture and national identity; to say nothing of the threat to the French television and film production industries.

Mention of the film industry brings us to another charge made against television: that it has severely affected cinema attendances. This is undeniable, but it must be remembered that television needs a healthy film industry and it is now repairing some of the damage it has caused. In France today television channels participate in the financing of one film in three and provide 10 per cent of the film industry's income (Alain Le Diberder and Nathalie Coste-Cerdan, *La Télévision*, Paris: La Découverte, 1986, p. 110).

Television is also accused of having been the major factor responsible for the decline in daily newspaper reading in France.

This may well be true, but why then should sales of dailies have *increased* over the past three decades in many other countries, notably Denmark, Norway, Holland, Germany, Sweden, Czechoslovakia, USSR and especially Japan?

In the domain of news reporting French television has justifiably been accused of being politically biased, given the fact that for so long it was considered by the French government to be its mouthpiece. Since the dismantling of the state monopoly, the setting up of an officially independent supervisory body (now the CSA) and the privatization of TF1, the charge of partiality is less often heard. The sheer power surreptitiously exercized by television is increasingly remarked upon with some alarm, however. François-Henri de Virieu has even coined a word to describe this phenomenon, *la médiacratie*, in his book bearing that title (Paris: Flammarion, 1990). The frequent use of the words *médiatiser* and *médiatisation*, more common neologisms, and certainly more common than their English equivalents, also illustrates the obsessive awareness of the French of the constantly increasing importance of the role played by television in their perception of current events. The fixed minimum length of the *journal télévisé* means that material has to be found to fill this slot even when it might not be newsworthy. In Médiamétrie's league table of the highest viewing figures for individual programmes in 1988, the top four programmes were four TF1 evening news bulletins which had scores ranging from 40.5 per cent to 42.6 per cent (Cayrol, p. 294).

Television has certainly made the French more vulnerable to personality cults in politics. Many attribute the success of the extreme right-wing party the *Front National* to the charismatic appearances on television of its leader Jean-Marie Le Pen. Fears have even been voiced that anti-parliamentarian (and by extension pro-Le Pen) sentiments, echoing past movements associated with Napoleon III, General Boulanger, the riots of 6 February, 1934, and Pierre Poujade, are perhaps being revived by the enormously popular (capturing over 40 per cent of the total television audience at times) satirical programme *Bébête Show* (TF1), which remorselessly caricatures both members of the government and the official opposition. In the mediatized atmosphere of French politics, particularly since the President of the Republic has been elected by universal suffrage (1965), image is vitally important. In December 1965 de Gaulle clinched his second round victory over Mitterrand thanks to the brilliance of his performance in three televised interviews (his first ever). Many claim that Mitterrand's success in May 1981 was partly due to cosmetic dentistry.

It is perhaps too early to draw any authoritative conclusions about the overall effect of television on French society. Two opposing theses have been put forward: television is either enslaving its captive viewers by imposing its uniform mass messages on them, or liberating them by enriching their lives through the sheer variety of its offerings!

Notes

1. Quoted by Yves Guillauma, *La Presse en France* (Paris: La Découverte, 1990), p. 20.
2. *Acquisition numérique de télévisualisation d'images organisées en pages d'écriture*, launched in 1973, also offers a sub-titling facility for deaf viewers.
3. Radio audience figures given in this section are quoted by Roland Cayrol, *Les Médias* (Paris: Presses Universitaires de France, 1991), p. 279.

Further Reading

Albert P., *La Presse Française* (Paris: La Documentation Française, 1990), *Lexique de la Presse écrite* (Paris: Dalloz, 1989), *La Presse* (Paris: PUF/Que sais-je? 8th ed, 1988)

Albert, P. and Tudesq, A-J., *Histoire de la Radio-Télévision* (Paris: PUF/Que sais-je? 1981)

Albert, P. and Terrou, F., *Histoire de la Presse* (Paris: PUF/Que sais-je? 1970)

Balle, F., *Médias et société* (Paris: Montchrestien, 1990)

Balle, F. and Eymery, G., *Les Nouveaux Médias* (Paris: PUF/Que sais-je? 2nd ed, 1987)

Boon, M., Ryst, A. and Vinay, C., *Lexique de l'audiovisuel* (Paris: Dalloz, 1990)

Bourges, H. and Josèphe, P., *Un amour de télévision* (Paris: Plon, 1989)

Cayrol, R., *Les Médias: Presse écrite, radio, télévision* (Paris: PUF, 1991)

Charon, J-M., *La Presse en France de 1945 à nos jours* (Paris: Seuil/Points, 1991)

Gaillard, J-M., *Zappons, enfants de la patrie!* (Paris: Fayard, 1990)

Gherardi, S., Guérin, S. and Pouthier, J-L., *La Presse écrite 1900–1991* (Paris: Connaissance des Médias, 1990)

Guéry, L., *Quotidien régional, mon journal* (Paris: CFPJ/ARPEJ, 1987)

Guillauma, Y., *La Presse en France* (Paris: La Découverte/Repères, 1990)

Le Diberder, A. and Coste-Cerdan, N., *La Télévision* (Paris: La Découverte/Repères, 1986)

Loiseau, Y., *Le Journalisme* (Paris: Marabout, 1991)

Mouillaud, M. and Tétu, J-F., *Le Journal quotidien* (Lyon: Presses Universitaires de Lyon, 1989)

Mousseau, J. and Brochand, C., *Le petit Retz du paysage audiovisuel français* (Paris: Retz, 1987)
Porcher, L., *Vers la dictature des médias?* (Paris: Hatier/Profil Economie, 1985)

CHAPTER 8

Food and wine

Stephen Mennell

Good food and great wine are very much bound up with the French national sense of *gloire*. They have been since the seventeenth century. The years after the Occupation and the Liberation, however, were no more a time of glory gastronomically than in other facets of national life. True, the great vineyards had for the most part survived. In the immediate post-war years, however, most Europeans were concerned with finding enough to eat rather than with sampling *premiers grands crus*. Even in France, which was better placed to feed itself than many other countries, these were times of thrift. Early issues of the women's magazine *Elle*, which began publication in November 1945, bear witness to the hard times: a dinner menu with a *croque monsieur* as the main course (12 December) and, in the Christmas issue, instructions on how to make turkey last over five days' dinners – dinde farcie aux marrons; abattis de dinde aux carottes et céléri; croquettes de dinde; risotto de dinde; soufflé de dinde. (In England, at the same time, the problem would have been getting the turkey, not making it last five days). Even French professional cookery was in a trough, though not only as a consequence of the war. Yet the 1950s and 1960s were to see vigorous gastronomic renewal in France – as they did in politics, the economy and intellectual life. And, viewed as a whole, the second half of the twentieth century has been one of rapid change in French culinary culture, though of course, in this as in so many other areas of French cultural life, the elements of continuity are also strong.

The historical sociology of French *haute cuisine*

What we now think of as the distinctively French tradition of great cooking first began to take shape in courtly circles during the last century and a half of the *ancien régime* (S. Mennell, *All Manners of Food*, pp. 62–133). The publication in 1651 of La Varenne's *Le Cuisinier françois* is usually taken as the first indisputable literary expression both of a clear break with medieval food and as the recognizable beginnings of a French style of cookery.

Jean-François Revel in *Un festin en paroles* (1979) describes the transition as one from a medieval 'cookery of mixtures' to a new 'cookery of impregnation' (p. 206). The technical details need not concern us here, but the gist of it is that instead of mixtures of many ingredients being thrown together, a growing diversity of dishes was favoured, but with greater simplicity of ingredients and more careful preparation of each, with the making of subtly flavoured sauces becoming central to the process. Also prominent in the æsthetic which emerged in the work of La Varenne and his immediate successors was a preoccupation with bringing order into the old and reprehensible disorder and superfluity of the earlier 'groaning board', and a sense of the correct and incorrect, the delicate and the vulgar in the serving of dishes. Within twenty-five years of La Varenne's book appearing, his recipes were already being denounced as rustic and vulgar by later authors.

Anything smacking of the rustic was of course deeply repugnant in courtly circles (Marie-Antoinette's frolics a century later at Le Petit Hameau were far removed from the real world of the countryside). In fact French cuisine as it developed in the hands of courtiers and their cooks was essentially an urban phenomenon: it depended on the availability of a wide variety of produce brought from far and near to the great markets of Paris. It had little in common with the rural tradition of eating the produce of one's own lands, according to the season – a tradition which persisted more strongly among the aristocracy and gentry in England, where continuities with medieval eating habits were in general more marked. For French courtiers, deracinated in the royal court under an absolutist monarch, knowledgeability about cuisine – as about music, art, manners or horsemanship – could serve as one vehicle for display of social rank. Virtuoso consumption, however, could no longer take the form of simply eating *more* food than inferiors: *robins* and merchants could now afford to stuff themselves too. And thus, in an era of increasingly intense social competition, prestige came to be attached to the variety and delicacy of the dishes one's chef served, and less to their sheer quantity. And, from an early stage, food served also as a badge of national pride. For example, Massialot wrote in the preface to his cookery book of 1691, *Le Cuisinier roïal et bourgeois*:

Only in Europe prevail the sense of what is proper, good taste and flair in the dressing of the foods found there . . . and only there, and especially in France, can one take pride in our excelling over all other nations in these matters, as we do in manners and in a thousand other ways already familiar to us.

These early origins of the great tradition of French eating have to be stressed because here, as much as in the metres of poetry or numerous other facets of French cultural tradition, the elements of continuity stretching right down to the present day are striking. As Norbert Elias remarked, 'In the conduct of workers in England, for example, one can still see traces of the manners of the landed gentry, and of merchants within a large trade network, in France the airs of courtiers and a bourgeoisie brought to power by Revolution' (*The Civilising Process*, II, 313). He could have added that today among the French truck drivers eating in a *routier* one can perceive traces of the gastronomic sensibility and discrimination and sheer enthusiasm for food which was once the privilege of the courtier.

Yet the track of development was not a linear progression. After a flurry of cookery books in the second half of the seventeenth century, the first three decades of the eighteenth saw few new ones appear. But then, in the 1730s and 1740s, people in fashionable circles began to speak of a *nouvelle cuisine*. In terms of actual technique, it may seem to have represented only small changes; for example, *fonds de cuisine* began to be used more flexibly as the basis of a greater variety of distinct sauces. But, interestingly, the new cookery books provoked the first gastronomic controversy among Parisian courtiers and intellectuals, in which styles of cooking were soon hijacked as emblems of more general cultural battles between 'ancients' and 'moderns' (S. Mennell, *Lettre d'un pâtissier anglois*). In the light of modern semiotics, that is not so surprising, and certainly such undercurrents to rival schools of taste in food persist into post-war twentieth-century France.

The next, vital, stage in the development of *haute cuisine* in France came after the Revolution, under the Directory, the Empire and the Restoration. Restaurants had begun to develop in Paris before the Revolution (oddly enough, partly in imitation of the great London taverns), but there is some truth in the old idea that their spread was the result of great chefs having to make a living after their aristocratic employers had fled abroad, lost their heads, or otherwise found themselves unable to enjoy the products of their own kitchen. Competition among Parisian restaurateurs for the patronage of a bourgeois gastronomic public now became the principal driving force for culinary change. The greatest chef of this period, Antonin Carême (1784–1833), was, however, not a restaurateur, but worked variously for Talleyrand, the Prince Regent, the Czar and M. de Rothschild. His books, notably *L'Art de la cuisine française au dix-neuvième siècle* (5 vols., 1833–5), codified a still more elaborate form of cookery. Recipes typically involved many stages of production, were extremely expensive and were presented highly disguised in architectural displays. Carême's works became the first bible for French professional cooks. But by mid-century, it was generally observed that the culinary tradition was becoming coarsened, even vulgarized by its ostentation and its routine, uninspired following of the style of Carême. One reason among others advanced for this coarsening was the deleterious effect of rich English tourists in Paris restaurants, who were said to be too indiscriminating to insist on the best. A more substantial reason may have been economic factors which made it more and more difficult for cooks to become proprietor-chefs owning their own restaurants, at least in Paris.

So, around the turn of the present century, yet another phase of renewal (and what was again occasionally called a *nouvelle cuisine*) emerged. This time it was codified by Georges Auguste Escoffier (1847–1935), whose *Guide culinaire* (1903) remains a central text in the training of professional cooks even to the present day. Unlike the cooks of earlier generations who had worked in noble kitchens or owned restaurants, Escoffier and his circle of collaborators – including his friend Prosper Montagné (1865–1948), author of the *Larousse gastronomique* (1938) – worked especially in the kitchens of the fashionable hotels which had been established in the major cities of Europe, notably by César Ritz, towards the close of the nineteenth century. Like the hotels, their cuisine catered for a less leisured clientèle. The heavy and elaborate style previously popular, wrote Escoffier in his preface to the 1907 English edition of the *Guide*, was inappropriate to

the light and frivolous atmosphere of the restaurants; was, in fact, ill-suited to brisk waiters, and their customers who only had eyes for each other . . . It is eminently suited to State dinners, which are in sooth veritable ceremonies, possessing their ritual, traditions, and – one might even say – their high priests; but it is a mere hindrance to the modern rapid service. (p. xii)

Escoffier therefore reorganized the kitchen, sub-dividing the work along lines consistent with the industrial principles of his contemporary Frederick Winslow Taylor, and played a leading part in the reorganization of the menu as it is familiar to restaurant-goers today – a sequence of courses from *hors d'œuvres* or soup through fish, meat usually with vegetables, sweet, savoury to dessert (or a sample therefrom). The dishes, especially the sauces, became generally lighter, although the ingredients remained often extravagantly costly: truffles galore and crayfish tails *ad lib*. It was in the Escoffier era that French *haute cuisine* achieved the undisputed international hegemony that it had begun to acquire since the Restoration.

Yet, by 1945, the Escoffier paradigm was also nearing exhaustion in its turn. Not only were some of its characteristic ingredients now absurdly expensive or temporarily unobtainable at all, but Escoffier had unwittingly in his turn 'decreed for all eternity laws that were applied blindly, sometimes with talent, too often with complete mediocrity', as Henri Gault and Christian Millau were to phrase it in *Henri Gault et Christian Millau se mettent à table* (p. 148). The scene was set for what may be counted – after the 1650s, the 1730s, the 1800s and the 1890s – as the fifth great renaissance of French professional cookery.

Nouvelle cuisine

This scarcely original label was applied in the 1960s by Henri Gault and Christian Millau to the new style of cookery they found in the work of such chefs as Paul Bocuse, Jean and Pierre Troisgros, Michel Guérard, Roger Vergé and Raymond Oliver. Their *cuisines* were quite diverse and individual, but one of the links between several of them was that they had been students of the great Fernand Point at *La Pyramide* in Vienne; although Point died in 1957, he has some claims to being the godfather of *nouvelle cuisine*. The historical geographer Jean-Robert Pitte, not one of *nouvelle cuisine*'s most fervent admirers, pinpoints 1964 in his *Gastronomie française* as a sinister year, when Raymond Oliver and other chefs returned from the Tokyo Olympics infatuated with Japanese cooking. Gault and Millau's contribution, much later, was to claim to have 'discovered the formula', which they then championed in their gastronomic guides and magazine. They listed ten common characteristics (pp. 154–7):

1 The *nouveaux cuisiniers* rejected unnecessary complication in cookery – an impulse for which there are many precedents.
2 They reduced the cooking time for most fish, seafood, game birds, veal, green vegetables and pâtés, aiming thereby to 'reveal forgotten flavours'. In this, and in the rediscovery of steaming as a method of cooking, *nouvelle cuisine* may owe something to the practice of Chinese cookery.
3 *Nouvelle cuisine* was (as the title of Bocuse's 1976 book indicated) a *cuisine du marché*. That is to say, the chefs insisted on buying the freshest ingredients available in the market each day. Many products had been bastardized and polluted by food technology and overproduction; the new chefs preferred to eliminate inferior ingredients altogether rather than mask them with aggressive sauces.
4 In order that each dish be of a high standard, the international hotels' gigantic lists of prefabricated dishes were abandoned, and a much shorter menu presented to the customer.
5 The new chefs abandoned strong marinades for meat and served game fresh, not 'high'.
6 They eliminated excessively rich and heavy sauces, especially the lingering *espagnole* and *béchamel*. They had a particular

horror of the use of flour roux, and made more use of good butter, fresh herbs, lemon juice and vinegar in dressing their dishes.

7   They turned to regional dishes and away from the pretensions of Parisian *haute cuisine* as a source of inspiration for new dishes.

8   The new chefs showed great curiosity about the most avant-garde techniques. Their kitchen equipment was ultra-modern. Bocuse made use of microwave ovens. Even their mistrust of frozen food was tempered by an interest in how to use it intelligently.

9   They tended to have the dietetic implications of their work constantly in mind: Guérard's *La Grande Cuisine minceur* (1976) sold hugely, both in France and in English translation.

10   A common characteristic of the leaders of *nouvelle cuisine* was their sheer inventiveness. The Troisgros brothers' recipe for Escalopes de Saumon à l'oseille (pp. 158–8) is representative of the sort of dish which has already become an international classic.

One characteristic of the *nouveaux cuisiniers* that Gault and Millau did not include in their list is that most of them are chef-proprietors of their own restaurants (often, following the example of Point at Vienne, in provincial towns), almost in the same way as some of the great names of the period after the Revolution. *Nouvelle cuisine* originated in rebellion against the Escoffier orthodoxy, particularly as stultified in international hotel cuisine. Perhaps it was inevitable that the bureaucratic pressures and accounting preoccupations within modern hotel chains would today make them unpromising sites for cooking at the highest level, however suitable an environment they had given Escoffier. Accountancy plays little part in *nouvelle cuisine*. By its nature it is expensive: it requires the finest ingredients and is extremely labour intensive.

Like the ideas of Carême and Escoffier before it, the influence of *nouvelle cuisine* has spread around the world, to western Europe, the USA, Australia and even Japan. Perhaps it is unavoidable that, as its ideas are adapted by lesser talents in less liberal contexts, *nouvelle cuisine* too has undergone routinization and become a dogma. Already by the 1980s, some writers were detecting signs of its exhaustion. The disenchanted diner, having sampled *nouvelle cuisine* at something less than its most inspired, might wish to add several characteristics to Gault and Millau's list. They might include visual impact taking precedence over the actual cooking, gimmicks like octagonal plates and the sauce being under rather than over the meat, and – worst of all – going home hungry after an expensive meal. The latter, to be fair, may be more a characteristic of *nouvelle cuisine*'s colonial impact in the anglophone world, where Guérard's *Cuisine minceur* became known in translation before most other texts of the genre.

It is striking that through the waves of renewal in French professional cooking, the continuities are very marked. The æsthetic aims of the post-war *nouveaux cuisiniers* are in summary not unlike those of Escoffier, Montagné and their collaborators, which in turn resemble those of Carême's. The aim of achieving a perfect balance between a few well-chosen flavours is simply a development from Carême's understanding that 'flavours and aromas must be judged not in isolation, but in their mutual relation', compared by Revel to the notion of 'values' in painting. In fact, in summary, the achievements of each successive 'revolution' in the history of French cuisine – from the age of La Varenne, through Carême to Escoffier and on to the 'nouvelle cuisine' of the present day – can sound remarkably similar: each of these so-called 'revolutions' involves (amongst other things) the pursuit of simplicity, of using fewer ingredients with more discrimination, moving towards enhancing the 'natural' flavour of principal ingredients, and in the process producing a wider range of dishes more differentiated in flavour because less masked by the use of a common cocktail of spices, or the same basic sauces. If the term 'revolution' implies a cyclical pattern in changing taste, it is the wrong word. For beneath the succession of dominant styles in French professional cookery is something more complicated than the random vagaries of fashion: each new spurt of development has involved not just the overthrow of some aspects of the previous one, but also the renewal of recognizably the same pursuit of refinement, simplicity, restraint and an increasingly conscious calculation of precisely how innovations will be received by an audience.[1]

Gastronomes and the gastronomic public

The creation of a gastronomic audience, or public, was fostered by what, rather than the restaurant *per se*, was arguably the decisive French contribution to eating as a social activity: the invention of gastronomic literature as a genre, and of the social role of the gastronome. Between them, two writers effectively founded the whole genre of the gastronomic essay. They were Alexandre-Balthazar-Laurent Grimod de la Reynière (1758–1838), and Jean-Anthelme Brillat-Savarin (1755–1826). Virtually everything of the sort written since quotes or harks back to these two authors in one way or another.

Grimod de la Reynière was the son of a rich farmer-general. In reduced circumstances after the Revolution, his genius for publicity led him to found the Jury des Dégustateurs, whose members met weekly at the Rocher de Cancales restaurant (later the similar Société des Mercredis met at Legaque's establishment) to pass judgement on the dishes before them. The ingenuity of the scheme lay in its revealing how eager were restaurateurs and food merchants of all kinds to supply their products for public evaluation by the Jury. The *Almanach des Gourmands*, published annually (except in 1809 and 1811) from 1803 to 1812, was a development of the same idea. It contained an 'Itinéraire nutritif, ou promenade d'un gourmand dans divers quartiers de Paris', covering not only restaurants and cafés but rôtisseurs and traiteurs, grocers, greengrocers and florists, butchers and tripières – food suppliers of every kind in Paris. Grimod apparently expected to be adequately and regularly rewarded for the praise he bestowed on restaurants and food shops. It was not until more than a hundred years later that the leading restaurant guides in France managed to establish a reputation for impartial and 'objective' evaluations uninfluenced by backhanders from the evaluated.

La Physiologie du goût (1826) by Brillat-Savarin has been in print ever since its first publication, and is by far the most famous of all gastronomic essays. Brillat-Savarin was a lawyer from Belley in the French Alps, who spent most of his life in Paris eating at the best tables. His book opens with a series of aphorisms, the most quoted of which is 'Tell me what you eat: I will tell you what you are'. These are followed by the 148 'Gastronomic Meditations' in thirty chapters which form the bulk of the book. Brillat-Savarin sets out the physiological knowledge of the day, on the sense of taste, appetite and the nutritional qualities of foodstuffs, but in a light and witty way enlivened by many anecdotes, and concluding with a highly speculative 'Philosophical History of Cooking' from the origins of mankind to his own day.

In France there has been a continuous line of successors to Grimod and Brillat-Savarin. Gastronomic literature possesses certain characteristic themes. One frequent component is the disquisition on what constitutes 'correct' practice at the time on such questions as the composition of menus, sequences of courses and techniques of service. A second component is dietetic, setting out what foods and what forms of cookery are good for one according to the prevailing knowledge of the day. This was a main theme in Brillat-Savarin, and it has been especially prominent in the work of the not inconsiderable number of medical men who have written on food and gastronomy, including columns on food and eating in French women's magazines.

A third component, and one probably more central to the gastronomic literary tradition, is a brew of history, myth and history serving as myth. The more solid kernel of this can be found in frequent potted biographies of historically famous eaters and, from the nineteenth century, cooks. Carême has always outstripped all others among the cooks. Only Vatel – the *maître d'hôtel* to the Prince de Condé – who, in 1671, according to Mme de Sévigné (*Correspondance*, I, 234–6), committed suicide when fish failed to arrive for a royal banquet, is mentioned more often, in a story used mythically to express the devotion of the French cooking profession to its art. Other stories, most of them lacking any solid foundation in history, are about the origins of particular dishes, techniques and their names. Favourites include mayonnaise (said by some to have been 'invented' by the Duc de Richelieu's cook and named in honour of his military exploits at Mahon – but there are alternative speculations).

A fourth and final component of gastronomic literature is the nostalgic evocation of memorable meals. Notable menus, lovingly amplified by discussions of why such and such a dish was so remarkable, are often a staple ingredient of gastronomic writing. This is one of several respects in which the literature of gastronomy resembles that of cricket: meals in place of memorable matches, cooks and gourmets of the past in place of the batsmen and bowlers of a bygone age – 'we shall not see their like again' – and so on.

An important development in the French gastronomic tradition took place between the wars through the activities of Curnonsky and his circle. Curnonsky was the pseudonym of Maurice-Edmond Sailland (1872–1956). The significance of Curnonsky and his friends Austin de Croze, Marcel Rouff and Maurice des Ombiaux was that they seized the opportunity of linking gastronomy and tourism, and thus initiated a great interest in and vogue for French regional cookery. Curnonsky tells how they

created the gastronomic press . . . and consecrated the holy alliance between tourism and gastronomy. This pioneering work benefited from two novelties: the 'democratised' motor-car and the taste for good fare which, after some years of anguish and privation, developed in France from 1919 onwards . . . The motor-car allowed the French to discover the cuisine of each province, and created the breed of what I have called 'gastro-nomads'. (*Souvenirs*, pp. 53–4)

The alliance of tourism and gastronomy was particularly to the advantage of tyre companies like Michelin and Kléber-Colombes, who began to publish their celebrated guides to the restaurants and hotels of France. Curnonsky and his friends had links with them, but also wrote their own guides. In the 1920s, with his collaborators, Curnonsky published a multi-volume series on the provinces of France entitled *La France gastronomique* (1921–) and a one-volume synopsis, *Le Trésor gastronomique de France* (1933). These authors have been credited with *inventing* the 'traditional' French peasant cuisine. What they gathered were the recipes of probably the 'festival dishes' which were anything but typical of the way peasants actually ate in the past.

In restaurant cooking, Curnonsky advocated more simplicity and less pompous show. The majority of diners, he wrote, no longer cared whether the dish bore the name of a famous diplomat or other celebrity: they were less impressed by the 'suprêmes', 'délices', 'financières', 'mousselines' and 'all the thingummys à la royale, à l'impératrice, or à la princesse'.

They ask simply that things taste of what they are, that a fricassée is called a fricassée, a matelote a matelote, a roast chicken a roast chicken, that nothing is substituted for butter, and that they do not have inflicted on them those abominable 'fonds de sauce' and those standardised 'ratatouilles' with which the cosmopolitan palaces and caravanserais stuff luckless tourists from Singapore to San Francisco, and from Cairo to Buenos Aires and Pernambuco. (*Souvenirs*, p. 274).

Although gastronomes are often seen as pandering to a social élite, they have always willy-nilly helped to popularize the taste for good food. Curnonsky was quite conscious of this, and of the gustatory pluralism that he was helping to create in France in place of the dominance of a single prestigious style. He wittily caught the flavour of this in his account of parties in gastronomy (*Souvenirs*, pp. 188–90). He distinguished five, ranging from extreme right to extreme left. The devotees of the *grande cuisine* were now to be counted as the extreme right. Their kind of learned, recherché, complicated cuisine required a great chef, and materials of the very finest quality; it was now to be found mainly in embassies and palaces – in hotels it was often only a parody.

The right was represented by traditional cookery: its adherents believed one ate well only at home, ate dishes cooked slowly over a wood fire by an old woman-cook who had served the family thirty years and their cellars were full of pre-phylloxera wines and brandy laid down by a great-grandfather.

The gastronomic centrists were those whose taste ran to the good *cuisine bourgeoise* of France; they were happy to admit that one could still eat well in a restaurant; they demanded that 'things taste of what they are' and never be adulterated or fussy; they were guardians of the great regional dishes.

The left were those who advocated cookery with no frips or frills, doing what one could with the minimum of time and whatever was to hand. They were quite content with an omelette, a chop, or a steak, or indeed with a slice of ham or a sausage. They did not ban the use of tinned food; they declared a good sardine in oil had its charms, and that such and such a make of tinned beans was at least as good as fresh ones. They looked for modest little restaurants where the proprietor did the cooking himself, and they recommended simple country cooking.

Finally, there was the extreme left: the eccentrics, the restless, the innovators, those whom Napoleon called ideologues. Always in quest of new pleasures and untried sensations, curious about all exotic cuisines, all foreign or colonial specialities, they wanted to taste the dishes of every country and every age. Above all, they loved to invent new dishes; and some were anarchists without bonds, who sought the overthrow of all out-of-date dishes.

Since the 1960s, there seems to have been a perceptible shift towards the left of Curnonsky's culinary spectrum. Gastronomic pluralism is much stronger. True, the *Guide Michelin* still assumes that there is an accepted set of traditional criteria against which the quality of a restaurant's cookery can be judged without further explanation. But there is also an extensive gastronomic press, including the Gault/Millau guides, which has campaigned for innovation and new approaches. Perhaps most striking of all was the advent of an iconoclastic magazine, *Néo-Restauration*, which soon became the most widely read journal among French caterers. It did not appear until 1972 – much later than corresponding publications in Britain or America. Unlike any earlier trade journal in France, *Néo-Restauration* openly looked abroad for its models – to the USA and, to a lesser extent, England. It was directed, as the first issue proclaimed, to the new commercial opportunities presented by 'les cafétérias, grills, snacks, fast-food de tous genres, coffee shops, "libre service" avec linéaire de distribution en continu ou en scramble, drugstores, quick-lunch, etc.' – in short, *cuisine à la franglais*! It blatantly challenged old assumptions. Its first editorial described it as: 'a monthly which brings a new image to the developing needs and tastes of a clientèle of consumers whose numbers, demands and mobility are constantly growing'. The stress was on the growth of meals eaten outside the home, fast-food operations, motorway service areas, microwave ovens. There had begun what the sociologist Pascale Pynson (*La France à table*, pp. 19–32) was later to call 'l'épopée Big Mac'. A simple walk around any town will reveal that French defences against Macdonalds, Pizza Hut and the rest are crumbling. Yet French traditions will not give up without a struggle: it is striking that even in *Néo-Restauration* there has always been an underlying concern for standards of cooking, a certain caution about frozen food for instance, and a persistent interest in relaying the recipes and latest ideas from the greatest restaurants. Even in the late twentieth century, as Jean-Paul Aron demonstrated happening in the nineteenth, the best and most expensive restaurants in France have continued to set the models to be distantly imitated by establishments far lower in the market – even if this trickle-down effect is to some extent offset by a small trickle-up of microwaves into Bocuse's kitchen.[2]

Domestic cookery

What, if anything, has all this to do with what most French people eat at home every day? One certainly should not expect to find housewives often preparing dishes in their own kitchens as elaborate and expensive as the masterpieces of French professional culinary art. A differentiation between *haute cuisine* and *cuisine bourgeoise* took place at an early stage, but the two codes never lost contact with each other. *Cuisine bourgeoise* is a difficult term to translate into English: it has overtones not just of 'domestic cookery' but also of 'middle-class' and 'urban' cookery. It is also often used to refer to the butter-based cookery of northern France as opposed to the regional cuisines of central, southern and eastern France based on olive oil, pork fat or goose fat, which are sometimes lumped together as *cuisine paysanne*.

Peasant cookery in the more general sense of the food of the countryside was not the principal source of the central tradition of French *cuisine*, which as I have argued took shape in courtly circles and in the urban restaurants. The matter is a subject of historical debate, but the balance of opinion (expressed strongly for example by Zeldin, *France 1848–1945*, II, 725) is that for centuries the French peasantry generally ate far from luxuriously; nor were the methods of cooking particularly elaborate or inspired, and meals were dominated by soup and the *pot-au-feu*. As Marc Bloch contended, it was only during the nineteenth century that it was possible to discern 'the beginnings of a trend towards greater uniformity in food – speaking in very relative terms – from the top to the bottom of the social ladder' ('Les Aliments', p. 232). The romantic image of 'French country cooking' was largely created by Curnonsky and his friends, who recorded what were probably the high spots of peasant eating – the dishes for special occasions and times of abundance. In the late nineteenth and early twentieth centuries, however, Escoffier and his contemporaries did sometimes find inspiration in traditional dishes of the *cuisine paysanne*, which through a process of 'butterization' – substituting butter for olive oil or *saindoux* and adding other more expensive ingredients – they transformed into dishes to set before the fashionable restaurant diner (see Elizabeth David, *An Omelette*, pp. 249–53). But this element of trickle-up was only a counter-current to the main trend.

Between *haute cuisine* and *cuisine bourgeoise*, on the other hand, there had long been an intimate connection dominated chiefly by trickle-down. Many of the cookery books of the eighteenth century were expressly written to make courtly fashions in eating known to a wider bourgeois audience aspiring to upward social mobility, and in the nineteenth century famous chefs sometimes divided their books into sections on *cuisine classique* and *cuisine bourgeoise*, explaining in detail how the former could be simplified for purposes of the latter (Mennell, *All Manners of Food*, pp. 69–83; 149–50). Perhaps more important than the simplified recipes that trickled down was the trickling down of enthusiastic attitudes towards eating. This is particularly evident in the cookery columns of French women's magazines compared with British ones, although the sense of cooking as a leaden burden has declined even in Britain during the 1970s and 1980s.

The sociologist and semiotician Roland Barthes described *Elle*, the women's magazine with the largest circulation in post-war France, as 'a real mythological treasure'. In a celebrated short essay written between 1954 and 1956 entitled 'Cuisine ornementale', Barthes described how the magazine *Elle* would, every week, delight its readers with a fine colour photograph of a prepared dish:

perdreaux dorés piqués de cerises, chaud-froid de poulet rosâtre, timbale d'écrevisses ceinturée de carapaces rouges, charlotte crémeuse enjolivée de dessins de fruits confits, génoises multicolores, etc. (*Mythologies*, Paris: Seuil, 1970, p. 128).

The principal characteristic of this 'ornamental' style of cookery was the glazing and rounding-off of surfaces, burying food under smooth coatings of sauces, creams, icings and jellies. Barthes maintained that this cookery was intended for the eye alone and that *Elle* wanted primarily to satisfy the dreams of its essentially popular readers. The various disguises were supposed to hide what Barthes calls the 'brutalité' of meat, the 'abruptness' of seafood. Country dishes were allowed only exceptionally to satisfy the rustic whim of the jaded city-dweller. Ornamentation proceeded in two ways – by altering nature itself: sticking shrimps in a lemon, making chicken look pink, serving grapefruit hot or, conversely, by attempting to recreate nature by what Barthes calls an 'artifice saugrenu':

[. . .] disposer des champignons meringués et des feuilles de houx sur une bûche de Nöel, replacer des têtes d'écrevisses autour de la béchamel sophistiquée qui en cache les corps. (p. 129)

By the mid-1950s, *Elle* had a vast circulation and was read in many working-class homes. Barthes believed that this could explain the 'ornamental' cookery in its columns. The role of the magazine was to present to its audience cookery which was a 'cuisine d'affiche, totalement magique' (p. 130). *Elle* was very careful not to take for granted the idea that cooking must be economical, although its working class readers were probably not expected to actually cook the more extravagant recipes. Barthes distinguishes the readers of *Elle* from the bourgeois readers of *L'Express*:

Elle donne la recette des perdreaux-fantaisie, *L'Express*, celle de la salade niçoise. Le public d'*Elle* n'a droit qu'à la fable, à celui de

L'Express on peut proposer des plats réels, assuré qu'il pourra les confectionner. (p. 130)

The 'ornamental' food Barthes described in the pages of *Elle* in the years when wartime shortages were finally disappearing was a degenerate survival of the *haute cuisine* of the mid-nineteenth century. As a powerful model or image of what cookery should be, in the 1950s it was completing its trickle down the social scale before becoming finally extinct. That is not to say, of course, that differences in styles of cookery have disappeared as a vehicle for the expression of distinctions between social classes. The great French sociologist Pierre Bourdieu has documented with a wealth of empirical survey data how the food people eat, as much as their tastes in music, art, films or furniture, remains strongly tied to social class – although perhaps, like Barthes, he underestimates how rapidly styles have been changing in recent decades.

Besides, the transitional 'ornamental' style was by no means the only kind of cookery to be peddled by French women's magazines in the post-war period. Not only were many of the recipes in an altogether simpler domestic style, but healthy eating became one of the most prominent themes. For many years – in fact until his death – *Elle* carried a weekly column by Dr Edouard de Pomiane (1875–1964), a medical doctor who in many books and voluminous journalism since the 1920s had been urging the French to adopt a healthy diet (see Elizabeth David, *An Omelette*, pp. 175–85). Pomiane seems to deserve much of the credit, for example, for the popularity of *crudités* as a first course in many French homes and unpretentious restaurants. Successors have continued to propagate his message. By the 1980s, fear of being overweight and a preoccupation with following a *régime* has become one of the French culinary traits best documented by sociologists. Pynson speaks of it as an *obsession inhibitrice* (pp. 121–80). Fischler writes of a *société lipophobe* ('fat-fearing society'), and documents the growth both of a terror of obesity among men and of the pressures on women that arise from their bodies being objects of fashion – pressures which can tip many young women over from the pursuit of slimness into eating disorders like anorexia nervosa and bulimia (pp. 297ff.).

Conclusion

The strength of traditions of great cooking in France has to some extent increased its kitchens' powers of resistance to the depredations of the food industry which are so evident in the USA, Britain and many other European countries. Until the late 1970s, casual observation suggested that frozen foods for instance occupied less space proportionally in the French than the British supermarket. Resistance, according to most observers, is crumbling, and manufactured and processed foods are finding their way into the French domestic kitchen, just as fast foods outlets are becoming as popular with young people in France as they are elsewhere. But all things are relative. Even Escoffier complained of the demand for faster service in the fashionable hotels of his day. The same pressures extend even to the domain of wine. As Alexis Lichine observes:

The present cry is for more of everything, turned out faster and more cheaply. If there is anything that does not respond to this call, it is wine. It can be made inexpensively, but it will not then be fine wine; it can be made in bulk, but cannot thus be great wine . . . The grower cannot obtain quantity and quality at the same time (*Encyclopaedia*, p. 228).

But despite what one may call *piatisation* of the wine market, as mediocre standardized wine is heavily advertised and delivered by bulk tanker, great wine will continue to be made and *premiers crus* vineyards prosper in niche markets. And, in the same way, the strength of traditions and French people's sheer enthusiasm for good food (buttressed by a culturally transmitted capacity to distinguish good from bad) are likely to safeguard excellent cooking both in French homes and French restaurants. I predict that they may even recover shortly from *nouvelle cuisine*!

Notes

1.   One is tempted to add that the 'increasingly conscious calculation of how innovations will be received by an audience' is a characteristic shared with the whole of post-war Parisian intellectual life.
2.   The terms 'trickle down', and by extension 'trickle up', often used by anthropologists and sociologists, seem largely to derive from the influential article by Fallers (1954), who however spoke only of the 'trickle effect'.

Further Reading

Jean-Paul Aron, *Essai sur la sensibilité alimentaire à Paris aux XIX siècle* (Paris: Armand Colin, 1967).

Jean-Paul Aron, *Le mangeur du 19ᵉ siècle* (Paris: Robert Laffont, 1973).

Roland Barthes, *Mythologies* (Paris: Seuil, 1970).

Marc Bloch, 'Les aliments de l'ancienne France', in *Pour une histoire de l'alimentation*, ed. by J. J. Hémardinquer (Paris: Armand Colin, 1970, (1st edition, 1954), pp. 231–5).

Paul Bocuse, *La Cuisine du marché* (Paris: Flammarion, 1976).

Pierre Bourdieu, *Distinction: A Social Critique of the Judgment of Taste* (London: Routledge and Kegan Paul, 1984 (1st French edition, 1979)).

J.-A. Brillat-Savarin, *La Physiologie de goût* (Paris: A. Sautelet, 1826).

Antonin Carême, *L'Art de la cuisine française au dix-neuvième siècle* (Paris: chez l'auteur, 1833–5).

Curnonsky [pseud. of Maurice-Edmond Sailland], *Souvenirs* (Paris: Albin Michel, 1958).

Elizabeth David, *An Omelette and a Glass of Wine* (Harmondsworth: Penguin, 1986).

Norbert Elias, *The Civilising Process*, vol. II, *State-Formation and Civilisation* (Oxford: Basil Blackwell, 1982, (1st edition, 1939)).

Georges Auguste Escoffier, *Le Guide culinaire* (Paris: L'Art culinaire, 1903; subsequent editions, Flammarion). (First English edition: *A Guide to Modern Cookery* (London: Heinemann, 1907)).

Lloyd A. Fallers, 'A Note on the "Trickle Effect"', *Public Opinion Quarterly*, 18 (1954), 314–21.

Claude Fischler, *L'Homnivore* (Paris: Editions Odile Jacob, 1990).

Henri Gault and Christian Millau, *Gault et Millau se mettent à table* (Paris: Stock, 1976).

A.-B.-L. Grimod de la Reynière, *Almanach des gourmands* (Paris: 1803–12).

Michel Guérard, *La Grande cuisine minceur* (Paris: Robert Laffont, 1976).

J.-J. Hémardinquer, 'Essai de cartes des graisses de cuisine en France', *Annales E-S-C* 16 (1961), 747–9.

François Pierre de La Varenne, *Le Cuisinier françois* (Paris: Pierre David, 1651).

Alexis Lichine, *Encyclopædia of Wines and Spirits*. 6th edn. (London: Cassell, 1985).

Massialot, *Le Cuisinier roïal et bourgeois* (Paris: chez Charles de Sercy, 1691).

Stephen Mennell, ed., *Lettre d'un pâtissier anglois et autres contributions à une polémique gastronomique du XVIIIᵉ siècle* (Exeter: University of Exeter, 1981).

Stephen Mennell, *All Manners of Food: Eating and Taste in England and France from the Middle Ages to the Present* (Oxford: Basil Blackwell, 1985).

Stephen Mennell, 'On the civilising of appetite', *Theory, Culture and Society*, 4 (1987), 373–403.

Jean-Robert Pitte, *Gastronomie française: Histoire et géographie d'une passion* (Paris: Fayard, 1991).

Pascale Pynson, *La France à table, 1960–86* (Paris: Editions La Découverte, 1987).

Jean-François Revel, *Un festin en paroles* (Paris: J.-J. Pauvert, 1979).

Waverley Root, 1958: *The Food of France* (New York: Alfred A. Knopf, 1958).

Mme Marie de Rabutin-Chantal de Sevigné, 1972–8 *Correspondance*. 3 vols., (Paris: Gallimard, 1972–8).

Jean and Pierre Troisgros, *Cuisiniers à Roanne* (Paris: Robert Laffont, 1977).

Theodore Zeldin, *France 1848–1945*. 2 vols. (Oxford: Oxford University Press, 1973–7).

CHAPTER 9

Popular music

G. Poulet

Popular music is a potential minefield for the average *rive gauche* nostalgic academic. Being witness to the beginnings of Jacques Brel at La Mutualité in 1958, being fascinated by the no-nonsense, take it or leave it kind of gentle artistic approach to his audiences by Georges Brassens in Roubaix in 1963, being impregnated by the so-called *veine poétique de la chanson française* from the evergreen Ferré of yesteryear to the Jonasz, Souchon, Cabrel *et al.,* do not necessarily make one the best guide to the trials of French pop music in the last forty years, but they do give good points of reference. The second half of the twentieth century in France has seen an extraordinary explosion of the *variétés françaises* as well as a steamrolling invasion of Anglo-American pop music, if that does not sound too much like De Gaulle or La Palisse. The concepts involved need to be defined, albeit briefly, if only to avoid the dangers of lexical looseness. Strictly speaking, in French, *la pop-musique ou musique pop* has designated globally musical forms stemming from the rock and folk idioms. In this particular chapter, popular music is taken in its broadest sense and is understood as covering every kind of *chanson* manufactured in France since the war. Our approach will be essentially qualitative, and will follow chronology, as well as providing some insight into the complexity of the musical idioms and the nature of political messages, where they exist.

The IVth Republic (1946–58) provides a convenient framework for the first part of our study. The war is over. France is living through paradoxical, traumatic moments of exuberant euphoria and painstaking rationing: difficult days of rebuilding her industrial base and developing her economic strength. The quality of post-war life is improving year after year: e.g., record-players, amazingly called *pick-ups* in French, invade a large number of homes. Hi-Fi crosses the channel and tip-toes its way onto the French market. In the 1950s, the first LPs and singles appear and soon the old *78 tours* will become a collector's item. The temples of yesteryear (music-halls, caf 'conc') will be virtually abandoned; five years is a long time in show-business. With the *libération* new habits will be formed, for financial as well as cultural reasons. In Paris, the Left Bank is in; the *cabaret* is where the new generation of *auteurs, compositeurs, interprètes* will flourish; space is limited; in no way can you expect the luxury of an orchestra (chamber or not). You may, at best, get a piano; so the singer will find the guitar the best instrument to accompany the lyrics.

However two music-halls will survive and prosper: Bobino and L'Olympia, *rive gauche* and *rive droite*. These have been the two 'temples' of French *variétés* for almost thirty years which have attracted two different kinds of worshippers and, to a certain extent, two different kinds of high priests. Bobino was in the Rue de la Gaité in Montparnasse (razed to the ground in 1984 in the constant urbanized Paris upheaval); *guinguette, café-concert* at the end of the nineteenth century, it becomes a fashionable music-hall between the wars. And with the arrival of Félix Vitry as its director, Bobino is enlarged to more than a thousand capacity and will be, until its demise, the theatre where the artists who graduated in the cabarets of the Left Bank seek final consecration: Georges Brassens, Juliette Gréco, Léo Ferré, Serge Reggiani and later Jean Ferrat, Georges Moustaki, Maxime Le Forestier, Claude Nougaro, Gilles Vigneault, Renaud, etc. . . . In spite of some relapses after Vitry's disappearance in 1973, Bobino has remained, according to Coulomb and Varrod in their informative *Histoire des chansons 1968–1988* (Paris: Balland, 1978):

le music-hall des consécrations d'une chanson différente, d'un autre langage, d'une autre folie, plus naïve souvent que celle de la chanson des Beaux Quartiers. (p. 126)

L'Olympia did not have such a prestigious history as Bobino, as a music-hall. For twenty-five years (1929–54) it was a cinema. Bruno Coquatrix is the legendary figure behind its renaissance as a 'temple' of *la chanson*. Bigger than Bobino, L'Olympia has outlived its rival too and is now the inescapable landmark of the Parisian show-business. Artists will for ever come back to the Boulevard des Capucines to test their popularity. L'Olympia is, par excellence: 'une arène barométrique où l'on prend des nouvelles des artistes à découvert' (Coulomb and Varrod, p. 118) – Edith Piaf (1961) and Charles Trénet (1971) are two examples of this phenomenon. In a way these superstars who began their careers under the IIIrd Republic – Piaf in 1937 and Trénet in 1933 – survived the digression of the war and dominated the scene in the 1950s. Edith Piaf continued to do so until her death in 1963 and the ever popular Trénet saw his legendary Douce France revamped in 1985 by Carte de Séjour in a version *beur,* (the new word which qualifies anyone and anything belonging to the second generation of North African immigrants.)

Charles Trénet (Narbonne, 1913) remains for many the master craftsman in terms of melody and lyrics and the initiator of the *auteur–compositeur–interprète's* reign in the domain of French song. There is a universal consensus amongst the critics on the original contribution of Charles Trénet. Even Pierre Dudan in his vitriolic pamphlet on the 'industry' *Vive le Show Biz bordel!* (Paris: Alain Lefeuvre, 1980) enthusiastically writes a qualified value-judgement on *Le Fou chantant:*

Trénet est un artisan du verbe, un orfèvre de la rime et du balancement des vers. Son inspiration est positive, gaie, saine, irrésistible. Son émotion est prenante, son charme léger. Il invente des mélodies inoubliables et interprète le tout avec une fougue à reveiller les fossiles. (p. 36)

From that particular period, three songs from Charles Trénet encapsulated the variety of his style and the international dimension of his popularity: *La Mer* (1945), *Une Noix* (1947) and *L'Ames de poètes* (1951). As Dudan remarked, his message is resolutely euphoric and his musical idioms new in the kingdom of the *bal musette.* He makes the French lyrics swing and introduces a variety of rhythms, some European (waltz), others more exotic. More than one song writer will later recognize his influence on their own craftsmanship: Brel, Brassens and later Nougaro.

Edith Piaf's undeniable contribution to this period in particular and to the French *variétés* in general is characterized, as I see it, by three main qualities: the persona is almost as important as the performer; her own private life is so entangled with her own career that the public fascination for this *petit bout de bonne femme en robe noire* is ambiguous. The last fifteen years have seen enough biographies, fictionalized shows, films, documentaries to ensure that Edith Gassion – genuine *saltimbanque,* on the game in Pigalle, singer as *la môme Piaf* in 1935, visiting artist during the war, American star in 1947, *monstre sacré* in France after her extraordinary concert at the Salle Pleyel in 1949, and thereafter until her death in 1963 and beyond – reached an almost mythical dimension. Her second quality is the extraordinary *présence* on stage which a few cinematographic archives demonstrate from time to time. She had a vibrating voice and an emotional delivery which made pathos respectable, because she sang like she lived and loved: passionately. She was essentially an *interprète génial* although she did write some of her lyrics, the best known being *L'Hymne à l'amour* written at the tragic end of her relationship with the boxer Marcel Cerdan. The third quality of her contribution is as an *accoucheuse de talent.* For example she contributed to the success of Les Compagnons de la Chanson, the French equivalent of the King's Singers, who between 1950 and 1980 imposed their choral expertise on the international showbusiness scene. Charles Aznavour and George Moustaki who both wrote for her and Yves Montand, emulated her infectious enthusiasm and the very human dimension of her talent.

Yves Montand was in 1991 the epitome of the versatile artist. He was no song-writer, nor a musician by trade; but he was highly successful as an actor (theatre and more importantly cinema) as well as a singer. He was first and foremost a rigorous and meticulous performer. In the 1950s he was one of the very few artists who could 'stay on' for six months on the trot, which he did at the Etoile in 1953 and in 1959 with a repertoire which varied from the political song to the surrealist boutade, from the love song to the humourous spoof. Some would argue, like P. Dudan that his leftish political lineage has made him an unnecessarily sacred monster among his talented peers like Philippe Clay, for example:

Il sait tout faire: interpréter, chanter, danser, se mouvoir, émouvoir. Il est grand, beau, a une gueule et 'de la gueule' . . . Eh bien je trouve presque autant de qualités à un autre très grand, qui lui n'a pas de convictions penchant viscéralement à gauche! et qu'on punit. Je veux parler de Philippe Clay. (p. 32)

Their common denominator is the presence in their 'creative environment' of sterling lyricists or composers. But this comparison between Montand and Clay is unkind to Montand. Could it be that, to be recognized, the artist must have leftish aspirations? In 1989, Yves Montand became a myth in his own lifetime, and Claude Berri in the film·*Trois places pour le 26,* made a panegyric of a film in which the main character was interpreted by the man himself.

As well as the consecration of pre-war talents, the 1950s in France saw the flowering of lasting talents who created what is often referred to nowadays as the golden age of *La chanson poétique française.* Their texts have all had entries in anthologies of Poésies et Chansons, which is the final accolade for these modern troubadours, even if they are the first to show humility and step down from the pedestal of the Parnasse where academia would put them. Jacques Brel himself, being interviewed by Jacques Chancel on France Inter's long lasting *Radioscopie* in 1972 said:

Parfois on m'a demandé ce que c'était qu'un artiste . . . je n'ai jamais pratiqué une discipline stricte . . . la chanson c'est une petite chose . . je crois qu'un artiste c'est quelqu'un qui a mal aux autres et dans les chanteurs il y a des chanteurs qui ont mal aux autres et des chanteurs qui n'ont pas mal aux autres et puis il y a aussi des gens qui ont du talent et des gens qui n'ont pas de talent . . . je crois que le talent c'est d'avoir envie de faire quelque chose mais ce n'est que cela et après il y a toute une vie à user pour essayer de faire ce quelque chose. (26 October, 1972)

Paris was an extraordinary culture medium for a whole generation of artists, now dead or in the twilight of their careers: Aznavour (1924), Barbara (1930), Béart (1930), Becaud (1927), Brassens (1921–81), Brel (1929–78), Léo Ferré (1916), Gainsbourg (1927–91) do stand out and deserve a pause in our marathon through popular music in France in the second half of the twentieth century.

Charles Aznavour had a background as a travelling artist among the Armenian milieu in Paris. Child performer with his sister, he started his career with Pierre Roche, a composer he met at the *Club de la Chanson* during the Occupation. The duo would survive after the war as song writers. In the late 1940s Aznavour wrote the lyrics and Roche the music for a series of quite successful numbers performed by others (E. Piaf for one). Soon he would write his own lyrics and music, but his debut as a singer was catastrophic. 'Get yourself a voice' seemed to be the advice he was given. Paradoxically it was his very cracked voice and his frail stature that made him a star who was internationally recognized. In 1954 he made his fourth appearance at the Olympia and by 1963 he was the king of New York with an extraordinary series of concerts at Carnegie Hall. Emulating Frank Sinatra, Charles Aznavour created some well manufactured songs, intelligently written, dynamically interpreted. The themes of his songs (the unsatisfied quest for happiness, the human suffering of estranged immigrants, lovers and artists in a ruthless world) have appealed to a very wide audience. In the 1970s and 1980s, Aznavour became the busiest showman in France. Showbusiness is business. Although manager of his own empire, Aznavour still produced some fine songs. In thirty years, some of the numbers have become great classics: *Je me voyais déjà, Les Comédiens, La Mamma, Après l'amour, Tu te laisses aller*.

Barbara (Paris 1930) is a very French phenomenon, the incarnation of *la femme fatale*. Typically for the period, she struggled for fifteen years in the *cabarets de la rive gauche* at the end of the 1950s. Her repertory was either contemporary (Brel, Brassens, etc.) or nostalgic (songs of la Belle Epoque). Accompanying herself on the piano, she offered to her small band of followers her own texts, unashamedly romantic, always discreet and elliptic, on a nostalgic quest for happiness, never fulfilled, but source and inspiration for masterpieces where the melodic line and sophisticated lyrics combined to leave the audience spellbound: *Nantes; Gottingen; Le Mal de vivre; Marienbad; Attendez que ma joie revienne; Pierre*.

Guy Béart (Cairo 1930) is another giant. He made it big, as it were, in 1958 with *L'Eau vive*, and never looked back. As with Aznavour, although the voice is technically lousy, it is remarkable. His trademark is the simplicity of his rhythmic melodies and the extraordinary versatility of its lyrics. He jazzed up a considerable amount of French *chansons de terroir ou folkloriques* (e.g., *Vive la Rose*) before embarking on a very ambitious, albeit messianic voyage through our modern predicament: ecology, spiritual renaissance, science fiction, as well as the tenets of our fragile human condition, namely love and death.

Gilbert Bécaud (Toulon 1927) a classical pianist, who, thanks to Edith Piaf, met one of his first lyricists Louis Amade, started singing, like everybody else, in the cabarets; significantly on the right bank. His performance at the Olympia in 1954 revealed an extraordinary performer who was to enthuse generation after generation of young people, from seventeen to seventy-seven, with his flamboyant energy on stage, his raucous voice, and the kind of positive euphoria, based on the mythical brotherhood of man, a private world where hope for a better world, close to a child's dreams, will make us forget the inescapable dreariness of life and create a magical illusion. In a way Bécaud is a magician, master of his art, musician more than a poet, who still draws the crowds to the Olympia. France Inter announced a special concert at the Olympia on the 16 and 17 November 1991, as compensation for disappointed fans who were turned away because chronic laryngitis forced him to cut short his performance. At sixty-four, the public still needs him, still wants him. He is like Charles Trénet, one of the greatest upholders of the music-hall tradition in France.

Brassens (1921–81) and Brel (1929–78) have had a parallel career and have already entered the *Panthéon des chanteurs-poètes*. Literary academics have harnessed, as it were, these two giants of post-war French *variétés*. Their songs are analysed and scrutinized in French lessons in colleges and lycées throughout France and beyond. Hatier have published books in the series *Profil d'une œuvre* on both of them (No. 52 on Brel, No. 71 on Brassens) alongside the great classics of French and European literature. However gratifying this academic accolade is to the lyrics of these modern troubadour and *trouvère,* it could blur the fact that the text should not really be severed from their music. The three to five minutes song should be experienced as a whole. This particular point is being emphatically made by G. Authelain in his book *La Chanson dans tous ses états* (Fondettes: Van de Velde, 1988) where he takes the novice as well as the expert through the creative phases of what is essentially a musical experience. Brassens and Brel were two different musical temperaments. The modern troubadour from Sète used basically a classical guitar, often accompanied simply by a double bass during his public appearances. To the unsophisticated ear, his melodies and accompaniment seem monotonous, whereas, if you study them attentively or try to play them, they display a learned and skilful musical expertise. They reveal too a contemporary musical influence: eg. *java,* blues and some of the jazz rhythms heard in Paris at the end of the war in St Germain des Prés. On the tenth anniversary of his death, in October 1991, RTL procured an interesting programme which gave evidence of these influences in a recording of a rehearsal with Brassens and some of his musicians which had not been previously broadcast. But the overwhelming impression in Brassens's songs is of sobriety, simplicity as well as sophistication; the music supports and follows the rhythm of the lyrics. On the other hand, when J. Brel composed and orchestrated the musical texture of his songs, he was often amplifying, sometimes caricaturing the meaning of his text, underlining the significance of his poetry. Brassens's technique is classical, Brel was more of a romantic. There is a certain convergence in some of the themes recurrent in both their songs. First, the generous appeal to friendship, brotherhood of man, good old-fashioned charity (Brassens: *La Chanson de l'Auvergnat; Les Copains d'abord;* Brel: *Quand on n'a que l'amour*); second, their general non-conformism and satirical vein against the values of a bourgeois society that has lost its soul. Their obsession with death is another common trait of their private world; but here Brassens exorcises this particular demon with humour and irony (*Les Funérailles d'antan; Le Testament; Supplique pour être enterré en plage de Sète*) while Brel reveals a feeling of revolt (*Le Dernier Repas; La, la, la,*) as well as a visceral attachment to life, (*J'arrive; Le Moribond*). Finally women and love will inspire many a fine poem, sometimes marked with a touch of misogyny, more evident perhaps in Brel (*Les Biches*) than in Brassens. Their final significant public appearances took place at the end of the 1970s. In 1967 Brel stopped performing and engaged himself in a short film career as an actor and director, then retired to the Marquises islands in the Pacific and masterminded a final comeback in 1977 with a final album simply called *Brel.* Brassens's last concert at Bobino was in 1976.

Léo Ferré (Monaco, 1916), a pianist for Radio Monte Carlo at the end of the war, came to Paris in 1946 and started in the cabarets. The initial period of his career was uneasy but the first two songs that give him notoriety (*Jolie môme, Merde à Vauban*) give a clear indication of his sensitivity as well as his permanent rebellious attitude towards established society. His aggressiveness is tempered by his musical and thematic versatility as shown in his best songs from the 1950s (*Le Bateau espagnol, L'Étang chimérique, La Vie d'artiste, Avec le temps, Le Temps du plastique*). The next turning point in his career was to be in the aftermath of the events of 1968, and in 1970 his album *Amour*

anarchie revealed his empathy with the rebellious youth as well
as his trademark: anarchy. Ferré will always remain an anarchist
at heart. The 1970s and 1980s see him embark on incredibly
ambitious projects as far as the length of his texts (e.g., *Il n'y
a plus rien*) or the volume and sophistication of his orchestration
are concerned. This grand patriarchal figure is still active and in
1991 he gave two special concerts in Paris. His own lyrics have
been a haunting mixture of slang and mannered language, and
his music goes from simple melodies (*C'est extra*) to lengthy and
intricate creations.

Serge Gainsbourg (1927–91) is the other iconoclast in the realm
of French pop music. Whereas there is a definite critical consensus
on the classical values of the 'Great' Brassens, Brel and Ferré,
who all started their careers in the 1950s, Serge Gainsbourg
only attracted any form of unanimous recognition on the day
of his funeral in March 1991. The essence of his persona is
mystification and provocation. What interests us here is the
originality and quality of his music and lyrics, beyond his taste
for decadence. Son of a Russian *émigré* nightclub pianist, failed
student of Fine Arts, he started to earn his living as a pianist
and guitarist at the cabaret Milord L'Arsouille in Paris at the
end of the 1950s. Musically he is a chameleon: he has skilfully
used every available contemporary idiom (rock, punk, reggae and
other exotic rhythms) and has always preceded changes in the pop
music public's tastes. Two albums among others mark his career:
Melody Nelson in 1972 and, in 1979, his reggae parody *Aux armes
et cætera* which caused a sensation as did, ten years earlier, his
erotic number *Je t'aime moi non plus* – a double musical act
with Jane Birkin, for whom he continued writing songs for some
time. The McCluhan aphorism is quite appropriate in the case of
Gainsbourg: 'the medium is the message', for both musically and
linguistically he found artistic fulfilment in juggling with words
and rhythms (e.g., **La Javanaise**).

From this particular period, the 1950s, it would be difficult to
ignore eminent lyricists like Jacques Prévert, Raymond Queneau
and of course Boris Vian who, as well as being a cult figure
novelist for the young generations, and a jazz critic, excelled,
with Henri Salvador, in parodying the burgeoning rock and
jazz idioms and wrote and interpreted **Le Déserteur** (which was
censored for a while during the Algerian conflict) before his early
death in 1959.

The years 1958 and 1968 are convenient landmarks for the
next phase of our study. The Algerian problem precipitated
the end of the IVth Republic and De Gaulle, who had been
waiting in the wings for twelve years, was called back. He
dissolved the assembly and called for constitutional reform.
The Vth Republic was born; new institutions gave France

a strong presidential system and the new elections gave the Right in France legislative power which they would hold until 1981, three presidents later. But after ten years of Gaullist rule, France was shaken by the events of 1968. Ten years had seen French society prosper economically and culturally. She slowly reconciled herself to the consequences of decolonization. France was a nation of young people following the post-war baby boom. Technologically the French had never had it so good in the routine of their daily lives: television and the transistor radio became very significant social and cultural factors and completely transformed showbusiness and the world of *variétés* in France. These two media become increasingly, overwhelmingly important as vehicles for songwriters and performers. Definitely a *mariage de raison* for better, for worse. A song or a singer can be promoted, hyped through radio, the state-run France Inter, or the so-called *radios périphériques*: Europe numéro 1, Radio Luxembourg, Radio Monte Carlo. Thanks to the transistor people found themselves listening to the same song time and time again, wherever they were and whichever longwave French-speaking station they were tuned into. Television made a different, but just as significant, impact on the promotion of the cultural product. In the 1960s television programmes such as *Age tendre et tête de bois*, *Discorama* or *Le Petit conservatoire de la Chanson* expanded the possibilities of indulging the young generations with their latest crazes, publicizing the established artists as well as giving a chance to the legion of hopefuls. Guy Béart had his own show *Bienvenue* where, as the title suggests, he invited fellow songwriters and performers. But the genuine innovative genius in the television presentation of the world of pop music during the 1960s was Jean Christophe Averty, skilfully using the televisual possibilities in terms of editing, filmsetting, etc. to the full. The same young generations were exposed increasingly, more through radio than television, to American–English pop music. Some of the present generation of artists readily admit that the idiom of their adolescence was Elvis Presley or the Beatles rather than Brassens or Brel and that they only discovered their 'masters' later on in life. Because most of these English or American pop songs punctuated their lyrics with 'yeah, yeah', the French fans digested the phenomenon and the concept of *la musique yé-yé* and French rock'n'roll was born. Their temple was Le Golf Drouot in the 9th arrondissement in Paris, on the Boulevard Montmartre, a bar and a dance hall combined, where the juke box as well as makeshift live performances made the young Parisians and *banlieusards* rock-a-round the clock. The first *habitués* J. P. Smet and C. Moine and others dreamt of recording their first album or hit; they soon did: the latter became Eddie Mitchell, the former Johnny Halliday. The Golf Drouot saw the first public appearances of Les Chaussettes Noires, Jacques Dutronc, Sheila; it welcomed pop music stars from abroad who were passing through Paris; and it was to be host to many a radio or television programme. Rock'n'roll is played by a group and listened to by many. It was a new way of life for a whole generation. Rock'n'roll music represented, in France as well as elsewhere, a political stance (political in the broader sense of the term) of a young and largely working-class generation; for them it was a social and individual liberation, before it was massively harnessed by managers and producers of showbusiness, given a fatal TWIST and degenerated into the *yé-yé* phenomenon. Daniel Filipacchi, producer of *Salut les Copains* on Europe numéro 1 masterminded the *yé-yé* consumer boom, and in 1962 *Salut les Copains* was not only a popular radio programme, but gave its name to a national institution: the first pop music magazine aimed at teenagers. The genuine rockers were a pain in the ears of *la France profonde*; not only because of the number of decibels their concerts generally generated but also because the adult public were used to more Latin sounds and the aggressiveness, enthusiasm and spontaneity of these American rhythms alienated them. Musically French rock was, at the beginning, a carbon copy of the original: unsophisticated 4/4 rhythm with the lyrics simply or approximately translated. The student generation, the privileged ones who were not on the shop-floor at sixteen or eighteen were wary of it. They tended to listen to the original product Presley *et al.* and contributed to the successful invasion of the Beatles in France in 1964. Nevertheless, rock'n'roll had a massive following and produced a few stars, some of whom lasted longer than others.

Johnny Halliday (Paris, 1943) made an extraordinary impact with the young rebels of the 1960s; from his debut at the Golf Drouot to the climax years of 1966–7, his style of songs follows the evolution of rock'n'roll in France. First the grapes of wrath followed by a gentler twisting image and sound. His greatest merit remains as a performer; he was and still is in the early 1990s a cathartic *bête de scène* genuinely seeking and achieving audience participation, American style. Many predicted that the Halliday product would soon go out of fashion; this great performer proved all his critics wrong and even sung, in 1981, a slightly tongue-in-cheek number entitled *Je suis toujours là.*

Eddie Mitchell (Paris, 1942) is the other great French rocker, first with Les Chaussettes Noires (1961–4) then as a solo artist; he sold American rock'n'roll hits, and then broadened his scope to country and western numbers, crooning blues, etc. and never really changed his confident humorous style as a performer. He proved to be a talented lyrics writer but has never abandoned the American musical idiom. Sylvie Vartan was commercially launched by the all-powerful D. Filipachi and learned her trade on the job. After humble beginnings and international tours in the USA and Japan she pleasantly surprised critics and fans. Her marriage to J. Halliday also contributed to the making of the legend and 1967 saw them both perform successfully at the Olympia. In 1968 she achieved her own success. Unlike the other two rock stars, she abandoned the exclusive rock idiom to blossom out in romantic ballads. As a performer she revived the tradition of the glorious *revues* of the 1920s and 1930s and was highly successful in Las Vegas. These three characters dominated the French rock scenes in the 1960s; but minor figures included popular voices like Dick Rivers, France Gall, Richard Anthony, Sheila and these could not really be ignored in an anthology of the new wave *yé-yé*.

Jazz was the other pervading influence on French pop music. Ten years earlier Boris Vian had been the genial *truchement*, but Claude Nougaro is without a shadow of a doubt the artist who once and for all proved that the French language and rhythm can cope with the syncopated musical idiom. He started writing lyrics for others; in 1962 sang himself; three years later he presented his own show at Bobino and has never looked back. Poet in the etymological sense, he plays on and with words to create a magical atmosphere as well as to shape his lyrics into the jazz mode. As a performer he reveals a rich voice and impressive phrasing. His private world is remarkably summed up in the invaluable dictionary on the last hundred years of French songs:

Les thèmes qui apparaissent dans l'œuvre de Nougaro permettent de cerner un nombre limité d'obsessions: l'érotisme, la mort, la difficulté d'être du couple . . . Le révélateur par excellence c'est la femme . . . La chanson devient alors célébration de l'Eve éternelle et, à travers elle, du désir de l'homme: tentative d'exorcisme pour qui aspire à réintégrer le paradis perdu. (Brunchwig, pp. 287–8)

Nougaro's success story was confirmed in the 1970s and he has outlived the *yé-yé* generation with which he was first identified.

Of the same period Claude Francois (1939–78) and Michel Polnareff (1944) deserve a place in the showbiz anthology, the former for his spotless career as a songwriter and performer idolized by generations of teenyboppers and the latter for his musical talent and originality inspired by the soul melodies. Meanwhile the old timers, as it were, Brel, Brassens and co., forged ahead. A newcomer on the scene of the traditional poetical song was Jean Ferrat (1930): he knew the same sort of humble beginnings as his peers in the cabarets; he wrote well-fashioned songs in a very conservative musical idiom; ironical in the sense that he is one of the best examples of the *chanteur engagé* and in a way exhausted the possibilities of the popular political song. More than a communist sympathizer, with his gentle revolutionary creed, he reached the climax of his career as a performer in 1970 at the Palais des Sports. But he has steadily produced albums every other year, until now. He was then and still is definitely in tune with the wave of anti-establishment protest.

The 1970s, or to be more precise the period which goes from the events of spring 1968 to the spring of 1981 cannot be easily summarized as far as pop music is concerned. They do start indeed with a new wave of protest songs in sympathy with the prevailing mood in France. The year 1968 is an expedient landmark, but it remains to be seen whether it signals any significant change in the world of pop music. S. Coulomb and D. Varrod in the *avant-propos* of their book make the point that:

La chanson est passée du statut d'expression ludique à celui d'un art consacré majeur jusque dans les plus hautes sphères des pouvoirs politiques successifs. (p. 11)

This passage was of course gradual and does not stem from 1968. Nevertheless after 1968 nothing would ever be quite the same again for the generation that lived through it. The American model, the Bob Dylan style protest song inspired writers and lyricists too. The hippy movement, love, peace and flower power, inspired the young generation, permeated or influenced as the Beatles were by mystical attitudes from India or tempted by the new drug culture. The concept of *société bloquée* branded by politicians in the Pompidolian France is useful to understand contemporary discontent. That is the other side of the coin of the affluent society. The alternative facing the adolescent confronted by the system is to rebel against it or live on the margin. The post-industrial society is pilloried by the modern gurus. These trends were reflected in the songs of the 1970s.

Most of the established figures of French pop music rode the new wave in comfort. Brassens, Léo Ferré, G. Béart, J. Ferrat are rebels at heart anyway and benefit from it. The stars of showbusiness, the French rockers or their *ersatz* will adapt or go back to their roots. But the vast movement of unrest, crystallized by the events of Spring 1968 generated a whole new contingent of songwriters and signalled the renewal of French folk music and regional cultural identities.

Not surprisingly, the linguistic and geographical marginals lead the way. Not necessarily in French either: Bretons, Occitans, Alsaciens, Basques. Alan Stivell and his Celtic harp has been seen by the Breton nationalists and sympathizers as a kind of eloquent symbol and spokesman for their plight of culturally colonized people. The Parisian eulogized this bard at L'Olympia in 1972, who exalts the mythical and legendary Brittany. Glenmor (*Princes, entendez bien*) and above all Gilles Servat (*La Blanche*

Hermine) followed Alan Stivell's brand of militant appeal for Breton identity as a Celt culture. The popular song became an academic object of study, either as a cultural or as a sociological phenomenon; it is symptomatic that in June 1973 in Royan, prior to the music festival, a colloquium was organized on the following theme: *La Chanson et les ethnies*. The Bretons were led by P.J. Hélias and the Occitans by Yves Rouquette. The *Occitanie* never really existed as a nation or as an independent state; it can only be circumscribed geographically and linguistically; the limits would follow a line going from Bordeaux, to Limoges, then south of Vichy, north of Clermont Ferrand and Valence, south of Grenoble and stopping at Vingtimiglia; in the South it stops where the Basque and Catalan language starts. Yves Rouquette himself would accept that the *Occitanie* covers more or less thirty *départments*. It is more a cultural homeland than a political entity compared to Brittany. But the protest songs signed and interpreted by Marti or Patric first in French then in Occitan are political. They have this common denominator with the Breton revivalists: their systematic opposition to centralized administration and their methodical defence of the oppressed, traditionally the workers on the land or on the shop-floor, as well as a strong appeal to regionalist language and culture. Without them the Breton and the Occitan would probably still be regarded as quaint *patois* rather than languages in their own right. Roger Siffert did the same politically and linguistically in his native Alsace, revamping traditional ballads or drinking songs. The musical idiom used by most of the revivalists is rock music seen as an enrichment of the local musical or vocal heritage rather than a commercial expedient. Alan Stivell looking back at his own career makes that very point:

J'ai suivi naturellement l'évolution de la musique; j'étais en réaction contre la variété jouée à la radio; puis est venu le rock: c'était un formidable espoir. Avant, les jeunes Bretons sifflaient des airs qui n'avaient rien à voir avec la tradition, le cha cha cha par exemple; puis la rock music a apporté des éléments qui remontent au Moyen Age, avec ses lois harmoniques et, brusquement la musique celtique. (quoted in R. Hoffmann, J.M. Leduc, *Rock Babies*, (Paris: Seuil, 1978, p. 170)

Another regional revival in the French speaking world is that of Quebec on the French scene. The year is 1976. Félix Leclerc (1914–88) was of course well known before that date. He started in Paris in 1950, before Brel, Brassens and Ferré, preferred cabarets and cultural centres (André Malraux's *Maisons de la Culture*) to the usual temples of French pop music but did appear triumphantly in 1966 at Bobino. He gave the image of the singing lumberjack, tough but gentle, ecologist long before the term had been coined, bard of the traditional values: family, love, life close to nature and our cultural roots. In December 1975 he was at the Théâtre de la Gaîté Montparnasse for six weeks and sang, among others, numbers from his latest album *L'Ile d'Orléans*, i.e., La Belle Province. These particular seasons of 1975 and 1976, saw an unusual and rich crop of French Canadian productions reaching the French market. Gilles Vigneault and Robert Charlebois were not unknown either. The first is, perhaps more than Félix Leclerc, the spokesman of French-speaking Canada as a distinct and independent cultural entity (*Mon pays*) and independent from any kind of cultural colonialism, being English, French or American. Brilliant storyteller and performer, he brings to his cousins in France the charm and robustness of Quebec folklore. The second goes beyond the model of his two elders; gone is the traditional French musical icon common to Brassens and Leclerc. His material is resolutely after the fashion of his North American culture, a kind of border territory where the Latin and European literary type of culture mingles, with the American world musically ruled by jazz and African rhythms, on the one hand, and country and western sounds introduced mainly by Irish and Scottish settlers at the end of the seventeenth century, on the other, with the exception of the Cajuns in Louisiana (some of their better known musicians were invited to Paris by Radio France in April 1976 too). There again, it is the rural folklore music which lies at the roots of a regional or ethnic identity, or considered so. Charlebois brilliantly fuses the *joual*, the working-class lingua, whether town or country in Quebec, with the rock'n'roll idiom. With him (his own show was a triumph at the Palais des Congrès in 1976) the French public welcomed a myriad of French Canadian artists: Pauline Julien, Louise Forestier, Diane Dufresne, the group Beau Dommage, (their interpretation of *La Complainte du phoque en Alaska* was a 1976 hit), Harmonium, Claude Dubois, etc. Songs from Quebec have found in France an ideal playing ground, because of their essential association of simple lyrics (i.e., in close touch with the forthrightness of its roots and the daily humdrum of life) and living music (i.e., the kind of music which is still heard in popular festivities or frolics and which has not lost its vigour in mixing American pop and reels). This success of the Canadian connection is a characteristic of the 1970s: Diane Dufresne was at the Olympia in April 1978, Pauline Julien visited Paris too with her show *Femmes de paroles* and Vigneault toured the provinces in the same year.

Provincial and traditional folk music in France was to know a revival too in the same stream of post-1968 heritage. If the movement did not last, some of the works achieved deserve a mention. One of the best-known groups, started in the shadow of Alan Stivell, Malicorne, around Gabriel et Marie

Yacoub and using suitably ancient instruments, has remained paradoxically pernickety about their sources but not particularly fundamentalist in their musical interpretation. Other groups Melusine and La Bamboche attracted an increasing number of enthusiasts too among the *soixante-huitards*. Some critics have not been particularly kind on the future of this particular trend of politically aware French folk music. Coulomb and Varrod give an uncompromising if slightly tongue-in-cheek conclusion to their analysis:

Pour résumer cette période un tantinet fromagère de l'histoire de la ritournelle, il n'est que de relire les textes, souvent écrits au bazooka, des militants de l'impossible . . . En 87, les mêmes ont changé de défroque. Quelques-uns sont députés, d'autres se retrouvent dans les couloirs des ministères, la majeure partie s'est fondue dans la masse et les plus héroïques ont ouvert des restaurants de nouvelle cuisine française avec -quand même- un coin bibliothèque. (pp. 111–12)

There is hidden censorship by the establishment, the showbiz moguls and the like. It might seem too much of a Manichean explanation to present the diffusion of songs and *variétés* in France as being clearly divided between, on the one hand, Mammon and its exclusively commercial and lucrative yardstick, successful by its own standards and, on the other, the marginal or the provincial efforts to promote singers who are not easily accessible or who refuse the commercial circuit (e.g., the marathon *Chanson en liberté* organized in Grenoble in February 1976, with Bertin, Colette Magny, the political French blues singer *par excellence*, etc.). Nevertheless it fairly accurately represents the reality of the 1970s. So, what did showbiz propose in the same period? Through elaborate but heavy plugging on the radio, Pop magazines and on Guy Lux television shows:

Voici éclore le profil 'minet', toujours propre, le sourire blanc comme neige, les cheveux longs agrémentés d'une mise en plis du plus bel effet, le costume deux pièces toujours impeccable. (p. 63)

Mike Grant is quoted by the authors as being the prime example. The excess of plugs on radio and television could explain why so many French youngsters preferred American, pop and/or folk music which invaded the French radio long wave stations anyway (Europe numéro 1, RTL, France Inter) providing 50 per cent of the available recorded music on late night shows.

The genuine *chanson à textes* is not dead of course and the 1970s have also seen the birth or confirmation of new talents, some less politically committed than others but all of them compromising with the showbusiness powers that be, the media and ultimately the public. The most *contestataire* of them all is Maxime Leforestier (1949) who has remained faithful to his anti-establishment, peace-loving, antimilitarist stand of his early career, while broadening his musical inspiration as well as his appeal. Ready to invent or try alternative means of distribution, ready to travel to risky places, Beirut for example, Leforestier reveals a genuine and essentially leftish sensitivity. Michel Sardou (1947) is at the opposite end of the political spectrum. In 1971 he had his first successful trial at L'Olympia and he appeared there again the following year. In 1976 a sordid murder story sent shock waves through French opinion and Sardou quickly composed a *chanson d'humeur* called *Je suis pour* advocating capital punishment. Not only is it not a very good song, even if it played on a sensitive chord among the silent majority in France, but it created negative waves for the talented and flamboyant singer among the liberals, aggravated by a following nostalgic number aptly entitled *Temps des colonies*. He is like an echo of the *franchouillarde* France, mildly xenophobic, misogynistic and chauvinistic. Among the other success stories of young artists in the 1970s, there is Joe Dassin (1938–80) who was considerably influenced by American folk songs; Gérard Lenorman (1948), Julien Clerc (1947), Michel Delpech (1946), Michel Fugain (1942), Serge Lama (1943), Yves Duteil (1949) all consistently scored hits; some have touched on the *comédie musicale* genre; they usually have in common a euphoric effect on their audience.

Towards the end of the 1970s a social and musical phenomenon hit the showbusiness world with a vengeance. After the box office triumph of the film *Saturday Night Fever* with John Travolta, Disco music reigned in Europe. In England, Germany, and France pop music writers found in this fad a new turning point in the business and the general transformation of American and English pop music into a universal yardstick. Most of the French neo *yés-yés* would start singing in English. The phenomenal example is Sheila with *Love me baby* and, in 1977, *Singing in the rain*. Sylvie Vartan followed suit recording in the USA. This craze alarmed those who had dedicated their artistic life to the defence and illustration of *La Chanson française*. The media as well as some governmental circles came to the rescue of that cause by organizing competitions, launching projects to stimulate creation in the French-speaking world. One of the most interesting initiatives saw its first realization in April 1977 and has, year in year out, pursued its objectives: *Le Printemps de Bourges* provided space for the discovery of new talents as well as confirmation of established stars, in a congenial atmosphere which combined performances, analyses and debates. The disco revolution changed the attitude of many song writers, too, technically speaking. If most of our traditional pop singers were quite happy to start with the lyrics and then put them to music (guitar or piano), the sound now became of primary importance.

The use of electronics and synthesizers was more universal; the beginning and the end of the songs had lengthy instrumental pieces so that people would have a decent chance to dance to it. Another evolution rather than revolution saw the diversification of the places for new talents to find the consecration they had been working towards. For example the wrestling arena of the Elysée-Montmartre saw the triumph of Yves Simon's brand of modern poetry (*Un autre désir*), Alain Souchon's disconcerting sense of humour (*Allo Maman Bobo, Poulailler's song*). Bernard Lavilliers had a concert in the modern church of Hérouville Saint Clair, the working-class suburb of Caen. Lucien Gibarra transformed public houses in the Quartier du Marais into cultural melting pots for the newcomers and old timers in the business: Blancs Manteaux, Pizza du Marais. Theatres, cultural centres opened their doors, while in Paris two newish temples were 'in': the Palais des Sports at the Porte de Versailles and the Palais des Congrès at the Porte Maillot.

In Giscardian France and to the same extent in Mitterrandist France the world of *variétés* drifted inexorably from an ebullient, sometimes idealistic, often political protest culture to a more egocentric, individualistic, realistic and laid back attitude to life, love and leisure. Socially the 1980s were meaner not greener. Solidarity was the new socialist concept after 1981, more present in the political discourse than in the tougher competitive economic world. It is tougher too for aspiring young artists. People with real musical talent like Catherine Lara and Véronique Sanson have struggled to make a lasting breakthrough. The state of the art as well as the tastes of the audience have been changed by two practical technical advances: first a round flat object, smaller than a gramophone record, on which musical sound is recorded; a CD is played on a special laser machine and the quality of reproduction is vastly superior to whatever came before. Secondly, the walkman, which is a trademark for a small personal, usually stereo, cassette player. This latest addition coincides uncannily with the new individualistic trait of young people, city dwellers in their majority. The very light headphones isolate you from the harsh, stressful, anonymous world beside you on the bus or metro, on your bike or in the crowd. Your favourite sounds accompany you in the hours lost used in transport, traffic and trivia. These two modern but by now completely commonplace instruments constituted then a progressive step forward towards receptive excellence. The production side of the industry has not seen great revolutionary devices since electronic synthesizers but one regional recording studio (Condorcet in Toulouse) made a greater impact than those of the capital and could, until its demise in 1985, rival the best studios in London, where a considerable number of French pop singers have always been tempted to go to find excellence. The diffusion of songs or albums is another matter; the new impact of radio and television needs to be scrutinized further. Their inspiration followed the socio-cultural trend of the 1980s. The concept of *pluralisme*, brought on the political scene by Valéry Giscard d'Estaing and enriched by his successor, is relevant to the world of pop music in France. Not only when one analyses the main musical genres; rock, blues, disco etc. but also in the sub-genres. Rock music, even in France, has seen every possible expression, usually trailing behind the American or English model: hard, punk, electro-funk, blue wave, etc. In the same way, as socialist models or ideals have been slowly eroded in the face of an uncompromising world economic situation, and through political realism, ideologies do not seem to generate enthusiasm any longer. The right to be different seems to be the essential human and cultural right in our relatively affluent western societies. Every possible kind of song is written: rebellious, escapist, socially aware, silly, provocative, gratuitous, funny, romantic, sad, euphoric, demystifying, mythifying – without any clear or significant consensus. The same essential fragmentation exists in the musical inspiration; the general impression is of a vast syncretism of rhythms and sounds borrowed and assimilated from the main western and eastern corpus, from Africa and South America, from central Europe to the Atlantic Arc. This diversity corresponds to the thematic plurality. The artistic coherence is, as always, created by the very personality of the song writer and/or performer, often the same person, even if music and lyrics are increasingly an act of cooperation between two similar artists. There is no doubt that to pass value judgements on the quality of creation and performance of the last decade is a risky business, but some characters have marked the 1980s and the early 1990s more than others. Using alphabetical order in the record of achievements is probably the least controversial.

Daniel Balavoine (1952–86). Perhaps his premature death during a Paris-Dakar rally where he was engaged in a humanitarian capacity, for the children of the Sahel, has made him greater than his career justified so far. His theme song is *L'Aziza*, charter of the anti-racist movement in France. Early in his career he was the central character of *Starmania*, a rock opera by Michel Berger and Luc Plamandon, but the album that encapsulates his generous message is *Loin des yeux de l'Occident*. The cover shows him sitting between an African and an Asiatic woman; two persons for whom he demands the right to be respected and to be free.

Marie-Paule Belle (1946) is the master of parody. Brilliant musician and performer, she finds her slot thanks to her lyricists M. Grisolia and the novelist Françoise Mallet-Jorris. Another great pianist is Véronique Sanson (1949) whose expertise lies in jazz, blues and rock music. Her association with Michel Berger was very fruitful, but this ended when she married an American musician, and embarked on settling down to a transatlantic performing career between France and the USA, while generally writing her own lyrics too. Catherine Lara (1945) plays the violin, started her career in the protest vein and folksy way but blossomed out in the early 1980s as the *Rockeuse de diamants*. Three distinctly gifted classy ladies whose voices are rich, modulated and energetic. Jane Birkin (1947) on the contrary is frustratingly successful thanks to an incredibly frail and very shrill voice. but the songs written for her by Serge Gainsbourg are well fashioned, sensitive or provocative, but always slightly mischievous.

Jazz, reggae, blues, samba and poetry have two stimulating exponents with Michel Jonasz (1947) and Bernard Lavilliers (1946). Jonasz has, through his grandparents, Jewish central European roots and a musical family background. His Hungarian heritage is rather diffuse. Ray Charles had a more lasting influence on him than Kodaly, Bartok or distant gypsy music. His career was long to develop but by 1977, after a recital at the Théâtre de la Ville, his reputation was solidly established. He reveals an original voice in the world of French pop music; unequivocably a bluesman with lyrics that poetically express a sensitive longing for universal unity (*Uni vers l'Uni*) as well as a humorous outlook on the human quest for happiness. His songs constitute more a moving ambiance than a message. He is a genuine altruist. Lavilliers has working-class roots in St Etienne, and humble beginnings in the boxing ring or on stage at the local rep. His musical world is first and foremost Latin American, following a long visit to Brazil, but his lyrics are packed with music of every kind (samba, salsa, reggae, etc.) He made a name for himself nationally the same year as Jonasz, in the same Parisian theatre and filled the Palais des Sports in 1980. He is a charismatic performer with an unmistakable hooligan look which masks a genuine poetical and political animal who has given a voice to some of the marginals in French society (*Les Barbares; French Vallée; Utopia*)

The new very French *chanson à texte* was presented in 1980 to the Cannes annual international market place (MIDEM) with Gilbert Laffaille (1948), Isabelle Mayereau (1947) and Francis Cabrel (1953). Of the three Cabrel has the greatest national impact. Jean-Jacques Goldman (1951) and Hubert-Félix Thiefaine (1948) have in common their reluctance to be submitted to media exposure, which probably explains their relative obscurity even if, in the summer of 1991, Goldman had a long-lasting hit, plugged for ever on the M6 channel. Their contrasting styles, Goldman rather multilingual *baba* cool,

Thiefaine multilingual surrealist, attract enthusiastic, diverse young audiences. Of the same generation, Renaud is a popular phenomenon too; popular in more than one sense, because he revived the tradition of the *chansonnier* in his own songs, with reference to household names like Madame Thatcher and in revamping realistic songs of the 1920s (*Le Petit Bal du samedi soir*). The twentieth-century gavroche skilfully uses slangy language, gives himself the image of a *marginal des faubourgs*, artistically recreates their world and looks upon our contemporary predicament with anarchistic cocky humour, in an indistinct or traditional musical idiom. Jacques Higelin (1940), late in his versatile artistic career, took over the suburban territory too, in a resolutely hard rock mode, in *franglais* and in great style.

French rock has always had dismissive comments in British pop review articles. Phrases like 'national embarrassment' or 'special talent for producing lousy rock music' crop up regularly in the appropriate gloss. The tune slightly changed, when Alain Bashung and groups like Téléphone, idolized by teenagers until their break-up in 1985, Starshooter, rather punky, Marquis de Sade in Rennes, Indochine, Rita Mitsouko, entered the scene in the 1980s. And since then the Gypsy Kings and the Négresses Vertes have successfully crossed the Channel but they constitute the exception rather than the rule. Nevertheless, in France in the 1980s, rock music was, commercially, the most lucrative sector in the industry. France, like most European countries, has been regularly invaded by American and British artists: Genesis, Police, Weather Report, Dire Straits etc. Confronted by the immense technical means, the huge success and colossal professionalism of these foreign bands, the local talents definitely played second fiddle, to the point where the cultural establishment voiced their concern over the apparent demise of the home-grown product. Jack Lang, the Minister for Culture, officially opened, in January 1984, the first Zenith, Porte de Bagnolet, a new space for rock concerts, with Higelin and Trénet heading the bill in the evening. Later, he took the unusual step, in the spring of 1989, of appointing Bruno Lion as *Chargé de mission pour le rock et les variétés* and in the arts budget provided ample provision for the promotion of concerts: new venues, cash assistance for creation, media guidance, management consultancy, etc. This controversial effort to subsidize pop music in France had seen his aims partly fulfilled in creating, outside Paris, centres of excellence like the Transmusicales and l'Ubu in Rennes. There is evidence that the 1980s had been a period *rétro* in the sense that people looked back to the 1960s and rediscovered the essence of rock music which was denigrated or misunderstood by the cultural establishment.

Patrick Mignon, a social science researcher in Paris, summed up the 1980s pertinently from that point of view:

La mise en avant des valeurs hédonistes ou individualistes fait apparaître la musique comme quelque chose d'important; il y a un grand choix et on peut y trouver des causes ou des expressions de soi. L'époque a fait sauter les blocages: le rock est le nom emblématique pour dire cela. Hédoniste et ludique, il porte en gros, toutes les valeurs de libération. (quoted by J. Stern in *Peut-on dire que le rock est un genre établi?*, article in Liberation, numéro hors série, May 1991)

Where French rock goes from here, subsidized or not, remains to be seen. For a French youngster who is eighteen in 1992, the artists mentioned in this chapter from the 1950s to the late 1980s might well seem like dinosaurs. What of the present generation? Among the successes of 1991 the choice is necessarily prejudiced; in my crystal ball I can see Patricia Kaas (1967) as an artist capable of outlasting her present commercial success as a modern Marlene singing the blues with a rich sensual voice. Patrick Bruel, Liane Foly, Pauline Ester, the Canadian Roch Voisine, all cited in the *Victoires 1991,* the French Oscars for the world of *Variétés,* are very promising too.

From the multiple ethnic communities of big cities in France are emerging new musical hybrids. The French originality there was ambiguous, if we look at second generation immigrants, *beurs* or South American, musicians, songwriters and performers, who create masterpieces reflecting both their ancestral musical heritage and their French context, but not necessarily in French. The most significant contribution comes from a second generation of Algerian, Tunisian or Moroccan artists, who successfully brew a stimulating mixture of cross-cultural influences (jazz, rock, funk, raï). The best-known groups or individuals are Carte de Séjour, Mounsi, Karim Kacel and Cheb Khaled. There is the Chilean connection (Corazon Rebelde), the Spanish connection (among others the group Mano Negra). From the French West Indies, the group Malavoi in 1985, later the group Kassav *et al.* From West Africa come Toure Kunda, Mory Kante successfully selling African rhythms and lyrics to the black and white French audiences. This array of new talents is an integral part of the French pop music scene to the extent that one could suggest that the national cultural flag should now read: black, *blanc*, *beur*.

One thing which any newcomer on the scene cannot easily ignore (or would ignore at their commercial peril) is the newish conditions of diffusion and packaging of pop music throughout the world. There is no need here to be too parochial. Contemporary pop depends more and more on visual imagery. Video clips are no longer subsidiary but vital to their commercial success and an art form in their own right. Television programmes as well as advertising jingles generate pop music too. The dictatorial discretion or hidden censorship of the media (be it radio or television) is obvious. In France the TOP 50 is like a huge distorting mirror, since it reflects the sale of singles in hypermarkets. If you have not made it the first week, forget it. It requires from the hopeful artist as well as from the established performer a constant prostitution to the plugging media. Since the liberation of FM Radio waves from the mid 1980s, the *Radios libres* offer a welcome but fragile counterbalance to the loaded dice of showbusiness marketing. They give the immense diversity of voices on the French pop scene a channel of expression. Is this enough to preserve the flowering of genuine and creative talent? Judging from the new buds burgeoning in these early 1990s, the question sounds too rhetorical. In 1984 Jean-Louis Foulquier (France Inter) initiated *Les Francofolies* in La Rochelle as an annual festival of French-speaking pop music and as an indispensable ferment of creativity. There is no real alternative in an increasingly global pop music market dominated by Anglo-American production. Jack Lang understood the urgency of the situation in terms of financial help to creativity, even if the criteria for selection remain unclear. Whether in French, in American English or in *Franglais* the *chanson* is here to stay. It would help the future of French culture and the sense of identity, if it was, in France, mostly written and sung in French. At its best it is the essence of modern poetry. It is most exclusively concerned with human experience; its poetical form, if any, is particularly adapted to our daily lives; it lasts three to five minutes. It can observe, imagine, accuse, wonder, marvel, protest, snarl, laugh. It can embrace man's dreams and fears. It spans the range of human feelings, invariably talks of love and the lack of it. It carries the uncertainties and phantasms of those who are looking for their identity or true self. It is a mirror of French society. (In such an overview it was difficult to contemplate detailed analysis of the last few years. In April 1991 Vicki L. Hamblin published a very pertinent and informative article, aimed at teachers of French civilization: 'Le clip et le look: popular music in the 1980s', with an excellent thematic anthology to which I would refer the reader.) At its worst it is a vast entreprise of cretinization.

On the threshold of the twenty-first century, French pop music is at a crossroads, as is French society. Its success lies in the future reconciliation of rhythms and sounds, coming from other continents and other cultures, with the vernacular idiom. This social and cultural coherence and cohesion must be achieved with respect to different but complementary outlooks on life and style. Not an impossible task if this civilizing activity that is, or should be, popular music is performed with the conviction that culture and/or society can do something about itself, can reform. A necessary utopia.

Further reading

Authelain, G., *La Chanson dans tous ses états* (Fondettes: Van de Velde, 1988)

Brunchwig, C., Calvet, L.-J., Klein, J. C., *Cent ans de chanson française* (Paris: Seuil, Collection Points, 1981)

Calvet, L.-J., *Chanson et société* (Paris: Payot, 1981)

Coulomb, S, Varrod, D., *Histoires de chansons 1968–1988* (Paris: Presses Pocket, 1987)

Decaunes, L., *Les Riches heures de la chanson française. Complaintes et refrains de la tradition populaire* (Paris: Seghers, 1980)

Dillaz, S., *La Chanson française de contestation* (Paris: Seghers, 1973)

Dudan, P., *Vive le showbiz bordel!* (Paris: Alain Lefeuvre, 1980)

Favre, P., Pirot, C., *Bourges, Histoire d'un printemps* (Paris: Pirot, 1986)

Hamblin, Vicki, C., 'Le clip et le look: popular music in the 1980s', *The French Review*, 64 (1991). 804–16

Hoffmann, R., Leduc, J.-M., Rioux, L., *50 ans de chanson française* (Paris: L'Archipel, 1992)

Rock babies: 25 ans de pop music (Paris: Seuil, 1978)

Rioux, L., *50 ans de chanson française* (Paris: L'Archipel, 1992)

Salachas, G., Bottett, B., *Le Guide de la chanson* (Paris: Syros Alternatives, 1989)

Sevran, P.,*Le Dictionnaire de la chanson française* (Paris: Carrère-Lafon, 1988)

Skoff Torgue, H., *La Pop-music* (Paris: PUF, Que sais-je?, 1984)

Seghers has a very rich series (Collection Poésies et chansons) on individual song writers and interpreters, e.g. Gainsbourg (L. Rioux), M. Jonasz (B. Kernel), Charlélie Couture (B. Soule) among others, Brel, Brassens, F. Leclerc, etc.

PART THREE

Cultural debates

CHAPTER 10

Paris versus the provinces: cultural decentralization since 1945

David Looseley

'Il ne faut pas envoyer aux provinciaux les miettes qui tombent de la grande table de Paris' (quoted in Gontard, p. 140).[1] As the respected theatre director Gaston Baty implied in 1945, the cultural relationship between Paris and the provinces was built upon injustice and its history since the war is that of a moral as much as a political crusade to right a wrong. This has taken two forms, both of which may be described as decentralization. The first, chronologically, has aimed to correct the uneven geographical distribution of cultural amenities (theatres, orchestras, libraries and so on); the second to transfer responsibility for such amenities from central to local government (Communes, Departments and more recently Regions). Put in these terms, cultural decentralization may appear a matter of dry administrative procedures. But my purpose in tracing its history is to show that it has in fact involved an ongoing debate not only about the right to culture but about the complex relationship between the national and the regional, the singular and the plural.

The tradition of political and administrative centralization in France is well known. It is deeply rooted in the nation's past, being strengthened with each major shift of regime from absolute monarchy through revolutionary jacobinism to the setting up of an administrative infrastructure under Napoléon. This tradition continued throughout the Third Republic and no doubt accounts for the pejorative sense the French terms *provincial* or *province* acquired during this period. However, the Liberation began a post-war challenge to centralism, slow to make any tangible impact at first but illustrated as early as 1947 by Jean-François Gravier's influential *Paris et le désert français* (2nd edition, Paris: Flammarion, 1972).

Culturally, the seeds of change had been sown well before 1944. Under the *ancien régime*, the Court, the Academies and the salons had concentrated artistic life on Paris. After the Revolution, the establishment of communes led to the development of a municipal network of cultural amenities independent of state aid: libraries, museums, theatres. Even so, by the end of the nineteenth century the capital remained the only real source of artistic legitimation and, like Balzac's Rastignac, artists were drawn to it in order to make their name. This Parisianism was aggravated by the ideology which prevailed after 1789. The Revolutionary tradition of the one and indivisible nation had been hostile to any expression of local identity or cultural specificity that might threaten national sovereignty. Consequently, regionalism and decentralization became identified with the counter-revolutionary right. The supposedly liberal Third Republic then perpetuated this suspicion. In the name of Republican unity, national cultural values were disseminated by *l'école républicaine*, which rejected regional languages and histories with the same zeal as it threw off the influence of the Church.

As for the arts, the state's role, financed by a paltry budget, was mainly limited to preserving the national heritage (*le patrimoine*), for the rest allowing itself to be guided by the conservative Academies, which centralized taste and disdained other styles and sources of contemporary creation. As the tradition of private patronage weakened, this state indifference gradually left the underfunded provinces with a lamentable shortage of orchestras, inventive modern architecture, museum space or good contemporary work to display. But it was above all in the theatre that the penury became acute enough to lead to action. As a result, theatre was to become the main focus of state intervention in the post-war period. In the early twentieth century municipal theatres, once flourishing centres for drama and opera with permanent troupes and even orchestras, began dying out, leaving many provincial towns with only some light opera and occasional, middle-of-the-road Parisian tours, both the preserve of a wealthy local elite. This meant that by 1945, the provinces had no permanent, professional drama companies. In the first decades of the twentieth century, however, a handful of individuals or groups, often inspired by a moral or populist position drawing broadly on the incipient socialist and trade-union movements, had begun to seek ways of remedying the loss. The most influential among them was the great catholic actor-director Jacques Copeau, who for five years (1924–9) chose to renounce his Parisian career and set up his own troupe, les Copiaus, in a small Burgundy village, working in an almost religious spirit of dedication and training, taking root in the region and touring with high-quality productions of classics together with material written or adapted to reflect local concerns. From the Copiaus and its ramifications emerged other *animateurs* who were to adapt these principles to their own regional theatre work over the next decades, most notably Jean Dasté, Copeau's son-in-law, and Jean Vilar.[2]

In the short term, what these early ventures could accomplish was limited. They did not constitute a movement and they were private, unaided by the state except during the brief interlude of the Popular Front (1936–7), a left-wing government committed to the right of every French citizen to enjoy the national heritage regardless of class or geography. During the Occupation, however, the division of France into two zones forced decentralization upon the French as huge numbers fled south and a new government was set up in Vichy. Although in practice Vichy was centralist, its ideology was provincialist. For many, the trauma of defeat brought about a desire to break with a decadent Republican past and rediscover a deeper-rooted national spirit that would reunite a divided people. Culturally, this meant the rejection of the effete Parisianism of the pre-war period and the rediscovery of a popular heritage in *la France profonde*. Policy therefore favoured the revival of regional folklore and gave limited encouragement to regional-language movements. For the same reason Vichy also subsidized a small, private cultural organization with high principles called Jeune France, which rapidly evolved into a semi-official unit. Aiming to renew France's tradition of artistic creation, its deeper mission was to train and thus remoralize a new generation of youth capable of unifying the nation and reconstructing it physically and spiritually. Many of those already active in theatrical decentralization joined or were aided by the group, including Vilar, Dasté and André Clavé. Theatre therefore became a major activity, but its ambitions were actually much wider and it brought numerous other arts and training activities to the regions. In this and in its deeper objectives, its work was close to the Resistance's own cultural creed.[3] Encouraged by a broad, socialist-humanist ethos and the social levelling clandestine activity naturally imposed, a number of Resistance groups working in deprived regions across the territory were similarly concerned with cultural dissemination and training, both to educate the population to resist tyranny and as a means of moral reconstruction for the future.

As a result of these various experiences, a number of cultural militants and artists emerged from the Occupation dedicated to decentralizing and more broadly democratizing culture. Combining the pre-war ideals of Copeau with those of the war-time movements, the democratization movement was distinguished by its moral, pedagogical and interventionist tone. Rather than being concerned with the popular cultures associated with diverse localities or classes, its objectives were generally unification and improvement. This ideology was perhaps best articulated by Jean Vilar, who believed in the civic mission of theatre to avoid facility and 'imposer au public ce qu'il désire profondément', restoring individuals to themselves beyond class and status and thereby conciliating all social groups in an uplifting, quasi-religious kind of communion (*De la tradition théâtrale*, Paris: Gallimard, 1963, p. 43).

Democratization took various forms which involved the provinces: the launch in 1944 of a nationwide network of Maisons des Jeunes et de la Culture, the creation a year later of leisure and cultural committees in firms (*comités d'entreprises*), and the rise of popular-education organizations, most notably Peuple et Culture which, formed from the Vercors maquis in Grenoble in 1944, made a long-term mark on culture in the provinces by training many of its future *animateurs*. But democratization was equally seen as the business of the state, culture being in Vilar's words a public service like electricity or water, and a number of administrative structures were also set up, usually within the Ministry of Education. One example was the Direction des bibliothèques, which in 1945 developed the Popular Front idea of *bibliobus*: mobile libraries fed by specially created Bibliothèques centrales de prêt (BCPs), bringing reading matter to deprived or remote areas. But by far the most significant official action for the provinces was taken by the Direction des spectacles et de la musique under Jeanne Laurent.

Despite a ruined economy and infrastructure, there were signs of renascent artistic activity in the regions by the late 1940s. New arts festivals were launched in Cannes, Avignon, and Aix-en-Provence. Musical activity was developing in Bordeaux, Strasbourg, Lyon. Through Laurent, however, it was once again theatre which was to be in the vanguard of change. Sharing the prevailing belief in democratization as a moral and civic mission, she was a firm critic of Third-Republic liberalism and advocate of state intervention. She also believed that the vitality and diversity of the provinces constituted one of France's major assets, having found evidence for this view in a sprinkling of local initiatives during the late 1940s.

In 1937, a Popular Front report on theatre in the provinces by the Parisian actor-director Charles Dullin had identified the need for theatre to 'aller vers le public' (quoted in Gontard, p. 136). Acting on its recommendations, Laurent's department asked for funds from the 1945 budget to set up a number of permanent provincial troupes, but the request was ignored. In July 1945, however, she was visited by an official of the Mulhouse town council in search of state help to develop French culture in his region, twice annexed by Germany and twice provided with exemplary German-language cultural activity. At stake here was more than a matter of cultural provision. It was politically expedient in the immediate post-war period for the Eastern regions of Alsace and Lorraine to reassert their cultural identity with the rest of France and decentralization was the ideal means. Laurent seized the opportunity and obtained a small budget for decentralization in 1946. To prepare the ground, she made regular visits to the area, discreetly encouraging local representatives to envisage setting up a permanent theatre structure. This painstaking work behind the scenes paid off when in October 1946 Colmar, Strasbourg and Mulhouse joined forces to set up a permanent troupe and drama school, jointly funded by the state and by the municipalities involved. This became the first decentralized Centre dramatique national, the Centre dramatique de l'Est (CDE). As principal patron, the state retained the right to choose the director, appointing first Louis Ducreux, another pre-war pioneer, then André Clavé who remained until 1952. Initially based in the municipal theatre of Colmar from where it toured the entire region, the CDE and its school moved to Strasbourg in 1954, laying the foundations for today's Théâtre national de Strasbourg.

The idea of a permanent provincial theatre troupe being created at municipal initiative was new and, though the formula was not repeated in precisely this form, it became the spur for four more 'Centres', or CDNs. At much the same time in Grenoble, another permanent company was set up under Jean Dasté, touring factories, villages and towns throughout the region. Here too, Laurent was discreetly supportive, though the Grenoble municipality remained blind to the benefits of regional theatre and refused to supplement the state subsidy, with the result that in 1947, the group moved to Saint-Etienne, establishing the second CDN, the Comédie de Saint-Etienne. The third, unlike its predecessors, was based on a local troupe, the Grenier de Toulouse, created by Maurice Sarrazin in 1945 and transformed into a CDN in 1949. Similar circumstances prevailed at the Centre dramatique de l'Ouest (CDO) in Rennes, which was officially opened with Laurent's assistance in 1949 by a director from Paris, Hubert Gignoux, but which in fact was linked with an earlier indigenous amateur troupe, les Jeunes Comédiens de Rennes, formed with the help of Jeune France by Guy Parigot and others. The last CDN, however, the Comédie de Provence based in Aix-en-Provence, was an entirely imported affair, set up only eighteen months before his death by Gaston Baty, like Dullin a member of the Copeau-influenced Parisian group, the Cartel des quatre. The conversion of so prestigious a Parisian figure, already in his 60s, to the cause of provincial theatre was eloquent testimony to the monumental shift that had already taken place.

The CDNs formed a more cohesive network than the pre-war initiatives. Touring each other's regions and faced with the same problems of how to take root in a region long deprived of serious theatre, their responses naturally had much in common: a repertoire based on accessible classics like Molière, techniques designed to help local people respond to their work and to stimulate the cultural life of the region, new types of contact with the population in the form of subscriptions, support associations and so on. All these approaches were to become the hallmarks of decentralization and their success made the central administration aware of the need for similar work in the Paris suburbs. In 1951, Laurent appointed Vilar to take over the Théâtre national populaire (TNP), set up in 1920 as an isolated democratization initiative. Already involved in decentralization of a kind with the Avignon Festival, Vilar had earned a reputation as a director with a fresh approach to the classics close to that of the CDNs, on which the TNP was to be modelled. Accordingly, he formed a company dedicated to performing a classical but also modern repertoire and set out to remove those architectural and psychological barriers which alienated ordinary people from theatre. He also made block-booking and subscription arrangements with workers' organizations or youth and educational establishments, often speaking in factories to make the TNP's work better understood. More importantly, in the first years he took the work of his troupe out into the working-class suburbs, organizing the famous 'TNP weekends', microcosms of the Avignon spirit offering suburban workers a package of plays, food and entertainment.

Laurent's readiness to obtain state finance for such initiatives (usually 60 per cent of a Centre's costs) was not always welcomed by the municipalities themselves. Local authorities had not been involved in financing permanent theatre for decades and some clearly feared the expenditure involved. Dasté's difficulties with the Grenoble town council were not an isolated case. Baty's generous action in Aix was delayed for a year by municipal doubts about the enterprise. And even the pioneering CDE found both its budget and its work kept under rigorous supervision by the municipal syndicate involved. Nor was Laurent's success greeted with universal enthusiasm elsewhere. The idea of decentralization went against deeply ingrained traditions and some, including dramatists, casino-managers, and representatives of trade-union interests, orchestrated a strident campaign against her. As a result, she was abruptly moved to another post in 1952. This heralded the end of official decentralization for the remainder of the Fourth Republic, though a handful of entirely private initiatives did spring up: Jo Tréhard in Caen (1949), Guy Rétoré's la Guilde in the eastern suburbs of Paris (1954), and Roger Planchon in central Lyon (1952), who moved to the suburbs at Villeurbanne in 1957 to launch the famous Théâtre de la Cité. Laurent's departure also coincided with a turning point in the wider democratization movement, as the Cold War made the Fourth Republic turn aside from social reform and as Americanized mass culture began to take hold. But a mentality of decentralization had none the less been generated which, although temporarily checked, could not be halted.

Of course, the extent of the decentralization achieved should not be overestimated. Firstly, although decentralization was not imposed on the regions and no *cahiers des charges* were required by central government in the early years, Denis Gontard suggests that this arm's length policy was somewhat deceptive since Laurent's work behind the scenes was often more pro-active than reactive (p. 147). The state also retained a decisive card by appointing the CDNs' directors. Secondly, the motive behind decentralization was national as much as regional. Not only was cultural deprivation nation-wide and therefore construed as the business of central government, but decentralization was arguably intended to restore a national culture after the Occupation (the case of Alsace here was an extreme but significant one). Like the nationalism of the Revolution, the consensualism underpinning the democratization ethos therefore went against the regionalist notion of a plurality of indigenous cultures, just as the post-Resistance Left at this time was opposed to the idea of regional devolution generally. Thus, the first CDNs were, in Hubert Gignoux's phrase, 'des sortes d'ambassades du théâtre national' importing not only directors (Clavé, Baty, Gignoux himself), but Parisian standards of excellence and broadly speaking a mainstream national or universal repertoire (Molière, Marivaux, Shakespeare, etc.), rather than drawing on specifically regional experience as Copeau sometimes had.[4] From the outset, then, there was in official decentralization and the wider democratization movement an unconsciously missionary attitude to the benighted provinces which it has never quite shaken off. Certainly, in the France of 1945, no other agent but the state had the vision or resources to carry out the task; but as time went by, its action increasingly came to be seen as 'boy-scoutist', centralist and paternalist. This became the main focus of debate in the 1960s.

The 1960s represented the second major phase of cultural decentralization for two reasons. The first was an explosion of provincial theatre companies as the work of the post-war pioneers bore fruit in a new generation, who chose to pursue regional careers. The second was a major reorganization of the state's cultural administration. De Gaulle returned to power determined to rebuild the country's international prestige. Culture was to become a vital instrument for achieving this and the creation in 1959 of a separate Ministry of Cultural Affairs under the novelist and *résistant* André Malraux (1959–69) was intended to be symbolic of the new esteem in which it was held. Malraux had been one of the left-wing intellectuals broadly associated with the

Popular Front. Later converted to De Gaulle's cause, he retained a commitment to democratization, all the more so as Gaullism entirely shared its consensualism.

Democratization was enshrined in the very definition of the new Ministry's mission. It was to be achieved by what became known as 'action culturelle' or 'développement culturel': intervention in stimulating both artistic expression and wider public participation in the arts and heritage. For Malraux, decentralization was its most important form. One of his more ambitious projects in this respect was the ten-year plan for musical development (1969–79) drawn up by Marcel Landowski, which provided for twenty-seven regional conservatoires offering a musical *baccalauréat*, quality orchestras and opera houses for each region, and a major regional dance company to be created every two years. Administratively, Malraux appointed the first 'Directeurs régionaux des affaires culturelles' in three major cities. For the theatre, he revived Laurent's initiative by creating fifteen more CDNs, one of them from Planchon's troupe, as well as giving smaller subsidies to a number of companies like Tréhard's which acquired the official designation 'Troupes permanentes de décentralisation'. But his most audacious action was the establishment of a network of Maisons de la culture (MCs) whose role, he proclaimed at the opening of the Amiens Maison in March 1966, was to eradicate the 'hideous' term '*Province*' once and for all.

The Maisons were designed to extend the achievements of the CDNs and TNP to all the arts. But Malraux went further, transfiguring decentralization with the help of his own visionary imagination. Initially, they were to be vast, regional arts centres located in every Department and equally funded by the state and the local authorities with a third source of income from box-office receipts. They were to attract and disseminate high-quality work to town and region (*diffusion*), but also to have their own creative units producing original new work (*création*). A further activity involved the elastic notion of *animation*: promotion of a dialogue between the Maison and the town intended to make each better aware of the other. This did not, however, imply involvement in local amateur activity. On the contrary, the Ministry stressed that the MCs were establishments of national excellence and creative research, capable of rivalling the best Parisian work. Finally, they were to be *polyvalent*, or multidisciplinary, having under one roof facilities for theatre, music, cinema, television, exhibitions and lectures, which would introduce a wide population to culture in all its highest forms (Bécane, pp. 8–9). For Malraux personally, these aims also had deeper, religious resonances articulated in his portentous speeches. The Maisons were to be 'cathedrals' of the modern age, as culture replaced faith in a godless world. He also likened them to the social transformation brought about under the Third Republic when Jules Ferry introduced primary education as a universal right. Transporting Paris to the provinces, the Maisons would enable children throughout France to encounter their cultural heritage unimpeded by origin or environment. Furthermore, they would combat the harmful potential of television and other mass-cultural forms and be the symbols of the greatness of the Gaullist nation, unifying its people in a common inheritance and allowing France to be true once again to its unique world mission. Not surprisingly, the reality was somewhat different.

After the prompt opening of the first MC in Le Havre in June 1961, only seven more had been inaugurated by May 1968 (though a number of others were scheduled): the Théâtre de l'est parisien (based round Rétoré's Guilde), Bourges, Caen, Thonon-les-Bains, Amiens, Firminy, Grenoble. In September 1966, the Minister claimed to be surprised at their success, with Bourges and Amiens having more subscriptions after only two years than the Comédie Française. But this could not disguise the problems the MCs were increasingly having. These were partly material. Some Maisons required magnificent new premises which were costly to build and maintain. Not only were they a drain on local resources, but, with the Ministry's overall share of central-government spending below 0.5 per cent and the three Parisian national theatres in 1966 absorbing almost double the subsidy to decentralized troupes,[5] the amount devoted to them soon proved inadequate and doubts began to be expressed about their viability.

The shortage of suitable staff was another impediment. The polymath skills required of the director, who needed to be a creator in one artistic form yet conversant with others and competent to manage a huge budget, were rare. In practice, most of the first MCs were built round a theatre company (Le Havre and Firminy were exceptions), with several based on existing CDNs or Troupes permanentes. But this was only a source of further difficulties. Given the objective of *polyvalence*, some were criticized for concentrating on theatre at the expense of other forms. More importantly, the decentralized theatre was dominated in the 1960s by Brecht, whose ideology and aesthetics raised some awkward questions. There was a growing perception among professionals that the Gaullist state's practice of decentralization was bourgeois, centralist and nationalist. But equally there was hostility to the municipalities, which, having often misunderstood their Maison's role in the advance guard of *création*, had a parochial view of the kind of entertainment or amateur facilities it should provide. The result was a web of tension between the three parties involved, illustrated in Saint-Etienne where the natural candidate for the directorship of the planned Maison was Jean Dasté. He was supported by the Ministry but not by the municipality because of policy disagreements and political reservations, with the result that the Maison was 'municipalized' (taken over by the town council) without Dasté as soon as it was inaugurated in 1968.

The mood of dissidence, fanned by a young, countercultural theatre inspired by Artaud, Grotowski and the 'Living Theater' troupe was channelled through events like Jack Lang's highly politicized Nancy World Theatre Festival. It grew into a challenge to the whole ideology of post-war democratization under the impact of the events of May 1968, when student unrest spread rapidly from Paris to the provinces and called into question every aspect of life in a society still suffocated by a paternalistic centralism. Despite a discourse of political revolution, it was a cultural Bastille the students mainly aimed to storm and with the Sorbonne and the Odéon-Théâtre de France occupied, it was inevitable that the Maisons too would be drawn in. Eschewing the class nature of the culture dispensed in France's institutions, protesters seized upon the MCs' failure to bring *la culture cultivée* to the masses either geographically, given the small number of establishments set up and their uneven distribution across the country (the entire south-west was ignored), or sociologically. All the evidence suggested that most of the provincial inhabitants who used the various new facilities, MCs or CDNs, were already culturally privileged: teachers, students, *cadres*. In 1967–8, students formed 35–40 per cent of MC users, while industrial workers made up only 2–3 per cent and agricultural workers less than 1 per cent (Simpson, p. 205).

Part of the problem was the recondite avant-garde work some directors indulged in. But this was only symptomatic of a deeper cause. The entire philosophy of decentralization since the Liberation was predicated on the belief that response to great art depends on a kind of spontaneous revelation, an immediate empathy which cannot be taught. Cultural deprivation, therefore, can be overcome quantitatively, simply by rectifying geographical distribution. For the militants of 1968, influenced by the sociology of Pierre Bourdieu as well as the didacticism of Brecht, this view was pathetically naive, ignoring the battery of social circumstances which condition individual responses to art: the family, class, working conditions, the absence in French schools of tuition in creative self-expression. This analysis was taken further towards the end of May when many directors of MCs and decentralized theatres, including some involved in the first decentralization like Dasté, Parigot and Gignoux, met in Villeurbanne at the instigation of Planchon to reconsider their position in the light of the events. Undertaking an *autocritique* of their objective complicity in their institutions' failure to reach the masses, they turned aside from 'le rassurant souci d'une plus équitable répartition du patrimoine culturel' (quoted in Jeanson, p. 119) and called for a radically different conception of *action culturelle*, its agenda defined not by a minority of *initiés* but by the unaddressed and unarticulated needs of the 'non-public'. True culture should not be a ready-made hand-me-down, but the means by which the non-public becomes politically aware of its situation, freeing itself from alienation and repossessing itself.

The key to achieving this was the notion of *animation*, now redefined. No longer just a way of establishing better relations between local people and the Maison's strictly professional activities, *animation* in post-1968 discourse acquired a much wider socio-cultural connotation. A Maison's resources should be turned outwards towards the factory, the youth-club or the school, involving improvised theatre or training in other expressive techniques. Unlike post-war democratization, the objective here was not improvement but to give local communities the tools to express their own experiences and socio-geographic identities. The actual building of a Maison, assembling within its walls all artistic forms and (supposedly) all social classes, therefore came to be seen as a Trojan horse of centralism, a symbol of the Gaullist, statist conception of a homogeneous national culture. 1968 proposed a pluralist alternative to this, in which true decentralization meant a deeper implantation: not simply Dullin's 'aller vers', but 'agir avec' (quoted in Simpson, p. 227).

In the aftermath of May, certain directors of decentralized establishments, like Jo Tréhard, active in Caen since 1949, were removed by exasperated local authorities. Nevertheless, permeation of some of the ideas of May soon began at official level. In a speech to the National Assembly on 13 November, 1968, shortly before he resigned, Malraux acknowledged the 'crisis' in the MCs, announcing a number of reforms which clearly represented a retreat from his original ambition. These included independence for the creative units within the Maisons, thereby allowing directors to concentrate on the artistic activity to which they were best suited, and the creation of smaller, more flexible structures to complement the Maisons, which themselves would now be limited to only one per region. These initiatives were taken up by his successors, notably Jacques Duhamel (1971–3), who developed a network of smaller 'Centres d'action culturelle' (CACs), less expensive to run and more responsive to local needs. For the MCs themselves, now nine with five more in preparation, he acknowledged their new concern with *animation socioculturelle* but recommended a greater concentration on serving as beacons of professional excellence rather than on a community function better carried out by structures like the Maisons des jeunes et de la culture. In 1972, he also drew up new, more flexible conditions for the CDNs based on three-year contracts and agreed to decentralize the TNP around Planchon's Villeurbanne company (now joined by Patrice Chéreau). But much more sweeping change was in the offing, as the entire cultural, socio-economic and political contexts in which the Maisons functioned began to shift.

With the onset of the 1970s, the history of the relationship between Paris and the provinces ceases to be the simple charting of a handful of major cultural establishments, CDNs or MCs, and becomes considerably more heterogeneous. This was the result of a number of factors. Firstly, Malraux's achievement, following on from Laurent's, had a domino effect, helping the idea of decentralized culture become established by fuelling demand for it at local level. To respond to this, local cultural associations blossomed and institutions like libraries and museums started to assume a socio-cultural role of their own, in some cases even becoming cultural centres. At the same time, new decentralized structures were springing up everywhere, partly as ministerial initiatives, like Landowski's ten-year plan for music, bore fruit, but also as the local authorities, taking advantage of the central funds being made available for decentralization projects, had begun to undertake their own cultural planning, with the result that by the mid 1970s they were playing a considerably greater role in cultural provision. In turn, central government took a number of measures designed to respond to this. In 1971, the FIC (Fonds d'intervention culturelle) was launched to fund experimental cultural action projects put forward by local associations or authorities. In the late 1970s, the network of field services, Malraux's 'Directions régionales des affaires culturelles' or DRACs, was developed with the aim of deconcentrating central funds and encouraging more effective communication with those involved on the ground.

Secondly, the rapid advance of mass leisure (television, pop music, video towards the end of the decade), and of the associated cultural industries, inexorably transformed the whole problem of decentralization by domesticating and in a sense democratizing cultural 'consumption'. Against this background, the recession which followed the oil crisis of 1973 and the election the following year of Giscard d'Estaing completed the transformation. Under Giscard, policy was oriented away from Malraucian interventionism. A more liberal cultural economy implied reducing the state's role in stimulating demand for traditional cultural forms like theatre, and a greater reliance on the free play of market forces, on private sponsorship, and on the more profitable cultural industries. It also appeared to mean a more prominent role for local government.

Under Michel Guy, Secretary of State for Culture from 1974

to 1976, an attempt was made to rationalize central and local spending through a system of pluriannual contracts, or 'chartes culturelles', in which the state (represented by the DRACs) and a tier of local government agreed to support a programme of one-off projects which the latter could not handle so effectively alone. Although limited in scope, the charters departed from the centralist model by acknowledging locally elected bodies as partners in policy-making rather than as mere recipients. Twenty-seven charters were signed between 1975 and 1979, resulting in new museums, regional conservatoires for music, and a multitude of restoration projects for rural buildings. The policy was then effectively abandoned, doubtless due to the inadequacy of the overall Culture budget.

Although welcomed at first, the charters were not without their critics. The left accused them of introducing a more insidious form of state interference in local affairs for only a minimum outlay. They also came to be seen in some local circles as a prelude to state 'disengagement' from the arts in general, with the local authorities being called on to make up the difference. This fear was fuelled when Jean-Philippe Lecat, Minister for Culture from 1978 to 1981, described decentralization as 'une idée dépassée'. Culture's share of state spending gradually fell from around 0.6 per cent in 1974 to 0.47 per cent in 1981, leaving the forty or so MCs and CACs hardest hit with a drop in real terms. There was also a concentration of resources on prestige institutions, particularly Parisian. Public reading was another problem in the provinces since all parties agreed that the national network of library provision was inadequate, with some sixteen Departments still without a BCP in 1981. Music, in which there was a surge of public interest in the 1970s, fared somewhat better, but the increased facilities were more the work of the Landowski plan and local-authority determination than of the Giscard administration.

In the light of this state of affairs, the gains by the left in a number of communes at the 1977 municipals were a watershed, as the new councils began to initiate and innovate, often with sizable culture budgets. In the run-up to the presidential elections of 1981, there were also hopes that a Socialist government would not only revive but redefine cultural decentralization. In the 1970s, the new Socialist Party (PS) had made the wider 'colonization' of France by Paris a live issue, proposing devolution of political powers at all levels of local representation. It had also been partially converted to the post-1968 revival of regionalism, under the slogan 'le droit à la différence'. Such hopes were fuelled after Mitterrand's victory by the appointment as Culture Minister of an arts figure with regional associations, the former director of the Nancy Festival, Jack Lang. He was quick to invoke the names of Vilar, Laurent and Dasté and to commit himself to 'irrigating' the national territory, even demanding that each province be autonomous in thought and action (*La Dépêche*, 6 July, 1981). In practice, however, his position proved somewhat more ambivalent.

The new PS government proclaimed political and administrative devolution to be 'la grande affaire du septennat'. Introduced in March 1982 and developed in 1983, its decentralization laws were intended to give greater freedom to the two established tiers of local government (communes and Departments) but also to strengthen the more recent regional councils by having them directly elected. Lang, however, like a number of other Ministers, did not see unconditional devolution as appropriate in his own domain. As a result, the impact of the laws where culture was concerned was limited.[6] Under the laws, transfer of power would entail transfers of central funds via a system of block grants which the authorities were to be empowered to spend as they wished. The Culture Ministry, however, mostly retained the traditional practice of specific subsidies, which allowed it to keep some degree of supervision over locally owned and financed amenities like museums and art schools as well as the MCs and CACs, causing a Senate report on the 1987 budget to complain of a return to dirigism. The only real transfer of power and finance was the handing over of the BCPs to the Departments (together with responsibility for Departmental archives). Even the subsidy to municipal libraries, ostensibly integrated in a block grant, was placed in a special category to ensure it could not be spent on anything else.

Alongside this limited devolution, alternative avenues were explored, such as the setting up of two innovative bodies designed to decentralize the purchase of works of art, the FRACs (Fonds régionaux d'art contemporain) and the FRAMs (Fonds régionaux d'acquisition des musées). More importantly, the Ministry also extended Michel Guy's contracts policy, despite the left's hostility to it in opposition. The new 'conventions de développement culturel' proved popular, providing an adaptable means of funding for projects that might otherwise have fallen outside the scope of state aid. The first were rapidly signed with all twenty-two Regions for a period of two years, later replaced by five-year agreements negotiated within the framework of the Ninth Plan (1984–8). Annual contracts were also signed with towns and Departments, reaching a total of 427 by 1985 and involving communes of every size.[7] One significant feature of the policy was the priority it gave to regional and minority cultures, following the Giordan report of 1982 entitled *Démocratie culturelle et droit à la différence* (Paris: La Documentation Française). Contracts with Regions like Brittany and Languedoc-Roussillon promoted regional identities by aiding associations concerned with minority languages or traditional musical forms and patrimonial amenities such as the Centre de documentation catalane in Perpignan. In the same spirit, a 'Fonds de promotion des cultures d'outre-mer' was set up in 1984, and a 'Conseil national des langues et cultures régionales' the following year. In practice, however, this spirit of *ouverture* could not go very far partly because regionalist movements were still in some cases extremist, even anti-republican, but also because the diversity of views on regionalization within the new Socialist party since the 1970s did not allow a more full-blooded approach. By 1985, Henri Giordan himself was claiming that the regionalist hopes placed in the new government had been disappointed.[8]

More generally, the contracts were criticized for retaining state superintendence and driving local authorities towards the Ministry's own predilections with the carrot of government funds. In 1985, an opposition conference on cultural decentralization held in Lyon rejected this approach as interference, calling for a more genuine transfer of power for all cultural facilities, with the Regions assuming the duties formerly carried out by the state. But this was precisely where the ambivalence of the Socialist position lay. Although genuinely committed to replacing state control with a form of partnership with localities more appropriate to today, they still wished to coax and shape home-grown policies according to a national design. In so doing, they were implicitly cleaving to the principle inherited from Laurent and Malraux, albeit in an attenuated and updated configuration, which saw a strong state as the indispensable guarantee of a national cultural identity. Of course, the Socialists differed from their predecessors in that their definition of 'national' was broader, embracing popular and minority arts and cultural industries as well as high culture. But this did not alter the basic desire for consensus even within diversity.

A further justification for preserving the state's role as harmonizer was that it also enabled the Socialists to tackle the other form of decentralization, the fairer distribution of cultural amenities, and in this regard their record has been impressive: new music schools, orchestras, cinemas, reading facilities (seventeen new BCPs have almost completed the Departmental network begun in 1945). Particularly significant has been the programme of *grands projets de province* launched by Mitterrand shortly after the announcement of his building programme for Paris in March 1982. Even here, of course, the will to decentralize had its paradoxes. Firstly, although the initiative for the provincial *grands projets* was intended to come from the local authorities, their plans usually only found favour when they matched the Ministry's own priorities. Furthermore, as the March 1986 elections approached, the opposition parties vigorously complained that, largely due to the Parisian *grands projets*, the disparity between spending on the capital and on the provinces was even greater than in 1981.

Since 1988, however, this imbalance has improved a little and, though it continues to cause comment whenever the Culture budget is discussed in the Assembly, the debate has generally become rather routine. In the case of the latest *grand projet*, the Bibliothèque de France, Mitterrand was initially challenged for siting yet another hugely expensive facility in Paris when, given its aim to irrigate the nationwide library network using the most advanced information technology, it might logically be situated almost anywhere. But the decentralization issue here has rapidly been eclipsed by other concerns. The contracts policy too is no longer contested as strenuously as it was at the 1985 conference, with some 500 local or regional authorities now involved. This is doubtless because, despite the state's spending less on it now, it has generally succeeded in stimulating local-council spending and policy initiatives as it set out to do. Nor is there any doubt about the status culture enjoys today both electorally and economically in the daily life of the regions. In fact, as culture thus flourishes and controversy withers, only Malraux's Maisons, so central to the whole decentralization debate, have continued to arouse some vestige of past passions.

Both the CDNs and the MCs have moved on from the utopianism of 1968. In the 1970s, administrative costs became predominant, new directors often began to reduce the usually unsubsidized *animation* work undertaken by their predecessors and there was a trend away from the regional touring and permanent companies through which the first CDNs sought to put down their local roots. During the 1981–6 period, both were also required to combine their original public-service aims with a more rigorous economic logic. Since 1981, the CDNs have increased from twenty-three to forty-two, with a few companies like Planchon's TNP achieving the status of 'Théâtres nationaux de région'. The network also includes, since 1985, a more flexible kind of structure, the 'Centre dramatique régional', in smaller towns such as Angers, Poitiers, and mostly recently Colmar. In the early 1980s, the state negotiated new contracts with the CDNs placing greater stress on their being commercial enterprises and requiring them to make at least 20 per cent of their income from box-office receipts. The contracts also contained measures to keep down overheads and a requirement to draw up a three-year, high-quality creative plan or *projet*.[9]

The fifteen MCs and thirty-eight CACs the Socialists inherited have generally derived less benefit from change, the MCs particularly appearing to some observers as dinosaurs. Only one new Maison has been created, Chambéry in 1987 (in preparation for twenty-four years), together with a number of new CACs and twenty-one smaller joint-funded structures called 'Centres de développement culturel' (CDCs). All three types of establishment were until very recently grouped under the heading of 'Etablissements d'action culturelle' (EACs). In 1982, a report to the Minister by Paul Puaux, *Les Etablissements culturels* (Paris, La Documentation Française), led to a major reform, as their budget more than doubled and they received new statutes intended to define 'une dynamique nouvelle' for the 80s. Firstly, there was a shift of power away from the previously dominant local associations – which hitherto had allowed representatives of the local community a say in their institution's financial management – to the director, who now assumed personal responsibility as a kind of *chef d'entreprise*, much to the disapproval of the associations themselves, represented by the Union des Maisons de la culture (UMC). Secondly, there was a shift of focus from a broad programme based on local implantation to the narrower but more universal notion of *création*, enshrined as with the CDNs in an agreed, fixed-term project drawn up in each case by an artist-director of national repute. For both types of institution, this emphasis on a finite, personal project as the basis for subsidy rather than on the establishment itself has in practice meant the regular importing and rotating among CDNs, MCs and national theatres of such 'national' figures and their work, together with a tendency towards costly, spectacular productions likely to attract attention and therefore funding.

Although in a sense recentralizing the EACs, the reform was welcomed by the SYNDEAC, the body which represents the directors of decentralized establishments. As creative artists, they were still wary of local-authority provincialism after the experiences of the 1960s and feared the consequences of the decentralization laws for their freedom to create. Such fears were partly confirmed after the 1983 municipal elections when the right made gains in a number of left-dominated towns and cities. In some cases, like Brest, Nantes, and Saint-Etienne, the new councils soon revoked past policies on the EACs, cancelled contracts, slashed budgets and even made closures, justifying their actions by citing poor management and unjustified costs, the elitist or otherwise unpalatable nature of the work produced, and the need to '*démarxiser*' decentralized establishments (*Le Monde*, 24–5 July, 1983, p. 14). This caused a wave of protest from the government and from numerous artists. It was, however, the last major ideological clash surrounding decentralization. The militancy of many of its key figures had largely disappeared by the early 1980s, as the new managerial and market-oriented values became accepted and the EACs began to suffer from a more material form of crisis. Shortly after March 1986, Jacques Chirac's government made a 4 per cent cut in the

Culture budget, the consequences of which were felt long after his departure despite subsequent increases. At the end of 1988, the public theatre sector generally had an overall deficit of eighty million francs, more than 40 per cent of which derived from six of the eleven surviving MCs, with La Rochelle and Rennes in particular peril. Lax management was evoked as a cause, but also problems aggravated by the recent reform, particularly the frequent changes of director and direction and the inadequacy of state funding, given the function of multidisciplinarity or the obligation to engage in creative work. Jack Lang had none the less issued a lugubrious warning the previous month in reference to the MCs, saying that 'certaines choses peuvent mourir' (*Le Monde*, 1 November, 1989, p. 13).

But the situation in the MCs was already changing fast. Firminy was municipalized in July 1989. La Rochelle went into liquidation and closed in December. The following month, it was announced that Rennes would cease to function as an MC and be grouped with Parigot's CDN under a new legal status. Nevers closed in December 1990. Earlier that year, the Ministry official responsible for the EACs, Bernard Faivre d'Arcier, had spoken of tighter financial supervision by the central authorities via audits and four-year mandates for directors of both CDNs and MCs entailing built-in procedures after the third year to assess management quality. In his annual address at the Avignon Festival in the summer of 1990, he had also announced the official launch of the 'Scènes nationales', grouping under a new name the sixty-two remaining EACs, including those former MCs which had already been redefined.[10] These latter changes appear to represent a refinement of the pre-1986 reform. The new name signals a narrowing of the notion of *polyvalence* to include only theatre, dance and, to a lesser extent, music. The Ministry justification for this is that it is merely responding to the evolution of the cultural environment by acknowledging the *de facto* specialization of most of these establishments in live performance and the involvement of other local institutions in *animation* and *diffusion*. The Scènes nationales are also meant to work more closely with the CDNs and independent theatre companies by such mechanisms as co-productions (already fairly common) and short-term residencies providing a venue for theatre or dance companies which do not have their own theatre. The Ministry continues to stress the centrality of the fixed-term 'project' and the executive responsibilities of the director, who is in charge of the budget as well as being the chief hirer and firer (some redundancies are likely). Stopping short of abolishing the EACs' association status (regulated by the 'loi 1901') as the SYNDEAC had demanded, the statutes now being recommended (they are not compulsory) make the director answerable to a *conseil d'administration* on which the representatives of the local population are outnumbered by those of the state and local authorities.

These latest innovations are still being applied, so it is difficult to be certain of their nature and significance. But one consequence of the package of changes since 1981 seems clear. The Maisons as Malraux conceived them, and which played such a key role in establishing the notion of decentralization after Laurent, have been transformed. For some, including the Ministry, this has merely been a natural evolution, for others a more fundamental change and a matter of regret. The last president of the UMC, Yoland Simon, believes that local democracy has been sacrificed to managerial efficiency and sees this as a return to state centralism. Deploring the lack of a national 'grand design' for the Maisons, he also considers that its replacement with a series of finite, costly, and often conventional *création* projects or short-term residencies ignores the specificities and expectations of the local community. The Maisons in his view have been stripped of the mystique given to them by Malraux and merely become 'des établissements comme les autres'.[11]

The story of the MCs is of course only one feature in the complex cultural landscape which characterizes the provinces today and which would be unrecognizable to the Laurent of 1945 or even the Malraux of the 1960s. New technology and media are disseminating a culture very different from that which they envisaged. But also the CDNs and MCs they set up have triggered a huge diversification of cultural provision in the regions: twenty-three regional orchestras and 132 national music schools and *conservatoires*, thirteen municipal opera houses and fourteen national dance centres (*Centres chorégraphiques nationaux*), arts festivals of every kind, new libraries and *médiathèques*, thirty-five *grands projets de province* finished or underway, and, most dramatically of all perhaps, local authorities spending more on culture than the state. But despite the enormous quantitative progress made in half a century, certain fundamental issues remain which are the latest avatars of the shifting but constant dialectic we have traced between the national and the regional, culture and cultures, state impulsion and local autonomy.

Some of these issues have recently been highlighted in the René Rizzardo report of February 1991, *La Décentralisation culturelle* (Paris, La Documentation Française), commissioned by the Ministry in parallel with the government's proposal for a second wave of administrative decentralization through its bill on 'l'administration territoriale'. Although Rizzardo expresses satisfaction with what has been achieved by decentralization, he argues that the dynamic created in the regions now requires to be completed by a 'nouvel élan'. This is primarily called for by the state's local partners who find the existing system of shared funding and responsibilities incoherent and who resent the resources expended on the Parisian *grands projets*. But it is also necessary in the context of 1992, since cultural relations within the new Europe will not be conducted uniquely between capitals but between other towns and regions; and France does not have regional centres to compete with the 'force de frappe culturelle' of great cities like Milan, Munich or Barcelona.

Even so, the report does not suggest a fundamental transfer of cultural power for the time being. Indeed, Jack Lang made it eminently clear when commissioning it that he still believes in the state as locomotive, maintaining that 'sa présence forte dans la vie culturelle stimule, et non limite, l'essor de collectivités locales entreprenantes' (Rizzardo, unnumbered pages). Working within these parameters, the report only seeks to rationalize existing procedures regarding the communes while recommending a limited number of new responsibilities for the Regions and Departments, particularly in specialist arts training and, for the Regions, as partners in financing the Scènes nationales. It also suggests that, when the existing Parisian *grands projets* are completed, the separate budget set aside for them be reserved for major projects with a specifically regional vocation.

Rizzardo believes this proposed redistribution of administrative responsibilities could become a new, mobilizing dynamic for the 1990s. But the history of cultural decentralization since 1945 is that of the gradual displacement of an ethical, democratic ideal by what Gilles Roussel has called its 'formalisation administrative' (p. 9), its technocratization and its institutionalization at local level as a factor in attracting investment. Administrative reform alone is therefore unlikely to rekindle its idealism without, as Roussel argues, an equal willingness to address more fundamental issues of pluralism and democracy.

One such issue is the opposition we have traced between decentralization as a purely spatial movement involving the wider dissemination of a 'national', but in fact Parisian, culture, and the need for a more organic, permanently implanted engagement with local cultural difference. A number of observers agree that with the circulation of work by national figures amongst regional establishments, with progress in transport and communications bringing the provinces and Paris ever closer, and with professionals today feeling safer with the national Ministry than their local authorities (who are themselves deeply concerned about the national *rayonnement* of the institutions they subsidize), artistic recognition, unlike in some European countries, is still essentially measured by a central, Parisian yardstick, despite all the progress made. Some even believe this has proportionally worsened as the commitment to implantation from Copeau to May 1968 has progressively weakened.

A related issue is democratization. Although supply has been improved by decentralization, it has not for all that been democratized. Not only is it still unevenly spread across the territory, but more importantly the audience for *la culture cultivée*, those art-forms like theatre and opera with which the movement has traditionally been concerned, is still largely made up of a minority privileged by social or educational status, just as it was in 1968. The crucial question here is no longer simply to do with cultural provision but with a national education policy for the creative arts at primary and secondary levels.

These are perceived to be the deeper issues to be faced if the cultural decentralization debate is to be re-energized as Rizzardo wishes. Both are predicated on the notion that in decentralization quality should count as much as quantity, content as much as form. The implication is that if they do not, the progress made since 1945 will prove to have been a mere shifting of furniture rather than the achievement of a true cultural democracy.

Abbreviations

BCP	Bibliothèque centrale de prêt
CAC	Centre d'action culturelle
CDC	Centre de développement culturel
CDE	Centre dramatique de l'Est
CDN	Centre dramatique national
CDO	Centre dramatique de l'Ouest
DRAC	Direction régionale des affaires culturelles
EAC	Etablissement d'action culturelle
FIC	Fonds d'intervention culturelle
FRAC	Fonds régional d'art contemporain
FRAM	Fonds régional d'acquisition des musées
MC	Maison de la culture
PS	Parti socialiste
SYNDEAC	Syndicat national des directeurs d'entreprises artistiques et culturelles
TNP	Théâtre national populaire
UMC	Union des Maisons de la culture

Notes

I would like to thank the following for kindly providing information for this chapter: Mesdames Jacqueline Boucherat, Elisabeth Raynal, Anna-Michèle Schneider, M. Alain Lennert (all from the Ministry of Culture), and M. Yoland Simon (formerly of the

UMC); together with the Leverhulme Trust and the University of Bradford for funding and facilitating leave of absence.

1. References to works cited in full in the Bibliography will generally be given in abbreviated form in the text and notes, as will shorter references such as press articles. In the text, I have adopted the practice of capitalizing the first letter of the English words 'Region' and 'Department' (and their derivatives) where they are used to refer to the respective tiers of French local government rather than in their more general senses.

2. Gontard, pp. 57–87 on Copeau, and pp. 89–120 on later troupes in the 1930s and 1940s. I am particularly indebted to this study in the analysis which follows of decentralized theatre in the pre-war and immediately post-war periods. Also D. Bradby and J. McCormick, *People's Theatre*, (London: Croom Helm, 1978) and Bradby's own *Modern French Drama* (Cambridge: Cambridge University Press, 1984).

3. Jeune France was in fact disbanded by Vichy in 1942 and some of its members, like Clavé, joined the Resistance. On Jeune France, see in addition to Gontard, pp. 120–7, C. Faure, *Le Projet culturel de Vichy: folklore et révolution nationale 1940–1944* (Paris and Lyon: Presses Universitaires de Lyon/Editions du CNRS, 1989) and V. Chabrol, 'L'ambition de "Jeune France"', in J.-P. Rioux, ed., *Politique et pratiques culturelles dans la France de Vichy*, Cahiers de l'IHTP, no. 8, Paris: CNRS, 1988. On a similarly influential group, formed at the Ecole nationale des cadres at Uriage and which also crossed the Vichy-Resistance divide, see in Rioux's volume B. Comte, 'L'Esprit d'Uriage: pédagogie civique et humanisme révolutionnaire'.

4. There were exceptions to this rule: Baty in particular aimed to encourage local forms like pantomime, but had little time to put this into practice: see Gontard, pp. 313–14. For the national dimension of the CDNs, see Gontard, p. 187. The quotation from Gignoux is from his book, *Histoire d'une famille théâtrale*. (Lausanne: Editions de l'Aire, 1984), p. 309.

5. J. Lang, *L'Etat et le théâtre* (Paris: Librairie Générale de Droit et de Jurisprudence, 1968), p. 252. Lang does point out that decentralized troupes also receive subsidy from local authorities, unlike the national theatres.

6. This was in fact true of a number of ministerial domains, but Culture was probably the most extreme case. For a fuller analysis of the decentralization laws and culture, see S. Mazey, 'Decentralisation: la grande affaire du septennat', in S. Mazey and M. Newman, *Mitterrand's France* (London: Croom Helm, 1987), pp. 117–18; M. Keating and P. Hainsworth, *Decentralisation and Change in Contemporary France* (London: Gower, 1986), pp. 79–88; and particularly Wangermée and Gournay, pp. 105–14 and pp. 126–32.

7. Ministère de la culture, 'La politique culturelle 1981–1985', booklet entitled 'La décentralisation et le développement culturel', pp. 7–9 and pp. 12–13; Wangermée and Gournay, p. 379.

8. 'La décentralisation et le développement culturel', pp. 16–19, and J. Forbes, 'Cultural policy: the soul of man under Socialism', in Mazey and Newman, pp. 153–4. For Giordan's 1985 comment, see

his 'Les minorités régionales', in Espaces 89, *L'Identité française* (Paris: Editions Tierce, 1985), pp. 89–91 (p. 89).

9. A. Busson, 'Le Théâtre en France', *Notes et Etudes Documentaires*, no. 4805 (1986), pp. 25–6 and pp. 107–20. See also the two booklets entitled 'Le Théâtre et les spectacles' in Ministry, 'La politique culturelle 1981–1985', pp. 4–5 and 'La politique culturelle 1981–1991', pp. 6–7 respectively.

10. For Faivre d'Arcier's statement about financial supervision, see *Le Monde*, 4 January, 1990 (Arts supplement), pp. 28–9. Little published information on the Scènes nationales is yet available. My main sources are a Ministry official in the Bureau des EAC and two Ministry documents: 'Bilan des Scènes nationales 1989–1991' and a copy of the 'statuts' being recommended by the Ministry. See also the Theatre booklet in Ministry, 'La politique culturelle 1981–1991'. pp. 13–14. The current situation of the ex-EACs is extremely complex partly because the changes are so recent, but also because the statutes of the different establishments vary a good deal.

11. M. Simon provided me with a written account of his views on the MCs and with the texts of various declarations he has made on the subject. Until 1990, he was also President of the Association of the Le Havre MC. The UMC has recently been dismantled as part of the Scènes nationales changes.

Further reading

Bécane, Jean-Claude, 'L'expérience des Maisons de la culture', *Notes et Etudes Documentaires*, no. 4052 (8 January 1974). Provides useful information on the principles and aims behind the MCs as well as a considerable quantity of more factual detail, including statistical data and extracts of speeches by Malraux and Duhamel.

Bradby, David, *Modern French Drama 1940–1980* (Cambridge: CUP, 1984). Written from an historical as well as dramaturgical standpoint, provides useful analysis of Laurent's and Malraux's initiatives regarding theatre, of the ideas and work of Vilar and Planchon, and of decentralized theatre in the 70s.

Gontard, Denis, *La Décentralisation théâtrale en France 1895–1952* (Paris: Société d'Edition d'Enseignement Supérieur, 1973). Is a minutely researched doctoral thesis, indispensable for an understanding of the pre-war pioneers of decentralization and of Laurent's setting up of the CDNs, each of which has a separate chapter.

Jeanson, Francis, *L'Action culturelle dans la cité* (Paris: Editions du Seuil, 1973). Contains discussion of the Maisons from the perspective of Jeanson's own experience at the Chalon-sur-Saône MC in the late 60s, but also a substantial selection of illuminating authentic documents concerning both Chalon and wider national issues.

Laurent, Jeanne, *La République et les beaux-arts* (Paris: Julliard, 1955). Indicts the cultural policy of the Third and Fourth Republics while remaining modest about her own achievements in decentralization. '1946–1976', *ATAC Informations*, no. 75 (March 1976), pp. 5–9. Usefully updates and extends this earlier account.

Roussel, G., 'La décentralisation culturelle ou la démocratie difficile', *Après-demain*, no. 322 (March 1990), pp. 9–14. Examines the decentralization movement's loss of direction and idealism since 1945 and puts a cogent case for its being reanimated today.

Saez, G., 'Politique culturelle: suivez le guide!', *Pour*, no. 101 (May–June 1985), pp. 36–45; and 'La politique de développement culturel de 1981 à 1986', paper read to the Séminaire du Centre de Recherches Administratives, Fondation Nationale des Sciences Politiques, 31 January 1987, typescript, 15pp. Contain an invaluable, expert analysis of the changes in the EACs during the 80s.

Simpson, N. J., 'The French Maisons de la Culture – an experiment in the decentralisation and democratisation of culture, from the inception of the Maisons de la Culture in 1959 until 1975' (unpublished MA dissertation, University of Bradford, 1978). Provides useful original material (including documentation) on the MCs in the 60s and 70s.

Wangermée, Robert, and Gournay, Bernard (Council of Europe), *Programme européen d'évaluation: la politique culturelle de la France* (Paris: La Documentation Française, 1988). Is an admirably thorough and indispensable two-part assessment of French policy, the first part by a Frenchman, the second by a team of European experts. Both have substantial analyses of decentralization, including statistical material.

Official documents:

Ministère de la culture, 'La politique culturelle 1981–1985' (collection of booklets), booklet entitled 'La décentralisation et le développement culturel'; and the more up-to-date 'La politique culturelle 1981–1991', April 1991 (collection of booklets), booklet with the same title and another entitled 'Développement et formations'. Both dossiers provide ample factual material and a revealing statement of the Ministry's own perspective on decentralization.

CHAPTER 11
Gender Issues

Alex Hughes

To analyse gender is to explore the multiple significations which we associate with the socio-sexual categories 'masculine' and 'feminine'. In practice, analysis of the gender issue in post-war France has focused more or less exclusively on what it means to be an *être sexué féminin* within a socio-cultural context which, even today, can be viewed as andro/phallocentric. This is mostly due to the fact that, in recent decades, French society has witnessed the (re)birth of a powerful feminist movement, and has seen the evolution of a current of feminist thought which has preoccupied itself with the related notions of feminine 'difference' and feminine linguistic specificity (*écriture féminine*). In the discussion which follows, I shall give an outline of the history of post-war French feminism, and of the movement's intellectual concerns. I shall also examine (i) the legal and social developments that have affected French women's lives since 1945 and (ii) some of the literary productions which grew out of women's desire to 'find a voice' – i.e., to explore, creatively, the nature of female experience, to chronicle the oppressive treatment the 'Second Sex' receives under patriarchy, and to forge representations of femininity or textual practices which interrogate those of the dominant male culture.

Historical and social landmarks

Until a surprisingly recent date, Napoleon's restrictive *Code Civil* still cast its shadow over the lives of French women. Instituted in 1804, the Code ensured that women in nineteenth-century France, particularly married women, were excluded from public life and condemned – unless they belonged to the privileged classes, or, like the writer George Sand, were daring enough to flout convention – to subservience and subordination. It left them with little control over what happened to them, and no chance of influencing the direction taken by the events of the outside world. One of its more (in)famous articles stated baldly that 'la femme doit obéissance à son mari', and another, equally draconian dictate (number 1124) granted women a legal and civic status identical to that of madmen and minors. As the feminist historians Maïté Albistur and Daniel Armogathe observe, 'avec le Code civil s'achev[a] l'œuvre d'avilissement de la femme commencée depuis le XVIe siècle' (Albistur and Armogathe, 1977, p.242). Not unsurprisingly, throughout the nineteenth and early twentieth centuries French women struggled to improve their legal and social situation, and by 1938 many of the outdated strictures of the Napoleonic Code had been revoked. The fact remains that the misogynistic attitude it exemplified was still very prevalent in France during the first half of this century. Manifestations of feminist activity were viewed with suspicion, and women were, to a large extent, still perceived as second-class citizens.

The advent of the Second World War brought about key changes in the social and sexual status quo. With their husbands and fathers away at the Front, women emerged from their kitchens and nurseries to work in the factories; later, many joined the Resistance and gave their lives for France. Recognition of their courage and their increased autonomy, together with a new distaste for the institutionalized misogyny which had been a feature of French life under Vichy[1] and an awareness that the Liberation would necessitate social change, provoked de Gaulle's Provisional government into giving women the vote in 1944. While political enfranchisement and the right to participate fully in party politics (by 1949, there were forty female members of the Assemblée, twenty-nine of whom were Communists) were clearly important gains for women, male politicians on both the left and right were wary of the consequences of female suffrage, and were less than enthusiastic about fielding women candidates. This gradually led to a sense of alienation on the part of those French women who sought to be politically active, and caused many to turn their backs definitively upon the established, official political scene.

During the decades that followed the end of the war, women's legal and social lot continued to improve. In 1965, lingering echoes of the Napoleonic Code were abolished – henceforth, a French woman could take full responsibility for her financial affairs, open her own personal bank account and exercise any profession she liked, without prior consent from her husband. In 1967, thanks to the campaign organized by the *Mouvement français pour le planning familial* and the passing of the *loi Neuwirth*, contraceptives became legally available to her. By 1974, she could, under certain circumstances, have an abortion. French women owe the acquisition of the right to control their own fertility and terminate an unwanted pregnancy to the lobbying activities of groups like *MLAC* (the movement for the freedom of abortion and contraception) and *Choisir*. *Choisir* was an association formed in order to protect the 343 women who put their names to the

Manifeste published in *Le Nouvel Observateur* in April 1971. The signatories of this document stated that they had had backstreet terminations – which was at the time a criminal offence – and called upon the government to make abortion freely available to all. It was signed by women (the writer Simone de Beauvoir and the actresses Catherine Deneuve and Delphine Seyrig, for example) who were very much in the public eye, and its existence illuminates the extent to which the abortion issue preoccupied and divided French society during the early 1970s.

By the mid-1970s, French women seemed to be making more rapid progress toward social, legal and sexual emancipation. In 1974, President Valéry Giscard d'Estaing established a (short-lived) *Secrétariat d'Etat à la condition féminine*, headed by the journalist Françoise Giroud. Viewed by many women as a 'token' institution, Giroud's secretariat was none the less responsible for recommending a series of anti-discriminatory measures. After the Socialists came to power in 1981, a Ministry for Women's Rights was inaugurated, and Yvette Roudy was put in charge of it. Laws were passed which ensured that abortions, like other operations, were paid for by the state and which combatted inequality between the sexes in the professional domain – although equal pay for women had become a legal requirement in 1972 ('à travail égal, salaire égal'), in practice many women were still earning lower salaries than their male colleagues. Increasing numbers of French women entered – or returned to – the job market, with the result that by 1987, 37.2 per cent of France's female population was professionally active. Women became more visible in the 'male' worlds of commerce, higher education, finance and industry; in 1984, for example, only 4 per cent of engineering diplomas were awarded to female students, but by 1986, the number had risen to 20 per cent. Women began also to play a much more prominent role in French political life. In 1988, although the number of female *députés* was proportionally smaller than it had been after the end of the Second World War, six women occupied key ministerial positions within the government of Prime Minister Michel Rocard. By August 1991, women made up almost half of President Mitterrand's senior governmental advisers at the Elysée palace, and Rocard had been replaced by Edith Cresson. As Elisabeth Guigou, the new Minister for Europe, commented, Cresson's success gave French women 'a feeling of pride. It's a sign for the future, a victory for a generation of women who don't have a conflict with their femininity' (*Guardian*, 17–18 August, 1991, pp.10–11). Unfortunately, however, the euphoria surrounding Cresson's appointment to the premiership did not last, and her recent departure took place in a climate of rancour and recrimination.

Clearly, major advances have been made – which explains why

91 per cent of the 800 women who took part in a recent survey of *la condition féminine* conducted by *Le Nouvel Observateur* replied in the affirmative to the question 'Etes-vous heureuse?'. This is not to say that women in today's France no longer encounter exploitation or discrimination. A report in *L'Evénement du Jeudi* (30 April, 1992) indicated that, in spite of the efforts of Véronique Neiertz, the current secrétaire d'Etat des droits des femmes, to discourage and legislate against sexual harassment in the workplace, it is a problem in France, where the phenomenon of the 'New Man' has yet to make much of an impact, and the conventional wisdom is that 'le flirt est notre sport national'. Access to education and training has become much more widely available to French women in the last few decades, but women tend, even today, to earn less than men (partly because many still opt for forms of employment which are traditionally reserved for women, and which attract low salaries). Their professional situation is more precarious, because they are more likely to take jobs with short-term contracts or temporary status – in 1988, 80 per cent of private-sector temporary posts in France were held by women. French women are less likely to achieve promotion than their male counterparts, and stand a greater chance of becoming unemployed – 54 per cent of France's *chômeurs* at the end of the 1980s were in fact *chômeuses*, and the majority of the long-term unemployed were also women. The *Grandes Ecoles*, France's most prestigious tertiary educational establishments, are all mixed these days, but have been slow to take in male and female students in equal numbers, which explains why France's professional élite is still largely dominated by men. This fact is reflected in a set of statistics published in the magazine *Le Point* on 1 May, 1989, as part of an article entitled 'Non, les femmes n'ont pas encore gagné!'. Of the 322 people holding the title of *Académicien* in that year, only eight were women. Forty per cent of France's judges were female in 1989, but only 7 per cent had penetrated the uppermost echelons of their profession. Many women were active in the previously male-dominated field of scientific research, but a mere one out of eleven had achieved the sought-after position of *Directeur de recherche hors classe*. Ninety per cent of the (poorly paid) nurses working for the *Assistance publique* in Paris were women, while 90 per cent of French surgeons were men.

Although these statistics are worrying, it would be absurd to claim that French women have not come a very long way indeed since 1945. That they have done so is due primarily to the rise, in France, of the feminist movement. It goes without saying that French feminism was not born in the post-war period. In the nineteenth century, bourgeois and working-class women were already struggling to free themselves from the limbo of insignificance in which they found themselves; women like Juliette

Adam, Claire Démar, Flora Tristan and Suzanne Voilquin, who took up their pens in order to denounce publicly the state of subjugation that was woman's lot. Nevertheless, it is true to say that French feminism really 'took off' after the end of the Second World War, and more particularly during the early 1970s. Certain key events were responsible for, and reflect, this phenomenon; notably the publication in 1949 of Simone de Beauvoir's *Le Deuxième Sexe*, the social upheavals that occurred during May 1968, and the subsequent evolution of what became known as the *Mouvement de Libération des Femmes* – the *MLF*. The following sections of this chapter will explore the development, and the multi-faceted character, of feminism in France.

'Femmes, vous lui devez tout!'

When Simone de Beauvoir died in 1986, one of the numerous obituaries that appeared in the French press bore the above, eye-catching title. In it, Elisabeth Badinter made the point that without Beauvoir, and particularly without *Le Deuxième Sexe*, women in the west would not have achieved the professional, social and legal autonomy they enjoy today. Yet when Beauvoir began to work on what became one of the bibles of the women's movement she was no feminist, even though she was to become one in the decades that followed. It was mostly due to Sartre's encouragement that she embarked upon her ground-breaking two-volume study, in which she analyses the structures patriarchy has evolved in order to subordinate the female sex, and suggests that the socio-sexual order is not immutable, but instead open to (much-needed) modification.

Le Deuxième Sexe is based upon two central propositions: (a) that 'femininity' is a socially determined rather than a natural state (hence Beauvoir's famous remark 'on ne naît pas femme, on le devient'), and (b) that the passivity, inferiority and alterity ('otherness') associated with femininity across the centuries are a product of the male-dominated cultures in which women have always found themselves. If women have been viewed – and have viewed themselves – as man's 'other', this relates less to the biological or psychological differences that exist between the sexes than to the fact that men have exploited those differences in order to construct a status quo precluding any form of sexual equality. In order to demonstrate the truth of these contentions, Beauvoir examines in detail the way women have been treated throughout history, deconstructs the myths that surround femininity, and analyses the experiences undergone by modern woman – marriage and motherhood, for example – as she is integrated into society, not as an autonomous individual, but as man's negative, object, or possession.

Beauvoir's critique of patriarchy is extremely wide-ranging; she was, for instance, one of the first women to question Freud's account of female psychosexual development, and to take issue with the controversial notion of 'penis envy' underlying his description of the feminine Oedipus Complex. However, her essay does more than illustrate the ways in which masculinist culture has defined and oppressed women, since it also indicates how things might change. Beauvoir suggests, for example, that the advent of a socialist, economic revolution, while this alone cannot resolve the problem of sexual inequality, is a necessary prerequisite of feminine emancipation (her opinion changed somewhat later on, once she adopted a more radical feminist outlook and ceased to view herself first and foremost as a socialist). She points out also that the modification of woman's economic condition is not enough; that moral, social and, above all, educational progress must occur if women are to be liberated. More importantly, she argues (and it is here that influence of the Existentialist philosophy which permeates her essay is most palpable) that if 'femininity' (= dependency, alterity, 'immanence') is not a *natural* given but a culturally elaborated *construct*, then women, however difficult their current situation, have the same basic capacity for freedom and 'transcendence' as men.[2] Freedom will be achieved once women recognize that the *condition féminine* (as it stands) is not fixed for all time, avoid the temptation to embrace an inauthentic mode of being based on resignation and submissiveness, and work for collective liberation.

Critics have disagreed about the impact of *Le Deuxième Sexe*. Anne Whitmarsh argues that if the book had never existed, 'on balance it seems unlikely that the women's liberation movement would have developed any differently'. Her belief is that Beauvoir's essay 'is not the sort of book to persuade anyone into militant action, partly because it was never conceived as anything other than an attempt to make people conscious of the traditional role of woman and rethink it' (Whitmarsh, 1981, p.152). Albistur and Armogathe, on the other hand, suggest that radical French feminism was virtually moribund at the end of the Second World War, and that the effect of *Le Deuxième Sexe* was to breathe new life into it and to offer fresh answers to the problem of women's oppression. Like Badinter, they stress the debt younger French feminists owe to Beauvoir, and maintain that 'il ne faut pas avoir peur de dire que tout le féminisme contemporain procède du *Deuxième Sexe*' (p.414). It seems fairly evident that the growth of the *MLF* in France in the early seventies was due at least in part to the change in awareness which Beauvoir's book (belatedly) helped provoke. It is also true, however, that the evolution of what became a very lively feminist movement was first and foremost the product of the cataclysmic events of May 1968.

'Plus rien ne sera jamais comme avant!' (popular slogan, May 1968)

During the late spring of 1968, France was hit by an explosion of anger, violence and social discontent which began in the Universities but rapidly spread to other sections of society. Feelings ran so high that it seemed for a time as if the country were going to fall into the grip of revolution. In Paris, students and workers demonstrated, rioted, and clashed with police; cars were burned and anarchy threatened to become the order of the day. Although the May revolt lost its momentum all too rapidly, it made people see that the status quo was not as stable and solid as they had believed, and sent shock waves through the educational, political and cultural institutions of France. One of its consequences was the birth of the *MLF*.

As Claire Duchen explains in her excellent study *Feminism in France from May '68 to Mitterant* (1986), the women who were involved with the May movement experienced the revolution which seemed to be within reach in both a negative and a positive way. On the one hand, May 1968 made them much more aware of the forms of oppression to which they, as women, were subject, and enabled them to see that a radical metamorphosis of the established sexual order could occur. Unfortunately, they also discovered (as women activists throughout history have discovered) that their male comrades were disinclined to abandon traditional, 'masculine' modes of behaviour – shouting women down in meetings, for instance, or making it plain that female comrades made better cooks than political tacticians. Disappointed with the limitations of what they came to perceive as a 'phallocratic', as well as short-lived, revolution, French women gradually began to form themselves into independent feminist groups. By the summer of 1970, the French media, aware of the existence in the United States of a Women's Liberation Movement, had begun to talk about the emergence in France of a *Mouvement de Libération des Femmes*.

The activities of the *MLF* were many and various during the 1970s. As women's groups that had come together in the late 1960s became more aware of each other's existence, large meetings (*assemblées générales*) began to be held. These were usually chaotic, but were, for a while at least, extremely good humoured. In August 1970, feminists placed a wreath on the tomb of the Unknown Soldier, dedicated not to this anonymous symbol of heroic French manhood but to his wife. Their action, which was viewed by many as gratuitously offensive or simply downright silly, was intended to make the point that in a society which privileges jingoism and male achievement, women, along with their sacrifices and values, are usually forgotten or ignored. In November of the same year, women from the *MLF* disrupted a conference arranged by the magazine *Elle* on the subject of Woman, because they objected to the reformist, insufficiently radical feminist line it adopted. Feminists demonstrated in 1972 against Mother's Day – probably western culture's most glaring symbol of the hypocrisy surrounding woman's domestic exploitation – and became increasingly involved in campaigns to legalize abortion, publicize the scandal of violence against women, and to achieve better pay and conditions for female workers. A plethora of feminist publications began to appear, including *Le Torchon brûle*, a journal launched in 1970 in order to offer women the opportunity of writing freely about their lives and experiences, *Les Pétroleuses*, which was a communist feminist paper, and *Questions féministes*, a periodical concerned with the theoretical analysis of oppression, edited by Simone de Beauvoir. The prestigious journals *Tel Quel* and *Les Temps modernes* each devoted special issues to feminism and women's writing. All over France, women joined feminist groups and began to organize collectively, in an effort to combat the sexual injustice they saw around them.

From its inception, the *MLF* was not a homogeneous organization, but rather an amalgamation of associations and groups of women who were dissatisfied with the traditional roles they were expected to play and were angry that the oppression of one sex by the other was still largely sanctioned in French society. That said, there were considerable differences separating the diverse elements within the Movement, and the existence of these differences led, inevitably, to disagreements. There were conflicts about what kind of action the *MLF* should take, and how it should be organized. Theoretical analyses of femininity and oppression based upon Marxist theory or psychoanalysis (the study of the unconscious and of human sexuality) were hotly defended by some groups and denounced by others as naive or ideologically dangerous. Women whose radical feminism caused them to embrace lesbian separatism as the only politically viable mode of existence felt alienated from feminists who were heterosexual and who did not accept that perceiving men as a hostile class made lesbianism a strategic inevitability.

In the wake of these dissensions, which became more pronounced by the late 1970s, various currents emerged within French feminism.[3] There were, for example, the 'tendance lutte de classes' feminists, who argued that the liberation of women could not and should not be divorced from the class struggle. A number of these socialist feminists belonged to the *Cercle Elisabeth Dimitriev*, a group which concerned itself with the relationship between patriarchal oppression and the capitalist system. In an attempt to attract greater numbers of 'ordinary' women and to popularize the feminist cause, the *Cercle* adopted an organizational structure based upon small, self-regulatory *comités de quartier*. Another important 'strand' of the *MLF* was constituted by the *Féministes révolutionnaires*, a broad-based group whose stated aim was the complete overthrow of the patriarchal order. The *Féministes révolutionnaires* distrusted the established socialist or revolutionary parties of the left and the feminists who maintained an allegiance to them. They were a vocal, high-profile band of women, who (amongst other things) played a key role in the demonstration against Mother's Day in 1972, disrupted a big anti-abortion 'Right to Life' meeting in the previous year, and organized the 'Journées de dénonciation des crimes commis contre les femmes' in May 1972. Unlike many of the 'class struggle' feminists, a large section of *Féministes révolutionnaires* were separatists, even though, as the American feminist critics Elaine Marks and Isabelle de Courtivron point out, 'the notion of working without, doing without, men is more scandalous in France than in the United States' (Marks and de Courtivron, 1981, p.9).

Féministes révolutionnaires and the class-struggle feminists found themselves at odds with what is probably the most famous of the French women's groups, *Psychanalyse et politique*, also known simply as *Psych et Po*. This organization, publicly launched in 1970 at the University of Paris at Vincennes, enjoyed a considerable degree of financial autonomy and was responsible for the establishment of the influential *Des femmes* publishing house and bookshops. In 1979, under the direction of the analyst Antoinette Fouque, *Psych et Po* more or less hijacked the French women's movement by registering the logo *MLF* as their own trademark. Their action provoked hostility amongst feminists who rejected the conceptual methodology favoured by the group and led, in the 1980s, to the existence of two, mutually antagonistic, *Mouvements de Libération des femmes*: the *Mouvement marque déposée* (i.e., *Psych et Po*) and the *Mouvement marque non déposée*.

Psych et Po were unusual in that they rejected the label 'feminist' – Antoinette Fouque argues that feminist women seek to be not only equal with but also *identical* to men, and to create a 'new' social order which effectively reproduces the same sexual power structures as patriarchy, only in reverse. As their name suggests, the group chose to base their analysis of gender relations upon psychoanalytic theory, even though they acknowledged the masculinist bias of much of what Freud had to say about the unconscious and psychosexuality.[4] Their explorations of femininity centred around a series of complicated assumptions, drawn largely from the writings of the French analyst Jacques Lacan (of whom more will be said later). These – at the risk of over-simplification – may be summarized as follows:

(a) Human subjectivity and sexuality, constructed at the level of the unconscious mind, are determined by and within the Symbolic Order which we enter as small children, via the resolution of our Oedipus Complex (a key stage in our psychosexual evolution). Oedipal resolution, whether we are male or female, involves a repudiation of the first relation of desire which binds us to our mother at the very start of our lives. It also involves a recognition of what Lacan calls the 'Father's Law', which bans the incestuous mother/child relation. Once the Oedipus Complex is resolved, we achieve subjectivity, i.e., become individual, social beings.

(b) The Symbolic, which we access through our unconscious internalization of the 'Father's Law', signifies the ensemble of rules and laws governing society/civilization as we know it. These are expressed in *language*, which is the vehicle through which the Symbolic inhabits/forms us. Language is acquired upon entry into the Symbolic.

(c) The Symbolic, socio-linguistic order, accession to which is dependent upon our acknowledgment of the Father's authority, is patriarchal and masculinist. Consequently, it allows no room for the conceptualization or articulation of feminine difference/specificity, except as that which is not masculine. Women's psychosexual identity is, moreover, warped and 'misogynized', because the process through which it is brought into being 'forecloses' (real) femininity. Feminine sexuality and identity are repressed/'phallicized' on entry into the Symbolic.

(d) There are nonetheless ways in which the Symbolic can be worked on so that this 'foreclosure' can be undone (*Psych et Po* depart from the Lacanian model here).

(e) The most effective ways for women to undermine the patriarchal structures of the Symbolic and 'liberate' the repressed feminine are:
  (i) to work to comprehend how they have been (socially and psychically) 'masculinized'. This necessitates a radical sep-aration from the dominant, patriarchal culture, e.g., by living and working in women-only spaces.
  (ii) to evolve writing practices which radically disrupt 'male' language in such a way that it no longer renders the feminine inexpressible and therefore non-existent.

The above, rather schematic overview of the theories of *Psych et Po*[5] indicates the extent to which the concerns of (some) French feminists differ from those of their Anglo-Saxon sisters, who generally adopt a more pragmatic, less abstract approach to the question of women's oppression. *Psych et Po*'s theoretical perspective was not endorsed by the *MLF* as a whole. The women writing for *Questions féministes*, for instance, argued that the stress placed by Fouque's group upon feminine difference/specificity/otherness (and upon the centrality of the female body) prevented them from truly contesting patriarchal ideology which – claimed *Questions féministes* – *also* foregrounds and 'politicizes' women's biological/sexual difference, specifically in order to legitimize the oppression of women that exists under the patriarchal system. *Questions féministes* also warned against an overemphasis on the concept of a female language.[6] Nonetheless, feminist interest in difference, and in the development of strategies which might 'feminize' the language of masculine culture, became fairly widespread in France during the 1970s and 1980s. This phenomenon mirrors the more general direction in which French thought was evolving, and is related to the growing importance accorded to the disciplines of linguistics, psychoanalysis and Derridean deconstruction. It is within an intellectual context circumscribed by these particular disciplines that the theoretical feminist writings of Hélène Cixous and Luce Irigaray – which provide the focus of the next part of this chapter – came into being.

Women and language: the quest for a 'langage autre'

Since the last war, linguistic matters have been of major concern to intellectuals on both sides of the Atlantic, so it is unsurprising that language should have become a key area of feminist debate in France. Since the 1970s, French feminists have denounced what has been termed 'la sexuation du discours' (Irigaray, 1977a, p.71) and have suggested that the linguistic sphere is not neutral but rather gendered, constituting a domain in which woman cannot easily find a place or voice. That women like Cixous and Irigaray (the former is a creative writer and theorist, the latter a feminist psychoanalyst) should claim this to be the case highlights the debt which they, like *Psych et Po*, owe to Jacques Lacan. Lacan believes that the patriarchal character of the Symbolic, socio-linguistic order, in which we are 'constructed' and 'positioned' as gendered subjects, means that the feminine somehow escapes definition, becomes inexpressible as a concept ('There is no such thing as *The* woman, where the definite article stands for the universal', Lacan, in Mitchell and Rose, 1982, p.144). This belief leads him to make a telling observation about the relationship which exists between women and language. In a characteristically hermetic passage, he comments that 'there is woman only as excluded by the nature of things which is the nature of words, and it has to be said that if there is one thing they themselves are complaining about enough at the moment it is well and truly that – only they don't know what they are saying, which is all the difference between them and me' (*ibid.*).[7] What Lacan seems to be saying here is that women and men do not have the *same* relation to the order of words – which, for him, is that of all reality – and that language is uniquely alienating for the *female* subject. His argument presumably reflects his belief that feminine reality cannot be articulated (and therefore cannot really 'exist') within an all-embracing signifying system that is intrinsically phallocentric. For Lacan, there is nothing to be done about this sorry state of affairs.

Cixous and Irigaray follow Lacan up to a point, in that they too consider the linguistic order (as it stands, at least) to be *sexué masculin*. Irigaray's critique of language is most in evidence in essays contained in *Ce Sexe qui n'en est pas un*, which appeared in 1977, and in various interviews and articles she has published more recently. Her aim is to reveal that a phallic/masculine bias exists within language, especially within the language of philosophical thought, which she calls 'le discours des discours' (Irigaray, 1977a, p.72). In the first place, she considers that (rational) discourse is underpinned by certain principles (linearity, non-contradiction) which, because they exclude ambivalence and ensure that meaning is always single, 'monolithic' and stable, may be symbolically equated with phallic sexuality rather than with woman's libidinal organization – which she views as plural and multiple. In a comparable way, she argues that the syntactical organization of language (which constructs sentences according to the subject–verb–object model) is quite alien to women, since 'female sexuality is not unifiable, it cannot be subsumed under the concept of subject – which brings into question all the syntactical norms . . .' (Irigaray, 1977b, p.65). Finally, she even suggests that language systems which, like French, involve grammatical genderization are somehow intrinsically 'sexist' because the feminine gender is consistently allocated to nouns associated with inferiority/ secondariness, while those which connote superiority are gendered masculine (*le* soleil cf. *la* lune, *le* ciel cf. *la* terre, *le* jour cf. *la* nuit, etc.). For all the foregoing reasons, Irigaray contends that women are 'exclues et niées par l'ordre linguistique patriarcal' (Irigaray, 1977, p.6).

Cixous analyses philosophical discourse and the secondary discourses it has spawned – literature and psychoanalysis, for instance – in a similar fashion. She considers that these particular signifying systems are subtended by an either/or logic and by a network of hierarchized binary oppositions which reveal their phallic nature. This is because such oppositions (activity/passivity, culture/nature, light/dark, etc. (Cixous, 1975, pp.115–17)) are always, in her opinion, related to the unequal couple man/woman and are therefore 'heavily imbricated in the patriarchal value system' (Moi, 1985, p.104). Both Cixous and Irigaray, in other words, perceive (rational) discourse/language more or less in the same way that Lacan does, i.e., as a masculine realm in which the feminine remains suppressed/repressed. Unlike Lacan, however, neither woman considers this situation to be irremediable, and both have produced texts which indicate that there may after all be linguistic practices which allow the feminine to be expressed.

For Irigaray, the (re)inscription within the linguistic order of the repressed feminine depends upon a radical 'travail du langage', whose function would be to 'désancrer le phallocentrisme, le phallocratisme, pour rendre le masculin à son langage, laissant la possibilité d'un langage autre' (Irigaray, 1977a, p.77). The kind of linguistic subversion she envisages works on two levels, since it involves an assault upon the *representations* of femininity which masculine discourse offers us and a modification of those *structural/syntactical* features of language which, she believes, betray its 'maleness'. As far as representation is concerned, Irigaray suggests that women should play ironically with the images of the feminine that the language of patriarchy offers us in such a way that their 'masculine' character is highlighted. She describes the parodic activity she recommends as 'mimésis', and explains that 'jouer de la mimésis, c'est [. . .], pour une femme, tenter de retrouver le lieu de son exploitation par le discours, sans s'y laisser simplement réduire. C'est se resoumettre [. . .] à des idées, notamment d'elle, élaborées dans/par une logique masculine, mais pour faire apparaître, par un effet de répétition ludique, ce qui devait rester occulté: le recouvrement d'une opération du féminin dans le langage' (*ibid*, p.74).

Irigaray obviously considers mimicry to be an important strategy, but argues in texts and interviews that it is above all the evolution of a new kind of writing which will enable women to disrupt the masculinization of language. If the 'phallicity' of (rational) discourse is evidenced by its privileging of stable, unambivalent meanings and its reliance upon a linear, logical syntactical organization, then a 'langage autre', for Irigaray, must be one whose style and structure allow fixed significations to be subverted. The sort of language she has in mind would 'undo the unique meaning of words, of nouns, which still regulates all discourse' (Irigaray, 1977b, p.65), would 'met feu aux mots fétiches, aux termes propres, aux formes bien construites' (1977a, p.76), and would have 'nothing to do with the syntax we have used for centuries' (1977b, p.64). It would be characterized by ambivalence and ellipsis, and would be the very antithesis of the rational.

Clearly, the plurivocal language Irigaray envisions when she talks about a '"style" ou "écriture" de la femme' is essentially *poetic* in nature. In addition, such language is (in her view) 'vulvomorphic', because its sinuosity and fluidity stand in (a metaphorical) relation to the non-unified form of woman's genital anatomy and to the decentred, multiple nature of female sexual pleasure.[8] The 'langage autre' she evokes *could* therefore be taken to represent a visceral body language, an 'unalienated language transparently expressing the real, a *parole* analogous to the female body, that would speak the body directly' – were it not for the fact that Irigaray's 'vulvomorphic' discourse 'is not predestined by anatomy but is already a *symbolic* interpretation of that anatomy' (Gallop, 1983, pp.78–9, my italics).

In her explorations of language in *La Jeune Née* (1975), Cixous agrees that the creation of multivalent, poetic discourse represents the means by which the feminine may be inscribed within the phallic symbolic. On the one hand, she argues that the kind of language she has in mind – an excessive, disruptive language which does not repress feminine difference and is consequently 'bisexual' – need not be equated with women. Male authors, she suggests, are capable of writing 'bisexually', of producing texts in which the feminine is decipherable, and some of them (she cites Genet and Kleist as examples) have already done so. Yet she also contends that it is in fact women who are more likely to produce the model of discourse in question, because they are psychically more open to bisexuality.[9] She implies moreover, like Irigaray, that there is a link between the female body/libido and the *écriture* she envisages, and that it is by 'writing the body' that woman subverts masculine language: 'Il faut que la femme écrive son corps, qu'elle invente la langue imprenable qui crève les cloisonnements, classes et rhétoriques, ordonnances et codes, qu'elle submerge, transperce, franchisse le discours . . .' (Cixous, 1975, p.175).

In summary, both Irigaray and Cixous privilege forms of language that are marked by polyvalence, ambiguity and poeticity, and relate these forms, however symbolically, to woman's anatomy and sexuality. Although compelling, their theories present certain difficulties. They invite accusations of biological/psychical essentialism, because they seem at times to indicate that a 'non-phallic' style directly echoes and derives from woman's physiological and libidinal make-up. They also set up an association between 'feminine' language and the anti-rational which, given the assumptions mainstream patriarchal culture traditionally makes about women and the *irrational* discourses they produce, is clearly problematic. Worst of all, perhaps, the writings of Cixous and Irigaray, because they are the product of an intellectual context which is unfamiliar to a great many people, can seem impenetrable, elitist and ultimately meaningless. Nevertheless, what these feminist theorists have said about language has proved extremely influential, both in France and elsewhere – not least because their writings help us to grasp why (some) French *écrivaines* of the post-war period have felt the need to write 'differently' and 'disruptively', and enable us to gain a clearer understanding of the kind of feminine *écriture* that has come into being during the last few decades.

Women's writing in the post-war period

The women authors most frequently cited in connection with the search for new, 'non-masculine' narrative and stylistic practices are Cixous (whose creative writing mirrors the vision of bisexual/poetic discourse contained in *La Jeune née*), Marguerite Duras and Monique Wittig. Duras does not consider herself a feminist, but a number of her novels have been taken by critics to represent textual 'inscriptions' of the feminine.[10] Works like *Le Ravissement de Lol V. Stein* (1964) and *Le Vice-Consul* (1966) depict worlds which are both coexistent with, and radically different from, the world of everyday reality as we know it; worlds in which passion, eroticism and madness characterize and dictate the actions of Duras's protagonists. These novels constitute a disturbing evocation of blackness and violence, of the 'unknown' – which is associated by Duras herself with women, and with feminine literature and desire.[11] It is also the case that certain formal and stylistic features of Duras's writing have been isolated as evidence of the 'feminine' character of her discourse. In particular, her use of ellipsis, of 'blanks', of the '*non-dit*' – in *Moderato cantabile* (1958), for instance – has been viewed as indicative of her creation of a kind of *écriture féminine*. This is because forms of language/narrative which are punctuated by gaps, suppressions and silences, and which are consequently illogical, non-rational, disrupted and disruptive, represent, for several French feminist critics, a 'rupture de la chaîne symbolique', 'quelque chose de femme, vraiment de femme'.[12] Duras has distanced herself from this kind of interpretation of her *œuvre*, which was very much a product of the 1970s, and it is on the whole rejected by contemporary Durassian critics – Trista Selous, for example, argues that there is no reason to regard the use of ellipsis as feminine *per se*.[13] Nevertheless, Duras's writing still tends to be associated with the evolution of a specifically feminine aesthetic.

Monique Wittig's *Les Guérillères* (1969) represents a landmark in contemporary women's writing. Margaret Atack views this work as 'a non-realist narrative, or rather complex of narratives, whose declamatory, stylized mode of writing creates a configuration of new forms of language, gender-specific language, a woman-centred sexual politics, new relations between the sexes, and a joyous celebration of women's collective power and strength'.[14] Atack's reading is perceptive, but obscures the fact that Wittig's intention was to develop a 'political' language, rather than a gender-specific 'woman's writing'. *Ecriture féminine*, for Wittig, is inextricably bound up with the concept of sexual difference as it is constructed and defined under patriarchy, and with the oppressive hierarchization of the binary unit man/woman. 'Political' writing must have nothing to do with this duality, which is predicated on the notion of feminine subordination, and 'must confront the structures of masculine culture, including the very structure that defines humans in terms of two castes'.[15] Such discourse is 'lesbian' – because the lesbian, according to Wittig, eludes categorization in terms of the masculine/feminine divide.

Les Guérillères tells of an Amazon society in conflict with patriarchy. The women who belong to it are determined to reject or reinvent the language men use and its representations of the feminine. Men are not absent from the text; indeed, peace is achieved in the last part of the work with members of a band of young male warriors. Yet masculinist culture comes under sustained assault in Wittig's narrative. Symbols associated with male heroism, the Holy Grail and the Golden Fleece, are 'reclaimed', because they are transmuted into metaphors for the womb and for female pubic hair. Myths tainted by patriarchal ideology are reworked: Eve, for instance, ceases to be responsible for the sufferings of mankind and is transformed into a symbol of women's quest for the knowledge patriarchy hides from them. The 'elles' who collectively represent the 'heroine' of *Les Guérrillères* dismiss the traditional images used to represent the female genitals ('Elles disent qu'elles n'ont pas à puiser leur force dans des symboles [. . .] Elles disent qu'elles doivent rompre le dernier lien qui les rattache à une culture morte' (p.102)), and provide their own/more clinical descriptions of women's sexual organs. Wittig's refusal of conventional figurative codes reflects her belief that 'lesbian writing' should subvert the obscuring metaphors associated with the female body in the language/texts of the dominant male culture, and thereby 'return' the body to women. Her rejection of (masculine) metaphoricity is expressed even more powerfully in *Le Corps lesbien*, a work that was published four years after *Les Guérrillères*.

Le Corps lesbien, which chronicles the violent homoerotic relationship between its first-person narrator and her female partner (known only as 'tu'), horrified many critics, including feminist critics. Its lovers, who inhabit a fantastic underworld that is empty of men, literally tear themselves and each other apart in the course of their sexual encounters, with the result that the female body is as split, flayed, and eviscerated as the 'j/e' who narrates.[16] Bits of bodies are everywhere in the text, yet no 'masking' images conceal anatomical reality. Organs, glands, muscles, secretions are constantly referred to, appearing sometimes in the form of simple lists, which interrupt the sequence of prose passages that make up *Le Corps lesbien*. Disturbing as Wittig's 'body-writing' is, it represents a carefully considered political/linguistic strategy. In male-authored erotic discourse, the female body is fragmented, but in such a way that it is reduced to a limited number of anatomical elements (breasts, lips, hair, etc.) which men deem desirable, and which are frequently subjected to metaphorical disincarnation. In Wittig's lesbian discourse, all of woman's anatomy is present, is directly named, and is presented as desirable, with the result that the (heterosexual) body-discourse of patriarchal culture is deconstructed. Wittig certainly evolves a 'different' (erotic) language in *Le Corps lesbien*, but it is not one that she chooses to view as 'feminine'.

Not every French woman novelist of the post-war period has displayed the concern with (the genderization of) language manifested by Wittig and Cixous. A number of modern French *écrivaines*, particularly if they were writing pre-1968, have produced texts which are formally/stylistically conventional, but which are, nonetheless, feminist productions. Simone de Beauvoir, who was profoundly mistrustful of the quest for an *écriture féminine* which so preoccupied her *consœurs* in the 1970s, chose to articulate her critique of patriarchy via the *thematic* focus of her fictional texts, most notably *La Femme rompue* (1967). In the three novellas which make up this work, Beauvoir presents us with middle-aged women who invest too much of themselves in the conventional roles – those of wife and mother – which society/men offer them, only to find that to do so is ultimately destructive. In *La Femme rompue*, Beauvoir weaves a complex analysis of the ways in which women are both the victims of, and complicit with, a socio-cultural order which encourages them to overestimate the importance of familial and emotional ties. What is problematic about this text, for feminists at least, is the way it seems primarily to blame the women themselves, rather than the social/ideological pressures that dictate their behaviour, for the bad faith they display. In the third story, Beauvoir seems doggedly determined to represent her heroine, Monique, as a 'criminal', whose self-deception and readiness to eschew freedom and autonomy provoke her husband's adultery and eventual departure. First and foremost, Beauvoir's novellas, especially this last one, are a criticism less of men's denial of independence to women than of the ease with which women renounce autonomy and transcendence. Beauvoir's treatment of her women protagonists is tinged with cruelty; a fact which reflects her ambiguous relationship with her own femininity, and which led one critic to comment that 'as an imaginative writer, she has not once, strangely enough, presented a female character whom we might admire, or merely remember lastingly as a complex, winning, mature, true woman'.[17]

Christiane Rochefort's *Les Petits Enfants du siècle* (1961), like *La Femme Rompue*, focuses on the influence of social and cultural factors on the development of feminine identity, and belongs to the realist tradition. However, Rochefort's novel is more obviously feminist than Beauvoir's text, and her adolescent heroine/narratrix, the ebullient Josyane, is portrayed with a good deal of sympathy. *Les Petits Enfants du siècle* explores what it means to grow into womanhood within a particularly disadvantageous socio-economic context. It is set on a large working-class estate in the Parisian suburbs, during a period when the falling birth-rate has provoked the government into encouraging (proletarian) women to breed like rabbits, by offering financial and material incentives. Josyane's mordant narrative evokes a world peopled with bovine mothers keen to keep on the maternal 'production line' long enough to acquire the full range of domestic appliances available, macho fathers and disaffected, squabbling children. Horrified by the model of femininity with which she is confronted – Josyane is highly contemptuous of her mother and the other married women on her estate – and by the destiny which awaits her, Rochefort's heroine pursues various escape routes. These include schoolwork, because doing her *devoirs* allows her to create her own space within her family's crowded apartment and affords an intellectual stimulation she is only dimly conscious of needing, and, later on, an almost obsessive promiscuity:

Ce qu'il y avait d'extraordinaire c'était d'être là debout dans l'ombre, la tête libre, le dos bien calé au mur, regardant le ciel, ne voyant que les étoiles quand il y en avait, seule en somme, et là-bas très loin tout en bas le garçon de plus en plus oublié à mesure que le plaisir vient et monte comme si c'était directement de la terre. Ça ça me transportait. (p.111)

Unfortunately for Josyane, neither of these escape routes lead anywhere; her family circumstances, unlike those of her friend Ethel, preclude her from staying on at school, and she comes to suspect that there's more to life than sleeping around. This, however, does not matter, because by the final part of the novel she has met Philippe, and has (re)discovered Love. She is also pregnant, and about to marry. The 'happy ending' of *Les Petits Enfants*, like the rest of the work, is ironic in the extreme, but Josyane is by this stage less the source of irony than its object. We sense (although Rochefort, by shifting the narrative focus to Philippe, avoids making this explicit) that Jo shares her fiancé's vision of the conjugal and parental bliss that awaits them, and is only too willing to embark upon a path which is not dissimilar to the one her mother has followed. As the reader reaches the text's conclusion, a (prophetic) image from an earlier part of the novel inevitably imposes itself: that of a photograph depicting Josyane's mother not as an overburdened, sickly *hausfrau* but as an insouciant, smiling teenager.

Mother/daughter identification and bonding have preoccupied a number of modern French women writers, including Beauvoir, Violette Leduc, Marie Cardinal and, more recently, Annie Ernaux. All of these women represent the dynamics of mother/daughter interaction in ways that echo contemporary psychoanalytic research on the subject. Both Nancy Chodorow (who belongs to the American object-relations school of psychology), and Luce Irigaray (whose analytic training is Freudian/Lacanian), view the tie between mothers and daughters as a powerful attachment, characterized by intersubjective continuity and entanglement, rather than by differentiation and individuation. The symbiotic, 'specular' nature of the mother/daughter relation is, according to these theorists, potentially highly problematic, as the opening lines of Irigaray's poetic text *Et l'une ne bouge pas sans l'autre* (1979) indicate:

Avec ton lait, ma mère, j'ai bu la glace. Et me voilà maintenant avec ce gel à l'intérieur. Et je marche encore plus mal que toi, et je bouge encore moins que toi. Tu as coulé en moi, et ce liquide chaud est devenu poison qui me paralyse. (p.7)

Issues of self/other mirroring, of symbiosis and separation, dominate the accounts of mother/daughter relations provided by Beauvoir, Leduc and Cardinal. All three writers confirm the point that 'to study the relationship between mother and daughter is not to study the relationship between two separate, differentiated individuals, but to plunge into a network of complex ties, to untangle the strands of a double self' (Hirsch, 1981, p.73). Beauvoir's *Mémoires d'une jeune fille rangée* (1958) chronicles a daughter's gradual rejection of the symbiotic intimacy shared in infancy with her maternal parent; an intimacy which blurred the boundaries between mother and child and which was both reassuring and terrifying:

Tout reproche de ma mère, le moindre de ses froncements de sourcils, mettait en jeu ma sécurité: privée de son approbation, je ne me sentais plus le droit d'exister. [. . .] Quand ses yeux brillaient d'un éclat orageux, ou quand simplement sa bouche se fronçait, je crois que je craignais, autant que ma propre déchéance, les remous que je provoquais dans son coeur. Si elle m'avait convaincue de mensonge, j'aurais ressenti son scandale plus vivement que ma honte [. . .]. (pp.56–7)

Beauvoir's pursuit of intellectual excellence, which is a central theme of the first volume of her autobiography, is inextricably bound up with her need to separate from her mother and move into a freer world associated with her father/the male sex. Beauvoir's *Mémoires* imply, moreover, that the separation she has sought is complete (and radical) once she encounters Sartre. Yet by the time she wrote *Une mort très douce* in 1964, after the death of her mother, her faith in the dissolubility of the mother/daughter tie had clearly been shaken:

Stupeur. Quand mon père est mort, je n'ai pas versé un pleur. J'avais dit à ma soeur: 'Pour Maman, ça sera pareil.'. . . Cette fois, mon désespoir échappait à mon contrôle: quelqu'un d'autre en moi pleurait en moi. Je parlai à Sartre de la bouche de ma mère, telle que je l'avais vue le matin, et de tout ce que j'y déchiffrais [. . .] Et ma propre bouche, m'a-t-il dit, ne m'obéissait plus: j'avais posé celle de maman sur mon visage et j'en imitais malgré moi les mimiques. Toute sa personne, toute son existence s'y matérialisait [. . .]. (pp.43–4)

If Beauvoir's *Mémoires* highlight a daughter's efforts to disentangle herself from her mother/mirror, Violette Leduc's equally autobiographical *La Bâtarde* (1964) reveals the intense nostalgia lost mother/daughter intimacy can provoke. The illegitimate child of an aristocrat and a housemaid, Leduc was brought up by a beloved grandmother and by her mother, whose 'regard bleu et dur' constituted a hostile mirror in which the young Violette's *bâtardise* and ugliness were confirmed and reflected. Nevertheless, the exclusive relationship Leduc enjoyed with her mother after her grandmother died is presented in *La Bâtarde* as a kind of quasi-erotic paradise and its dissolution, occasioned by the mother's marriage, is likened both to a wound and – significantly – to a birth:

Ma blessure: toi arrachée de moi. Jalouse? Non. Nostalgique jusqu'au vertige. Répudiée malgré tes bontés, ma mère. Oh oui, exilée de notre édredon qui nous réchauffait [. . .]. (p.57)

Leduc's autobiographical and fictional writings, especially her first novel *L'Asphyxie* (1946), have been read as a denunciation of a mother who failed to provide the emotional sustenance her daughter craved. Above all, however, Leduc's *œuvre* constitutes a sustained cry of pain at the ineluctability of mother/daughter division, described by Adrienne Rich as 'the essential female tragedy' (Rich, 1977, p.237). As the following extract from *La Bâtarde* indicates, a key facet of Leduc's textual project is the attempt to regain access to, and reconcile herself with, the mother her birth has 'shamed':

Retournons en arrière, ouvre-toi le ventre, reprends-moi. Tu m'as tant parlé de ta misère quand tu cherchais une chambre, quand tu ne la trouvais pas parce que tu n'avais plus la taille fine. Souffrons encore ensemble. Foetus, je voudrais ne pas l'avoir été. Présente, éveillée en toi. C'est dans ton ventre que je vis ta honte de jadis, tes chagrins. Tu dis parfois que je te hais. L'amour a des noms innombrables. Tu m'habites comme je t'ai habitée. (p.25)

Marie Cardinal's *Les Mots pour le dire* (1975) is a *récit d'analyse*, and recounts the seven-year *cure* she underwent after suffering a mental and physical breakdown. In the course of her therapy (as it is recounted in the novel) Cardinal's narratrix recreates not only the child and adolescent she once was, but also her adored, detested mother, Solange. She discovers that her sickness, 'la chose', was born out of the disparity between the woman she became, and the woman her mother – a product of the French colonial system and a rigidly devout Catholic – wished her to be:

C'est entre cette femme qu'elle avait voulu mettre au monde et moi que la chose s'était installée. Ma mère m'avait dévoyée et ce travail avait été si bien fait, si profond, que je n'en étais pas consciente, je ne m'en rendais plus compte. (p.86)

Analysis helps Cardinal to come to terms with the profound ambivalence that characterizes her feelings for her mother, and to understand the complexity of the ties that bound them together during her youth. Psychotherapy, and its retelling in textual form, also enables her to achieve at her mother's graveside the reconciliation sought by Violette Leduc – which suggests that for both authors (and for Beauvoir too?), writing about the mother is first and foremost a highly emotional rite of passage, engendering exculpation (of self *and* mother) and resolution:

Soso, comme vous étiez belle un soir de bal où vous étiez venue me montrer votre robe dans ma chambre. J'étais déjà dans mon lit. Vous m'aviez éblouie. [. . .] Je vous aime. Oui, c'est ça, je vous aime. Je suis venue ici pour vous déclarer ça une fois pour toutes. Je n'ai pas honte de vous parler. (p.340)

Cardinal's *Les Mots pour le dire* is one of a number of contemporary women's texts in which the relationship between femininity and insanity is explored. Jeanne Hyvrard and Emma Santos, who has had personal experience of psychiatric treatment, have both produced strange, experimental novels in which the brutalization suffered by female patients in mental institutions is vividly and shockingly evoked. Santos's *La Malcastrée* (1973) and Hyvrard's *Mère la mort* (1976) depict doctors and psychiatrists as insensitive beings devoid of human(e) feeling, whose aim is simply to 'normalize' the women in their care and to reintegrate them, as quickly as possible, into mainstream society:

La Dame Psychiatre vend ses mots d'amour sortis de ses lèvres vertes de courtisane, la pute gardienne de la Société, chienne fidèle des Sécurités sociales. La Dame Psychiatre qui me donnait des nourritures psychiques dans ses mains est devenue machine psychiatrique, acier, une machine qui crache des sandwichs, jambon, rillettes, saucisson contre une pièce d'un franc. (*La Malcastrée*, p.121)

For Hyvrard and Santos, 'normalization' involves acceptance of the conventional codes of feminine conduct their narrator-protagonists refuse. It also involves an acceptance of 'male' discourse, i.e., of a rational, logical, grammatically 'correct' mode of language. Interestingly, both *Mère la mort* and *La Malcastrée* foreground the 'different' language that is valorized by their heroines but suppressed by and within the institutions imprisoning them; a 'langage du corps' which is presented less as a symptom of female madness than as a transgressive mode of expression capable of authentically articulating female reality. Both texts suggest strongly that psychiatric 'healing' involves women in a kind of linguistic indoctrination, destined to protect the sociolinguistic status quo from the threat of destabilization embodied by their 'other' words. In the final part of *La Malcastrée* (in which the narrative shifts to the third person) Santos makes this clear:

Elle veut bousculer, déranger, inverser, renverser, désarticuler désatomiser les mots, les anéantir détruire sécouer démolir vider, les pulvériser les mots. [. . .] Ah, si vous ne lui aviez pas donné vos sales mots, si vous ne lui aviez pas appris vos mots, si vous ne lui aviez pas dicté ce roman, Madame la Surveillante, si vous ne lui aviez pas torturée, matraquée, droguée jusqu'à ce qu'elle répète vos mots à vous, si vous l'aviez laissée vivre sans médicament elle aurait son langage. Le sien celui que vous avez fait dedans, il est manqué. (p.124–5).

A third dimension of female experience on which French women writers of the post-war period have chosen to focus in their texts is feminine homoeroticism. Obviously, lesbianism had been written about in France before 1945 – most famously by Diderot, Baudelaire and Proust. However, what these authors produced was, in essence, a literature of lesbian denigration, which had little or nothing to do with women's experience of homoerotic love. Colette went some way towards 'correcting' the (stereotypical) images of lesbianism offered by these male authors, but, as Elaine Marks observes, the radicalism of her lesbian writing is attenuated by the fact that 'women who love women come together in Colette's world because they are fleeing from a painful experience with a man and are looking for a *retraite sentimentale* [. . .] Lesbianism is a *pis aller*. It is a copy of either mother–daughter or male–female love or both' (Marks, 1979, p.369).

The modern French women authors most commonly associated with the creation of new and subversive images of lesbianism are Violette Leduc and (as we saw above) Monique Wittig. Neither writer is content to depict the lesbian union simply as a bond which mimes a heterosexual or mother/daughter relation. Leduc's *Thérèse et Isabelle* (1966) is a less 'political' and less challenging work than Wittig's *Le Corps lesbien* (1973); nevertheless, like its successor, it presents the relationship between its heroines as one which admits violence (because the erotic *is* violent) but which eludes the taint of hierarchization. For Leduc, as for Wittig, feminine homoeroticism precludes a (damaging) master/slave relation – with the result that the adolescent lovers she creates in *Thérèse et Isabelle*, although they play with and exchange the roles of dominator and dominated, enjoy a privileged union based upon mutuality and assent. It is this which enables them to achieve a degree of sensual ecstasy that is unparalleled in Leduc's *œuvre*. In those sections of *Thérèse et Isabelle* where homoerotic pleasure is evoked, Leduc's language is at its most lyrical. This reflects her desire to evolve a poetic, 'translational' mode of erotic writing which, she believed, would convey more palpably the sensations she was exploring – which in turn suggests that she, like Cixous, Santos and Hyvrard, was alive to the need to evolve a (feminine) 'langage du corps'. The following extract from the novella typifies the rich sensuality of Leduc's homoerotic discourse – and provides a fitting conclusion to my investigation of contemporary French *écriture féminine*:

Nous avons effleuré et survolé nos épaules avec les doigts fauves de l'automne, nous avons lancé à grands traits la lumière dans les nids, nous avons éventé les caresses, nous avons créé des motifs avec de la brise marine, nous avons enveloppé de zéphyrs nos jambes, nous avons eu des rumeurs de taffetas au creux des mains. Que l'entrée était facile! Notre chair nous aimait, notre odeur giclait. Notre levain, nos bulles, notre pain. Le va-et-vient n'était pas servitude mais va-et-vient de béatitude. Je me perdais dans le doigt d'Isabelle comme elle se perdait dans le mien. (pp.31–2)

Conclusion

A student recently told me, in a seminar on modern French women's writing, that she was disturbed by the violence she perceived in and behind some of the texts referred to in the last part of my discussion. She felt, she said, that women writers like Wittig, who have sought so obviously to disrupt the male literary space, were displaying a rejection of men which she found unsettling. I was also struck by the reactions of a group of French male writers and publishers, who were asked in 1981 by the *Magazine Littéraire* to comment on whether or not contemporary women authors were producing an 'autre écriture'. Several of their number dismissed the question as uninteresting and inconsequential – 'Ça n'a pas beaucoup de sens, de se demander s'il y a une écriture de femme' (Georges Lambrichs, director of the Gallimard NRF collection); 'Ça n'a pas de sens de faire une distinction entre les livres écrits par les hommes et ceux écrits par les femmes' (Gérard Mordillat, literary critic for *Libération*); 'Il n'y a pas de littérature de femme; pour moi, ça n'a aucun sens' (Pierre Ajame, editor on the *Nouvel Observateur*) – while the writer Claude Louis-Combet suggested that *écriture féminine* represents less an affirmatory discourse of female specificity than 'l'écho d'un mal-être dont les vicissitudes sociales, sentimentales et érotiques constituent la multiple image spéculaire' (*Magazine Littéraire* 1981, no. 180, p.33). All of the above responses suggest that the flowering in France of 'la parole des femmes' in the last few decades has been met with wariness (whether acknowledged or not), and even hostility. Why? It is undoubtedly the case that the feminine *venue à l'écriture* of the 1970s and 1980s, like the feminist activity of the 1970s, is related to a desire on the part of French women to assert themselves, and to vent, in textual form, their rage at the enduring androcentrism of the culture in which they live and write. Since rage, however obliquely it is expressed, is an uncomfortable emotion, it is perhaps unsurprising that a fair proportion of the texts produced by female French creative writers and theorists of the post-war period have provoked unease in their readers.

Notes

1. During the Vichy régime, the place of French women was very definitely in the home, and it was considered preferable that they should also be surrounded by children. Pétain's government made abortion illegal (an abortionist was executed in 1943) and instituted the 'fête des mères'.

2. 'Immanence', for Beauvoir, means 'the urge toward passivity, toward the being of a thing'. 'Transcendence', on the other hand, involves 'the forward movement into the future of a willing subject' (Pilardi, 1989, p.21). Beauvoir argues in *Le Deuxième Sexe* that the invidious situation in which women find themselves under patriarchy makes it all too easy for them to renounce transcendence/subjectivity and succumb to passivity and subjugation.

3. We need to bear in mind, when studying the complex trajectory followed by the contemporary French feminist movement, that divergences of opinion can be productive. As Marks and de Courtivron point out, 'dissensions, which must be recognized, are not necessarily indications of weakness. Indeed it has often been stated that radical feminism is the only revolutionary force that has maintained the exuberance of May 1968: it is the only movement in France that combines the conviction of a cause with a serious theoretical quest and unlimited occasions to test the relation between theory and practice' (Marks and de Courtivron, 1981, pp.33–4).

4. In a recent interview, Fouque commented that 'l'idéologie de la masculinité qui pesait sur la révolution psychanalytique ne parvenait pas à me faire rejeter un tel instrument de connaissance, surtout pour lui opposer une contre-idéologie féministe' (Fouque, 1990, p.131).

5. For an extensive discussion of the group's approach to the question

of feminine identity and difference, see Claire Duchen, (*Feminism in France*), p.32 and *passim*. Interesting insights into *Psych et Po*'s theoretical position are also contained in Nicole Ward Jouve's 'Contemporary Women's Writing in France and the Editions des femmes', in Atack and Powrie, 1990, pp.128–40.

6. *Questions féministes*'s desire to attack feminist groups like *Psych et Po* which valorized the concept of feminine difference (and related this to the female anatomy/libido) is apparent in the lead article of their first issue, 'Variations sur des thèmes communs', which is translated in Marks and de Courtivron 1981, pp.212–30. The collective points out, for example, that privileging feminine otherness, as *Psych et Po* did, involves falling into a trap set by men: 'Now, after centuries of men constantly repeating that *we* were different, here are women screaming, as if they were afraid of not being heard and as if it were an exciting discovery: "We are different!" Are you going fishing? No, I am going fishing' (*ibid.*, p.219). Their critique of the notion of a feminine language is articulated in the following excerpt from the same piece: 'Some women declare that "language must be shattered", because language is supposed to be male as it is a conveyor of, among other things, male chauvinism. They claim for themselves "another" language, that, in its new form, would be closer to woman's lived experience, a lived experience in the center of which the Body is frequently placed. Hence the watchwords: "liberate-the-body" and "speak-the-body". It is legitimate to expose the oppression, the mutilation, the "functionalization" and the "objectivation" of the female body, but it is also dangerous to place the body at the center of a search for female identity. [. . .] [Bodily] difference has been used as a pretext to "justify" full power of one sex over another.' *Ibid.*, p.218.

7. The original, French version of the text in which Lacan made these remarks is *Encore, Le Séminaire XX* (Paris: Seuil, 1975) – see p.68. I have quoted them in English because of their extreme complexity, using Jacqueline Rose's translation.

8. The association of feminine pleasure with multiplicity (and the opposition of multiplicity to the sexual norms of the dominant/phallic libidinal 'economy') occurs throughout Irigaray's theoretical writings, for example in the following extract from *Ce Sexe qui n'en est pas un*: 'Or, *la femme a des sexes un peu partout* [. . .] La géographie de son plaisir est bien plus diversifiée, multiple dans des différences, complexe, subtile, qu'on ne l'imagine . . . dans un imaginaire un peu trop centré sur le même' (Irigaray, 1977a, p.28).

9. 'Je dirai: aujourd'hui l'écriture est aux femmes. Cela n'est pas une provocation, cela signifie que: la femme admet qu'il y ait de l'autre. Elle n'a pas effacé, dans son devenir-femme, la bisexualité latente chez la fille comme chez le garçon' (*ibid.*, p.158).

10. In her essay 'The Laugh of the Medusa' (see Marks and de Courtivron 1981, pp.245–64), Cixous argues that the only twentieth-century French authors who 'write the feminine' are Duras, Colette and Genet.

11. Duras states in a 1975 interview with Susan Husserl-Kapit which appeared in *Signs* and is reproduced in *New French Feminisms* that: 'I think "feminine literature" is an organic, translated

writing . . . translated from blackness, from darkness. Women have been in darkness for centuries. They don't know themselves. Or only poorly. And when women write, they translate this darkness. [. . .] The writing of women is really translated from the unknown, like a new way of communicating rather than an already formed language' (Marks and de Courtivron, 1981, p.174).

12. Xavière Gautier, 1974, p.12. Marcelle Marini, a Lacanian critic, reads Duras's use of ellipsis in the same way – see Marini, 1977, p.69.

13. 'I do not think that such a way of using language can be called specifically "feminine" in itself; for it works in the same way as innuendo or jokes, by controlling and using the power of the unconscious, and I do not see why or how such universally found phenomena can be gendered' (Selous, 1988, p.137).

14. Atack, 1991, p.185. Atack's article provides a wide-ranging overview of post-war French feminist theory and women's writing.

15. Diane Crowder, 1983, p.118. Crowder's article is essential reading for anyone seeking to familiarize herself with the different theories of women's writing that burgeoned in France during the 1970s.

16. In her Author's Note in the English translation of *Le Corps lesbien*, Wittig explains that her slashed narrating j/e is an emblem of woman's problematic relationship with (masculine) language: '*Je* as a generic feminine subject can *only* enter by force a language which is foreign to it [. . .] The 'I' (je) who writes is alien to her own writing at every word because this 'I' (je) uses a language alien to her . . . . J/e is the symbol of the lived, rending experience which is m/y writing, of this cutting in two which throughout literature is the exercise of a language which does not constitute m/e as subject' (Wittig, 1975, p.10).

17. Henri Peyre, in Leighton, 1975, p.7. I agree, on the whole, with Peyre's analysis, but it is flawed by his hostility towards Beauvoir and women writers in general.

Further reading

Albistur, Maïté and Armogathe, Daniel, *Histoire du féminisme français* (Paris: Des Femmes, 1977).

Atack, Margaret and Powrie, Phil eds., *Contemporary French Fiction by Women* (Manchester: Manchester University Press, 1990).

Atack, Margaret, 'Aux Armes, Citoyennes', in *Textual Liberation: European Feminist Writing in the Twentieth Century*, ed. Forsas-Scott (London: Routledge, 1991).

Beauvoir, Simone de, *Le Deuxième Sexe* (Paris: Gallimard, 1949).
Mémoires d'une jeune fille rangée (Paris: Gallimard, 1958).
Une Mort très douce (Paris: Gallimard, 1964).
La Femme rompue (Paris: Gallimard, 1967).

Cameron, Deborah, *Feminism and Linguistic Theory* (London: Macmillan, 1985).

Cardinal, Marie, *Les Mots pour le dire* (Paris: Livre de poche, 1975).

Chodorow, Nancy, *The Reproduction of Mothering* (Berkeley and Los Angeles: University of California Press, 1978).

Cixous, Hélène, *La Jeune Née* (with Cathérine Clément) (Paris: Union Générale d'Éditions, 1975).

'The Laugh of the Medusa', *Signs*, I (1976), pp.875–93.

Crowder, Diane, 'Amazons and Mothers?', *Contemporary Literature*, 24 (1983) pp.117–44.

Duchen, Claire, *Feminism in France from May '68 to Mitterrand* (London and Boston: Routledge and Kegan Paul, 1986).

Duras, Marguerito, *Moderato cantabile* (Paris: Editions de minuit, 1958).

Le Ravissement de Lol V. Stein (Paris: Gallimard, 1964).

Le Vice-Consul (Paris: Gallimard, 1966).

Fouque, Antoinette, 'Femmes en mouvements: hier, aujourd'hui, demain', *Le Débat*, 59 (1990), pp.126–43.

Gallop, Jane, 'Quand nos lèvres s'écrivent: Irigaray's Body Politic', *Romantic Review*, 74 (1983), pp.77–83.

Gauthier, Xavère (with Marguerite Duras), *Les Parleuses* (Paris: Editions de Minuit, 1974).

Hirsch, Marianne, 'Mothers and Daughters: Review Essay', *Signs*, 7 (1981), pp.200–22.

Hyvrard, Jeanne, *Mère la mort* (Paris: Editions de Minuit, 1976).

Irigaray, Luce, *Ce Sexe qui n'en est pas un* (Paris, Editions de Minuit, 1977a).

'Women's Exile' (Interview with Couze Venn), *Ideology and Consciousness*, I (1977b).

Et l'une ne bouge pas sans l'autre (Paris: Editions de Minuit, 1979).

Lacan, Jacques, *Ecrits* (Paris: Seuil, 1966).

Encore: le Séminaire XX (Paris: Seuil, 1975).

Leduc, Violette, *L'Asphyxie* (Paris: Gallimard, 1946).

La Bâtarde (Paris: Gallimard, 1964).

Thérèse et Isabelle (Paris: Gallimard, 1966).

Leighton, Jean, *Simone de Beauvoir on Woman* (New Jersey: Fairleigh Dickinson University Press, 1975).

Marini, Marcelle, *Territoires du féminin* (Paris: Editions de Minuit, 1977).

Marks, Elaine, 'Lesbian Intertextuality', in *Homosexualities and French Literature*, ed. by Marks and Stambolian (Ithaca and London: Cornell University Press, 1979).

Marks, Elaine and Courtivron, Isabelle de, eds., *New French Feminisms* (Brighton: Harvester, 1981).

Mitchell, Juliet and Rose, Jacqueline, *Jacques Lacan and the Ecole Freudienne: Feminine Sexuality* (Basingstoke and London: Macmillan, 1982).

Moi, Toril, *Sexual/Textual Politics* (London: Methuen, 1985).

Pilardi, Jo-Ann, 'Female Eroticism in the Works of Simone de Beauvoir', in *The Thinking Muse*, ed. by Allen and Young (Bloomington and Indianapolis: Indiana University Press, 1989).

Rich, Adrienne, *Of Woman Born* (London: Virago, 1977).

Rochefort, Christiane, *Les Petits enfants du siècle* (Paris: Livre de poche, 1961).

Santos, Emma, *La Malcastrée* (Paris: Des Femmes, 1973).

Selous, Trista, *The Other Woman: Femininity and Feminism in the Work of Marguerite Duras* (New Haven and London: Yale University Press, 1988).

Whitmarsh, Anne, *Simone de Beauvoir and the Limits of Commitment* (Cambridge: Cambridge University Press, 1981).

Wittig, Monique, *Les Guérillères* (Paris: Editions de Minuit, 1969).

Le Corps lesbien (Paris: Editions de Minuit, 1973), trans. David LeVay, *The Lesbian Body* (London: Peter Owen, 1975).

CHAPTER 12

The French language since 1945

D. A. Trotter

Few students of the French language can have failed to notice one of its most striking features: the division between its spoken and written forms. Such a discrepancy is not, of course, an exclusively French phenomenon. Written language always has a tendency to diverge from the spoken language. Historically, and genetically, the spoken language came first, and from this point of view the written language must be seen as a secondary development. If there is any such thing as 'French', it is only the spoken language which can lay claim to being it. But this does not mean that the written form is simply a transposition of speech. If this were the case, the differences between written and spoken French would be much more limited, and, in practice, would just reflect the inability of conventional writing to represent the full complexity of speech. Obviously, this is a factor: for example, written French is at a loss to know how to convey intonation, emphasis, and gesture. Another factor is the conservatism of written languages, which are slow to reflect (for example) changes in pronunciation, if, indeed, they ever do register them. French, like English, has a thoroughly archaic spelling system: the pronunciation suggested by it approximates to that current in the late twelfth century. The vast majority of pronunciation changes since then have left little or no mark on the orthography of the language: for example, the spelling -oi-, first used to denote the diphthong [oi], like English voice, has passed through [w ɛ] and is now (usually) [w a], without the spelling ever having been modified from the Middle Ages onwards. No recent attempt at spelling reform, including the latest suggested rationalization of certain apparent anomalies such as double consonants and circumflex accents, has so far commanded sufficient support to make its introduction a realistic possibility.

Closer inspection of the French language leads to the conclusion that the differences between spoken and written forms are rather more substantial; it is not merely a matter of archaic spelling. A number of features are often cited to back up this claim. Verb morphology, for example, is much less complex in spoken than in written French, with, in the case of most -*er* verbs (which make up 90 per cent of French verbs), a considerable reduction in the distinctions between different persons. In the present indicative of *donner*, the range of five oppositions provided by written French is severely curtailed: instead of *donne* – *donnes* – *donne* – *donnons* – *donnez* – *donnent*, spoken French produces only three distinct forms, *donne/donnes/donnent* (all pronounced the same), *donnons*, *donnez*. The scope for confusion exists not only in this oft-quoted case of the present indicative. In, and between, the imperfect, conditional and future tenses, and not just in -*er* verbs, the same problem arises, with phonetically identical endings on (for example) *contiendraient* (condit. 6) *contiendrez* (fut. 5) and *contiendrai* (fut. 1), or *contenais* (imperf. 1) and *contenaient* (imperf. 6). The famous French clarity is re-introduced, to some extent, by the use of pronoun subjects (*je chante* – *tu chantes*), but such elucidation is absent in the important third person forms, where *il/elle donne* and *ils/elles donnent* are pronounced identically. The crucial distinction between singular and plural is thus abolished. Indeed, this is a distinction which spoken French, in many respects, systematically undermines. Plural nouns and adjectives in -*s* are only differently pronounced from their singular counterparts under certain circumstances (in liaison), and the singular–plural opposition thus has to be conveyed by the article (*le/la/les*). The article, of course, is not always used (for example, after negatives), so that confusion can easily creep in. Feminine and masculine are not always distinct either, since many adjectives (though fewer than in the past) are invariable, at least to the ear: *bleu/bleue, rouge, facile, compliqué/compliquée* and indeed all the numerous participial adjectives derived from -*er* verbs. Many parts of these same -*er* verbs are actually no longer differentiated, being all pronounced with a final [e]: thus, for many French speakers, *donner, donné(e), donnait, donnez* are indistinguishable. Yet the distinctions between persons, between singular and plural, masculine and feminine, and between completely different parts of the verb, can hardly be regarded as luxuries which the language can happily do without. They are fundamental structural principles of the French language. It is not that spoken French dispenses with them, merely that the spoken language finds other ways of expressing them. Reduplication of subjects, for example, is just one, increasingly frequent, solution. The originally emphatic forms of *eux, ils chantent* and *lui, il chante* serve the purpose, not of emphasis, but of retaining a distinction which would be lost without the addition of the extra pronoun.

Differences such as those outlined above have led some to talk of two distinct 'codes', a *code parlé* and a *code écrit*, functioning by their own rules, and equally valid systems of communication in the right context.[1] What creates problems is when only one of these codes is accorded real status, with the consequence that the other is devalued, excluded from the educational system and relegated to the uncertain role of non-prestigious form. Thus, in French, it is not the spoken language but the written language which is the more prestigious, official variety, the object of educationalists' and politicians' attention. This is despite the fact that, as we have seen, the written language is necessarily, from the point of view of the development of the French, a secondary form. It is worth considering how this situation has come about; for come about it has, with far-reaching and, in some respects, disastrous consequences.

In societies with a well-developed literary culture, it is perfectly normal that the spoken language should depart from the model provided by this cultural tradition. It would be absurd to imagine that the medieval French texts which survive can do more than hint at the reality of spoken medieval French, or, for that matter, that seventeenth-century Frenchmen ever actually spoke as Racine, or even Molière, wrote. In addition to this initial divergence between the two codes (if we may use the term), there is the question of historical development over time. We have already seen how written French has signally failed to incorporate into its orthographic system many sound-changes which took place centuries ago. Small wonder that it has not yet caught up with developments in the twentieth century. One of the main reasons why the spoken language inevitably develops faster than the written variety is precisely that it has lower status, and that it is consequently much less subject to the restraining influence of the combined forces of tradition and education. The written language has been standardized, settling on one regional variety as the accepted basis for literary and documentary purposes; it has been grammatically codified, so that writers are only too aware that some forms are 'correct' and others 'incorrect', and will thus exclude the latter from their usage. In part, too, the divergence arises simply because the register or level of language adopted as the norm in written French is significantly higher than that found suitable for most speech. The written language is inherently more formal than the spoken, because of the contexts in which it is deployed. This perhaps lies at the heart of the distinction between the two forms. The elegant model presented by the written language is quite inappropriate to most occasions on which spoken French is used. This is not to say that the written variety is never followed as the basis of how French should, ostensibly, be spoken, and respected as the underlying model for all careful speech. Paradoxically, this can only exacerbate the division between written and spoken forms of the language, since this formal spoken French, calqued as it is on written French, is in the end a strictly limited, highly literary code. Moreover, for all the rhetoric of anti-elitism in the educational system, education in France is manifestly not something to which all speakers, in practice, have equal access. For social, cultural, economic, political and intellectual reasons, the linguistic competence of the French population is not, and cannot be, a matter of complete *égalité*. Thus the form of spoken French which enjoys most prestige is, in many ways, a transposition of written French, in an ironic reversal of the natural evolutionary process. Needless to say, this form of French is only appropriate to certain quite limited circumstances. In most contexts, to say of a speaker that *il parle comme un livre* is not a compliment: rather, it implies that the restrictions governing the use of this specialized variety have been misunderstood. In the same way, it is not usually effective to use colloquial language in formal, written communication, or, for that matter, in formal situations such as job interviews. In many respects, the situation seems to have developed where written and spoken French are aspects of a continuum of different registers of the language, between which, by definition, substantial differences are inevitably to be found. The hallmark of the competent speaker is the ability to select a register appropriate to the context; and this, of course, presupposes competence in as wide a range of registers as possible.

'Correct' French is not only linked to a particular register of speech: it is also geographically defined, being now, as throughout the history of the language, essentially the educated French of the Ile-de-France region. Historically, the educational system has always been deployed as one of the state's principal weapons against regional varieties and languages. Thus, the majority of French people, insofar as they use such regional varieties of the language, in however attenuated a form, speak, some of the time at least, a version of French which is removed not only by register, but also by other important features, from the norm represented by the written language. Typically, a regional French speaker will employ items of vocabulary not found in the standard language, and probably not known outside the area, or will use words in different senses to those of standard French; he or she will pronounce words differently (with what is normally called a regional accent), and may display limited syntactic divergences from the norm represented by 'standard' French. The upshot of this is often a marked sentiment of linguistic insecurity and inferiority, frequently made worse by the concomitant existence of other extra-linguistic prejudices concerning (for example) the inhabitants of the Auvergne or of the north-east.

This situation is not one which has suddenly arisen since 1945. Its roots go back to those of the French language itself. This language is the direct descendant of *francien*, the medieval dialect of the Ile-de-France region. Certain elements have entered into standard French from other dialects, notably vocabulary, but it is nevertheless broadly correct to claim that modern French derives directly from *francien*. At first, *francien* was simply a dialect amongst many, in no sense superior to (for example) Picard or Burgundian or Norman, and spoken as a true vernacular by a very small percentage of the population of the territory which would eventually become present-day France. The first literary texts written in French do not, in fact, come from the Paris area, but from the provinces. The earliest administrative documents in the vernacular, rather than in Latin, come from north-eastern France, not from Paris. It was only because of non-linguistic factors (notably the establishment of the court at Paris after the accession of Hugues Capet in 987 and the concomitant emergence of Paris as the administrative centre of the then much smaller area known as France) that this particular dialect came to acquire additional status, and began slowly to be used as a means of supra-regional communication. There is evidence, from the middle of the twelfth century onwards, that writers were aware of the pressure to conform to the new literary standard represented by *francien*. A pressure, in this case, dictated not by central authority but by the need, presumably, to enable their work to reach as wide a public as possible, and by what one can only term literary fashion. From about the thirteenth century, admittedly isolated comments are found from which it is apparent that *francien* was also beginning to be considered the standard for the spoken language. At the end of the Middle Ages, during the fifteenth and sixteenth centuries, the government intervened actively with a series of measures, culminating in the Ordonnances de Villers-Cotterêts of 1539, which sought unequivocally to establish *francien* as the exclusive language of the courts and of legal documents. Initially intended to safeguard the rights of individuals unfamiliar with Latin (in many cases still the language of the judicial process), the consequence of this policy was that regional languages, such as Basque or Breton or Occitan (the language of southern France), as well as regional dialects of French, came increasingly to be used only in speech, being supplanted in writing by French. Inevitably, this led to still further decline in their status, so that the regional varieties, which once had equal status with *francien*, were reserved for unofficial use, and those who spoke only such varieties (the majority) were unlikely ever to attain high social positions outside the region of their birth. The legislation of the sixteenth century thus paved the way for a major onslaught on the very existence of such regional varieties which followed the French Revolution. The pattern, then, is one of the initial emergence of distinct dialects, and of the subsequent superimposition of one of them, *francien*, on the other regions. In many parts of France, especially in the Midi, the effect of introducing French in this manner was tantamount to the imposition of a foreign language on the inhabitants. During the seventeenth century, the French language itself (as opposed to its disparate dialectal relatives scattered across France and now restricted to spoken use) had been subjected to detailed attention by a new breed of grammarians. The result of their deliberations, encapsulated in the famous notion of *le bon usage* coined by the most celebrated and most enduring of the grammarians, Vaugelas, was that standard French was henceforth not only the French of Paris (or rather of the court at Versailles), but also the French of only certain sections of Parisian society, buttressed by, and enshrined in, the writings of *les bons auteurs*. Thus it was defined not only geographically, but also socio-culturally, and became doubly exclusive. The situation begins to resemble that of modern French. It is these same *bons auteurs* who figure so prominently in modern grammars of French, and whose collective influence, via the educational system, has so retarded the development of the written language. It is perhaps unfortunate that this era of literature should be the one aptly called classicism, when the *bons auteurs* wrote in closely controlled style about only certain subjects. By the end of the seventeenth century, then, what was thought of as 'the French language' was a singularly limited entity, and one whose geographical and social extension did not reach far beyond the elevated Parisian circles whom Vaugelas had identified as the exponents of this idealized linguistic variety. There were voices who spoke against so limited a vision of the language (which bore, of course, little relationship to what was really going on in the spoken language), but they appear to have had little impact. In 1694 the French Academy, founded by Cardinal Richelieu nearly sixty years earlier, produced its first dictionary, the preface to which compares the exalted heights of perfection attained by the French language to the golden days of the languages of Greece and Rome. The comparison is not fortuitous: the intention of the Academy was, precisely, to ensure that French remained at that stage of development; or, to put it another way, that all further development would be discouraged and, as far as possible, prevented. It is hard to avoid the feeling that this is a goal which the Academy still largely espouses. The problem, for modern French, is that the language of the *bons auteurs* of the seventeenth century, which successive generations of schoolchildren have been exhorted to emulate, bears little resemblance to everyday speech or even everyday writing. It did not do so in the seventeenth century, and it certainly does not do so in the twentieth century.

The linguistic impact of the French Revolution has already been alluded to.[2] It is no accident that the Revolution of 1789 was followed by a project whose declared aim was 'to annihilate the *patois*' – a far from neutral term loosely used, then as now, to cover both minority languages and French dialects (still widely spoken at the end of the eighteenth century). Both were, and are, perceived as a threat to the unity, and indeed status, of the one and indivisible Republic. The more virulent campaigners against minority languages spoke of superstition speaking Breton, the counter-Revolution speaking Italian, and fanaticism speaking Basque: language and speakers are one and the same, identified as enemies of the Republic, and the extirpation of the former is, logically enough, thought to be a means of reducing the threat posed by the latter. It is worth mentioning, in passing, that similar policies, and similar sentiments, were produced with regard to Scots Gaelic in the aftermath of Culloden. As a manifestation of Scottish opposition to the Hanoverians, Gaelic (together with traditional Highland dress) was proscribed. The eighteenth century, whether republican or monarchist, was well aware of the link between language and nation. The connection between these two means that non-standard varieties of language are, in the ideology of the nation-state, stigmatized and treated as incorrect or defective, with (in the case of French) the often derogatory term *patois* being used to refer indiscriminately to anything which is neither standard French nor a recognizable, foreign standard language.[3] In France, governmental measures and educational policies have been systematically deployed since 1790 in an attempt to eradicate regional aberrations from the national linguistic norm. Yet the Revolution was, in this respect, less revolutionary than perhaps it thought. In the first place, as in other areas of national life, the centralizing tendencies of the French Revolution have simply continued, and extended, what was in practice the policy of the Ancien Régime. There was nothing radically new in the policies adopted; they had, in fact, already been tried by the monarchy in territories such as Alsace-Lorraine, which had come under French control in the seventeenth century. The influence of such attitudes is still only too apparent. Comments which still emerge from modern surveys of speakers of regional varieties of French suggest that they perceive themselves as guilty of mutilating the French language (*estropier le français*), or even of damaging France itself (*donner des coups de pied à la France*). If this seems an extreme reaction, the counterpart of sometimes disturbing official comment in the same vein, then we should perhaps remember that the most linguistically intolerant states are very often those which are the most repressively authoritarian in general. Totalitarian regimes, whether of the right or of the left, rarely welcome linguistic diversity, which they regard as a menace to stability and unity.

The present situation in France is, then, by no means a recent phenomenon. It is, rather, the continuation and extension of a long-standing discrepancy between supposedly 'standard' French (which must surely be regarded as a hypothetical commodity) and the French, or the forms of French, spoken by the overwhelming majority of the population. The discrepancy is on several levels: geographical; socio-cultural; and in terms of register, insofar as cultivated spoken French is very much dependent on an essentially written tradition where the amount of education received determines, to a very large extent, whether one has access to this tradition or not.

It would, moreover, be astonishing, in the light of all the social changes which have occurred, if spoken French itself had not changed since 1945. The most obvious, and most easily documented, developments affect vocabulary, the most famous, or infamous, aspect of which is the incorporation into French of a substantial number of words of English origin. Borrowing between English and French has been going on since before the Norman Conquest, with an earlier high-point of Anglicisms in French during the so-called *Anglomanie* of the eighteenth century. Most of the words appropriated by French at this point have now become fully naturalized and assimilated into French phonology, with the result that their status as borrowings is often concealed from both the French and English speaker. The pronunciation of *la redingote*, like *le boulingrin* from the previous century, does little to suggest their Anglo-Saxon provenance. Modern borrowings are inevitably more apparent, because the assimilation process has not yet had time to take place. The hostility provoked by the alleged invasion of modern French by *franglais* reveals not just an objection to indiscriminate borrowing of foreign terminology, frequently with a confusing change in meaning in French; it also uncovers a fierce and often conscious resistance to a perceived threat to the French way of life and even to national honour. The words borrowed are seen not so much as filling a linguistic need, but as forerunners of an overbearing Anglo-American, particularly American, culture which threatens to swamp France. It goes without saying that such an apocalyptic vision, dear as it may be to the popular press, scarcely corresponds to linguistic reality either in terms of the durability or the number of imported words. Most such words belong to specific domains, mainly technical, and it is hard to see how the introduction of Anglicisms impedes comprehension any more than it is obstructed by the reconstructed Greek and Latin (and often Græco-Latin) words habitually suggested as an alternative. *Oléoduc* and *logiciel* are scarcely less opaque to the average Frenchman than the Anglicisms they replace, *pipeline* and *software* (the latter of which means precious little to many an English speaker). What is more, vocabulary, despite first impressions, is one of the least important elements of a language. It would be possible to replace virtually every French word one used and still speak French.

However, official resistance to the flow of Anglicisms has been unremitting. Between 1972 and 1989, there were no fewer than thirty-nine *arrêtés* establishing *commissions de terminologie* for fields as diverse as the *langage des techniques spatiales* (1972), the vocabulary of *les activités des femmes* (1984), or that of *composants électroniques* (1986).[4]

Vocabulary may be the most outward and visible sign of linguistic change. It is not the only one. There is abundant evidence, now well-documented by a series of studies since the pioneering investigation by André Martinet, of other types of change.[5] Both pronunciation (of 'standard' French) and syntax, especially, although in this case by no means exclusively, of spoken French, are undergoing significant alterations. Many of the structures of modern spoken French have little in common with their written equivalents; and it is, of course, the written equivalents which are embedded in the grammars used in the educational process. It is now very rare, for example, to hear the negative particle *ne*, or the full form *cela* in speech unless of a very formal nature. For the negative, the other particle (*pas*, *jamais*, and so on, originally included to reinforce *ne*) suffices. As a result, *plus* meaning 'more' and *plus* meaning 'no more', 'no longer' have to be kept distinct by pronunciation of the final -*s* when the word retains its positive sense. *Ça* is the normal spoken equivalent of *cela*, even in quite formal situations. Likewise, the construction of interrogatives in spoken French is predominantly based on intonation (*Tu as* (or *T'as*) *l'heure?*), often with no change of word-order, rather than by using the convoluted introductory formulae of literary French (*Est-ce que tu as l'heure?*). Complex sentences with subordinate clauses give way to short, separate, simple clauses with no obvious logical or grammatical connection between them, and scattered with strictly redundant emphatic pronouns: not *S'il pleut demain, je n'y irai pas* but *Alors, demain, s'il pleut, moi, j'y vais pas*. Rare and difficult verb forms are eliminated in favour of more regular alternatives: the imperfect subjunctive, for example, has vanished from all but very formal speech, and 'irregular' verbs (*choir, moudre*) are increasingly replaced by neologisms whose paradigms are more familiar (*chuter* derived from the noun *chute*, itself from the old verb *choir*; *mouler* from the stem of *moudre*). Future tenses are formed not on the synthetic model traditional in French, but by use of *aller* + infinitive, thereby retaining, at least in appearance, the predominant present tense of spoken language. Typical of modern spoken French, too, is what is sometimes referred to as the *nous, on* formula, whereby the first person plural is expressed by using the morphologically more familiar third person singular: not *nous allons* but *nous, on va*. Again, *on* is in a sense redundant here, at least as far as meaning is concerned; but its introduction permits the use of a less complex form of the verb. All these economies of grammatical effort are available to the spoken language because additional information can be imparted by other means, intonation, gesture and facial expression. None of them can really now be regarded as belonging exclusively to the lower registers of the spoken language: they are part of normal, informal spoken French *tout court*.

Pronunciation, too, is changing, with a general tendency towards a broadening of the range of acceptable pronunciation. The *Dictionnaire de la prononciation française dans son usage réel* compiled by André Martinet and Henriette Walter (Paris: France Expansion, 1973) gives some idea of the possible, and often quite different, pronunciations of words in supposedly 'standard' French. The difference between this reference work and the *traités de prononciation* designed for more normative and didactic purposes is striking. The latter, destined in many cases for foreign students of the language, indicate an (often outmoded) pronunciation to be adopted, without betraying the fact that this is not how most Frenchmen would pronounce a given word. This is no doubt helpful to the foreign student, but it does not tell us much about the reality, and above all the diversity, of modern pronunciation. The *Dictionnaire de la prononciation française dans son usage réel*, on the other hand, attempts to convey at least some idea of the acceptable range of pronunciations which may nevertheless be considered to fall within the increasingly flexible norm; that is, pronunciations which would not immediately identify the speaker as uneducated or provincial or both. What is increasingly apparent is that spoken French, in general, is becoming less formal, or that the less formal registers of spoken French are becoming acceptable in circumstances where, a generation or two ago, they would have been avoided. In many cases, what is perceived as pronunciation change is nothing of the sort, it is simply the growing use of types of French which once had a more restricted circulation.

There have nonetheless been some real changes to the phonological structure of the language (the way in which distinctions between sounds convey meaning). Certain of these distinctions, which would once have been regarded as part of 'standard' French, belong now only to the speech of an older generation: for example, the distinction of length of vowel between *maître* and *mettre*; or the difference in pronunciation between *pâte* and *patte*; or, more and more, the distinction between the more open *e* of *contiendrais* and the more closed sound of *contiendrai*, both of which tend now to be pronounced, by younger speakers at least, as [e]. The four distinct nasal vowels of French are fast reducing to three: one, the sound found in *un*, its compounds and a few other words, has all but disappeared in normal speech of at least the Paris region, with consequences, not yet fully developed, for the other nasal vowels. A very characteristic feature of French phonology is thus under attack. The change, by which *un* is pronounced like *ain*, was first noted in the mid-seventeenth century, and was becoming common towards the end of the last century in popular (working-class) Parisian speech. The traditional pronunciation of *un* and other words with the same sound persists in the provinces, and it persists amongst older speakers from the higher social classes in Paris. An interesting case is presented by the phenomena of liaison and the pronunciation of final consonants. These are related. Liaison, the pronunciation of a normally silent consonant at the end of a word when followed by a vowel at the beginning of the following word, is compulsory (*ils ont*), optional (*pas un chat*) or prohibited (before *onze*, before *h aspiré*); the compulsory and prohibited variations are largely unchanged, but the important optional category is increasingly disappearing in informal spoken French. It continues to be retained in more careful speech. Political speeches, or formal addresses, will thus preserve liaison, whereas everyday conversation will not. Liaison, in other words, has become a stylistic marker and indicator of register, one of the devices used by speakers in elevated speech. An apparently contradictory development is that of the widespread pronunciation of final consonants, especially on monosyllabic words (*août, but*). Historically, French has gradually lost its final consonants over the centuries, of which, in many cases, only liaison preserves the last spoken evidence (for example, the now very stylized pronunciation of the final *-r* in *-er* infinitives in liaison with a following vowel). There is thus something paradoxical about a tendency, on the one hand, to reduce liaison and, on the other, to pronounce, indeed to reintroduce, final consonants even where no liaison is involved. Here, there may be some influence from the written language: some commentators have seen in this aspect of modern French a spelling pronunciation, whereby pronunciation is affected by orthography. Such interference between the written and the spoken codes is quite common: witness the widespread, though mistaken, pronunciation of the purely orthographic *-p-* in *sculpteur*. Finally, but importantly, there is some evidence that the stress pattern of spoken French is undergoing potentially far-reaching modifications. French is characterized by a rigid use of oxytonic stress, where the accent falls on the last syllable of the word or group of words (*une histOIRe*, but *une histoire impossIBLe*, with a transfer of the stress). Popular French of the Paris region has long had a tendency to stress, and to lengthen, the penultimate syllable, particularly for reasons of expressivity (*il s'est barré, le sAlaud*). For reasons of emphasis (in spoken French more generally) the first syllable is often stressed (*c'est*

IMpossible). Both these pronunciations are beginning to threaten the primacy of the oxytonic pattern. In the case of days of the week, for example, the pronunciation which stresses the first syllable (*LUNdi*, *SAMedi*) is becoming very common. Since the phonetic development of the French language, from Latin onwards, has always depended to a large extent on stress, with unaccented syllables traditionally vanishing over the centuries, it remains to be seen what the implications of a wholesale shift in the pattern of accentuation will be.[6]

These developments of pronunciation and syntax belong in a different category from the changes in vocabulary mentioned above. In many, if not all cases, they can be traced back to the popular spoken French of the last century or before, whereas vocabulary changes are often more recent. In practice, 'popular spoken French' means the language of the Parisian working classes, thought by some to be simply a continuation of historically evolved normal spoken French, untrammelled (in an era of mass illiteracy) by the controls and restrictions which bodies such as the French Academy endeavoured to impose on the standard language. We must not forget that, during the seventeenth, eighteenth and nineteenth centuries, standard French, even more than nowadays, impinged only on a very small section of the population. There thus existed, in parallel to the French of literature, non-literary documents and grammars, an increasingly distinct spoken language, the only language accessible to most French speakers, and one which continued to evolve oblivious of the glories of classical French as extolled in the Academy dictionary's preface. What seems to have happened is that forms originating in this spoken French of the masses have now become more widespread in the informal speech of all social classes. Perhaps, more generally, this form of spoken French has expanded from its original environment to become a new, colloquial norm for most informal situations. Together with the general process of democratization which has affected France as well as other European countries in the last forty-five years, the effect of this is to give the impression that spoken French has been dramatically transformed since the Second World War. In reality, what has changed, above all, is speakers' attitudes, and the extent to which certain forms, hitherto socially marked, are now accepted across a broader section of society and in contexts from which they would formerly have been rigorously excluded. Naturally, there are exceptions, areas of usage which remain within certain social groups. This arises, in part, because language not only serves as a means of communication, but also as an essential element in the establishment of group identity. That group may be the nation: hence the evolution of national languages, and the attempt by many states to suppress separate, minority languages within their boundaries. Or the group may be smaller, a profession, perhaps, a particular social class, or an age-group. Each will tend to have its own, specific language, or at least specific forms of what one might call the parent language. Thus, originally *français populaire* was the language of the Parisian working classes. We have seen that it is now tending to climb the social scale, increasingly becoming one of a number of informal registers of spoken French, between which distinctions are harder and harder to draw. The meaning of *français familier, français courant, français populaire, français vulgaire* is very much in the eye (or ear) of the beholder. What is *vulgaire* to one speaker is *courant* to another. The idea that uttering the word *con* in public (not, of course, in its now lost etymological sense) could create a scandal is now absurd; yet, as recently as 1955, just such a scandal occurred when the singer Georges Brassens transgressed that particular linguistic taboo. *Français populaire*'s function of providing group identity still persists, however, since there is evidence that it now fulfils the role of archetypical working-class speech, indicative of (particularly) male, class solidarity in other parts of France. A study in Touraine demonstrated this conclusively, and all the more ironically, because Touraine is traditionally (though wrongly) held to be the centre of 'standard' or 'correct' French (Nicole Gueunier *et al., Les Français devant la norme* (Paris: Champion, 1978)). A more problematic concept is that of *argot*, a term widely used to refer to what are in reality very different forms of French, ranging from criminal slang and the vogue slang of adolescents to familiar vocabulary or even familiar, informal speech in the most general sense. *Argot*, a term at first referring to a hermetic criminal code which was born in and used by the organized underworld, is, by definition, a language whose original intention is to create group solidarity and above all to exclude outsiders, particularly outsiders who happen to belong to the forces of law and order. The most common *argot* terms of the nineteenth-century *milieu* have now largely passed into familiar spoken French, in many cases being given a new lease of life, and wider circulation, by the authors of twentieth-century *polars* (*romans policiers*); but newer forms have emerged, to supersede a language now too well understood to be able to provide secrecy and group identity. The most prolific generators of modern argot are the young; the most famous modern development, *le verlan*, is, ironically, not modern at all, but dates from the early twentieth century. Research suggests that it is now particularly favoured by young second-generation Maghrebin immigrants. Consisting in the inversion of syllables (*verlan* = *l'envers*), it is one of a number of forms of *argot* which function by deformation, another being the less common, and equally venerable, *javanais* (in which -*av*- is inserted in each and every syllable). The expertise required in order to speak, and especially to decode, such a form of French ensures that, with the exception of a few well-known words (*meuf* = femme, *keum* = mec, *ripou* = pourri, *chébran* = branché, or *bléca* = câblé), themselves often slang words even before their encoding, *verlan* can only with difficulty penetrate informal spoken French. The likelihood of its becoming a widespread variety of such French, in the way that much of the *argot* of the nineteenth century has done, seems remote. What it and other slang forms reveal is that slang, by its very nature, tends constantly to need to innovate, whether for reasons of secrecy or simply for amusement. It is an element of spoken French which naturally does little to narrow the gap between spoken and written registers of the language.[7]

Needless to say, the literary language has not changed to anything like the same extent as has the spoken language. The gap between written and spoken French is thus generally thought to be widening. Yet, at the same time, many of the developments which have originated in spoken French are encroaching on the written medium, most conspicuously in newspapers, magazines and in the only semi-oral media of radio and television. This is not, of course, to the liking of official bodies such as the Academy, or indeed of those who, in general, represent the French cultural establishment. The conflict between the two varieties of French is thus also a contest between conservative and progressive tendencies, as the guardians of the language of a rich but increasingly inaccessible literary heritage struggle to retain control over the rapidly-developing and heterogeneous modern language. The inescapable conclusion is that there are not simply two forms of French but, instead, a continuum of registers from the formal to the informal, with the possibility of writing, or speaking, formally or informally according to context. It is naive to suppose that written French and spoken French are inevitably poles apart, and that the written language is always the formal, carefully constructed classical French of the literary canon, whilst spoken French is invariably the throwaway informality of the *Café des Sports*. Spoken, and written, French, both come in a wide variety of styles ranging from the very formal to the very informal. Yet, as has already been suggested, the dichotomy between the two forms persists, for most French speakers, in part because of the contexts in which most writing and most speaking tend to be carried out. These ensure that the former is predominantly formal, the latter predominantly informal.

A second major conflict, and also a long-standing one, arises from the tension between centripetal and centrifugal forces. France is, of course, a highly centralized state, and the French language is, as we have seen, one of the national assets over which Paris claims control. 'Standard French', taught in schools throughout France, is the French of the educated Parisian. Moreover, it is not only the educational system, but also, by and large, the speakers of the language themselves, who recognize and accept the hegemony accorded to this particular variety. It has to be said that the situation in the Midi is a little different from that in the northern half of France, since the Midi has evolved a sort of southern French standard which enjoys considerable status. Throughout northern France, though, regional forms of French (regional accents), the last vestiges of the dialects which have almost entirely vanished, have little prestige. Whether in towns or in the countryside, regional pronunciation, whilst not synonymous with social class, is nevertheless closely associated with it. Just as *français populaire* used, at least, to be the spoken French of Parisian workers, so, too, what have come to be called *français régionaux* are, by and large, spoken by the working classes, and particularly those who live in the country. And of course *français régionaux* are exclusively spoken forms, thus accentuating still further the divide between spoken and written varieties in those areas where the regional pronunciation diverges widely from that of 'standard' French. Broadly speaking, these are, logically enough, the areas furthest from Paris, and in particular those areas where minority languages are, or were, spoken: Brittany, Flanders, Alsace, the Midi in general. In most of these regions, the situation is that two languages coexist, one (Breton, Flemish, Alsatian, Occitan) being predominantly used in less formal situations, the other (French with a more or less strong regional accent) being employed in formal circumstances.[8] This presents a classic situation of what is known as *diglossia*, where one language (French) occupies the higher or prestige role, the other (the minority language) the lower or non-prestige function. The minority language will be used in informal conversations (with family, friends etc.) while French is used in more formal situations (dealings with official bodies like banks, post offices etc.). In such areas, the strength of a speaker's regional accent is usually related to his or her use of the minority language; not surprisingly, since the regional accents of minority-language areas are the outcome of the superimposition of French on parts of France where other languages were originally spoken. In those regions where what used to be spoken were dialects, genetically related to French but emphatically not derivatives of (still less, aberrations from) 'standard' French, regional accents are, similarly, the product of the introduction of the national language in the nineteenth and, especially, twentieth centuries. In these areas (most of northern France, except the minority language areas), *français régional* coexists with standard French in a state of diglossia. Abundant scientific evidence about the state of dialects and regional variations is available from the turn of the century, with the publication of the pioneering *Atlas linguistique de la France*, compiled by Jules Gilliéron and Edmond Edmont and published between 1902 and 1910. Studies carried out since then, whether in the Midi or in the north, all point in the same, predictable direction: throughout France, 'standard' French (or, usually, French with a regional accent) is gaining ground rapidly, and the minority languages and dialects are declining fast. In the early years of the twentieth century, an investigation in the Vosges mountains concluded that the Romance dialect of Lorraine was not spoken, in practice, by anyone born after 1880 or so: elementary arithmetic suggests that there are, therefore, no speakers of this dialect still alive. A study of the Franche-Comté region (published in 1983) came up with similar findings. The *patois* is now spoken only by the oldest inhabitants, the pre-war generations who are now grandparents and great-grandparents. Like the Vosges, the Franche-Comté is a fairly remote and predominantly rural, and conservative, area. Here, too, the dialect seems doomed to die out with its last speakers. French has advanced less overwhelmingly in the Midi; but there, to judge by recent research in the departments of the Tarn and Cantal, it is abundantly clear that one of the principal criteria which divide Occitan speakers from those who speak only (regional) French is age. The younger generations do not often speak, and sometimes do not even understand, Occitan: it is a language predominantly spoken by the old. In the space of perhaps three generations, Occitan-French bilingualism is giving way to monolingual French-speaking. It is hard, under these circumstances, to be optimistic about Occitan's future as a living language. The imminent disappearance of Occitan must, then, be reckoned one of the significant post-war developments in the linguistic history of France.[9] Elsewhere in France, minority languages (rather than dialects) are holding up well: in Alsace, for example, a survey carried out in 1979 showed that fully three-quarters of the population claimed to speak Alsatian, a Germanic dialect closely related to the form of German spoken in the neighbouring Black Forest. It seems likely that the continuing survival of Alsatian owes something to the fact that it enjoys support from the existence of a virtually identical Germanic dialect, and indeed of standard German itself (which functions as the written version of Alsatian), in an adjacent country. In very general terms, however, there is little doubt that the future survival of minority languages, dialects and even regional forms of French has become markedly less promising since 1945. In particular, the dialects of northern France (as distinct from minority languages, Breton, Alsatian and Flemish) have all but disappeared. It seems only a matter of time before the regional forms of French which represent them, albeit in attenuated form, are gradually erased.

The reasons for this development, common to much of Europe including Britain, are several. Amongst those commonly cited are the French enthusiasm for centralization, which means, for example, that education is controlled by Paris, and that teachers are appointed, centrally, all over France, where they can disseminate 'standard' French; military service, which brings together (at least in theory) young Frenchmen from the whole of France; improved communications; the importance of Paris as an economic as well as political capital, which ensures that many people spend at least some time working or training there; the advent of media such as the radio and television, which expose the population all over France to 'standard' French in a way which was not hitherto the case. Another factor which might be adduced, and which is sometimes overlooked, includes the stigma attached to a strong regional accent, and *a fortiori* to a dialect. It is hard to overestimate the significance of such prejudices. Increasing social mobility contributes substantially to the eradication of non-prestigious regional variations, because the upwardly mobile consider the use of such forms detrimental to their own professional and social advancement. In most cases so far investigated, in France and elsewhere, there is a sex difference in this regard, with women consistently more aware of, and more inclined to modify, the socially or regionally marked features of their speech. This is as true of developments in modern Parisian French as it is of the use made of non-prestigious Occitan in the Midi. Women consistently favour more prestigious forms; and this normally means something more akin to 'standard' French than will be spoken by their husbands. Thus women are apparently at the forefront of linguistic change in Paris,[10] and women speak Occitan far less than men. The pattern holds good with *français régional* as well. That speakers modify their language in an attempt to disguise or obliterate regional features points strongly to a perceived correlation between regional accent and social class, with the former serving as a marker not only of geographical origin, but also of social status and educational attainment. Naturally, the attitude towards regional varieties of French varies from place to place, as it does in Britain, and it is probably broadly correct to claim that regional accents are a less reliable indicator of social class than they are in Britain. It is true, however, that a strong Lille or Strasbourg accent is unlikely to be found amongst the professional classes in those towns. It is not by accident that academic studies of regional French tend to concentrate on old, poorly-educated, working-class men who live in the countryside and who have (preferably) never strayed far from the village of their birth. They are the people who speak a *français régional* most differentiated from 'standard' French. Not all *français régionaux* are equally looked down on. The existence of a southern French standard, in a sense a rival to the Parisian standard throughout the Midi, has already been mentioned. As in Britain, it seems that attitudes towards regional accents are largely the result of non-linguistic suppositions and prejudices, with the greatest opprobrium being reserved for those accents perceived as 'foreign' (Alsace) or arising from allegedly disagreeable, impoverished industrial towns (the north east), and greater tolerance being displayed towards accents from regions with positive connotations (the Midi: sun, sea, pétanque and pastis). It goes without saying that such attitudes are neither rational nor scientifically founded; but that does not stop them exerting considerable influence.

Official hostility towards dialects dates back, as we have seen, to well before the French Revolution. It was the post-Revolutionary period, however, which introduced the principal measures which would, in practice, undermine the existence of dialects and of regional varieties of French more generally. Above all, it was through educational measures, the deployment of the *hussards noirs de la République* (as the teaching profession was called at the end of the nineteenth century) that the government hoped to impose the 'language of liberty' in all its standardized glory on the recalcitrant dialect-speaking citizenry of the new Republic. It is, therefore, gratifyingly ironic that it should now be through education that the resurgence of minority languages is being promoted. Regionalism, partly encouraged by Socialist governments since Mitterrand, partly prompted by the development of the European Community and a concomitant reduction in the importance of national frontiers, and indeed of the concept of the nation-state itself, has provoked a renewal of interest in regional languages.[11] Since 1951, a degree of tolerance or even encouragement has been extended, at least in theory, to such aberrant linguistic varieties as Breton or Occitan. 1951 is the date of the so-called Loi Deixonne, introduced in order to 'favoriser l'étude des langues et dialectes locaux dans les régions où ils sont en usage'. In fact, only Occitan, Basque, Breton and Catalan were included in this seemingly catch-all category, and all the law introduced was the possibility of a weekly hour of language-teaching and the inclusion of these languages in the baccalaureate, with the development of the teaching of the same languages at university level. Subsequently, the measures were extended to German (not Alsatian) in Alsace (1952) and to Corsican (1974). It could be argued that such measures are of largely academic interest: the fact that minority languages now have to be taught in schools can be seen as eloquent and unfortunate proof of their demise as living vernaculars outside the classroom. Similarly, the regional movements which have sprung up in various parts of France (Brittany, Corsica, the Midi, for example) include amongst their aspirations the holding back of the tide of linguistic evolution and the resuscitation of moribund minority languages. These organizations themselves often seem to be a minority activity in regions which have largely gone over to the cause of French. Perhaps the minority languages which enjoy the support of an adjacent hinterland in neighbouring states may survive: this includes Alsatian, Catalan (much revitalized in Spain since the end of the Franco era) and Basque. But, rightly or wrongly, the loss of dialects which are not in such a privileged position is part and parcel of twentieth-century progress, and is unlikely to be reversed by political action unless the would-be speakers themselves embrace the cause, and even then, it is probably too late. It seems reasonable to suppose that the regional accents of France will survive for some time yet, but that here, too, a gradual reduction of divergences between these regional accents and 'standard' French will occur. Policies ostensibly in favour of minority languages, and which perforce threaten the absolute rule of 'standard' French, are hard to reconcile with other governmental intervention in the area of the language. Official policy remains one in which minority languages are at best tolerated, at worst surreptitiously suppressed. When an EEC survey of minority languages (or 'lesser-used languages' [*sic*] as the EEC sometimes calls them) was carried out in the 1980s, based in Rome, the French embassy there initially informed the investigators that there was no minority language problem in France because everyone in France spoke French. The reply may have revealed more than was intended about French official thinking. *Liberté* and *égalité* have never been much in evidence in the policies of the five French republics to date, where concern for unity has led to a desire for linguistic uniformity which looks likely to be realized before very long.

Notes

* References are not intended to be exhaustive; they aim simply to direct the reader to the sources of specific information in this chapter. Further references will be found in the works listed under 'Further Reading'.

1. See Bodo Müller, 'Gesprochene Sprache und geschriebene Sprache', in Günter Holtus *et al.*, ed., *Lexikon der Romanistischen Linguistik*, V, i: *Französisch* (Tübingen: Niemeyer, 1990), 195–211 for a general survey and copious bibliographical references.
2. See Michel de Certeau *et al.*, *Une politique de la langue française. La Révolution française et les patois* (Paris: Gallimard, 1975). A number of important Revolutionary documents are reprinted in this volume.
3. An interesting illustration of the problems still surrounding the term *patois* is provided, perhaps unwittingly, by Henriette Walter, 'Patois

ou français régional?', *Le Français Moderne*, 52 (1984), 183–90.
4. Lists of decrees emanating from the various official bodies (with references to the *Journal Officiel*) are conveniently assembled in Christian Schmitt, 'Sprache und Gesetzgebung: Frankreich', *Lexikon der Romanistischen Linguistik*, V, i, 354–79.
5. André Martinet, *La Prononciation du français contemporain. Témoignages recueillis en 1941 dans un camp d'officiers prisonniers* (Paris and Geneva: Droz, 1945). Martinet is responsible for the useful concept of *synchronie dynamique* to describe the state of a changing language studied at a particular moment.
6. A most impressive survey of pronunciation changes from a historical perspective is provided by Georges Straka, 'Sur la formation de la prononciation française d'aujourd'hui', *Travaux de Linguistique et de Littérature de l'Université de Strasbourg*, 19/i (1981), 161–248.
7. On *français populaire* and *argot* generally, see Müller, *Le Français d'aujourd'hui*; on *verlan*, see Vivienne Méla, 'Parler verlan: règles et usages', *Langage et Société*, 45 (1988), 47–72.
8. A series of articles concerning Alsace illustrates the point: see Gilbert-Lucien Salmon, *Le français en Alsace. Actes du Colloque de Mulhouse (17–19 novembre 1983)* (Paris and Geneva: Champion-Slatkine, 1985).
9. See Oscar Bloch, *La pénétration du français dans les parlers des Vosges méridionales* (Paris: Champion, 1921); Peter Scherfer, *Untersuchungen zum Sprachbewusstsein der Patois-Sprecher in der Franche-Comté* (Tübingen: Narr, 1983); Trudel Meisenburg, *Die soziale Rolle des Okzitanischen in einer kleinen Gemeinde im Languedoc (Lacaune/ Tarn)* (Tübingen: Niemeyer, 1985); Wolfgang Markhof, *Renaissance oder Substitution? Eine soziolinguistische Untersuchung zur Stellung des Okzitanischen im Departement Cantal* (Geneva: Droz, 1987).
10. This emerges quite clearly from a Pennsylvania Ph.D. thesis by M. Lennig, *Acoustic measurement of linguistic change: the modern Paris vowel system* (1978). For Occitan, see the studies cited in the previous note.
11. See Mathée Giacomo, 'La politique à propos des langues régionales: cadre historique', *Langue française*, 25 (February 1975), 12–28 and the issue of this periodical devoted to *Les parlers régionaux*, 18 (May 1973), ed. Alain Lerond.

Further reading

Ager, Denis, *Sociolinguistics and Contemporary French* (Cambridge: Cambridge University Press, 1990)

Batty, Adrian and Hintze, Marie-Anne, *The French Language Today* (London and New York: Routledge, 1992)

Désirat, Claude and Hordé, Tristan, *La Langue française au 20e siècle* (Paris: Bordas, 1976)

Müller, Bodo, *Le Français d'aujourd'hui* (Paris: Klincksieck, 1987).

Offord, Malcolm, *Varieties of Contemporary French* (London: Macmillan, 1990)

Rickard, Peter, *A History of the French Language*, 2nd edition (London: Unwin Hyman, 1989)

Walter, Henriette, *Le Français dans tous les sens* (Paris: Laffont, 1988)

C H R O N O L O G Y

Years	Part I Literature	Theatre/ Cinema
1945	Suicide of Drieu La Rochelle Execution of Robert Brasillach Birth of Modiano Beauvoir, *Le Sang des autres, Les Bouches inutiles* Camus, *Lettres à un ami allemand* Jean-Paul Sartre, *L'Age de raison, (Le Sursis)* Vailland, *Drôle de jeu*	Camus, *Caligula*
1946	Beauvoir, *Tous les Hommes sont mortels* Sartre, *L'Existentialisme est un humanisme, Réflexions sur la question juive*	Founding of CNC (Centre National de la Cinématographie)
1947	Birth of Grainville Beauvoir, *Pour une morale de l'ambiguïté* Camus, *La Peste* Sartre, *Situations, I; L'Homme et les choses* Sarraute, *Portrait d'un inconnu* Vailland, *Héloïse et Abelard*	Genet, *Les Bonnes* Autant-Lara, *Le Diable au corps* Clouzot, *Quai des Orfèvres*
1948	Beauvoir, *L'Amérique au jour le jour; L'Existentialisme et la sagesse de nations* Sarraute, *Portrait d'un Inconnu* Sartre, *Situations, II*	Sartre, *Les Mains sales*
1949	Blondin, *L'Europe buissonnière* Beauvoir, *Le Deuxième sexe*, 2 volumes Sartre, *La Mort dans l'âme; Situations, III* Nimier, *Les Epées*	Camus, *Les Justes* Melville, *Le Silence de la Mer*
1950	Duras, *Un Barrage contre le Pacifique* Nimier, *Le Grand d'Espagne; Le Hussard bleu* Vailland, *Bon pied, bon oeil*	Ionesco, *La Cantatrice chauve* Bresson, *Journal d'un curé de campagne* Cocteau, *Orphée*
1951	Camus, *L'Homme révolté* Courtade, *Jimmy* Nimier, *Les Enfants tristes* Vailland, *Un Jeune homme seul* Yourcenar, *Mémoires d'Hadrien*	Ionesco, *La Leçon* Sartre, *Le Diable et le bon Dieu*
1952	Blondin, *Les Enfants du bon Dieu; Le Chemin des écoliers* Duras, *Le Marin de Gibraltar* Sartre, *Saint Genet, comédien et martyr*	Adamov, *La Parodie* Ionesco, *Les Chaises*

Years	Part II Popular Culture	Part III Cultural Debates
1945	*Radiodiffusion française* (RDF) created *Elle* created	Creation of the Bibliothèques centrales de prêt, coupled with the relaunch of the Popular Front 'bibliobus' initiative February: the *Comités d'entreprises* are created by law August: the *Direction des spectacles et de la musique* is set up under Jeanne Laurent
1946		October: the first CDN is created: the Centre dramatique de l'Est
1947	France Inter created	Creation of the Avignon Festival by Jean Vilar July: the Comédie de Saint-Etienne, the second CDN, is founded under Jean Dasté
1948		The Aix-en-Provence Festival is created
1949	*Paris-Match* started	January: the Grenier de Toulouse becomes the third CDN November: the Centre dramatique de l'Ouest is founded, becoming the fourth Simone de Beauvoir publishes *Le Deuxième Sexe*
1950	Government decree stipulating that all Physical Education teachers in secondary schools should devote three hours of their weekly contractual time to work with the *Associations sportives*	
1951		Jean Vilar is appointed by Laurent to lead the reformed TNP Loi Deixonne introduced to favour study of minority languages
1952	RDF becomes RTF (*Radiodiffusion-Télévision française* started)	March: the fifth CDN, the Centre dramatique de Sud-Est, is set up under Gaston Baty Laurent is removed from the Ministry's theatre administration; as a result the first wave of official decentralization is halted until 1959

Years	Part I Literature	Theatre/ Cinema
1953	Barthes, *Le Degré zéro de l'écriture* Bonnefoy, *Du mouvement et de l'immobilité de Douve* Courtade, *La Rivière noire* Duras, *Les Petits chevaux de Tarquinia* Nimier, *Histoire d'un amour* Robbe-Grillet, *Les Gommes* Sarraute, *Martereau* Vailland, *Expérience du drame*	Adamov, *Le Professeur Taranne* Beckett, *En Attendant Godot* Tati, *Les Vacances de M. Hulot*
1954	Camus, *L'Été* Beauvoir, *Les Mandarins* Butor, *Passage de Milan* Sagan, *Bonjour tristesse* Sarraute, *Martéreau* Vailland, *Beau Masque*	Becker, *Touchez pas au Grisbi*
1955	Beauvoir, *Privilèges* Duras, *Le Square* Robbe-Grillet, *Le Voyeur* Vailland, *325,000 Francs*	Adamov, *Ping-Pong* Ionesco, *Jacques ou la soumission*
1956	Camus, *Requiem pour une nonne, La Chute* Butor, *L'Emploi du temps* Sarraute, *L'Ere du soupçon*	Vinaver, *Aujourd'hui, ou les Coréens* Vadim, *Et Dieu créa la Femme*
1957	Barthes, *Mythologies* Camus, *L'Exil et le Royaume; Réflexions sur la peine capitale* Beauvoir, *La Longue marche: essais sur la Chine* Butor, *La Modification* Robbe-Grillet, *La Jalousie* Simon, *Le Vent*	Beckett, *Fin de Partie*
1958	Aragon, *La Semaine sainte* Camus, *Discours de Suède*, his acceptance speech for the Nobel Prize for literature Beauvoir, *Mémoires d'une fille rangée* Duras, *Moderato Cantabile* Levi-Strauss, *Anthropologie structurale* Simon, *L'Herbe*	Planchon, *Les Trois Mousquetaires*
1959	Camus, *Les Possédés* Robbe-Grillet, *Dans le Labyrinthe* Sarraute, *Le Planétarium* Sollers, *Une Curieuse Solitude*	Arrabal, *Pique-nique en campagne* Genet, *Les Nègres* Gatti, *Le Crapaud-Buffle* Truffaut, *Les Quatre cent coups* Godard, *A Bout de Souffle* Resnais, *Hiroshima mon amour* Chabrol, *Le Beau Serge*

Years	Part II Popular Culture	Part III Cultural Debates
1953	First *classes de neige* *L'Express* started	
1954	Transistor radios first appeared in France	Simone de Beauvoir wins Prix Goncourt with *Les Mandarins*
1955	Europe I created	First woman tax inspector *(percepteur)*
1956	Number of TV sets in France: 442,433	The founding of *Le Mouvement pour le Planning Familial*
1957	Guy Béart, *L'Eau Vive*	Simone de Beauvoir publishes *La Longue Marche*
1958	France came third in World Cup in Sweden. Fòntaine top scorer with 13 goals	Six women elected to Assemblée Nationale (out of 465)
1959	France wins 5 Nation Rugby Tournament for the first time	January: André Malraux is appointed Ministre d'État in charge of the newly-created Ministère des affaires culturelles November: Malraux addresses the National Assembly on the need for one Maison de la culture in each Department

Years	Part I Literature	Theatre/ Cinema
1960	Death of Camus Butor, *Degrés, Répertoire: études et conférences 1948—1959* Duras, *Hiroshima mon amour, Les viaducs de la Seine-et-Oise, Dix heures et demie du soir en été* Beauvoir, *Brigitte Bardot and the Lolita Syndrome, La Force de L'Age* Sartre, *Critique de la raison dialectique*, Vol. 1 Simon, *La Route de Flandres* Deguy, *Fragments du cadastre*	Beckett, *Le Dernière Bande* Genet, *Le Balcon* Ionesco, *Rhinocéros* Rouch, *Chronique d'un été*
1961	Founding of *Tel Quel* Courtade, *La Place rouge* Duras, *Une Aussi longue absence* Jaccottet, *L'Obscurité* Robbe-Grillet, *L'Année dernière à Marienbad* Sollers, *Le Parc*	Resnais, *L'Anneé dernière à Marienbad*
1962	Death of Roger Nimier Cardinal, *Ecoutez la mer* Du Bouchet, *Dans la Chaleur vacante* Duras, *L'Après-midi de Monsieur Andermas* Jaccottet, *Airs* Simon, *Le Palace* Deguy, *Poèmes de la presque-ile*	Ionesco, *Le Roi se meurt* Truffaut, *Jules et jim*
1963	Beauvoir, *La Force des choses* Cardinal, *La Mule de corbillard* Le Clezio, *Le Proces-verbal* Robbe-Grillet, *L'Immortelle: Pour un nouveau roman* Sarraute, *Les Fruits d'or* Sollers, *L'Intermédiaire* Bonnefoy, *Pierre écrite*	Obaldia, *Le Satyre de la Villette*
1964	Beauvoir, *Une Mort très douce* Butor, *Répertoire II: études et conférences 1959—1963* Duras, *Le Ravissement de Lol V. Stein* Lévi-Strauss, *Mythologiques: Le Cru et le cuit* Sartre, *Les Mots; Situations, IV; Situations, V; Situations, VI; Qu'est ce que la littérature?*	Gatti, *Le Poisson noir*
1965	Death of Roger Vailland Camus, *Essais* Butor, *6810000 litres d'eau par seconde* Cardinal, *La Souricière* Robbe-Grillet, *La Maison de rendez-vous* Sartre, *Situations, VII* Sollers, *Drame*	Duras, *Des Journées entières dans les arbres* Obaldia, *Du Vent dans les branches de Sassafras* Godard, *Pierrot le fou*

Years	Part II Popular Culture	Part III Cultural Debates
1960	*Télé 7 Jours* started	Marc Boegner proposes that women be admitted to the Académie des Sciences morales et politiques
1961	Creation of *Association du sport scolaire et universitaire* (ASSU)	June: the first MC is inaugurated by Malraux in Le Havre, followed by seven more between this date and May 1968
1962	First issue of *Salut les Copains*, teenage magazine Johnny Halliday becomes a social phenomenon	First woman elected to the Académie des Sciences: Marguerite Perey
1963	Death of Edith Piaf	February: the Comités régionaux des affaires culturelles are created, allowing local cultural officials to be involved in national planning
1964	ORTF (Office de Radio-Télévision Française) created Second TV channel opened	Inauguration of Théâtre de l'est parisien and the Maison de la Culture de Bourges
1965	First televised soccer match in France	Aspects of Napoleonic Code are revoked: women more autonomous, legally and financially

Years	Part I Literature	Theatre/ Cinema
1966	Beauvoir, *Les Belles images* Deguy, *Actes* Duras, *Le Vice-Consul* Foucault, *Les Mots et les choses* Lacan, *Écrits* Le Clézio, *Le Déluge* Lévi-Strauss, *La Pensée sauvage* Simon, *Femmes*	Arrabal, *Le Cimetière des voitures* Genet, *Les Paravents* Rivette, *La Religieuse*
1967	Barthes, *Systémes de la mode* Cardinal, *Cet été-là* Cixous, *Le Prenom de Dieu* Derrida, *De la grammatologie,* *L'Écriture et la différence* Duras, *L'Amante anglaise* Lévi-Strauss, *Mythologiques: Du Miel aux cendres* Sarraute, *Le Silence, suivi de Le Mensonge* Simon, *Histoire* Tournier, *Vendredi ou les limbes du Pacifique* F. Mauriac, *Un Adolescent d'autrefois* Etcherell, *Elise ou la vraie vie*	Gatti, *V comme Vietnam* Bresson, *Mouchette*
1968	Beauvoir, *La Femme rompue. L'Age de discretion. Monologue* Butor, *Répertoire III* Cixous, *L'Exil de James Joyce ou l'art du remplacement* Du Bouchet, *Ou le soleil; Dans la chaleur vacante* Jaccottet, *L'Entretien des Muses* Lévi-Strauss, *Mythologiques: L'Origine des manières de table* Modiano, *La Place de l'Étoile* Sarraute, *Entre la Vie et la Mort* Sollers, *Logiques; Nombres*	Barrault, *Rabelais* Chabrol, *Les Biches*
1969	Butor, *Essais sur le roman* Cixous, *Dedans* Deguy, *Figurations* Duras, *Détruire dit-elle* Mauriac, *François, Un Adolescent d'autrefois* Modiano, *La Ronde de nuit* Simon, *La Bataille de Pharsal* Yourcenar, *L'Oeuvre au noir* Tournier, *Vendredi ou les limbes du Pacifique*	Césaire, *Une Tempête* Soleil, *Les Clowns* Rohmer, *Ma Nuit chez Maud* Ophüls, *Le Chagin et la pitié* (released 1971)

Years	Part II Popular Culture	Part III Cultural Debates
1966	Bob Dylan and Joan Baez make a large impact on French Radio	The fifth Plan calls for eight more MCs to be opened (as well as the twenty already scheduled) March: Malraux inaugurates the Amiens MC with a speech that outlines his cultural ideology
1967	Colour TV introduced on second channel	Legalization of contraception
1968	First 'open' tennis tournament at Roland Garros	The newly-opened Saint-Etienne MC is immediately taken over by the town council. The first Equipement intégré is set up and the first Directeurs régionaux des affaires culturelles appointed May and after: the eight MCs already opened are implicated in the cultural critique of the May movement. The directors of decentralized establishments meet in Villeurbanne. Jo Tréhard is sacked from Caen and the MC transformed after incidents during the May events November: Malraux addresses the National Assembly on the 'crisis' in the MCs and announces a number of reforms Feminist group *Psychanalyse et Politique* formed
1969	Publication of the 10-year Landowski plan for music (1969 – 79) setting up new structures for music in the regions	April: Resignation of General De Gaulle June: Malraux officially resigns Publication of Monique Wittig's *Les Guerillères*

Years	Part I Literature	Theatre/ Cinema
1970	Barthes, *S/Z* Beauvoir, *La Vieillesse* Cixous, *Le Troisième corps. Les Commencements* Jaccottet, *Paysages avec figures absentes* Le Clézio, *La Guerre* Robbe-Grillet, *Projet pour une révolution à New York* Simon, *Orion aveugle* Tournier, *Le Roi des aulnes* Modiano, *La Ronde de nuit*	Soleil, *1789* Grand Magic Circus, *Zartan*
1971	Butor, *Dialogue avec 33 variations de Ludwig van Beethoven sur une valse de Diabelli* Camus, *La Mort heureuse* Cardinal, *La Clé sur la porte* Cixous, *Un vrai jardin* Duras, *L'Amour* Jaccottet, *Poésie: 1946—1967* Lévi-Strauss, *Mythologiques: L'Hommu nu* Sartre, *L'Idiot de la famille: Gustave Flaubert de 1821—1857*, 3 vols. *Situations, VIII* Sollers, *L'Écriture et L'expérience des limites* Tournier, *Vendredi ou la vie sauvage* Yourcenar, *Discours de réception à l'Académie royale belge de langue et de littérature françaises, 19 mars 1971*	Renoir, *Le Petit Théâtre de Jean Renoir*
1972	Du Bouchet, *Qui n'est pas tourné vers nous: essai sur Albert Giacometti* Cixous, *Neutre. La Pupille* Beauvoir, *Tout compte fait* Deguy, *Le Tombeau de Du Bellay* Duras, *India song: texte-théâtre-film. Nathalie Granger, suivie de La Femme de la Gange* Grainville, *La Toison* Modiano, *Les Boulevards de ceinture* Sartre, *Situations, XI. Plaidoyer pour les intellectuels*	Grand Magic Circus, *Les Derniers jours de solitude de Robinson Crusoë* Soleil, *1793*
1973	Barthes, *Le Plaisir du texte* Cixous, *Tombe* Deguy, *Poèmes: 1960—1970* Grainville, *La Lisière* Le Clézio, *Les Géants* Simon, *Triptyque* Wittig, *Le Corps lesbien*	Grand Magic Circus, *De Moïse à Mao* Vinaver, *La Demande d'emploi; Par-dessus bord* Eustache, *La Maman et la Putain*

Years	Part II Popular Culture	Part III Cultural Debates
1970	Léo Ferré a success at La Mutualité	*MLF* place wreath on tomb of Unknown Soldier, dedicated to his wife First issue of feminist paper, *Le Torchon Brûle*
1971	Liebermann takes over direction of Paris Opera	January (– April 1973): Jacques Duhamel becomes Minister of Cultural Affairs March: official launch of FIC Feminists demonstrate against Mother's Day. In April, 343 women sign manifesto declaring they have had abortions Formation of *Choisir*, a pro-abortion group
1972	Merger of the *Comité olympique français* (COF) and the *Comité national des sports français* (CNSF) to form the *Comité national olympique des sports français* (CNOSF) FR3 created *Le Point* started *Paris-Jour* ceased publication	March: reorganization of subsidized theatre: the TNP is to be moved to Villeurbanne under Planchon and Patrice Chéreau (Jack Lang takes over its former premises at Chaillot) July: law on the creation of Regions October: a decree defines a new constitution for the CDNs, including pluriannual contracts
1973	*Libération* started	*Psyche et Po* establish publishing house: *Des Femmes* MLAC (Mouvement pour la libération de l'avortement) formed

Years	Part I Literature	Theatre/ Cinema
1974	Butor, *Répertoire IV* Cixous, *Portrait du soleil. Prénoms de personne* Duras, *Les Parleuses* Grainville, *L'Abîme. Les Flamboyants* Modiano, *Lacombe Lucien*	Grand Magic Circus, *Goodbye Mr Freud* Grumberg, *Dreyfus* Malle, *Lacombe Lucien* Blier, *Les Valseuses*
1975	Cardinal, *Les Mots pour le dire* Cixous and Catherine Clément, *La Jeune Née* Cixous, *Le Rire de la Méduse. Souffles* Jaccottet, *A Travers un verger* Modiano, *Villa triste* Simon, *Leçon des choses* Tournier, *Les Météores*	Grumberg, *En r'venant de l'Expo* Soleil, *L'Age d'or*
1976	Cixous, *LA. Partie. Portrait de Dora* Grainville, *Les Flamboyants* Sartre, *Situations X: Politiques et autobiographie*	Deutsch, *La Bonne Vie. Dimanche* Wenzel, *Loin d'Hagondange*
1977	Cardinal, *Autrement dit* Cixous, *Angst. La Venue à l'écriture* Duras, *Le Camion; suivi de Entretien avec Michelle Porte. L'Éden cinéma* Jaccottet, *A la lumière d'hiver. Leçons. Chants d'en bas* Modiano, *Livret de famille* Tournier, *Le Vent paraclet. Canada-Journal de voyage. La Famille des enfants*	Gatti, *Le Cheval qui se suicide par le feu* Vinaver, *Iphigénie Hôtel*

Years	Part II Popular Culture	Part III Cultural Debates
1974	ORTF split into seven autonomous organizations: TF1, A2, FR3, TDF, Radio France, SFP and INA	May: Valéry Giscard d'Estaing becomes President June: (– August 1976): Michel Guy becomes Secretary of State for Culture. Later this year, his 'chartes culturelles' are launched The *Loi Veil* repeals anti-abortion law Irigaray publishes *Speculum de l'autre femme* *Secrétariat à la condition féminine* formed, headed by Françoise Giroud
1975	Number of TV sets: 15,000,000 (including 3 million colour sets). Now in 89.9% of homes	Hélène Cixous and Catherine Clément publish *La Jeune Née*
1976	Guérard published *La Grande cuisine minceur* *Chanson en liberté* organized in Grenoble Creation of the *Fonds national pour le développement des sports* (FNDS) *Télé Star* started *Le Matin*, *VSD* started	Françoise Giroud made Minister of Cultural Affairs First woman made General in Air Force
1977	Death of Jacques Prévert End of Parisien Libéré conflict after 20 months	Irigaray publishes *Le Sexe qui n'en est pas un* *Questions féministes* started February: publication of the Giordan report, *Démocratie culturelle et droit à la différence* March: publication of the Puaux report on the EACs. Decentralization law on the 'droits et libertés des communes, des départements et des régions'

Years	Part I Literature	Theatre/ Cinema
1978	Cardinal, *Une Vie pour deux* Cixous, *Chant du corps interdit, le nom d'œdipe. Préparatifs de noces au dela de l'abîme* Grainville, *La Diane rousse. Images du désir* Le Clézio, *Mondo et autres histoires. L'inconnu sur la terre* Modiano, *Rue des boutiques obscures* Sartre, *Sartre: Images d'une vie* Tournier, *Le Coq de Bruyère*	Grand Magic Circus, *Les 1001 Nuits* Vinaver, *Diussident, il va sans dire. Nina, c'est autre chose* Truffaut, *La Chambre verte*
1979	Beauvoir, *Quand prime le spirituel* Cixous, *Ananke. Vivre l'orange* Duras, *Le Navire Night. Césarée. Les Mains négatives. Aurélia Steiner, Aurélia Steiner, Aurélia Steiner* Tournier, *Des Clés et des serrures*	Grumberg, *L'Atelier* Soleil, *Méphisto*
1980	Death of Sartre Cardinal, *Au pays de mes racines* Cixous, *Illa* Duras, *Vera Baxter ou les Plages de l'Atlantique. L'Homme assis dans le couloir. Les Yeux verts. Cahiers du cinéma, no. 312—313* Grainville, *Le Dernier Viking, Au long des haies de Normandie. Bernard Louedin* Jaccottet, *La Promenade sous les arbres* Le Clézio, *Désert* Sarraute, *L'Usage de la parole* Tournier, *Barbedor. Gaspard, Melchior et Balthazar*	Vinaver, *A la Renverse. Les Travaux et les jours* Godard, *Sauve qui peut*
1981	Duras, *L'Été 80. Agatha. Outside* Grainville, *L'Ombre de la bête* Modiano, *Une Jeunesse, Memory Lane* Beauvoir, *La Cérémonie des adieux, suivi de Entretiens avec Jean-Paul Sartre* Butor, *Répertoire V* Cixous, *With ou l'art de l'innocence* Simon, *Les Géorgiques* Tournier, *Le vol du vampire, Morts et résurrections de Dieter Appelt, Vues de dos* Yourcenar, first woman elected to *Académie française; Discours de réception de Mme Marguerite Yourcenar à l'Académie française et réponse de M. Jean D'Ormesson*	Chekhov, *The Cherry Orchard* (Brook) Deutsch, *Partage* Molière, *Le Bourgeois Gentilhomme* (Savary)

Years	Part II Popular Culture	Part III Cultural Debates
1978	School and university *associations sportives* separated into two bodies: the *Féderation nationale des sports universitaires* (FNSU) and the *Union nationale des sports scolaires* (UNSS) Death of Brel	Jean-Philippe Lecat becomes Minister of Cultural Affairs
1979	First Paris-Dakar rally	Women allowed to do night work in industry
1980	*L'Aurore* merged with *Le Figaro*	Marguerite Yourcenar first woman to be elected to the Académie Française
1981	Physical Education in schools placed under the sole authority of the Ministère de l'Education Nationale Death of Brassens	Mitterrand elected President Creation of Ministère des Droits de la Femme

Years	Part I Literature	Theatre/ Cinema
1982	Bonnefoy, *Poèmes: Du Mouvement et de l'immobilité de Douve. Hier régnant désert. Pierre écrite. Dans le leurre du seuil*, préface de Jean Starobinski Cixous, *Limonade tout était si infini* Duras, *L'Homme Atlantique. Savannah Bay. La Maladie de la mort* Grainville, *Les Forteresses noires* Modiano, *De si braves garçons* Tournier, *Pierrot ou les secrets de la nuit*	Demarcy, *L'Etranger dans la maison* Shakespeare, *Twelfth Night* (Soleil)
1983	Cardinal, *Le Passe empiété* Charef, *Le Thé au haarem d'Archi Ahmed* Cixous, *Le Livre de Promethea* Jaccottet, *Pensées sous les nuages* Modiano, *Poupée blonde* Sarraute, *L'Enfance* Sartre, *Cahiers pour une morale. Les carnets de la drôle de guerre* Sollers, *Femmes* Tournier, *Gilles et Jeanne. Les Rois mages* *Tel Quel* folded	Duras, *Savannah Bay* Koltès, *Combat de Nègres et de chiens* Kurys, *Coup de foudre* Pialet, *A nos amours*
1984	Death of Foucault Bouzid, *La Marche* Duras, *L'Amant* Grainville, *La Caverne céleste* Jaccottet, *A travers un verger. Les Cormorons* Beauregard, *La Semaison: carnets 1954—1979* Modiano, *Quartier perdu* Sollers, *Portrait du joueur* Tournier, *Le Vagabond immobile*	Shakespeare, *Henry IV, Part I* (Soleil) Zidi, *Les Ripoux*
1985	Duras, *La Douleur. La Musica deuxième. La Muette de Tchekhov* Le Clézio, *Le Chercheur d'or* Tournier, *La Goutte d'or. Marseille, ou Le Présent incertain*	Bourdet, *Station Service* Brook, *Le Mahabarata* Cixous, *Norodem Sihanouk* Duras, *La Musica* Kantor, *Qu'ils crèvent les artistes* Varda, *Sans toit ni loi*

Years	Part II Popular Culture	Part III Cultural Debates
1982	2 March: decentralization laws End of state monopoly of television Minitel launched *Prima* started	Publication of Giordan Report, *Démocratie culturelle et droit à la différence*
1983	Creation of an *agrégation* in Physical Education	After the municipal elections of 6 and 13 March, in which the PS loses a number of towns, conflict breaks out between several EACs and their new municipal authorities July: a further decentralization law specifies the responsibilities of the communes and Departments in the cultural field
1984	Physical Education placed amongst the first group of subjects for marking the Baccalauréat Creation of Canal Plus, first private TV channel First French communications satellite launched, Télécom 1A *L'Evénement du jeudi, Femme Actuelle* started	Bobino demolished
1985		Creation of the Conseil national des langues et cultures régionales

Years	Part I Literature	Theatre/ Cinema
1986	Death of Simone de Beauvoir Begag, *Le Gone du Chaâba* Belghoul, *Georgette* Cixous, *Entre l'écriture* Deguy, *Poèmes II: 1970—1980* Du Bouchet, *Ici en deux, Air, Défets* Duras, *Les Yeux bleus cheveux noirs.* *La Pute de la côte normande* Grainville, *Le Paradis des nuages* Le Clézio, *Voyages à Rodrigues* Modiano, *Dimanches d'août. Une* *Aventure de Choura* Simon, *Discours de Stockholm* Tournier, *Le Médianoche amoureux,* *Petites Proses. La Goutte d'or*	Jaques, *Elvire Jouvet 40* Koltès, *Quai Ouest* Berri, *Jean de Florette. Manon des* *Sources*
1987	Death of Marguerite Yourcenar Boukhedenna, *Journal: nationalité:* *immigré(e)* Cardinal, *Les Grands désordres* Duras, *La Vie matérielle. Emily L* Jaccottet, *Une Transaction secrète.* *Autres journées* Modiano, *Une Fiancée pour Choura* Simon, *L'Invitation*	Cixous, *L'Indiade* Koltès, *Dans la solitude des champs* *de Colon*
1988	Cixous, *Manne* Grainville, *L'Atelier du peintre* Modiano, *Remise de peine* Tournier, *Le Tabor et le Sinai;* *essais sur l'art contemporain*	Beshehard, *Arromanches* Koltès, *Le Retour au désert*
1989	Begag, *Béni ou le paradis privé* Cardinal, *Comme si de rien n'était* Charef, *Le Harki de Meriem*	Besset, *Villa Luco* Copi, *Les Escaliers du Sacré-Coeur* Larivey, *La Fidelle*

Years	Part II Popular Culture	Part III Cultural Debates
1986	Creation of La Cinq, TV6 and La Sept. *Loi relative à la liberté de communication* (Léotard; The Haute Autorité replaced by CNCL (Commission nationale de la communication et des libertés))	March: legislative elections bring down the Socialist government, marking the beginning of 'cohabitation'. Replacing Jack Lang, François Léotard becomes Minister of Culture and Communication
1987	Privatization of TF1	
1988	*Le Matin* ceased publication	May: the re-election of Mitterrand to the Presidency brings Lang back to the Ministry of Culture and Communication
1989	Law creating the new *Instituts universitaires de formation des maîtres* (IUFM), subsuming the old *Ecoles Normales* and the *Centres de pédagogie régionaux*. Apart from three pilot institutions (Grenoble, Lille and Reims functioned from September 1990), a new IUFM in every French *Académie* in September 1991 CNCL replaced by CSA (Conseil Supérieur de l'Audiovisuel)	July: the Firminy MC is officially municipalized December: closure of the La Rochelle MC (later reborn as Coursive)

Years	Part I Literature	Theatre/ Cinema
1990	Grainville, *L'Orgie, la neige* Guibert, *A L'ami qui ne m'a pas sauvé la vie* Modiano, *Voyages de noces*	Shakespeare, *The Tempest* (Brook) Besnehard, *L'Ourse blanche* Grumber, *Zone libre* Rappeneau, *Cyrano de Bergerac*
1991	Death of Hervé Guibert Cixous, *L'Ange au secret* Duras, *L'Amant de la Chine du Nord* Le Clézio, *Onitscha* Modiano, *Fleurs de ruine*	Novarina, *Je suis* Strauss, *Le Temps et la chambre* Feydeau, *La Dame de chez Maxim* (Murat and Françon) Carax, *Les Amants de Pont-Neuf*
1992	Cixous, *Déluge* Grainville, *Colere* Guibert, *Cytomégalovirus: journal d'hospitalisation. L'Homme au chapeau rouge* Tournier, *Le Crépuscule des masques*	

Years	Part II Popular Culture	Part III Cultural Debates
1990	Hervé Bourges appointed director of both public TV channels Opéra – Bastille opened with Berlioz's *Les Troyens*	January: *Le Monde* (4th) reports on the financial difficulties in three other MCs out of the ten remaining: Le Havre, Nevers, Rennes. Later (26th), another article announces that the Rennes MC is to disappear as such (it will later reappear as the Théâtre national de Bretagne) July: the official launch of the Scènes nationales network (announced by B. Faivre d'Arcier at the Avignon Festival) December: closure of the Nevers MC
1991	Death of Serge Gainsbourg and Yves Montand	February: publication of the Rizzardo report December: the government's 'projet de loi sur l'administration territoriale' passes its second reading in the National Assembly Edith Cresson becomes France's first woman prime minister
1992	Television: La Cinq folded and was partly replaced by La Sept, renamed Arte	

INDEX